EXTRAORDINARY
BEHAVIOR

EXTRAORDINARY
BEHAVIOR

A Case Study Approach to
Understanding Social Problems

Edited by Dennis L. Peck
and Norman A. Dolch

Westport, Connecticut
London

Library of Congress Cataloging-in-Publication Data

Extraordinary behavior : a case study approach to understanding social problems / edited
by Dennis L. Peck and Norman A. Dolch.
    p. cm.
    Includes bibliographical references and index.
    ISBN 0–275–97015–9 (alk. paper).—ISBN 0–275–97057–4 (pbk. : alk. paper)
    1. Social problems—United States—Case studies. 2. United States—Social
conditions—1980– I. Peck, Dennis L. II. Dolch, Norman A. (Norman Allan)
HN59.2.E97   2001
361.1'0973—dc21   00–029840

British Library Cataloguing in Publication Data is available.

Library of Congress Catalog Card Number: 00–029840
ISBN: 0–275–97015–9
      0–275–97057–4 (pbk.)

First published in 2001

Praeger Publishers, 88 Post Road West, Westport, CT 06881
An imprint of Greenwood Publishing Group, Inc.
www.praeger.com

Printed in the United States of America

The paper used in this book complies with the
Permanent Paper Standard issued by the National
Information Standards Organization (Z39.48–1984).

10 9 8 7 6 5 4 3 2 1

A special thank you is due to Peggy for her understanding and support during
the various phases of this undertaking as well as several other projects.
She is a special person, large in wisdom, and a great teacher
from whom I have learned a great deal of sociology.
—Dennis L. Peck

I dedicate my efforts in this project to Cindy, Kris, Ed, Susan, and Nicki,
who in their special way helped me to understand the relationship
between personal troubles and social issues.
—Norman A. Dolch

Contents

Introduction

The idea that led to the creation of a case study approach to the study of social problems first began to develop when the co-editors met to deliberate a set of evaluations for another project. This discussion involved an assessment of the various attributes of the case study approach for evaluating social problems. The content of this book is the result of this discussion.

Except for the coverage of the general concepts that serve as the foundation for the discipline of sociology, currently it is difficult to differentiate between the topics included in most social problem and introductory level textbooks. In covering a wide-ranging number of topics the authors of most social problem books focus on three or even four theoretical perspectives, even though one or more of these perspectives offer little by way of discussion and explanation of the process through which social problems evolve or why they persist without solution. Our purpose in seeking contributions from a distinguished group of researchers and practitioners was to draw upon their considerable expertise to create book-length chapters in which each author would be able to assess the extent of a specific social problem and then bring to life some of the numerous factors and issues involved in the evolution of the social problem.

The topics selected for this book differ not only by virtue of the case study approach employed, but also from the standard topics included in general social problems books. When examples of the topics included here are found in social problems books, they are often used in passing reference to other issues. Our purpose is to explore selected social problems and related issues of importance to the body politic and to provide concrete case study examples of individuals who, to a lesser or greater extent, have been defined as engaging in extraordinary behavior. In each chapter, the unique characteristics and factors involved in a social problem are illustrated to explain how the individuals came to be at risk. Although the case study approach allows each author the opportunity to describe important aspects in the lives of specific individuals, the social problems under consideration are distributed throughout society without regard to age, gender, race, or social class. By reviewing the extent of a particular problem and then developing a case study using the symbolic interaction perspective, our intent is to offer an enriched and perhaps more palatable explanation.

Although the recognition, nature, and understanding of social problems may change over time, the subjects covered in the following chapters are currently viewed as social issues, and to many analysts each is considered a social problem in need of a solution. Illustrative of a public attitude that something should be done to solve these problems is the increase in federal and state research funding to encourage research to assist in determining the magnitude and range of drug, homeless, divorce, harassment, child support, and family abuse problems.

With the discovery of the child abuse problem during the 1960s and 1970s, similar research funds were channeled into studies of this social problem as well as suicide, juvenile delinquency and crime, sexually transmitted diseases, alcohol and drug abuse, and civil liberties. Government-supported assistance centers also were financed during this period. During the 1980s, research and other forms of government support focused on areas such as the AIDS/HIV pandemic, legal rights, mental illness, wife abuse, and then, spousal abuse. Throughout the 1990s, various forms of family abuse, including abuse of the elderly, a renewed focus on drug abuse, a closer look at the victims of crime, judicial abuse, and issues relating to the unique problems experienced by women gained much of the same kind of support. Such examples are illustrative of a shift in the public conscience, not only in challenging traditional social values but also in addressing issues relating to human rights and the dignity of the individual.

Consistent with this shift in social values is yet another public reaction to what became known as an "entitlement mentality" and a reduced public tolerance for individuals who choose to violate the law. During the 1990s, this public reaction caused governments to create policies in which the focus of accountability and responsibility shifted back to local communities and, subsequently, to individuals. However, the consequences of previous government initiatives, such as releasing thousands of individuals from state mental health institutions and reducing the length of time people receive public assistance now render unanticipated social problems such as the increased numbers of homeless persons.

Of course, some social problems are so identified from one generation to the next. Crime and violence are examples of social problems that always seem to capture public attention and imagination. These kinds of social problems are not bound to any specific temporal period or spatial milieu and, for this reason, are included here as well.

PERSPECTIVE OF THE BOOK

Two traditional sociological approaches are employed in this book. First, the symbolic interaction paradigm is employed through using the case study approach. Applying the case study method, a respected analytical technique, allows each contributor to focus on the symbolic experiences, situations, and circumstances of real people within the context of a more general social problem. A microinteractionist interpretive analysis of what most analysts consider to be macrolevel problems is challenging, and each contributor discusses the national data to establish a foundation for their evaluation at the individual level. Each does so following the lead of Hartmut B. Mokros (1995), who wrote:

It is with the context of social bonds that we experience the self—through the actions and reactions of the other (including the self as other) to the self . . . The "mind" becomes a theater in which the self takes the role of the other in relation to the self. In other words, the self reflexively problematizes it-self by looking through the "expectational" lens of the other. Through interactional and reflexive self-other experiences, we evolve a sense of identity that is most adequately understood in terms of social bonds. (Pp. 1094–1095)

The contributors examine social problems as a subjectively problematic social process. This social process highlights the character of human behavior and signifies the need for an empathetic understanding in the study of human behavior. In turn, as analysts of human behavior we can gain an appreciation for why people behave in the manner they do through achieving what Charles Horton Cooley (1964 [1902]) argued for: an appreciation of the orientation toward this behavior from the perspective of those individuals involved in this process. On occasion these orientations may challenge our objective understanding, but they nonetheless emphasize the active character and self-awareness of human conduct. This subjective problematic approach to understanding social problems, according to Jerome Manis and Bernard Meltzer (1978), is distinguished by its symbolic interactionist orientation.

The Symbolic Interaction Perspective

The symbolic interaction perspective serves as the primary theoretical explanation for each social problem. Coined by Herbert Blumer, the term symbolic interactionism is a part of the social psychology of human behavior, and it represents the first chapter in the ongoing development of a distinctly American brand of sociology. It is a tradition which, in the words of Randall Collins (1994, pp. 242–243), "concerns the human subject and builds the social world out of human consciousness and human agency. . . . it upholds the fluidity and meaningfulness of humanism." With the individual as the unit of analysis, this perspective enhances our understanding of the important symbolic world that affects everyday life.

The legacy of the social interaction perspective can be traced to the social philosophy of Charles Horton Cooley (1964 [1902]) and the efforts of George Herbert Mead, a pragmatist and social behaviorist who, unlike the focus on outward behavior emphasized by eminent psychologists (e.g., John Watson) of the day, explored the nature and function of the mind. In his sociology of thinking, Mead (1934) theorized that language and control serve as the basis for a social psychology of the mind, self, and society. Social actors construct norms unconsciously in their everyday interactions with others or through conscious decision making.

More recently, Neil MacKinnon (1994) enhanced Mead's contribution by acknowledging the crucial theoretical link between language and emotional experiences. Language, according to MacKinnon, plays an important role in eliciting emotional experience: "Language functions as a linguistic warehouse . . . for strong affective meaning. . . . Symbolic interaction involves the processing not only of cognitive information about objects and events, but also, and perhaps even more fundamental, their affective associations" (p. 3).

A second branch of social interactionism, known as role theory, explains the self in relation to the social structure (Collins 1994). Developed by more abstract theorists who related their ideas to the then-dominant sociological functionalist paradigm, role theory explanations relate human behavior to role sets. Role theory explains that each person holds a number of statuses simultaneously and, based on these statuses, they play out a number of distinctive roles. On occasion, role conflict and role strain are experienced when individual statuses and/or roles compete with one another as the individual attempts to carry out day-to-day responsibilities and obligations inherent in each role set.

Aspects of both kinds of symbolic interactionism can be found in the case studies presented here. That is, the reader will be exposed to the fluidity and spontaneity of situations and a brand of symbolic interactionism in which the primary reality develops as individuals negotiate social situations. Thus, the self-fulfilling prophesy of W. I. Thomas takes on great significance for the actor. According to the Thomas theorem, "social life has the quality that what people think it is, it tends to become" (cited in Collins 1994, p. 261). The reader also will find the abstract theoretical model of the role theorists useful to understand the relationship between the individual and structure and complexity of the social conditions explored in each chapter.

The contributors address issues relating to subjective meanings, motivations, and actions. In most instances one or two cases are used. In other instances, the case study analysis is based on a small group of individuals simply because this approach captures the range of human characteristics involved. Thus, the symbols that shape subjective meanings and interpretations of human interaction, and the importance these interpretations and meanings have on emotions and experiences, can be understood more readily.

Given that culture represents the symbolic aspect of social life (Black 1976, pp. 61–79), these human problems represent a part of this cultural reality even if they are not expressions of all that is good and beautiful. Each author is able to capture the essence of what C. Wright Mills (1940) referred to as vocabularies of motives. These motives are strategies of action and the motivational accounts represent a system of justification for behavior by which people attempt to position themselves within an accepted cultural matrix. These motivational accounts are expressed in face-to-face encounters (symbolic interaction) which, according to Nachman Ben-Yehuda (1985, pp. 211–213), "provide . . . the bridging mechanism for the macro-micro analysis and . . . a way for boundaries to change or stabilize." Although macrolevel social problems serve as the focal point of analysis, knowledge of the changing vocabularies of motives is useful for understanding why some social conditions always seem to be a cause for public concern while other conditions become a problem only when a change in social values, morality, and interests occur.

The Case Study Method

In a book entitled *A Case for the Case Study* (Feagin, Orum, and Sjoberg 1991) the co-editors explain why the case study approach serves as a valuable research tool within the social sciences. As a research strategy the use of case studies has a rich sociological legacy, and this technique is again proving to be a useful method as researchers explore new areas of inquiry. The case study, whether the content is created through ethnographic field research, life histories of individuals and families, or information pertaining to a large group, offers a unique opportunity to assess a wealth of information pertaining to beliefs, social meanings, customs, structure, social networks, social continuity, and change in natural settings (Sjoberg et al. 1991, pp. 4–7). And, as noted by Feagin, Orum, and Sjoberg (1991), case studies can assist in the development of more general theories of human behavior.

These case studies illustrate the relationship between the individual and the general society. They are also useful to enhance our understanding of the nature of social problems by grounding the learning experience in the reality of in-depth, multidimensional investigation and analysis. As stated by Joe Feagin et al. (1991, p. 39): "(we) . . . find how the case study approach has expanded our understanding of 'others' and 'ourselves.' " The reader will be able to reflectively think about the issues involved based on a *verstehen* or understanding achieved from the perspective of the subjects.

The social problems and cases are not merely descriptions of one individual or even a small number of individuals. Rather, each example represents that which Emile Durkheim (1938; 1951 [1897]) referred to as social facts or things that are specific to a social problem. Unlike Durkheim, however, the contributing authors operate within the realm of a tradition established by another eminent sociologist, Max Weber (1968), whose analysis of ideal types provides the general umbrella under which these case studies are presented. In so doing, the authors address the negative sphere of each documented case, noting the effects of the interaction between the person and the public and social realms (Maris 1997). From this interaction, the social (realm) produces symbolic meanings, each of which hold greater or lesser importance. As noted by Donald Black (1976, pp. 63–83), the more culture one experiences, the more individual conventionality takes root. Because one's symbolic reality is grounded in culture, some people respond to a greater extent to these symbolic meanings than do others, but each responds. The seriousness of what is considered to be extraordinary behavior depends upon the conventionality of both the individual actor and those who are offended by such behavior.

Each chapter is crafted around the social constructionist approach to understanding extraordinary behavior and each offers some practical insight into the social dynamics involved. The contributors enhance our understanding of the dynamics involved in social problems at the abstract level as well as personal issues using the recorded experiences of the unit of analysis, namely, the individual. By first surveying the nature of the problem under consideration, the contributors then place the case study examples within a general social context.

In each chapter, one or more of the principles of the case study approach is applied. These principles, as outlined by Feagin, Orum, and Sjoberg (1991), are: (1) the study of people in natural settings, (2) a holistic study of the complexities of action and meaning, (3) a sense of time and history, and (4) theory generation and/or generalization. Although each chapter is written in a manner devoid of technical jargon, concepts are applied for interpretive purposes, and these are useful for understanding the motives and interests of individuals whose stories are told through the use of questionnaire data, diaries, written correspondence, and personal interviews. In a manner of speaking, the reader becomes a part of what Erving Goffman (1983) refers to as the interaction order. This interaction order represents the interactive life experiences of individuals whose personal cognitive world and behavioral responses to the symbolism that constitutes this world become, for a brief time, face-to-face experiences that can be shared in a meaningful manner.

Health-Related Issues

Part I, Health-Related Issues, captures the attention of the public either because of media exposure or because a specific health-related issue becomes part of a political agenda. These health issues are grouped in this section because each occurs as a result of human motivation. With few exceptions, it can be argued, people choose to behave in the manner they do even if the result is viewed by others as undesirable. Thus, without a desire and the requisite motivation to engage in a specific act or pattern of behavior, the resulting problem would not occur.

Specific programs are created often in the wake of community response to a social problem. Each of these health-related issues generated sufficient public concern that either research-related or applied programs were created to address the problem. However, without appropriate individual desire and motivation, people would continue to engage in excessive behavior, or could fail to recognize the support available that could assist them in solving the problem at the personal level. The resulting aggregate of each person involved culminates in what is then declared to be a problem of national importance in need of further attention.

The decade of the nineties represented a period during which an increasing number of people became conscious of their health. It was also a period during which a great deal of federally supported medical research occurred. The result was significant evidence and other more tentative findings that supported the contention that health is affected by long-term stress resulting from events and conditions associated with the family, school, and work. Not only are people affected psychologically and socially, but physiologically as well.

Within this context, perhaps it can be argued that grouping suicide, anorexia nervosa, alcohol/drug use and abuse, and AIDS together as health-related issues does not make these topics mutually exclusive. Such an argument is not without merit because the consequences of each of the social problems included in this section not only affect the health and well-being of certain individuals, but others as well, including family members. The same outcome may be true for each of the topics presented in this book.

Chapter 1 takes a look at the growing problem of suicide. Changing social values often lead to conflicting public perceptions of this social problem. For example, recent public attention has been directed toward suicide committed by individuals who experience pain related to health problems and other individuals whose symbolic world portrays a future that is presumably devoid of emotional and physical relief. Such situations are replete with varied community reactions and many legal consequences for both the survivors and the body politic. The discussion of suicide as officially documented during the past several decades illustrates the extent of this problem for those age groups most at risk for suicide and provides a review of theoretical explanations that contribute to our understanding of why suicide occurs, including the rational aspects that enter into the decision to commit suicide. To illustrate the multitude of emotional experiences related to the motivation to commit suicide, a case study of Nancy, a middle-aged woman, whose suicidal thoughts are documented in a diary, is used to portray the backstage behavior of one whose symbolic world at the time pales in comparison to the promising prospects of her earlier life.

In chapter 2, anorexia nervosa, a major health problem among youthful American females, is discussed by noting the numerous social, psychological, and physiological consequences involved. The social and psychological factors that influence young females, the physical consequences experienced, and the family characteristics of individuals who suffer from this eating disorder are described. A case study of Sarah, a former anorexic, is presented to illustrate the complex factors involved in the process that leads to the anorexia nervosa problem, the conflict individuals experience as they attempt to cope with their problem and, in this case, the eventual success in overcoming this problem.

Chapter 3 is based on an extensive review of the research literature and a national data base, each of which is used to compare the characteristics identified in the alcohol and drug use literature with those of four teenagers. Each teenager was introduced to alcohol and/or drug use during their early teenage years and later experienced alcohol and drug abuse problems severe enough for them to be admitted to a treatment program. The subjects were interviewed while undergoing treatment, and the authors frame their interviews to address the relationship between early alcohol and substance use and the period during which the subjects applied that which previously had been learned to complete the process of becoming an alcohol and/or substance abuser. The authors address issues relating to circumstantial factors, individual characteristics, and the role of parents and peers in either contributing to substance abuse or in modifying the process that leads to substance abuse.

When the first case of AIDS was reported officially in mid-1981, a massive worldwide effort to discover a cure for the AIDS virus ensued. This effort also led to the diversion of research funds from the study of other sexually transmitted diseases in order to provide greater financial resources in support of the AIDS research effort. In chapter 4, we look at some of the reasons traditional medical tactics in support of the concerted effort to treat and control the spread of the acquired immune deficiency disease in the United States failed. As we move into the new millennium the AIDS virus continues as a major health problem in the United States.

This lack of success in controlling AIDS can be attributed to at least two reasons. First, the magnitude of the AIDS problem initially may have been misunderstood. Thus, the research commitment initiated by the federal government paled in comparison to the nature of the problem. Second, as noted by the contributor, the traditional organizational responses within the medical community did not take into consideration the unique features of the disease and of those who are most prone to be infected.

The contributor addresses a unique effort to understand better the AIDS virus and to provide convenient evaluation of and treatment for infected patients. Cast within a health care delivery context, the focus of the discussion centers on a federal program in which evaluation, treatment, and research were integrated into a single health care delivery model. This unique medical arena involves community-based research within a treatment setting established outside the traditional health care delivery context. Central to this discussion is a process of cooperation between local and federal officials that fostered a treatment/research relationship with patients by establishing a new professional role for practitioners who also served as clinical researchers. This research and treatment setting was intended to eliminate the bureaucratic hierarchy characteristic of the medical field by combining a nontraditional community-based diagnostic, treatment, and research program with private practitioner resources.

Family Issues

Part II, Family Issues, is consistent with the topics included among family problems currently found in standard social problems books. The American family has been undergoing a transition, and is now taking on forms that differ from the traditional conception of what the family should look like and what it represents. However, community and state level data strongly support the contention that each of these family issues represent important social problems in need of a solution. In 1996, for example, some state jurisdictions reported that more than 50 percent of recorded live births were to unwed teenagers. Nationally, unwed teenagers account for one-third of all recorded live births.

And of the myriad problems said to be related to the American family, those included in this section can be counted among the most pressing issues. Each problem adds to a public concern which, during the final decade of the millennium, led to the creation of public policy. No longer can unwed mothers expect to receive long-term public assistance. Similarly, spousal abuse and domestic violence are subject increasingly to public scrutiny and official sanction. Nonpayment of child support prompts yet another form of official reaction that includes, in some cases, a term in jail. Even the homeless, once viewed with empathetic understanding, are subject to ordinances intended to control the range of their activities.

An American value system that includes an orientation promoting the unique development of each individual and avoids invading individual integrity also emphasizes achievement, success, individualism, conformity, and freedom. Such a value system, however, is destined to experience a contradiction; a contradiction that appears to be a public hue and cry for a reinstatement of norms that require morality, responsibility, and accountability as a measure of what a society should expect from its citizens. Yet another American value of importance is humanitarianism. The utility of this value is not lost in the case studies.

The chapters in this section portray life events that represent a process through which some individuals could conceivably move. Although this combination of social problems is not intended to represent such a process, cumulative family problems such as spousal abuse and domestic violence, divorce and poverty, and a lack of child support could indeed result in entire families becoming homeless.

Despite the fact that most people view children having children as a societal problem, the right-of-passage issue so important within certain portions of the American society is not easily understood. To many individuals, children becoming impregnated and bearing children represents an unacceptable part of social reality. Chapter 5 illustrates the significance of this reality as presented through the thoughts and experiences of three teenagers, two of whom, similar to the majority of single parents, chose to raise their babies. A discussion of the role of professionals who teach teenage mothers appropriate parenting skills and encourage them to attend to the needs of their children illustrates the importance of such programs. This is especially true for teenagers whose personal experiences do not include the requisite insights or encouragement to learn the skills essential to appropriate parenting.

The topic of domestic violence and spousal abuse, as examined in chapter 6, represents a fairly recent area of inquiry, having become a social problem of public interest only within the past two decades. Having been so recognized, domestic violence is now thought to be of epidemic proportion in the American society. An estimated two to four million American women are at risk of abuse by their current or former partners. The serious nature of the injury that occurs includes physical and psychological harm and social consequences for the female victims involved in the abusive relationship. The scope of this problem reaches far beyond families, affecting our schools, hospitals, businesses, and prisons.

Domestic violence involves battering, male power and control, and other general factors relating to institutional inequality. Although spousal abuse is not limited to male perpetrators, most perpetrators are male, and the majority of domestic violence victims are female. The two case studies illustrate that domestic violence is not related to specific family background, social class, or level of education. The first case, involving a well-educated professional couple and their infant child, covers the stages involved in the cycle of violence. The second case involves a family of relatively little education, meager financial means, and even more limited life opportunities. Although the two families differ dramatically in their background, in both instances the wife and children were threatened and/or otherwise victimized. Factors involved in the domestic cycle of violence are identified and special attention is given to the power and control-oriented behavior characteristic of male-dominated relationships.

The decline in the standard of living experienced after divorce, especially by women, is a well-documented phenomenon, but it is a problem that has only recently been addressed by governments. The public misconception that 50 percent of marriages end in divorce has had an unintended, albeit important, consequence inasmuch as this myth stimulated research efforts in which the social and economic consequences of divorce have been explored. In chapter 7, the author describes the major financial problems and social factors that affect many women soon after a divorce occurs.

In the first part of the chapter the incidence and social causes of divorce are examined; in the second part, the general distribution of poverty among the American population is discussed as are social factors known to be associated with divorce. The divorce and poverty data provide the base upon which the three case studies are presented. Each of these cases illustrates the range of individuals who are affected, as well as noting the social, financial, and legal consequences of divorce.

In chapter 8, on child support and deadbeat dads, our attention is drawn to the role of governments that seek to reduce dependence on public assistance. This effort includes enforcement to ensure that parents paying child support uphold their court-mandated obligations. The results of this effort are generally noted by the public only when high profile, well-to-do professionals and government officials are targeted. Although little public attention and consideration are given to the noncustodial parents who are least able to provide for their children, this chapter brings such parents to our attention.

The Child Support Enforcement program (CSE) is making progress toward ensuring that the welfare of each child is provided by the responsible parent. However, one question that is unanswered is: what of the fathers? Recent child support legislation, intended to curb national and state spending for public assistance also may be responsible for creating an unanticipated, but perhaps even greater, problem. This problem is that stringent enforcement guidelines fail to take into consideration that some fathers, who are targeted as "deadbeats," may be victimized by a system of bureaucratic rigidity.

The case study composite presented in this chapter offers an assessment of noncustodial child support–paying fathers who are least able to fulfill their financial obligations. As largely unrecognized members of a much greater group of eligible child support–paying fathers, low-income fathers nevertheless represent a significant portion of the child support enforcement caseload. This chapter is based on the circumstances of fathers, portraying the problem from the fathers' perspective. The author suggests that the CSE program may be too rigid in working with low-income fathers who desire to support their children but, because of their financial situations, are unable to pay at the level dictated by the courts and enforced by CSE program officials.

Beginning in the 1960s many of the nation's inner cities began to experience high rates of crime and other forms of deviance that led to abandonment by the middle class and withdrawal of investments by the business community. A decreased base of taxable commercial businesses and properties, social disorganization, and an overall decay in the urban infrastructure resulted. However, conditions are again changing inasmuch as the central portions of many older cities are experiencing revitalization. One of the problems faced by city administrators that carries over from the past is that of homeless people. This problem is discussed in chapter 9.

Homelessness emerged as a social problem during the 1970s when the number of homeless people substantially increased. Caused in part by personal choice and drug usage, the number of homeless increased as people fell victim to a changing economy, corporate restructuring, and federal court orders that called for the release of thousands of patients from state mental health facilities. The extent of the visible homelessness problem places governments in a need to know the magnitude of the situation, requiring that city officials hire researchers to count the homeless. Sissy's personal experience as a homeless person illustrates how easy it is to fall from grace and how difficult reentry into a productive community of citizens is without benefit of public assistance. Sissy's case serves the authors well in shaping our knowledge of the homelessness problem, a problem that they argue seems to defy solution.

Behavior Beyond the Boundaries

A certain amount of crime is expected and even tolerated in a civil democratic society. As societies grow in size and complexity, so too does the incidence of recorded crime. However, specific types of behavior do not receive the same kind of official and public reaction as do others because certain behavior is neither expected nor tolerated by most adults. It is this kind of behavior that can be thought of as behavior beyond the boundaries.

A portion of the material included in this section deals with classic social problems. That is, these problems are included because each has received much public and scholarly attention throughout the nineteenth and twentieth centuries. For example, because of their potential predatory and violent nature or because they create a public nuisance, problems such as street hustling occasionally gain the attention of the public and authorities. Other crimes, such as murder and repeat criminal offenders, always seem to gain our attention in that such behavior is considered to be beyond the boundary of public indifference and tolerance. Some overlap in the consequences of specific problems occurs, for example, chapter 12, street hustling, with chapter 15, serial killers, where it is possible to see that street hustling can place one in harms way. Still other problems, such as equal protection under the law and sexual harassment, are included in this section because these are more recent discoveries. However, these problems are no less pressing in importance as our society strives to ensure that social justice and civility will prevail.

Chapter 10 presents sexual harassment, a problem of importance in the workplace. During the past several years sexual harassment has gained exceptional national prominence. The Equal Employment Opportunity Commissions's (EEOC) claims against alleged harassers have increased dramatically, as have civil suits demanding compensation for damages. Although sexual harassment is illegal, specific behaviors associated with such actions vary widely and are open to interpretation. Gender, as well as other characteristics of the person assessing the behavior, influence whether or not the behavior is judged to be sexually harassing. Moreover, blame assigned to the victim of harassment varies with characteristics of the perpetrator, as well as with characteristics of the victim. This chapter illustrates well the all too common dilemma associated with the interpretation of undesirable attention such as sexual harassment and the subsequent disposition of allegations claimed by the victims of sexual harassment, their supervisors, and the courts.

The Constitution of the United States represents a theory for how Americans can live without prejudice or oppression. Impartial legal justice is a significant part of the theory upon which this document is based, and this issue remains important today. In chapter 11, on equal protection and racial exclusion, it is noted that the Sixth Amendment to the Constitution ensures that individuals accused of violating the criminal law shall be judged by an impartial jury and that this jury shall be comprised of one's peers. The Fourteenth Amendment guarantees equal protection under the law. However ideal these principles are, the theory and social reality often do not correspond.

The two case studies, one criminal and one civil, raise questions pertaining to this impartial system. These cases illustrate a process that includes legal actors and citizens called upon to engage in a ritual intended to ensure truth and justice will prevail. The scene includes potential jurors who, if selected, judge the merit of the evidence presented both for and against those who stand accused of wrong-doing. To preclude any able-bodied, willing person from participating in this ritual is to deny equal protection and due process, each of which is in violation of a document that symbolizes the essence of democratic society. Voir dire is one symbolic factor in this process. Despite many legal challenges raised during the past three decades, voir dire, or the process during which potential jurors are questioned by opposing attorneys, continues to be a matter of social concern, as indicated in the case studies presented in this chapter.

Public discussions of homosexuality and prostitution usually result in varied reactions, and in terms of prostitution, at least, the assignment of this topic to the illicit category. Despite the fact that homosexuals benefit from changing social perceptions and legal actions that provide greater protection for this minority group, much of this form of sexual expression remains hidden. Prostitution, on the other hand, remains a criminal activity in most jurisdictions.

The focus of chapter 12 is on one type of male prostitution, namely the male street hustler who engages in impression management strategies to protect his identity and to avoid social stigma. Created from personal interviews and field observations, this case study material includes graphic language spoken to explain the subjects' perception of self (their true sexual identity), their perception of other hustlers, and their perception of their clients' sexuality. The language of the street hustler expresses the attitudes and values held by this group while offering an insider's view of a symbolic world that generally escapes public attention.

In chapter 13, on career criminals, a discussion of the kind of people responsible for the decade of the 1990s becoming known as the punishing decade is presented. During the final two decades of the millennium, policies intended in part to deal with repeat offenders led to the incarceration of nearly two million individuals by the end of 1999. Although the majority of these inmates are first-time drug offenders, a significant proportion of the nation's felony offenders are career criminals.

In the past, criminality was perceived as a transient, part-time phase of life or, if engaged in criminal activity on a regular basis, the career criminal was thought to be a professional whose skills were known largely only to members of the underworld. Today, however, the public perceives the career criminal as a troubled individual whose only goals in life are to commit crime and to achieve immediate gratification.

The career criminal represents a heavy financial and social burden and, for these reasons, an increasing number of states enacted habitual felony offender laws similar to California's "three-strikes" legislation. Although the sentencing consequences differ by state, each of these life-without-parole policies is intended to ensure that repeat offenders are kept off the streets for an extended period of time.

The focus of this case study is on the adaptive mechanisms career criminals employ to avoid detection from the police and follows their cases as they are processed by the police and through the courts as well as during their periods of incarceration. The case study discussion of the career criminal problem is enriched through the insights provided by inmates who are well acquainted with the criminal justice system and also explores their criminal mind-set and symbolic world.

Chapter 14 examines the phenomenon of mass murder (the murder of three or more individuals in a limited spatial area) in public settings. Although the media and popular culture portray the mass murderer as a deranged individual who randomly kills people, a significant number of mass murders occur during the commission of a felony offense. Addressing public and academic misconceptions and news media distortion of mass murderers, the authors reconstruct the image of mass murder.

Using this case study and examples of other high-profile incidents, the authors deconstruct the mythology surrounding the mass murder phenomenon. Comparing the popular misconceptions of mass murder with fact, the authors create a reality that stands in stark contrast to the mythical effect produced by the mass media through its use of sensational descriptors of the event and of the mass murderer. Of particular interest is the focus on word choice used by the media in describing mass murderers and the killer stereotypes they created.

Despite the notoriety sought by some serial killers and the strong community reaction to this heinous crime, knowledge of the serial killer remains limited. In chapter 15, the author discusses the evolving definition of the serial killer concept, the characteristics and methods of serial killers, the difficulties legal authorities encounter in their attempts to apprehend serial killers, and provides the foundation for introducing a case study of serial killer John Wayne Gacy.

John Wayne Gacy, who was interviewed by the author just prior to Gacy's execution, is considered the most prolific serial killer in history. The discussion of Gacy's early life, employment history, and early sexual experiences is developed directly from these interviews and from personal correspondence conducted between the author, Gacy, and Gacy's sister. These interviews are used to illustrate Gacy's early response to the environmental influences that would eventually lead to his criminal sexual activities and later to the killing of at least thirty-three victims. A discussion of the emotional conflict Gacy experienced is employed to illustrate the symbolic meaning attributed to homosexual behavior learned during Gacy's early home life, his involvement in homosexual sex, and of the motivations used to justify the killing of street hustlers.

REFERENCES

Ben-Yehuda, Nachman. 1985. *Deviance and Moral Boundaries*. Chicago: The University of Chicago Press.

Black, Donald J. 1976. *The Behavior of Law*. San Diego: Academic Press, Inc.

Collins, Randall. 1994. *Four Sociological Traditions*. New York: Oxford University Press.

Cooley, Charles Horton. 1964 [1902]. *Human Nature and the Social Order*. New York: Schocken Books.

Durkheim, Emile. 1938. *The Rules of Sociological Method*. Translated by Sarah A. Solovay and John H. Mueller. New York: The Free Press.

———. 1951 [1897]. *Suicide: A Study in Sociology*. New York: The Free Press.

Feagin, Joe R., Anthony M. Orum, and Gideon Sjoberg, eds. 1991. *A Case for the Case Study*. Chapel Hill: The University of North Carolina Press.

Frazier, Charles E. 1976. *Theoretical Approaches to Deviance: An Evaluation*. Columbus, Ohio: Charles E. Merrill Publishing Company.

———. 1978. "The Use of Life Histories in Testing Theories of Criminal Behavior: Toward Reviving a Method." *Qualitative Sociology* 1: 122–142.

Goffman, Erving. 1983. "The Interaction Order." *American Sociological Review* 48:1–17.

Kasler, Dirk. 1989. *Max Weber: An Introduction to His Life and Work*. Chicago: The University of Chicago Press.

MacKinnon, Neil J. 1994. *Symbolic Interaction as Affect Control*. Albany: State University of New York Press.

Manis, Jerome G., and Bernard N. Meltzer. 1978. *Symbolic Interaction: A Reader in Social Psychology*. Boston: Allyn and Bacon.

Maris, Ronald. 1997. "Social Suicide." *Suicide and Life-Threatening Behavior* 27: 41–49.

Mead, George Herbert. 1934. *Mind, Self, and Society*. Chicago: The University of Chicago Press.

Mills, C. Wright. 1940. "Situated Actions and Vocabularies of Motives." *American Sociological Review* 5: 904–913.

Mokros, Hartmut B. 1995. "Suicide and Shame." *American Behavioral Scientist* 38: 1091–1103.

Ragin, Charles C. 1987. *The Comparative Method: Moving Beyond Qualitative and Quantitative Strategies*. Berkeley: University of California Press.

Ragin, Charles, C., and Howard S. Becker, eds. 1992. *What is a Case?: Exploring the Foundations of Social Inquiry*. New York: Cambridge University Press.

Sjoberg, Gideon, Norma Williams, Ted R. Vaughn, and Andree F. Sjoberg. 1991. "Introduction." In J. R. Feagin, A. M. Orum, and G. Sjoberg, eds., *A Case for the Case Study*, pp. 1–26. Chapel Hill: The University of North Carolina Press.

Weber, Max. 1968. *Economy and Society: An Outline of Sociology*. Edited by Guenther Roth and Claus Wittich. New York: Belminster Press.

PART I

HEALTH-RELATED ISSUES

The topics selected as health-related issues, namely suicide, anorexia nervosa, alcohol and drug use and abuse, and AIDS all are grounded in a number of theories that explain certain cultural aspects and social demographic character-istics of these problems. In some instances, such as suicide, the problem is placed in a comparative theoretical context in which sociological (e.g., anomie), psychological (e.g., alienation), sociopsychological (e.g., frustration-aggression), and, more recently, biochemical theories (e.g., an imbalance in serontonin levels) have proven useful in exploring the dynamics involved in the actions and re-actions that lead to the taking of one's life. None of these theories, however, offer the same sensitizing, humanistic effect for understanding the problem of suicide than that of the symbolic interaction perspective.[1]

The intellectual roots of symbolic interaction include the idea that people construct their world and, therefore, their reality. That is, people construct their world of reality based on their perceptions and conceptions. If their behavior is unpredictable, as is often the case, then it is incumbent on analysts of human behavior to recognize that the influence of the environment and the manner in which people selectively react to symbols and signs in adapting to their envi-ronment, differ. Although affected by this same environment, human beings are active and creative. This means they can, and, do, play an active role in creating their own future destiny. As the noted sociologist C. Wright Mills wrote (1940, p. 907): "When an agent vocalizes or imputes motives, he (she) is not merely stating 'reasons'. He (she) is influencing others—and himself (herself). Often he (she) is finding new 'reason' which will mediate action." Accordingly, the motives that prompt human behavior lie in the vocabularies of motives verbalized by people in specific situations. Although analysts can, and do, input or attach some imagined real motive to behavior, such analytic attribution may be inappropriate. Based on Mills' assessment of situated actions and vocabularies of motives for different situations, words are the determinants of conduct.

In chapter 1, the case study of Nancy well illustrates the insights of C. Wright Mills. Nancy vocalized her motives through documenting the reasons why she intended to end her life. These reasons included a broken relationship with a man who rejects Nancy, her physical disability, and an inability to secure some form of employment that would, in turn, provide Nancy with the requisite resources to again establish her independence and, ultimately, regain her sense of self-worth.

In *Strategic Interaction* Erving Goffman observes that, "Individuals typically make observations of their situation in order to assess what is relevantly happening around them and what is likely to occur. Once this is done, they often go on to exercise another capacity of human intelligence, that of making a choice from among a set of possible lines of response" (1969, pp. 85–86). Although Nancy had the love and attention of a daughter and grandchildren, these important relationships were insufficient to counter or diminish the negative aspects of her immediate symbolic world, a world that caused Nancy to experience a diminishing sense of self. The definition of the situation of which W. I. Thomas spoke, from Nancy's perspective, translated into a view that the future would be devoid of the kind of social interactions and events that previously characterized Nancy's life.

The social dynamics and the complex process leading to the anorexia nervosa problem and subsequent recovery of Sarah, as noted by Diane E. Taub and Penelope A. McLorg in chapter 2, is encumbered with competing cultural meanings, socially contrived icons, and individual motivations and actions as well as physiological consequences. The case study demonstrates how the reactions of others, especially parents, siblings, and peers to something as basic as eating and physical exercise can, and do, lead to the creation of meanings that cause unanticipated behavior. Nevertheless, these meanings hold important consequences for the person defined or labeled as one who engages in behavior thought of by the actor as healthy but considered by others as extraordinary. Denial of this reality also is characteristic of the estrangement that can occur between individuals who share the same environment but fail to share similar meanings and experiences.

The use of drugs and alcohol not only have had an historical swing throughout the American experience, but the current perspective of the public and government reaction to any form of mind-altering drug continue to challenge the American conscience. Throughout the past two centuries, especially during the twentieth century, we have witnessed changing and oft-times conflicting shifts in the social norms based on public and official perceptions of the appropriateness of such consumptive behavior. The present era is no different from that of the past; the American society continues to struggle to identify the most appropriate legal and/or medical response to individuals who become involved in a process leading from social experimentation to, in many instances, habit-forming, addictive behavior (Musto 1991).

A conflict of social values, the guidance of parents, the influence of peers, and the vocabularies of meanings youth attach to drug use cannot be underestimated as factors in the process leading to substance abuse. As noted by Celia Chun-Nui Lo and Gerald Globetti in chapter 3, substance abuse assists some youth in compensating for, or overcoming, some deficiency in their perception of self or life situation and may lead them to accept definitions favorable to drug use. Role behavior and the expressed attitudes of significant others influence a modeled lifestyle that for many youth may lead to substance abuse. As demonstrated by the case studies of Jim (a drinker), Judy (a marijuana user), David (a multiple drug user), and John (also a multiple substance abuser), youth might, because of the influence of role models and peers, be influenced to drink or use drugs. Motivated to use drugs to escape from a routine or an environment perceived as boring, because of an alienated state of mind, or perhaps as a form of rebellious repudiation or redefinition of the meanings attributed to their behavior, these youthful individuals first rejected the label attributed to their own behavior and that of their peer associates (Rogers and Buffalo 1974). Lo and Globetti describe the paths through which these youthful alcohol and drug users entered into, and then negotiated an exit from, a process that involved substance abuse through first modifying and then altering their behavior. According to the process of adaptation theorized by Joseph W. Rogers and M. D. Buffalo (1974), the teenagers acquiesced by first acknowledging and then moving toward accepting the validity of the claim that their behavior was problematic. They accomplished this by entering into rehabilitation. In the end, this entire process is best understood in reference to the negotiated meanings or vocabularies of motives people attach to their actions.

In chapter 4 we learn that traditional approaches to communicable diseases that threaten the community do not always receive the required reaction from public officials, nor are these traditional methods of control as beneficial as medical administrators would lead us to believe. In 1981, a phenomenon emerged from what was first identified by the medical community as a new form of cancer found among male homosexuals, a disease that later was to became known in some circles as the "gay plague." This socially debilitating stigma, now known as the AIDS virus, also redefined, in some measure, traditional medical and public health delivery and research models during the final decade of the millennium.

Although the AIDS virus is now known to affect individuals regardless of age, social standing, or racial background, Mary-Rose Mueller aptly points out that the traditional health model excluded or underrepresented many at risk and infected people from screenings and clinical trials oriented around traditional academic-based treatment projects. The program upon which this case study is based represents a new medical health reality that was created because control of this communicable disease necessitated a fresh approach to study the effects of the AIDS virus and to reach out to the large divergent population at risk. Drawing on the insights of Manis and Meltzer (1978), the result of complex negotiations between policymakers, clinicians, practitioners, and patients became humanized as was the creation of a program that promoted a new scientific approach to evaluating the AIDS problem. This redefinition of the situation resulted in what Rogers and Buffalo (1974) identify as an alteration of style or, in the words of Mary-Rose Mueller, an alteration in the normative structure of modern medical practice. The result was an integration of the scientific clinical research model with community-based care practice.

NOTE

1. The basic propositions of the symbolic interaction perspective outlined by Jerome G. Manis and Bernard N. Meltzer (1978, pp. 5–9), are aptly demonstrated throughout each of the three sections of social problems. These elements are:

1. Human behavior and interaction are carried on through the medium of symbols and their meanings

2. Individuals become humanized through a process of interaction with other individuals

3. Human society consists of people in interaction

4. Human beings actively shape their own behavior

5. Interaction with oneself involves conscious thinking

6. Human beings construct their behavior in the course of its execution

7. An understanding of human conduct requires knowledge of the motivations that cause the behavior.

REFERENCES

Goffman, Erving. 1969. *Strategic Interaction*. Philadelphia: University of Pennsylvania Press.
Manis, Jerome G., and Bernard N. Meltzer. 1978. *Symbolic Interaction: A Reader in Social Psychology*. Boston: Allyn and Bacon.
Mills, C. Wright. 1940. "Situated Actions and Vocabularies of Motives." *American Sociological Review* 5: 904–913.
Musto, David F. 1991. "Opium, Cocaine, and Marijuana in American History." *Scientific American* (July): 40–47.
Rogers, Joseph W., and M. D. Buffalo. 1974. "Fighting Back: Nine Modes of Adaptation to a Deviant Label." *Social Problems* 22: 101–118.

1

Suicide

Dennis L. Peck

INTRODUCTION

In a letter to "Dear Abby" ("Sister" 1998, p. 7D), a contributor wrote:

Two months ago my youngest sister called me—collect again—sobbing that she felt alone and frightened in the world. She asked if we could meet for tea or if I could visit her. As a mother of twins and self-employed, I reminded her that having tea in a cafe is a luxury I cannot afford. Last month she called me again. She wanted to spend Saturday night with us and make pancake breakfast "for old times' sake." She told me she missed me and felt blue. (Abby, Saturday nights are reserved for my husband.) Two weeks ago, my sister invited me to a matinee—her treat. She tearfully informed me that she was not sleeping well (she was being treated for depression and chronic fatigue syndrome.) I told her "working people don't go to matinees, but when you get your life together, you'll know what 'chronic-living-life-fatigue' is."

My little sister will never call again. She took her life last week.

My sister had some of the best medical help available, and I know she was ultimately responsible for her own life. But I also know that I'll never again brush her hair out of her sleepy blue eyes or trade my blouse for her mauve lipstick, or tell her she's not fat— she's beautiful. Most of all, I will never forgive myself for not realizing how suicidal my sister was. Perhaps this letter will prevent others from making the mistakes I made.

Perhaps no social problem captures the attention and emotions of acquaintances and loved ones as much as the act of suicide. Those individuals who knew the committer often question whether they could have assisted the individual in some way to cope with whatever pain or problems led to this act. The act of suicide also indicates that, for some individuals, life symbolizes a hopeless, meaningless existence, especially for those individuals who consider their present condition unacceptable and believe this condition will continue in the future.

The letter to Dear Abby represents a symbolic reaction that encompasses guilt and self-blame as well as pity for a loved one. This reaction is not atypical among those who survive the suicide of a friend or loved one. Most people are unprepared for such an event. The question that begs an answer is: How can we better understand and prevent this kind of social problem?

OVERVIEW OF THE SUICIDE PROBLEM

Although long the subject of scholarly analysis, acts of suicide or the intentional taking of one's life remain a matter of vexation. Jack Douglas (1967) identified suicide as one of the most researched topics of the previous 250 years; the contemporary experience is similar in that the act of suicide continues to be highly scrutinized, and remains a subject of considerable and varied community reaction and debate. As we move into the new millennium, suicide undoubtedly will remain a controversial topic over which diverse social, religious, medical, legal, and scientific perspectives will continue to be in conflict.

Suicide is committed primarily by white males at almost twice the rate of black males (*Statistical Abstract of the United States, 1997*, p. 102). However, suicidal behavior has been engaged in increasingly by elderly persons as well as terminally ill individuals regardless of gender. In the United States, suicide rates have increased since 1980 in only two age-specific age groups: 15–19 years and 65 years and older (Public Health Service, 1996, p. 3).

Historically, age-specific rates of suicides in the United States have been highest among the elderly, specifically, among older males. During the 1980–1992 period, males accounted for 81 percent of the suicides among elderly persons 65 years of age and older. During this same period, a total of 384,262 suicides occurred in the United States of which 74,675, or 19 percent, were elderly persons.

According to a federal government Annual Summary Report, during the 1990s the number of suicides recorded each year increased while the rate remained relatively stable. For example, during the 1990 to 1995 period, the rates of suicide for all races and both sexes were 11.5, 11.4, 11.1, 11.3, 11.2, and 11.0 respectively (*Statistical Abstract of the United States, 1997*, p. 95 Table 128). During 1996, 29,280 persons (rate = 11.1) died from a self-inflicted death, the number of suicides increased during 1997 to 29,580 (rate = 11.1), and a similar rate is projected each year for the remainder of the decade (National Center for Health Statistics, 1998).

Suicide is a social problem that is much larger in scope than is homicide, and it is one category of death that is preventable. Symbolic of diminished hope among those who choose to end their life, suicide also is viewed as a tragic end to the human experience. Although the very young and the very old are at greater risk, the risk factors for the elderly differ from those among the young. For example, older suicide victims have a much higher prevalence of alcohol abuse, depression, and social isolation while younger victims of suicide experience more stress related to competition for resources and disparity between their high expectations for success and material gain as opposed to their ability to meet these expectations. Accordingly, the youthful suicide rate has increased threefold during the past four decades (Clark and Mokros 1993).

Theoretical Issues and Explanations

Long the topic of scientific inquiry, the topic of suicide has led to numerous theoretical explanations. The first sociological theory developed to explore this phenomenon was created by Emile Durkheim (1951 [1897]). Strong social ties such as those created through work, marriage, having children, and engaging in other social commitments protect against suicide, according to Emile Durkheim (1951 [1897]), who demonstrated that suicide rates are relatively low and even decrease during the stages of the life cycle between late adolescence and old age. Durkheim's proposition continues to be supported. As noted above, only among the youthful and elderly age-specific categories have the rates of suicide increased.

A partial explanation for this increase among the youthful population may be the improved documentation that some analysts have observed. Until recently many coroners and medical examiners were hesitant to accept suicidal behavior among the very young, but reporting procedures currently reflect a different perspective among those trained to investigate cases of equivocal death.

Less general explanations that facilitate the assessment of the factors and conditions leading to the suicidal act are varied. Some of these explanations are based on interviews conducted with attempters, while others are based on statements documented in notes and letters crafted by individuals who made the decision that death provides the ultimate solution for whatever difficulties are experienced on a day-to-day basis. Included are causal explanations that identify failure (Breed 1967), anomie (Durkheim 1951 [1897]), diminished hope (Farber 1968) or hopelessness (Shneidman 1985), guilt (Henslin 1970), an imbalance existing between social conditions (Mestrovic and Glassner 1983), fatalism (Peck 1980), imitation and elitism (Stack 1987), shame (Mokros 1995), and the interaction between the individual with public and social forces (Maris 1997). After combining several of these social psychological components, yet another explanation introduces a rational decision-making component to suicidal behavior (e.g., Battin 1982; Maris 1982; Peck 1983; Kevorkian 1991; Werth and Cobia 1995; and Werth 1996). Although this rational explanation challenges more traditional views that argue suicide represents impulsive, nonrational behavior, the rational component of suicide may be deemed to be a plausible explanation if considered from the perspective of the principal actor involved, namely the committer.

Suicide evokes strong emotional reactions among family survivors and others and, despite what appears to be an increasing understanding and tolerance among, for example, members of the medical community, some analysts continue to report a negative view of suicide among college-age students (Lester, McCabe, and Cameron 1991–1992) and the membership of religious groups (Barry 1994). A similar attitude currently exists among some policymakers and concerned citizens.

Certain types of suicide may also be of greater concern to the community at large, especially those committed by juveniles, dyatic deaths (homicide/suicide), and the increasing number of elderly persons who choose to terminate their lives because of pain and loneliness, occasionally assisted by individuals (such as Dr. Jack Kevorkian) who are attempting to present a different understanding of suicide to the public based on rational decision making. However, Kevorkian's deviant label, Dr. Death, symbolizes the emotional chasm and legal interpretations that continue to divide public, political, and scientific views of this topic. Witness, for example, the view offered by Barry:

From the Roman Catholic perspective suicide is not compassionate, just, rational, or of social merit because it does not protect the weak and vulnerable from self-inflicted harm . . . (I) will question claims that suicide can be rational, and . . . (I) will . . . espouse the view that the real-world situations in which suicide could be construed as a rational act are so few as to be insignificant. (1994, p. xx)

But as we progress into the twenty-first century it is clear that some behavior previously considered to always be deviant is now the subject of evaluations that differ from those of the past. Included among the normative reactions to suicide is that for a variety of reasons people do make a conscious, rational decision to take their life. Not all individuals need be considered so depressed that they cannot think "properly" and, therefore, are not rational.

Although the motives for suicidal behavior vary, one factor common among those who attempt suicide is the influence of significant others upon self-esteem. According to Dukes and Lorch (1989, p. 316), "low self-esteem predicts a diminished sense of purpose in life," and, in turn, low self-esteem fosters suicidal behavior as a response to stress and role conflict (Jacobs 1967; Maris 1971; 1981; 1982; Breed 1972; Newman, Whittemore, and Newman 1973; Wilson 1981; Battin 1982; Droogas, Siiter, and O'Connell 1982–1983; Peck 1983, and Mokros 1995). Moreover, stress-related research has demonstrated that the absence of a bonding influence between an individual and their significant other(s) diminishes the well-being of individuals who are encumbered by stress, thereby inhibiting their problem solving skills (Thoits 1982; Ritter 1985) as well as their ability to respond to and cope with changing social conditions (Peck and Folse 1990).

Personal control, as Reynolds and Farberow (1976) note, is instrumental to healthy self-esteem and a positive view of life, while escalating problems could, according to Topol and Resnikoff (1982, p. 149), "lead to an increasing sense of hopelessness and importance about effecting solutions . . . eventually ending in a suicidal mental set."

The influence of significant relationships upon one's self-esteem, as evaluated by Kaplan and Pokorny (1976, p. 23), indicates "the adoption of suicidal responses tends to be preceded by negative self-attitudes." These analysts argue that a positive relationship exists between "suicidal behaviors and the experience of self-derogation in the most recent past" (p. 33), further noting that suicidal responses to negative self-attitude represent an attempt to avoid further self-devaluing experiences. Self-demand, levels of aspiration, standards of performance, expectations of significant others, and self-judgment produce what Farber (1968, p. 299) theorized as the probability that suicidal behavior will vary inversely with the level of one's sense of competence.

Almost six decades ago Davidson (1941) observed that suicidal behavior was not uncommon among individuals who extended themselves to the limits of available resources, but failed to achieve an acceptable level of performance. Similarly, Breed (1968) estimated that one-half of the suicides committed each year in the United States qualify as failure suicides. Failure suicide is conceived on the foundation of a self-attitude that, according to Breed (1968), involves a sequence of behaviors, reactions by others, and negative self-perception. Factors that influence failure suicide include "great sensitivity to failure and the shame which accompanies it; the inability to change goals and roles; and worsening of interpersonal relations" (Breed 1968, p. 287). In addition, as noted by Peck and Folse (1990), self-derogation and feelings of low self-worth are causes for individuals to view themselves as insignificant and, therefore, unworthy of living. Corder and Haizlip (1984) and Eth, Pynoos, and Carlson (1984) suggest that suicide represents a final, impulsive behavioral act by individuals who had attempted to repair negative self-perceptions while inhibited by a stress level that interfered with normal coping mechanisms. Such conceptual issues serve as the focal point for the symbolic interactionist approach to understanding suicidal behavior.

Suicide Notes

According to Shneidman and Farberow (1957) and Yessler, Gibbs, and Becker (1960) less than 25 percent of committers communicate their intent through the use of a suicide note. Nevertheless, for analysts such as Leenaars (1988, p. 34), suicide notes represent the ultrapersonal document, unsolicited productions of suicidal persons usually written minutes before the suicidal act. Moreover, Bauer et al. (1997) report that through the use of suicide notes, analysts are privy to information that enhances our understanding of the complex issues involved in the decision to terminate one's life. Assuming these analysts are correct, suicide notes represent a valuable starting point for understanding the symbolic social factors influencing those who choose to end their lives.

In the case study that follows, the information contained in the suicide diary pertains to ideation, personal problems, and other issues utilized by the author to establish the reasons for her suicidal act. Nancy died at age 48, an age when many individuals are at their peak performance. Nancy's legacy continues through the presentation of her thoughts as they were documented over several days just prior to her death. She left behind a message that is intriguing and perhaps somewhat perplexing.

NANCY: A CASE STUDY

Experiencing an unstable childhood, Nancy E. married for the first time at age 17. This union led to the birth of her only child; the marriage ended after a two-year period.

Gifted with exceptional athletic ability as a gymnast, Nancy earned a college scholarship and later secured a berth on the U.S. Olympic team. Soon thereafter, Nancy again fell in love and married a second time. This marriage also ended in divorce.

Several years later, Nancy married her third husband, entering into a union that offered ample opportunity for travel and a lifestyle that allowed her to demonstrate a graceful athletic ability and superior intellect. Identified by Nancy's daughter as the happiest period of Nancy's life, these years were short in number. At age 42, a cerebral aneurysm left Nancy partially paralyzed. Her youthful, attractive appearance and intelligence eroded; Nancy's pleasing personality also changed resulting in periods of memory loss, prolonged sullenness, and hostility. Later attributed to periodic ischesmic attacks, these problems led to her third divorce. Brain surgery followed, and three years later a traffic accident resulted in Nancy suffering severe leg and facial injuries that required radical surgery.

Upon her discharge from the hospital Nancy co-habited with a male as a means to pool her limited financial resources. She again fell in love, but this time the target of Nancy's affection was unaffected by her overtures, and the couple continued to co-habitate. Disappointment resulting from this failed attempt to establish a relationship and frustrated over her inability to secure a job to ease her financial plight, Nancy also experienced menopause.

As noted above, the cumulative effect of factors such as these affect interpersonal relationships with others, causing alienation from friends and acquaintances who could provide people such as Nancy the succorance so urgently desired. Within this context, the self-assessment of personal well-being and rationality seem crucial to understanding the motivation to engage in self-destructive behavior. As will be demonstrated in the following section, many of the characteristics common to those vulnerable to suicidal behavior can be identified in the thoughts documented by Nancy.

In the following, the verbatim text of a suicide diary drafted over a period of several days serves to demonstrate the process by which self-derogation results from interactions within the social environment, including one individual whom Nancy viewed as a significant other.

A SUICIDE DIARY

November 23, 7:35 p.m.
God knows, I don't want to die. But I've simply just run out of time. The ideal solution would be to just disappear. However, I can't even do that.

Bob, your suggestion that I commit suicide sounds like a logical reasonable solution. The first time you asked me why I didn't, I just ignored you. But the second time it registered. After all, Bob, isn't that the way of a liar, cheat & a thief.

Same day, 1:00 a.m.
I managed to talk myself out of suicide tonight. I have to admit the Paris helps. I wish (almost) that I were an alcoholic. If so, then I could accommodate this horrendous pain & find an excuse (justify) for what I am sure seems like irrational drinking & more asinine uncontrol & weakness.

I found the gun tonight. Now, all I need is the bullets. God, I don't want to die. However, again tonight I had to smile (oh shit that's the Kessler incoordination) & make small talk (about the weather, the cats,—"who Mr. Gordon is"—etc. (to Bob before he left, this is). I have given myself until Jan 1 . . . to get my act together. Please, Bob, be gone by then. I hope I have the strength & fortitude to daily recoup my self-esteem go on living, regardless of the pain. By the pain, of course, I primarily mean the mental anguish. The super horror of realizing that I am and have been duped by the only (that sounds pretty dramatic Nanc) love of my entire 48 years.——

But that's another category & era; one that is too personal & painful to divulge indiscriminately. I haven't eaten in 28 hours—& common sense tells me that I must eat & try to rest now. It's 1:30 a.m. on the day before Thanksgiving. . . .

P.S. Simmy Cat isn't home yet, either.

Thanksgiving morning, 8:00 a.m.
I've just re-read what I wrote yesterday. In retrospect, it sounds so incoherent. When I wrote it I wasn't babbling, but this shows one how important the human voice is to convey integrity, mode, and meaning.

I've tried to think of alternatives to death. I did manage to sleep about 3 hours last night. I woke up & it was daylight and immediately gagged. God, I hope my self-control will improve; the physical aspects of this ugly mess could be the straw that finally breaks my back. By this I mean: The pain is so overwhelming, sometimes I'm afraid I won't be able to conceal it. I'm referring to the physical pain, now. Egad—my head, chest, (back) it goes straight through so really can't discern where one stops & the other begins, ankles, wrist, some fingers. This is a ridiculous rhetoric (sp.?) I didn't mention the super hurts—but what difference does it make. I'm merely talking to this paper with this pen trying to fend off the next wave of despair.

I'm so humiliated that Bob really & sincerely does believe that he must lock up his wallet when he's here. Oh God—how did we get so far apart. That last statement was a typical dumb ineffectual pointless remark from me.

We got so far apart because of mutual inability to communicate. Perhaps its more dis-inclination than inability on Bob's part. Is there such a word as dis-inclination?

I just thought of the fact that Bob will probably say that he's afraid that I'll shoot him when he finds out I have the gun. I'd like to think that he knows that I would never do anything to hurt him. But, of course, he either doesn't know or doesn't believe that. I have too strong altruistic tendencies to vent any ill feelings toward him. Just cause Nanc loves Bob doesn't mean Bob has to love Nanc.

If he would just go & stay gone the constant daily heartbreak of seeing the disgust and, yes, the revulsion at times takes every bit of strength I have. His actions reflect all of the above, as does his mouth on occasions. Please, please, please go out of my life Bob. I've begged, cajoled & considered threatening him with legal action but his stock answer is no. No reasons, just no. However, he does say things that I know he feels I can't get by financially if he goes. Yes, as I think back, I know thats what he's told me.

He has told me repeatedly how my family (my children (his children, I mean) don't love me and what a lousy other (step-mother) I was. "He gave me the responsibility of raising Mike & I did such a terrible job I ruined him". I don't feel totally responsible for Mike, I honestly & lovingly did the best I could. I see now that I apparently was a lousy Mother. Deb has told me a couple of things that I did that startled & dismayed me. According to Bob Mile & Sue really do have no use for me. When I think about it I was the one (after the divorce) who has always pushed for the relationship. I invited them, but they came to see their Dad. I didn't really care since I got to see them too. In a milder degree than Bob has told me I know Mike & Sue have no deep affection for their step-mother but I had no idea they felt so intensely against me. It shouldn't have been a surprise tho, considering Bob's low opinion of me. I absolutely must eat something & keep it down!!

Happy Turkey Day, Foo!

I managed to get Bob Ettl out of my system once; *I can do it again.* It's 9:45 a.m. & he isn't here yet. I wonder if he'll be here to eat any of the turkey I'm cooking (he didn't know).

As I think of things I write them down. This happens over a period of hours. Therefore, that accounts for the apparent ramblings which, of course, I am doing, too.

Oh God—I wish I understood.

11–24; 11:45 a.m.

Again I say I don't want to die. Oh I baked the turkey & made the gravy. I sliced the turkey & fed some to Foo. He was delighted. Simmy is asleep.

I couldn't eat any myself dammit. So here I sit = what a mess I've made of my life. Neither Mike nor Jimmy has called me back. It's been 2 hours for Mike and 1 ½ hrs since I called Jim. I wanted to invite Mike over to eat (Grandma isn't eating until tonight.) It's silly for me to make a pie for just me. I was going to ask Jimmy if he wanted a lemon merrange (sp?) pie. I should have told Bobby when he answered & said Jim was busy—so he'd know I wasn't calling with car trouble. I really wanted to ask him where my grandchildren are—no one answers at Deb's. I'm kinda worried. Joe & Pat are in California—they can't be there. If Jim has the kids where's Deb?!

Noon
I've decided to indicate the time so this is more congruent. I just ate some turkey & it stayed down. I'm starting to get a little weak. The *damn pains* in my head!!! I think they're from a lack of food this time. I generally do get a headache when I don't eat.

4:45
Hot damn! I beat the grim reaper again today. I think I'll be alright for a few days (hours?) now I've thought & thought about it—If I can get a decent paying job I'll get a good deal of my self respect back. How the hell could anyone like, let alone love me. I don't even like myself. Come on *Career Works!!*

Nov. 25; 1 A.M.
Before I even write anything—let me say I have had too much to drink in antici-pation of finally being able to eat & sleep. I must do this in order to sleep & eat & finish school. I must sleep & eat to finish school.—& I must finish school to prove to Bob & myself that I am not a total retard, dummy and/or totally disgusting.

Bob came home (showed up) pretty drunk tonight about 5:30 p.m. I left because I really didn't know what else to do with my drunken son, Mike at about 6:45. I wanted to get Mike out of Bob's way & vice versa. They were both so drunk; they would possibly have said things that neither one of them meant. Mike was doing a pretty damn good job of that all by himself & Bob would have eventually have to either defend or retaliate.

God—I wish I wouldn't have talked myself out of buying the bullets today.

I really must give the job club a chance regardless of the fact that I do exactly the same thing on my own time at home. These people don't know that I have the self-discipline & integrity to do the same darn thing at home. But then, what can you expect of a liar, a cheat & a thief.

I need to stop writing now & have a cup of coffee & a cigarette.

I'm really not so sure that my success against the "grim reaper" (as my inept attempt at humor calls it is really a success in the long run.

The same nausea, inability to eat, diaherria (sp?) terrible spelling. & I don't really even care to look it up. (I wonder if I'll refrain from buying food, cigarettes and or liquor until Monday. Bob threw $10.00 (Mike took the $. He was drunk I know he didn't realize it.) gas money at me so that I can go to the job club Monday.

Oh dear God (for an agnostic I sure as hell say that often enough in here. However, dear God—that is if I can manage to keep myself alive until then.

1:35 am.
I must drink some more coffee & go check to see if Mike is home or if Bob is at Wolffs—why in the hell do I have to see if Bob is at Wolffs Gardens. (compulsive time passer) It's none of my damn business.

But then—I'm terrified that he might go without paying the back rent that he owes. I can make the payments on the Titanic!!!!!

11–29; 2:30 a.m.
So much has happened. I closed the Paris at 9:00 p.m. on Sunday evening. Thank the lord for friends, I didn't spend a dime. I cleaned off tables. I thought I was going to be sick until I got close enough to the house to see that Bob was here when I came home. I went to sleep & he made the bed & remade it in a fashion so that he wouldn't

have to sleep under the covers with me. (my interpretation or does he have another reason reasonable I mean)

8:00 a.m.

The above was Sunday. I must back track to Saturday. I drove to the gun store but it was too early & they weren't open yet. So I drove around just looking for the caddy for hours. I don't know what I thought that was going to accomplish. I'd die of humiliation if Bob saw me drive by—he's not dumb, he'd know I was looking for him. He's entitled to do as he pleases with his life. I keep telling myself that & I do believe it—but I guess I can't accept the rejection.

I broke down in front of Chloie & Evelyn—(at different times but in front of their husbands, too) I feel it best I do die—how can I ever see them again. I looked so piteously weak & disgustingly out of control. Oh well—enough of that.

On Monday I went to the job club with high hopes of being able to find a job.

Sunday afternoon I called about the apartment next door. He met me at 1:00 p.m. to se it—Its so nice & roomy & clean. It was so hard to keep it all together & not break down. I'm afraid perhaps I wasn't too coherent at times; I kept trying to make jokes. (Did they come off?) The landlord was willing to rent to me in a minute if Bob would come, too. He agreed to accept me alone, but he had reservations—rightly so—I have no visible means of support. God—I have wanted out of here for so long!!

11–29; 3:00

Repeat: On Monday I went to the job club with high hopes of being able to find a job. However, my first observation is that its another phony agency that drags out services in order to receive government funds. They statistically credit themselves with a success ratio of 68% in job placement. Regardless of their spiel; that's a better percentage than I've encountered anywhere else or by myself. I'll do anything they suggest = please, please don't let this be another blind alley. I hope I have the patience & ability to cope a couple more weeks.

I went to school Monday evening; I was there physically if not mentally I made my mind up to talk to Bob the next time I saw him. I was so frantic I was seriously considering not driving for fear I might hurt someone in another car. But, then I sat & my car & reasoned that the goal is to see Bob so I was alright to conduct myself.—& he was here! I was so delighted & at the same time scared that I'd say the wrong thing or not be able to convey what I wanted to say in a collected respectable manner.

8:00 p.m.; 11–28

He said "The spark is gone" "I don't love you like that" "I'm concerned for your welfare as a friend." "He assured me he wouldn't leave without giving me plenty of time to tell welfare." God—I tried so hard to find consolation in that. "He restated that he would finish the Titanic if I would come up with the money." I slept for a whole 6 ½ hours. Soundly & restfully. He was here & okay.

Monday a.m. 11–28

I went over to Helen Gordon's at 7:45 a.m. to ask her to borrow $1000.00 I threw up in her alley. Thank God not her house. The conversation was spattered with the conventional pleasantries & it was truly not so horrible & difficult as I anticipated. She wasn't judgmental at all & seemed to almost sympathize with my emotional involvement. She said she would check her *special* fund to see if she had enough to loan me.

I made it through job club very well some how. I offered a woman a ride downtown 7 we came out to a flat tire on Patrick. I went in Whatney school and called Helen to tell her I couldn't stop by to see about the loan as planned. I also called Barb McCormich to say I couldn't stop by to pick up my letter of reference from Travel Host; & Steve Gibson, Stautzer herger Counselor to cancel my appt. top discuss a work-study program. I called Bob & he showed up & God—again—what would I have done if he hadn't. (I need to be able to join Triple A so badly).

4:00 a.m.; 11–29

As I'm writing this Bob worked in this freezing cold weather, & with his bad shoulder for an hour & couldn't break the damn tire loose. (Too many problems encountered to recount them all) Sufficient to say that he put forth a super-human effort & told me what to do. He even gave me money to pay for the tire. He left; I came home & boiled potatoes to fix salmon patties & fried 'taters' (one of his favorite) for supper. I wrote him a note (I asked him to tell me if he was not going to be here so that I wouldn't cook & waste food) to that effect & went to school. Again I managed to get through classes. I only had to run to the john once & not to throw up—to keep from crying. I was successful; no one had any idea I was losing control.

I gagged all the way home & was nauseated—but no upchuck. He was here! I rehearsed telling him about moving all the while I prepared dinner. I did prepare a decent meal & then totally destroyed my good intentions by not turning the stove completely off under the salmon frying pan. The house filled with smoke.

Perhaps he left because the smoke annoyed him & irritated his eyes so. But—I'm rationalizing & I know it. Of course he had plans. Probably had them even before I interfered with his schedule to fix my tire.

This happened at 12:30 a.m.

11–29

I came home . . . & fixed supper. I ate a helping and a half & kept it all down. He was undressed & in his jamies when I came in. He read the paper. He got up at 7 shaved & monkeyed around for a few minutes with the Shammy Burt lay-out on the drawing board. I realized that he had shaved when he came out pulling on his pants & carrying clean socks. Oh dear God!!!!!!! He's leaving. I asked "are you going out now?" I sat up & said "Well, I had better talk to you now cause I don't know when I'll see you again. I told him about borrowing the money & wanting to rent the apartment next door. (God almighty I'm so very tired of living like a pig & a gypsy). Bob's comment when I told him how roomy & clean it was:—"You'll fuck that place up, too."

I don't understand—I can keep a nice house when I have something to work with. He said he didn't know if he would move (in quotes) "with me" or not as he didn't want to move again until it was to a place with a garage & studio—I don't see how I can stand living here for one more day with the cockroaches, mice, & the marijuana smoke through the registers.

He was very affectionate & petted the cats when he left. He took a long time (maybe it just seemed like it to me tying and re-tying his shoes, finding his gloves & adjusting his sweat shirt hood. He stopped at the door & gave me a big smile & said "see you later."

I didn't even bother to ask him "are you gone for the night?" He always says he doesn't know whenever I ask him anything—even the simplest questions merit a perfunctory distasteful reply.

5:00 a.m. Tues. eve/Wed morn.

I wish I could sleep—I managed to keep most of my supper down by telling myself that he would be back by 3:00 a.m. Management by objective has helped me get through a lot hours that seem to pass by frantic, desparing seconds at a time. Shimmy came back

I've called for & looked for Simmy cat several times, he must have gone out when Bob did.

He asked me this afternoon while he was fixing the tire if I had done his laundry. I was so embarrassed to have to say no. He knows I've told him that I won't wash his farty shorts so he can look pretty for his dates. When he left at 12:30 a.m. I killed an hour or so by doing a load of his laundry. Looks like I'll have it dried & put away before he needs to change again.

5:30 a.m.

The nausea is better but I'm shaking so damn hard & my eyes look terrible (swollen) from crying. I have to get it together for the rest of this day. I hope I can physically hold up with no sleep for another 14 hours till I'm home again. *I have to study my accounting so* that I understand Chap 8 & can pass the test on Thurs. Oh—I have a test on chap 18 & 19 in econ, too.

Good luck, Nanc.

I always thought love was fulfilling & a beautiful experience based on what I see I most other relationships. Am I incapable of such a relationship? For 30 years, Bob Ettl & sex & family & joy & pleasure & on & on & on have been synonymous to my head & heart. I never lost the damn "spark."

11–29; 8:00 a.m.

When I write it down, it sounds childish & juvenile & wimpy. I wish it were not true I don't want to die—but I'm too old & too tired to change now. I would shun a lily-livered spineless, whining dumb broad like me if I were a man. That's a perfectly normal & honest reaction to an unpleasant situation. Neither Bob nor I ever dealt in losers.—Since I am a loser now; it follows that he should seek a winners. My God, I do love him so very very much. I'd give anything to be able to make him proud of me again.

11–30; 9:00 am Wed

I called Job Club & said I would be late. I called Mr. Kirkbride (landlord next door) & told him to rent the apt if he can—but that I would call him "if I got my check." I fed him a bunch of bull-shit about waiting for a check that the government was holding up from Travel Host. I also called Kowalka & found out they open at 10:00. I have obviously elected to stop struggling.

Wed. 11–30

I have to stop writing now & go to Kowalkas. Its 10:35 a.m. & Bob hasn't come home yet. I must go & get the bullets & hurry right back so as to be sure & not miss him. I'm aware it means nothing to him but I simply must see him one last time. Egad, I've written the great American novel. But now I really must go . . .

11–30; Noon

I went to Kawalkas & got the bullets & got smokes at Avalos. Then I took a ride & looked for Bob. Naturally he isn't—whatever. It has been almost a full seven days now since Bob left for the long Thanksgiving week-end & I went into this ridiculous blue funk. It will be a week in exactly seven hours & ten minutes.

I have my plans all made. All I have to do now is wait for Bob to get here. When he does, I'll run over & mail however much I've written. This has to be the longest suicide note in the world. I'll come back & say goodbye & force myself on him one last time. I don't mean sexually. I mean a hug & with luck, a quick kiss.

Goodbye, my dearest. At last you'll be free completely & under no obligation to me. Even though you originally imposed the obligation on yourself, it isn't fair to have you feel morally responsible for me. You can't just dump me—your conscience won't let you do that. I think I understand now why you suggested suicide to me a couple of times. As Helen Gordon says, she can't understand this strange influence you have over nice girls, Bob.

The world knows that self-destruction is the work of an emotionally deranged mind, so you're exonerated. I don't mean that sarcastically—or facetiously, either. Merely a statement of a judgment that you are responsible in a way but you really aren't.

11–30; Wed.; 2:00 p.m.
Bob is finally here. He's in the bathroom so I'll take a minute for one last word. God, I still don't really want to die. But as usual Bob is right. No sarcasm. His batting average is way over 1,000%—(maybe 400?) This is hardly the time to be cracking jokes

Practical Particulars
Bob-
Please take care of Foo.
Donate me to M.C.O
Everything I have left is Debs.
I m sorry & I love you all.
It really is better this way.

2:20 p.m
Bob just left. I really lucked out. For the first time in weeks I asked if he would be here for supper & he said yes. I'm settled down & have a definite goal. The end is finally in sight. I can't think of anything more that I would have to say that would be pertinent or that anyone would really care to hear.—I know—you really don't care to hear any of this. However, I may get to see Bob more than for just a minute.—I'm going to load all the chambers in the gun just in case I'm so shaky I miss. That way I'll have another shot (at least) to make sure. Oh God, I misplaced the firing pin. I was right when I said I couldn't even commit suicide right. Well I guess its the other way, now. You're free, Bob. Crazy as I am, my love is healthy. I want only the best for you—You're free now.   NE

Sometime later Nancy was found by her daughter who admitted Nancy to a hospital where her stomach was pumped after which she was placed under observation. While hospitalized, Nancy obtained a substantial number of pills that she ingested and then died.

Consistent with the findings that rejected individuals choose active methods (firearms, hanging, and stabbing) to end their lives (Leenaars and Lester 1988–1989), Nancy's initial method of choice was a firearm. However, as noted, she misplaced the firing pin. The "other way" meant taking an overdose of pills, a less active method but similar to that chosen by her mother. Did Nancy really intend to die?

DISCUSSION AND CONCLUSION

Many reasons are documented or inferred to others by individuals who decide when their lives will end. Among these reasons are illness and pain, the loss of a career position or community stature, indebtedness, a troubled relationship, a lack of meaning for one's life with a future deemed to bring more of the same, a low self-concept, and a lack of direction. The list appears endless.

Stress factors known to contribute to emotional instability include financial crisis, personal ineptitude, and repeated failure. Some analysts suggest that the suicide rate affects older women more than males, especially when socioeconomic factors such as labor force participation are controlled (e.g., Newman, Whittemore, and Newman 1973; Yang and Lester 1988; Lester and Yang 1992). This lack of economic opportunity also appears to hold severe consequences for individuals, such as Nancy, whose chronic unemployment lead them to financial dependency on others.

As people age, those who are preoccupied with their perceived inability to cope with change and the concomitant social expectations to adapt to changed conditions become increasingly distressed (Peck and Folse 1990). As age-specific stressors accumulate, such as physical illness, dependency caused by financial difficulty, and a diminished mental capability, those prone to seek suicide as a final solution experience great emotional pain (Leenaars 1997). Nancy possessed these characteristics. She also experienced a diminished sense of self. Drawing upon the insights of Mokros (1995, pp. 1094–1095),

It is within the context of social bonds that we experience the self through the actions and reactions of the other (including the self as other) to the self. This omnipresent experience of the self in relation to the other is "internalized" early in the life of a child. The mind becomes a theater in which the self takes the role of the other in relation to the self. In other words, the self problemizes it-self by looking through the "expectational" lense of the other. Through interactional and reflexive self-other experiences, we evolve a sense of identity that is most adequately understood in terms of social bonds.

Based on her eventful past, Nancy also had a great deal of pride, but the present condition offered a different set of circumstances which included the lack of a significant other in her life. As noted by social interactionist theorists such as Charles Horton Cooley (1964 [1902]), George Herbert Mead (1934), and Erving Goffman (1983), establishing and maintaining social bonds serves as a fundamental goal of human motivation. Nancy's life was shattered and her previous focus destroyed. Torn apart by a series of deleterious events and less than desirable interactions with others, her goals of resuming a career and once again establishing a significant relationship were all but eliminated. Again, drawing on the insights of Mokros (1995, p. 1096), Nancy's present situation became a source of shame for her.

Feelings aroused along the shame-pride continuum are regulatory in the sense that they call attention to one's place and responsibility to the social bond. Through the experience of pride, we experience integration into the social bond. Through shame, we experience separation and distance and the pull toward social reintegration. Shame may thus be regarded as a 'routine' regulatory component of everyday experience that brings to awareness one's sense of place and self as contingent upon others within the social bond.

Nancy's attempts at reintegration failed. Unable to secure employment, to rent a place of her own, or to gain the attention of Bob underscored this failure.

Because of a diminished ability to control important aspects of her life, Nancy experienced so many stressful moments that the level of pertubation, described by Leenaars (1997, p. 77) was high which may explain why Nancy initially selected a firearm as the method of choice for committing suicide. Rejecting the many options available that could reduce her level of stress, Nancy chose to die. While perhaps unconvincing as a rational decision to some, the choice seems logical, at least from Nancy's perspective.

Nancy's choice also is consistent with the findings reported by Leenaars and Lester (1988–1989, p. 312): "In the suicide note, the person communicated that the root cause of his [sic] self-destruction is the sense of total rejection, in a personality that already depreciates itself." Nancy's symbolic world, so dependent on the evaluation and interpretation of her housemate, apparently weakened the effectiveness of those individuals who held more supportive views, including her loving daughter. The inability to secure gainful employment, her social marginality, and a recognized rejection by her housemate served to reduce even further whatever self-respect Nancy may have had during this crucial period of her life. The solution, suicide, became in this instance a meaningful solution for her many problems. Nancy's words suggest that by actively seeking to terminate her life she was involved in planning a rational act.

Consistent with the findings reported by Vella, Persic, and Lester (1996), Nancy's low self-esteem became associated with a desire to end her life. One important difference in this instance is that Nancy's inability to recognize that Bob's view of her and actions toward her symbolized failure to such an extent that she was incapable of recognizing that others viewed her differently.

The effect of interpersonal relationships can not be underestimated. Responding to the negative, condescending statements of her housemate, Nancy's evaluation of his behavior was all consuming. Her own thoughts portray a damaged, low conception of self and negative self-esteem. The future, from Nancy's perspective, did not appear to offer much in the way of improvement over her current situation, leaving her without any meaningful alternative choices.

Margaret Battin (1982) describes several criteria which should be taken into consideration when tendering an assessment regarding the utility of the rational explanation of suicide. Summarizing these criteria, Werth (1996, p. 292) states the person must have an ability to reason, have a realistic world view, have adequate information, avoid harm, and be acting in accordance with her or his fundamental interests. This insight currently serves as the substance for serious discussion among those who evaluate suicidal behavior from the perspective of the actress/actor. Going beyond philosophy, one recent empirically based discussion emphasizes three components: (1) the presence of an unremittingly hopeless condition, (2) a suicidal decision as a free choice, and (3) the presence of an informed decision-making process (Werth and Cobia 1995, pp. 235–238). These criteria are based on an attitude survey of psychotherapists, 88 percent of whom, in responding to the rational suicide question, indicated they believe people do engage in a rational decision-making process when committing suicide (Werth and Cobia 1995, p. 234). Central to our discussion, each of the three criteria discussed by Werth and Cobia are found in Nancy's documented thoughts.

Although suicide is a social act rather than the act of a private, subjective individual (Maris 1997, p. 41), it is important to consider the emotional dynamics that exist between the individual and his or her public and social components. It is within this context that the quality of a person's symbolic world is best understood. Nancy's thoughts symbolize what the measured quality of her world meant for her. Nancy's symbolic world changed as did the quality of her interactions. It is within this context that Nancy's low conception of self affected her ability to negotiate a satisfactory position within the social bond. Shame appears to have served as the fundamental motivation for Nancy's suicidal act. Based on the standard of rationality referred to, Nancy chose to remove herself from this painful existence.

The question raised at the beginning of this chapter is: How can we better understand and prevent this kind of social problem? The is not an easy task, but it is one that has undergone analytical and clinical scrutiny for an extended period of time. Recently much has been written about suicide prevention, especially among adolescents and young adults. However, suicide is not a phenomenon bound to any age, racial, or gender category and, although greater understanding has been achieved, it remains a matter in need of further scrutiny.

Can we create a world without suicide as suggested by Pender (1996)? Or should efforts even be considered in directing our efforts toward reducing the number of suicide victims? As a much younger person seeking permission to enter a Medical Examiner's office for the purpose of securing a data set on suicide to be used to write my M.A. thesis, a question posed to me by the veteran deputy medical examiner was: And how do you intend to commit suicide? Surprised by this question, my response was something to the effect that

I had not given any thought to the matter and my purpose in calling was that I sought these data for analytical use in achieving the goal as stated. In turn, this old man responded: "Everyone thinks of taking their own life at some time. Everyone experiences depression." Perhaps the old veteran observer was correct and, if so, it is reasonable that much recent effort has been directed toward establishing creative means to prevent suicide in adolescents, age 12–18 (Berman and Jobes 1995), young adults, age 18–30 (Lipschitz 1995), adults, age 30–65 (Maris 1995), and the elderly, age 65–99 (McIntosh 1995). However, the strategies for suicide prevention among each of these age groups are usually based on the assumption that the suicidal person is depressed, perhaps for many of the reasons cited earlier in this chapter. Based on the research findings of numerous empirical assessments and clinical evaluations this approach to identifying and dealing with depressed individuals is reasonable. However, not all who may think of committing suicide do so because of a depressed state of mind; all depressed people do not commit suicide. Can we state with confidence that depression is the cause for all or most acts of self-destruction?

The vast range of interdisciplinary theories and empirical findings notwithstanding, the act of self-destruction continues to serve as a major challenge for interested students of this phenomenon. Like all social problems, no single perspective or prevention strategy may prove absolute for eliminating or controlling whatever is identified as *the* most important cause of suicide. Rather, suicidal behavior arises in the complex dynamics involving social factors and the individual, as the case study of Nancy demonstrates.

REFERENCES

Barry, Robert L. 1994. *Breaking the Thread of Life: On Rational Suicide.* New Brunswick, N.J.: Transaction Publishers.

Battin, Margaret Pabst. 1982. *Ethical Issues in Suicide.* Englewood Cliffs, N.J.: Prentice-Hall.

Bauer, Martin N., Antoon A. Leenaars, Alan L. Berman, David A. Jobes, J. Faye Dixon, and James L. Bibb. 1997. "Late Adulthood Suicide: A Life-span Analysis of Suicide." *Archives of Suicide Research* 3: 91–108.

Berman, Alan L., and David A. Jobes. 1995. "Suicide Prevention in Adolescents (age 12–18)." *Suicide and Life-Threatening Behavior* 25: 143–154.

Breed, Warren. 1967. "Suicide and Loss in Social Interaction." In Edwin S. Shneidman, ed., *Essays in Self-Destruction*, pp. 188–201. New York: Science House.

———. 1968. "The Suicide Process." In Norman L. Farberow, ed., *Fourth International Conference for Suicide Prevention*, pp. 286–291. Los Angeles: Delmar Publishing Co.

———. 1972. "Five Components of a Basic Suicide Syndrome." *Suicide and Life-Threatening Behavior* 2: 3–18.

Clark, D. C., and Hartmut B. Mokros. 1993. "Depression and Suicidal Behavior." In P. H. Tolan and B. J. Cohler, eds., *Handbook of Clinical Research and Practice with Adolescents*, pp. 333–358. New York: John Wiley & Sons.

Cooley, Charles Horton. 1934 [1902]. *Human Nature and the Social Order.* New York: Schocken Books.

Corder, Billie F., and Thomas M. Haizlip. 1984. "Environment and Personality Similarities in the Histories of Suicide and Self-poisoning by Children Under Ten." *Suicide and Life-Threatening Behavior* 14: 59–66.

Davidson, G. M. 1941. "The Mental State at the Time of Suicide." *Psychiatric Quarterly Supplement* 15: 41–50.

Douglas, Jack D. 1967. *The Social Meanings of Suicide.* Princeton, N.J.: Princeton University Press.

Droogas, Athena, Roland Siiter, and Agnes N. O'Connell. 1982–1983. "Effects of Personal and Situational Factors on Attitudes Toward Suicide." *Omega: Journal of Death and Dying* 13: 127–144.

Dukes, Richard L., and Richard D. Lorch. 1989. "Concept of Self-Mediating Factors and Adolescent Deviance." *Sociological Spectrum* 9: 301–319.

Durkheim, Emile. 1951 [1897]. *Suicide: A Study in Sociology.* Translated by George Simpson. New York: The Free Press.

Eth, Spencer, Robert S. Pynoos, and Gabrielle A. Carlson. 1984. "An Unusual Case of Self-inflicted Death in Childhood." *Suicide and Life-Threatening Behavior* 14: 59–66.

Farber, Maurice L. 1968. *Theory of Suicide.* New York: Funk and Wagnall.

Goffman, Erving. 1983. "The Interaction Order." *American Sociological Review* 48: 1–17.

Henslin, James M. 1970. "Guilt and Guilt Neutralization: Response and Adjustment to Suicide." In Jack D. Douglas, ed., *Deviance and Respectability*, pp. 192–228. New York: Basic Books.

Jacobs, Jerry. 1967. "A Phenomenological Study of Suicide Notes." *Social Problems* 15: 60–72.

Kaplan, Howard B., and Alex D. Pokorny. 1976. "Self-attitudes and Suicidal Behavior." *Suicide and Life-Threatening Behavior* 6: 23–25.

Kevorkian, Jack. 1991. *Prescription Medicine—The Goodness of Planned Death.* Buffalo, N.Y.: Prometheus Books.

Leenaars, Antoon A. 1988. *Suicide Notes: Predictive Clues and Patterns.* New York: Human Sciences Press.

———. 1997. "Suicide Notes of the Elderly and Their Implications for Psychotherapy." *Clinical Gerontologists* 17: 76–79.

Leenaars, Antoon A., and David Lester. 1988–1989. "The Significance of the Method Chosen for Suicide in Understanding the Psychodynamics of the Suicidal Individual." *Omega: Journal of Death and Dying* 19: 311–314.

Lester, David, Colleen McCabe, and Marilyn Cameron. 1991–1992. "Judging the Appropriateness of Completed Suicide, Attempted Suicide and Suicidal Ideation." *Omega: Journal of Death and Dying* 24: 75–79.

Lester, David, and Bijou Yang. 1992. "Social and Economic Correlates of the Elderly Suicide Rate." *Suicide and Life-Threatening Behavior* 22: 36–47.

Lipschitz, Alan. 1995. "Suicide Prevention in Young Adults (age 18–30)." *Suicide and Life-Threatening Behavior* 25:155–170.

Maris, Ronald W. 1971. "Deviance as Therapy: The Paradox of the Self-destructive Female." *Journal of Health and Social Behavior* 12: 113–124.

———. 1981. *Pathways to Suicide: A Survey of Self-Destructive Behaviors.* Baltimore: Johns Hopkins University Press.

——. 1982. "Rational Suicide: An Impoverished Self-transformation." *Suicide and Life-Threatening Behavior* 12: 4–16.

——. 1995. "Suicide Prevention in Adults (age 30–65)." *Suicide and Life-Threatening Behavior* 25: 171–178.

——. 1997. "Social Suicide." *Suicide and Life-Threatening Behavior* 27: 41–49.

McIntosh, John L. 1995. "Suicide Prevention in the Elderly (age 65–99)." *Suicide and Life-Threatening Behavior* 25: 180–192.

Mead, George Herbert. 1934. *Mind, Self, and Society*. Chicago: The University of Chicago Press.

Mestrovic, Stjepan, and Barry Glassner. 1983. "A Durkheimian Hypothesis on Stress." *Social Science Medicine* 17: 1315–1327.

Mokros, Hartmut B. 1995. "Suicide and Shame." *American Behavioral Scientist* 38: 1091–1103.

National Center for Health Statistics. 1998, January 28. *Monthly Vital Statistics Report* 46, no. 6. Hyattsville, Md.: National Center for Health Statistics.

Newman, John F., Kenneth R. Whittemore, and Helen G. Newman. 1973. "Women in the Labor Force and Suicide." *Social Problems* 21: 220–230.

Peck, Dennis L. 1980. "Towards a Theory of Suicide: The Case of Modern Fatalism." *Omega: Journal of Death and Dying* 11: 1–14.

——. 1983. "The Last Moments of Life: Learning to Cope." *Deviant Behavior* 4: 313–332.

——. 1988–1989. "Evaluation of a Suicide Diary: A Content and Situational Analysis." *Omega: Journal of Death and Dying* 19: 293–309.

Peck, Dennis L., and Kimberly A. Folse. 1990. "Teenage Suicide: An Evaluation of Reactive Responses to Change and a Proposed Model for Proactive Accommodation/Adaptation." *Sociological Practice Review* 1: 33–39.

Pender, Sheryl B. 1996. "The Possibility of No Suicide." *Suicide and Life-Threatening Behavior* 26: 155–160.

Public Health Service. 1996, January 12. *Morbidity and Mortality Report* 44, no. 6. Hyattsville, Md.: Public Health Service.

Reynolds, David K., and Norman L. Farberow. 1976. *Suicide Inside and Out*. Berkeley: University of California Press.

Ritter, Christian. 1985. "Occupational Stress and Depression Among Vietnam Veterans." *The Journal of Sociology and Social Welfare* 11: 826–852.

Shneidman, Edwin S. 1985. *Definition of Suicide*. New York: John Wiley and Sons. "Sister of Suicide Victim Has to Live with Her Own Guilt." *Tuscaloosa News*. 1998. February 15: 7D.

Shneidman, Edwin S., and Norman L. Farberow. 1957. *Clues to Suicide*. New York: McGraw-Hill.

Singh, Gopal K., et al. 1995. "Annual Summary of Births, Marriages, Divorces, and Deaths: United States, 1994." *Monthly Vital Statistics Report* 43, no. 13. Hyattsville, Md.: National Center for Health Statistics.

Stack, Steven. 1987. "Celebrities and Suicide: A Taxonomy and Analysis, 1948–1983." *American Sociological Review* 52: 401–412.

Statistical Abstract of the United States, 1987. 107th ed. Washington, D.C.: U.S. Bureau of the Census.

Statistical Abstract of the United States, 1989. 109th ed. Washington, D.C.: U.S. Bureau of the Census.

Statistical Abstract of the United States, 1997. 117th ed. Washington, D.C.: U.S. Bureau of the Census.

Thoits, Peggy A. 1982. "Conceptual, Methodological, and Theoretical Problems in Studying Social Support as a Buffer Against Life Stress." *Journal of Health and Social Behavior* 23: 145–159.

Topal, Phyllis, and Marvin Resnikoff. 1982. "Perceived Peer and Family Relationships, Hopelessness, and Locus of Control as Factors in Adolescent Suicide Attempts." *Suicide and Life-Threatening Behavior* 12: 141–150.

Vella, Maria L., Sue Persic, and David Lester. 1996. "Does Self-Esteem Predict Suicidality After Controls for Depression?" *Psychological Reports* 79: 1178.

Ventura, Stephanie J., Kimberly D. Peters, Joyce A. Martin and Jeffrey D. Maurer. 1997, September 1. "Births and Deaths, 1996." *Monthly Vital Statistics Report* 46, no. 1, supp 2. Hyattsville, Md.: National Center for Health Statistics.

Werth, James L., Jr. 1996. "Can Shneidman's Ten Commonalities of Suicide Accommodate Rational Suicide?" *Suicide and Life-Threatening Behavior* 26: 292–299.

Werth, James L., Jr., and Debra C. Cobia. 1995. "Empirically Based Criteria for Rational Suicide: A Survey of Psychotherapists." *Suicide and Life-Threatening Behavior* 25: 231–240.

Wilson, Michele. 1981. "Suicidal Behavior: Toward an Explanation of Differences in Female and Male Rates." *Suicide and Life-Threatening Behavior* 11: 131–140.

Yang, Bijou, and David Lester. 1988. "The Participation of Females in the Labor Force and Rates of Personal Violence (Suicide and Homicide.)" *Suicide and Life-Threatening Behavior* 18: 270–278.

Yessler, Paul G., James J. Gibbs, and Herman A. Becker. 1960. "On the Communication of Suicidal Ideas: Some Sociological and Behavioral Considerations." *Archives of General Psychiatry* 3: 612–631.

2

Anorexia Nervosa

Diane E. Taub and Penelope A. McLorg

INTRODUCTION

With an increasing occurrence over the past three decades, the eating disorder of anorexia nervosa is currently considered a major health and social problem (Gordon 1988; Wiseman et al. 1992; Wiseman, Harris, and Halmi 1998). Approximately 2.5 percent of college students are anorexic (Schlundt and Johnson 1990); 5 to 20 percent of anorexics die (Haller 1992; Hobbs and Johnson 1996). Representing 90 to 95 percent of cases, females are much more likely than males to become anorexic (Hobbs and Johnson 1996; Leichner and Gertler 1988). As a concern virtually limited to females, anorexia nervosa provides an excellent example of the interrelationships among cultural norms, family life, and health.

Anorexia nervosa consists of a fear of weight gain and a refusal to maintain body weight above a minimum for age and height; the diagnostic guideline is a weight of 15 percent below normal. Physical effects from anorexia nervosa include constipation, abdominal pain, hypotension, hypothermia, dry skin, lanugo, bradycardia, edema, cardiac arrhythmias, and anemia (Hobbs and Johnson 1996; Wiseman, Harris, and Halmi 1998). In addition, amenorrhea in menstruating females occurs (American Psychiatric Association 1994; Wiseman, Harris, and Halmi 1998).

OVERVIEW OF THE ANOREXIA NERVOSA PROBLEM

The usual ages of onset for anorexia nervosa are the early teens and early twenties (Leichner and Gertler 1988), with a mean age of onset of 17 years

(Hobbs and Johnson 1996). Anorexia nervosa is reported most often among young, white, affluent (upper-middle to upper-class) females in modern, industrialized countries (Gard and Freeman 1996; Hobbs and Johnson 1996; Schlundt and Johnson 1990).

Contributing to the prevalence of anorexia nervosa are women's role models and the mass media. These images serve as a frame of reference for the ideal body type while setting an example of thinness that is unrealistic for most women (Taub and McLorg 1997; Wiseman, Harris, and Halmi 1998). Socialized within a "cult of thinness" (Hesse-Biber, Clayton-Matthews, and Downey 1987), females internalize the ideal body shape. They desire to be slim and are critical of their figure, regardless of actual body size (Hobbs and Johnson 1996; Wiseman, Harris, and Halmi 1998).

In general, women are likely to overestimate their weight, without regard to their actual weight (Connor-Greene 1988; Hobbs and Johnson 1996). The social pressure to be thin, combined with the low rate of success for dieting, results in persistent weight-loss efforts by females (Hobbs and Johnson 1996; Taub and McLorg 1997; Wiseman, Harris, and Halmi 1998). A history of dieting, beginning in one's teens, is common among anorexics (Crisp 1977b; Wiseman, Harris, and Halmi 1998). Individuals who are anorexic typify "weight phobia" (Crisp 1977a) and can be viewed as extensions of the slim body ideal for females.

Individuals with anorexia nervosa have a body image disturbance, perceiving their entire body or portions of their body as very large. In addition, anorexics emphasize achievement and perfection (Hobbs and Johnson 1996; Wiseman, Harris, and Halmi 1998). Many of these individuals maintain high grades and experience considerable business success (Humphries, Wrobel, and Wiegert 1982; McLorg and Taub 1987). However, their accomplishments often go unrecognized by families, friends, and coworkers as such achievements are considered normal for them (McLorg and Taub 1987).

Common family background characteristics of anorexics include excessive preoccupation with eating, exercising, and body weight and shape (Humphries, Wrobel, and Wiegert 1982; McLorg and Taub 1987). Many families of anorexics appear intact, close, and supportive—the "all-American family" (Humphries, Wrobel, and Wiegert 1982). This superficial image, however, belies the impaired interaction that occurs at a deeper level (Wiseman, Harris, and Halmi 1998). Feelings, especially negative ones such as hostility and anger, are generally not expressed (McLorg and Taub 1987).

Another feature of the families of anorexics is excessive interdependency. Individuals who become anorexic often have a history of overdependency on their same-sex parent, which is actively reinforced by the parent (McLorg and Taub 1987). By failing to discourage such dependency, parents reinforce their children's underdeveloped self-esteem, need for approval, and desire to fulfill other's expectations. Obsessions with eating, compulsive exercising, and extreme attempts at weight management provide anorexics with an "adaptation" (Schwartz, Thompson, and Johnson 1982) to their families' weight consciousness, behavioral rigidity, and encouraged dependency. Their bodies and eating behaviors become vehicles for expressing personal insecurities and impaired family interactions (McLorg and Taub 1987).

The case study that follows details the experiences of one woman, Sarah (a pseudonym), a former anorexic. Her story illuminates the anorexic's definition of the situation and clarifies the processes involved in her becoming anorexic and eventually overcoming anorexia nervosa.

SARAH: A CASE STUDY OF AN ANOREXIC

The focus of this case study is the experiences and perceptions of one individual. Case studies are useful to illustrate the life history of an individual, the life and activities of a group of individuals, or the social history of a particular group or collectivity. Such studies are valuable in that they can be richly chronicled, provide detailed information covering a period of time, and illustrate how individual-level problems are connected to larger social structures (Feagin, Orum, and Sjoberg 1991; Stake 1995; Yin 1989).

The following discussion involves a 38-year-old woman, Sarah, who was anorexic for a period of four years beginning during her senior year of high school and continuing into her junior year of college. Sarah was interviewed three times by the senior author (Taub); each session averaged three hours. These informal interviews consisted of broad, open-ended questions. Detailed notes were taken during each meeting. Moreover, follow-up questions or clarification of comments were asked of Sarah during the writing of this chapter. In this case study, Sarah describes the precipitating factors of her anorexia nervosa, her experiences as an anorexic, and her journey into recovery.

The Early Years

Sarah was the third youngest of four children and the oldest girl. She had always been a good girl—obedient, helpful, conscientious. As a child, Sarah did have a few rambunctious friends with whom she would engage in rebellious activities such as eating a Pop-Tart or drinking a can of soda pop. Such foods and beverages were not allowed in her own home; her mother simply would not purchase them. Treats available at home, like tapioca pudding or Jello, were very healthy. Thus, from an early age, Sarah became aware of "rules" about food. The family eating experience was primarily functional, not pleasurable. Even before widespread appreciation of the nutritious aspects of food, Sarah's mother (who selected and prepared foods and managed the family's eating) provided the family with whole unprocessed breads and cereals, lean protein sources, and plenty of fruits and vegetables. As a young girl, Sarah did not fully grasp the rationale behind her family's eating habits, but she was aware that there existed enjoyable foods that only her lucky friends ate.

All four children in Sarah's white, affluent family were encouraged to pursue physical activity. Her father was an avid runner before running was a popular activity, and her mother was a regular walker. The children swam and biked every day during the summer, and tobogganed and ice-skated throughout the winter. Sarah found physical activity enjoyable, but she was aware that there was also a duty to be active. An attitude inculcated by her father, especially, was that the body was to be exercised.

Immediately prior to puberty, Sarah moved with her family to a very different geographic and cultural setting from that of her childhood. She left behind several close friends and did not easily make new ones at her new location. She just did not feel very connected with the new girls and boys, did not share their concerns, and felt marginal in social groups. Sarah spent most of her leisure time at home, playing the piano, practicing the cello, sewing, and completing jigsaw puzzles. She also regularly went on long walks with her mother.

Although Sarah had always been an industrious and inquisitive student, she became acutely aware of the performance aspects of school after the family relocation. The grading system now involved A, B, C, etc., instead of numerical ranges; and "B" was quite different from, and inferior to, "A." She became even more concentrated on school and did exceptionally well, outcompeting other students for awards and recognition at the three schools she attended in her new city. However, Sarah was not consciously trying to surpass other students; rather, she felt that straight "As" were the only acceptable grades because they were the highest one could achieve. Perfect scholastic performance was very attainable for Sarah, and she felt any less an achievement would disappoint not only herself but also her parents and teachers. Although Sarah's mother and father did not insist on straight As, they did convey the idea that such grades were expected.

Adolescence

Unlike her siblings, Sarah shared an appreciation of classical music with her parents. She alone took piano lessons at an early age, later taking up the cello and playing in the school and community orchestras. Sarah also accompanied her parents to symphony concerts, something her siblings were never interested in doing. Also unique among the children, Sarah followed her father and mother into playing tennis. Although she sometimes played with peers, Sarah usually played tennis with her mother and her mother's friends. In general, throughout junior high and high school, Sarah began to relate more to teachers and other adults and less to her peers. While her siblings established several close friendships, Sarah either rejected overtures from other teens or had her overtures rebuffed. At the time, however, she did not feel socially bereft. She saw her siblings engaging in what she considered risky behavior with their friends. To Sarah, it was much safer and better to binge on Spanish peanuts than to smoke cigarettes or marijuana.

During high school, Sarah had classes each year with a teacher who was both feared and admired. While continuing to do well in her schoolwork, Sarah concentrated on her performance in classes with this particular teacher. As the workload was intense and continual, success in these classes was rare and exceptionally satisfying. Every week involved a build-up of tension, culminating in the completion of a paper. Sarah began a ritual of listening to music and eating an entire row of Saltine crackers as a stress release each time she turned in a paper to this teacher. It was comforting to know that she could eat again in a couple of hours at dinner.

Predictably, as she continued these eating behaviors through high school and experienced postpuberty changes, Sarah began to gain weight. Her increased size resulted from eating large quantities of low-fat foods, rather than from high-calorie foods. Also, she began to take notice of a girl in school who was exceptionally thin and rumored to be anorexic. For the first time in her life, Sarah began to believe she had a problem with her weight. She initiated some efforts at food restriction, none of which was sufficiently effective. Requiring a size 13 pants was a disgusting milestone. Sarah envied the "anorexic girl" who was able to freely tuck tops into her pants, something that Sarah had started to avoid. She began to entertain fantasies of being abducted and starved, so that her body would be forced to lose weight.

During her childhood and early teens, Sarah, like other family members, had been lean. Now she became the family member whose size was not appropriate and who ate too much. In comparison with her younger sister, Sarah felt large and less attractive. Her sister was of a slighter build with very slim hips; she also was more confident about her appearance and more popular.

By the final semester of her senior year, Sarah had instituted some major weight control efforts. She began to rise before the rest of the family to engage in stationary exercising. In addition to being a regular walker, Sarah started using an exercise bicycle. She also bicycled everywhere possible, even at night and on busy thoroughfares. She would bike to a distant health club, swim for a couple of hours, and then bike home.

Regarding food consumption, Sarah adopted stricter and stricter rules of her own. Her meals became sparse and functional, with gradual removal of anything not absolutely essential to good health. She became quite knowledgeable about nutrition and the caloric expenditures of various activities. Sarah measured foods precisely and kept meticulous records of everything she ate, usually allowing herself a maximum of 900 calories a day from only nutritiously dense foods. Each meal consisted of only a few permitted food choices. Initially, family members thought Sarah's conscientious weighing of food and composing food intake charts were amusing. Eventually, however, her parents gave Sarah a food scale for her birthday.

Young Adulthood

Sarah entered the university located in her hometown during the fall following high school graduation; she did not seriously consider any other college. On campus, Sarah would not allow herself to eat lunch indoors or with others; she had to eat her meals alone outside, even during the winter. Sarah would not deviate from self-imposed eating rules to consume what she knew were pleasurable food items, such as home-baked treats. Her sister observed that Sarah usually performed family chores like mowing the lawn because of the calories expended, a charge Sarah denied but vaguely recognized as accurate.

Sarah's intense weight control efforts yielded results fairly quickly. As had been true of her approach to other pursuits, Sarah went "all out" in her new campaign. With her visual success, however, came some psychological problems. Unusual things began to bother her, such as the sound of her mother's slippers in the morning as Sarah exercised and the sight of her brother eating. Conversely, she received unexpected pleasure from things like the appearance of the mixture of unprocessed grains in her cereal bowl.

After several months of strict eating and exercising, Sarah stopped menstruating. This change was no cause for alarm; in fact, she was glad not to be bothered with this monthly ritual. The cessation of menstrual function reinforced the detachment from her body that Sarah was feeling in general. Her body was no longer out of control, too big and with its own needs; Sarah was now in control. She could ignore feelings of hunger and of pain from great physical exertion.

With Sarah's weight loss, her breasts had become much smaller; it seemed reasonable to Sarah that she avoid wearing a bra whenever possible, including the time she accompanied her father and brother on a camping trip. It even seemed appropriate to discard her top when the three went swimming in a river, an action quickly halted by her male family members. While others still related to her as a young woman, Sarah lost awareness of herself as a sexual being, a feeling reinforced by the loss of menstrual period and her reduced breast and hip size.

Emotionally as well as physically, Sarah's feelings were stifled. She was not able to be touched or to feel empathy. When her father was required to increase the frequency of the family's meals due to a medically induced ulcer, Sarah felt only resentment at having her own eating plan disrupted. Because her dinners usually differed from those of the rest of the family, Sarah often ate by herself in her bedroom. There she could study in peace and not have to endure the disgusting sights and sounds of other people eating.

Becoming progressively thinner was now Sarah's overriding purpose in life. She felt ultra healthy, much healthier than others who did not control their eating and exercising as much. Sarah's weight eventually declined to 95 pounds. With her 5'5" height and medium frame, she appeared very lean and had to alter many clothes. Her gauges of thinness included the circumference of her wrists and gaunt neck and hips. The more bones she could observe through her skin, the better. Sarah did not feel she was too thin; on the contrary, only now was her "true" body emerging. She brushed off or denied comments that she had become too skinny or that her clothes hung too loosely, although she was pleased people had noticed.

When either her sister or mother would hint that something might be wrong with her behavior, Sarah would vigorously protest. She did not view any of her actions as extreme. And, although Sarah knew she had become estranged from her brother and father and did not feel as happy as she once had, she did not view these changes as her fault.

During the summer following her freshman year in college, Sarah's parents insisted that she leave home for a while to visit an aunt's family living in a distant city. The tension in her own family created by Sarah's eating and exercising rituals and unabashed repugnance at other family members had become intolerable to her parents. The idea of her being anorexic was sometimes verbalized and always hovering. Even Sarah recognized that she did not enjoy being so intolerant of others and inflexible with herself, but she resisted the label of anorexia nervosa.

The change of environment provided by the lengthy visit with a favorite aunt was useful for developing a new perspective. Immersed in the novelty of her trip, Sarah allowed herself to eat new and previously forbidden foods. Back home, however, she reverted to her old rules as her sophomore year began. It seemed that more friends and acquaintances were noticing her thinness in disapproving ways and whispering the "a" word.

Sarah met a new male friend the next spring with whom she later became involved romantically. For the first time in the two-and-a-half years since her strict weight control regimen began, Sarah had a desire to enjoy eating and to allow herself to experience some pleasure. She remained restrictive, but loosened her rituals.

That summer, Sarah worked at a small restaurant preparing salads. Waitresses would query, "How do you stay so slim?" to which she gave what she thought was the obvious response of eating carefully and exercising a lot. At the restaurant, however, Sarah began to eat forbidden foods such as morsels of the restaurant's specialty pie. At the end of her shift, she would take a few miniloaves of bread to eat while she walked home. Sarah had begun to break her own restrictions about eating, believing she deserved more food.

When the restaurant closed that fall, Sarah found a job at a fabric shop where she employed knowledge from her many years of sewing. She became a part-time college student, earning enough money at her job to move out of her parents' home for the first time the following spring. In her apartment, Sarah could buy her own food and eat anything she wanted including large quantities of carbohydrate food such as crackers.

After a two-year absence, Sarah's menstrual period returned. She gradually gained weight and returned to her highest preanorexic weight of approximately 140 pounds. The family doctor, who had not seen Sarah for years, commented he did not want her to become any heavier. During the time she was eating more, Sarah justified her intake; she deserved it after years of denial. She also felt oddly detached from her body again, as if she were watching somebody else. To her mortification, however, she now needed to borrow her mother's bigger pants, while her mother in comparison had recently lost a sizable amount of weight due to a medical condition.

After ignoring her larger body size for a year, Sarah began to dislike her size. Experiencing difficulties with her roommate, she moved back in with her parents while continuing to work and attend school on a part-time basis. She no longer bought her own food, and her intake declined. But Sarah was ready to again be more restrictive. Socially, she felt isolated living at home and that summer moved out for the last time. When Sarah stopped eating large amounts of carbohydrates, she became steadily smaller to 115 or 118 pounds. Then, as Sarah became older, her weight increased to approximately 125 pounds, a level at which it has essentially stayed without any particular effort.

Life after Anorexia Nervosa

Reflecting upon the period in her life during which she was anorexic, Sarah believes that breaking away from the family home environment was critical to her recovery. Having new close relationships, becoming more independent, and living in her own household encouraged Sarah to set her own standards, including those for eating. Ironically, while on her own, Sarah broke the eating rules she established during the period of anorexia nervosa. She was free to experiment with the other extreme of eating behavior, namely overeating. Moreover, having new social contacts helped Sarah enjoy life again, which included allowing herself the pleasures of eating.

In the decade and a half since her extreme weight preoccupation and fluctuation, Sarah continues to be conscious of her food intake, but not fanatical. She maintains a very nutritious diet and often allows "treats"; she appreciates the social and pleasurable, as well as functional, aspects of eating. Sarah occasionally increases or decreases her food intake slightly when her body reacts to situations or seasonal factors, such as work overload or reduction in caloric need during warm weather.

Sarah also continues to exercise regularly, especially fitness walking and cycling. However, her primary exercise motives genuinely are fitness and cardiovascular/muscular health, in contrast to her anorexic years when her stated purpose was health while her actual concern was caloric expenditure. Over the years since Sarah's anorexia nervosa, she has achieved a balanced approach in which her thoughts about eating and exercise have become a routine part of life rather than a consuming passion. She still finds herself looking at people's hips first, the area of her own body about which she was most concerned. However, instead of being detached from and at odds with her body, Sarah is now in tune and content with her body. She thinks of herself as slim but not skinny, healthy, even athletic; and she takes care of her body.

Sarah currently is in a long-term, committed relationship and has an enjoyable social life with a few friends. Her parents and siblings live almost 1,000 miles away. Sarah is close to her sister, but communication with other family members is infrequent. In her employment setting of higher education, Sarah is quite successful and considers herself a high achiever with a tendency toward perfectionism.

DISCUSSION AND CONCLUSION

Sarah's life history can be interpreted on varied levels. Many of the socio-demographic, family, and personal characteristics associated with anorexia nervosa are reflected in her case (see for example Hobbs and Johnson 1996; Wiseman, Harris, and Halmi 1998). Sarah is a white female from an affluent background whose onset of anorexia nervosa occurred during her senior year of high school, a time period in which she was 17–18 years of age. Her family relationships appeared to be extremely close, but actually were enmeshed and dependent. For example, rather than socializing with peers, Sarah participated in leisure and exercise activities with her mother and father. The family's relocation exacerbated Sarah's dependence on her parents as she did not integrate well with a new peer group.

Further embodying the family features of individuals who experience anorexia nervosa, Sarah's parents did not express negative emotions or discuss problems. The strategy of sending Sarah during the summer to visit a favorite aunt demonstrated an overall family pattern of not effectively confronting problems and issues.

Both Sarah and her family illustrate many situation factors associated with anorexia nervosa. Her parents were concerned with their weight and maintained an exercise program. Sarah's father was an avid runner, and her mother was a regular walker. Sarah recognized there was a "duty" to be active. Concerning academic pursuits, Sarah was a very high achiever and perfectionist in her work. She earned many awards and much recognition for her scholastic abilities and accomplishments.

Sarah's case also can be evaluated in terms of symbolic interactionism, specifically the tenet that individuals act according to their interpretation, or the meaning, of social interactions, events, or situations (see, for example, Blumer 1969; Cooley 1964 [1902]). In illustration, Sarah did not perceive that she was thin enough to be anorexic or that her eating behaviors and rituals were extreme. Thus, she ignored comments by family members and others about her skinniness, and she denied that her compulsive physical activity was motivated by weight loss. Acting in accordance with her "definition of the situation," Sarah altered her interpretations of food and eating at different periods in her life. For example, during the height of Sarah's anorexia nervosa, many foods were forbidden and her food intake was minimized. Before and after her eating disorder, food including taboo items was considered deserved and indulged in or even overindulged. Similarly, while Sarah was anorexic, eating was defined and performed as purely a functional activity, whereas prior to and following anorexia nervosa, eating was interpreted as a functional and pleasurable part of life.

Sarah was very concerned that others would stigmatize her if they believed she was overweight; thus, she sought to avoid the stigma associated with obesity. Stigma, or an attribute that is deeply discrediting, generally spoils the social identity of the possessor (Goffman 1963). When Sarah gained weight to require a size 13 pants, this attainment symbolized "a disgusting milestone"; the occurrence was so repugnant that Sarah had fantasies of being abducted and forced to starve. During this period, Sarah's view of self was that of an overweight person. Regularly comparing her body with those of other family members and classmates, Sarah began a rigorous regimen of excessive exercising and food restriction. To Sarah, any stigma of fanatical weight control was preferable to the stigma of being fat.

Distinguishing types of stigma, Goffman (1963) describes two forms, namely discredited (visible) stigma and discreditable (invisible) stigma. To control a stigma, the discredited individual attempts to manage tension while the discreditable individual manages information. Due to her gaunt appearance as an anorexic, Sarah primarily experienced discredited stigma. For example, she found it difficult to interact spontaneously with others and increasingly isolated herself, even avoiding eating meals with others. Sarah also attempted to control discreditable stigma, as she was constantly on guard against discussing topics related to eating and body size and diminished suggestions by others that she was excessively skinny.

Through her anorexic-type behavior, Sarah engaged in "identity work," or strategies individuals employ to construct, maintain, or transform identities which are consistent with their self-definitions (Sandstrom 1990; Snow and Anderson 1987; Tewksbury 1994). With her reduction in body size, Sarah redefined herself from a fleshy teenage girl to a svelte, asexual individual. The more flesh that disappeared, the more she thought her true physical self had emerged. By regimenting and manipulating her physical self, Sarah believed she was "in control" and a very healthy, disciplined person. She no longer succumbed to hunger or to the pleasures of eating. As an anorexic, Sarah believed she embodied the epitome of health; her rituals of meticulous, minimal eating and frequent, compulsive exercising reinforced this new identity.

In her life after anorexia nervosa, Sarah again perceives herself as a healthy individual. However, her approach to exercising and eating currently is balanced and moderate. Thus, Sarah's identity work in the aftermath of her eating disorder consists of maintaining a reasonable, healthy self. This approach dramatically contrasts with the transforming identity work in which she was previously engaged to achieve an extreme, anorexic "healthy" self.

Sarah's case facilitates our understanding of the symbolic experiences of those who develop anorexia nervosa, specifically, what it is like to be anorexic, and what meanings are attributed to the individuals and to the circumstances involved. The case study further demonstrates how Sarah's personal problems surrounding eating and food are related to larger structural issues such as cultural and familial meanings attributed to thinness and health. Such an investigation illustrates how social problems are not simply macrolevel phenomena disembodied of individual-based behavior.

Although symbols and numerous external stimuli influence attitudes and values, not everyone will respond as did Sarah to stimuli that emphasize a slim or skinny physique. For those who do, however, the potential that the anorexia nervosa problem may influence all aspects of their life is very great. Young people are especially impressionable and susceptible to embracing the symbolic stimuli that encourage people to engage in the kind of behavior that could lead to the anorexia nervosa problem. Members of the adult world should understand that their beliefs and actions influence individuals who, although gaining in maturity, may be incapable of discriminating between stimuli that could be detrimental to their social, psychological, and physical well-being.

REFERENCES

American Psychiatric Association. 1994. *Diagnostic and Statistical Manual of Mental Disorders.* 4th ed. Washington, D.C.: American Psychiatric Association.

Blumer, Herbert. 1969. *Symbolic Interactionism: Perspective and Method.* Englewood Cliffs, N.J.: Prentice-Hall.

Connor-Greene, Patricia Anne. 1988. "Gender Differences in Body Weight Perception and Weight-loss Strategies of College Students." *Women and Health* 14, no. 2: 27–42.

Cooley, Charles Horton. 1964 [1902]. *Human Nature and the Social Order.* New York: Schocken.

Crisp, A. H. 1977a. "Anorexia Nervosa." *Proceedings of the Royal Society of Medicine* 70: 464–470.

———. 1977b. "The Prevalence of Anorexia Nervosa and Some of its Associations in the General Population." *Advances in Psychosomatic Medicine* 9: 38–47.

Feagin, Joe R., Anthony M. Orum, and Gideon Sjoberg, eds. 1991. *A Case for the Case Study.* Chapel Hill: The University of North Carolina Press.

Gard, Maisie C. E., and Chris P. Freeman. 1996. "The Dismantling of a Myth: A Review of Eating Disorders and Socioeconomic Status." *International Journal of Eating Disorders* 20: 1–12.

Goffman, Erving. 1963. *Stigma: Notes on the Management of Spoiled Identity.* Englewood Cliffs, N.J.: Prentice-Hall.

Gordon, Richard A. 1988. "A Sociocultural Interpretation of the Current Epidemic of Eating Disorders." In Barton J. Blinder, Barry F. Chaitin, and Renee S. Goldstein, eds., *The Eating Disorders: Medical* and *Psychological Bases of Diagnosis and Treatment*, pp. 151–163. New York: PMA.

Haller, Ellen. 1992. "Eating Disorders: A Review and Update." *Western Journal of Medicine* 157: 658–662.

Hesse-Biber, Sharlene, Alan Clayton-Matthews, and John A. Downey. 1987. "The Differential Importance of Weight and Body Image Among College Men and Women." *Genetic, Social, and General Psychology Monographs* 113: 511–528.

Hobbs, Wendy L., and Cynda Ann Johnson. 1996. "Anorexia Nervosa: An Overview." *American Family Physician* 54: 1273–1279.

Humphries, Laurie L., Sylvia Wrobel, and H. Thomas Wiegert. 1982. "Anorexia Nervosa." *American Family Physician* 26: 199–204.

Leichner, Pierre, and A. Gertler. 1988. "Prevalence and Incidence Studies of Anorexia Nervosa." In Barton J. Blinder, Barry F. Chaitin, and Renee S. Goldstein, eds., *The Eating Disorders: Medical and Psychological Bases of Diagnosis and Treatment*, pp. 131–149. New York: PMA.

McLorg, Penelope A., and Diane E. Taub. 1987. "Anorexia Nervosa and Bulimia: The Development of Deviant Identities." *Deviant Behavior* 8: 177–189.

Sandstrom, Kent L. 1990. "Confronting Deadly Disease: The Drama of Identity Construction Among Gay Man with AIDS." *Journal of Contemporary Ethnography* 19: 271–294.

Schlundt, David G., and William G. Johnson. 1990. *Eating Disorders: Assessment and Treatment*. Boston: Allyn and Bacon.

Schwartz, Donald M., Michael G. Thompson, and Craig L. Johnson. 1982. "Anorexia Nervosa and Bulimia: The Socio-cultural Context." *International Journal of Eating Disorders* 1, no. 3: 20–36.

Snow, David A., and Leon Anderson. 1987. "Identity Work Among the Homeless: The Verbal Construction and Avowal of Personal Identities." *American Journal of Sociology* 92: 1336–1371.

Stake, Robert E. 1995. *The Art of Case Study Research*. Thousand Oaks, Calif.: Sage.

Taub, Diane E., and Penelope A. McLorg. 1997. "The Influence of Gender Socialization in Eating Disorders." In Leonard Cargan and Jeanne H. Ballantine, eds., *Sociological Footprints: Introductory Readings in Sociology*, pp. 44–51. 7th ed. Belmont, Calif.: Wadsworth.

Tewksbury, Richard. 1994. " 'Speaking of Someone with AIDS . . . ': Identity Construction of Persons with HIV Disease." *Deviant Behavior* 15: 337–355.

Wiseman, Claire V., James J. Gray, James E. Mosimann, and Anthony H. Ahrens. 1992. "Cultural Expectations of Thinness in Women: An Update." *International Journal of Eating Disorders* 11: 85–89.

Wiseman, Claire V., Wendy A. Harris, and Katherine A. Halmi. 1998. "Eating Disorders." *Medical Clinics of North America* 82: 145–159.

Yin, Robert K. 1989. *Case Study Research: Design and Methods*. Newbury Park, Calif.: Sage.

3

Alcohol/Drug Abuse

Celia Chun-Nui Lo and Gerald Globetti

INTRODUCTION

The use of alcohol among the nation's youth has remained relatively stable since the beginning of this decade while the use of illicit drugs has shown a resurgence to its mid-1980s level. About three in four twelfth graders in a 1997 national survey had used alcohol in the previous year while more than two in five (42.4 percent) had used at least one illegal drug (Johnston, O'Malley, and Bachman 1997). Research has accumulated to demonstrate that regardless of its prevalence, substance abuse is associated with a variety of behavioral and health problems among the young (Lee and DiClimente 1985; Windle, Miller-Tutzauer, and Domenico 1992; Arria, Tarter, and Van Thiel 1991; Augustyn and Simons-Morton 1995). Moreover, some researchers suggest that one's initial and early experiences with drugs and alcohol may play a significant role in later teenage and early adult practices relative to substance abuse (Robins and Przybeck 1985; Humphrey and Friedman 1986; Newcomb and Bentler 1989; Samson, Maxwell, and Doyle 1989; Hartnagel 1996). Continued effort, therefore, has been exerted over the years to identify relevant factors leading to the onset of substance use among young people with the intent to develop strategies to deter or to modify potentials for future abuses (Chou and Pickering 1992).

In this chapter, we attempt to transform information from the more quantifiable research literature to the everyday life experiences of four teenagers diagnosed by clinicians as having problems with substance abuse. The objective is to see how closely the survey research corresponds to the subjective accounts of young substance abusers as revealed in their own words. This method provides a way to understand the "vocabulary of meanings" youth attach to drugs as well as an insight into the process of becoming a substance abuser.

The interpretive framework utilized in this study is symbolic interactionism that combines meanings of one's sociocultural environment with personal experience and definitions of one's situation (Vold and Bernard 1986; Einstadter and Henry 1995). From this perspective an understanding of why young people use and abuse substances must involve the meanings of the act that they attach to it (Einstadter and Henry 1995). A young person has an affinity to abuse substances because they think it will bolster or remove some deficiency in their self-identity or life situation. Moreover, they may have family and peer experiences which lead them to accept "favorable" attitudes or meanings of substance abuse and rule breaking. Thus in Mead's words "meanings determine behavior" (Vold and Bernard 1986). Experiences in one's life, although similar in many respects mean different things to different people. It is these meanings and how they are shaped or learned over time that allow us to understand deviant reality from the individual's perspective. This perspective lends itself to the more naturalistic and qualitative method of data collection employed in this study (Einstadter and Henry 1995).

OVERVIEW OF THE ALCOHOL USE PROBLEM

Alcohol is the drug of choice among the nation's teenagers although it is illegal for them to drink in each of the states. Initial use occurs in early adolescence usually around the age of 13 and eventuates from "tasting" and experimentation to a somewhat regular use around the age of 16 (Milgram 1990). First time use is generally in the home with parental supervision although more frequent and unsupervised usage increases with age as peer influences grow stronger (Milgram 1982; 1990).

Since the onset of drinking starts at an early age, family dynamics and relationships are viewed as crucial factors in what kind of drinker the adolescent may eventually become. Parental drinking behavior, for example, has been shown to be especially influential in their children's behavior and attitudes about alcohol (Wechsler and McFadden 1979; Barnes, Farrell, and Cairns 1986; Lo 1995). In general, youth reflect their parents' behavior regarding alcohol (Barnes and Welte 1990), with problem use showing up at the two extremes of the drinking continuum. In other words, youth from homes characterized by either a militant abstinence attitude (Kinney and Leaton 1983) or one with an over-permissive drinking style run a greater risk in developing problematic drinking (Bales 1946; Globetti 1967; 1969; Hanson 1973). This does not mean that teens from a more moderate posture concerning parental drinking or abstinence attitudes do not develop problems with alcohol but simply they are less likely to do so. More moderate positions about alcohol provide guidance that assists adolescents to resist peer pressures to either drink and/or to abuse alcohol (Kinney and Leaton 1983).

In addition to parental drinking behavior and attitudes, the youths' initial experience with alcohol has also been shown to be a crucial factor in later drinking styles. Ullman (1952) identified the first drinking experience as the step necessary to elicit addiction symptoms in individuals psychologically or physiologically prone to it. As they use copious amounts of alcohol to reduce stress, such individuals can become addicted. Since ethnic groups use varying means to reduce stress and anxiety, and since alcohol has diverse meanings for different groups, the first drinking experience may prove to be important in distinguishing "normal" drinkers from incipient alcoholics (Ullman 1960). Based on his study, Ullman (1953) suggested that alcoholics are more likely than "normal" drinkers to start drinking later in life. At the time of their first drink, alcoholics were more likely than normal drinkers to drink outside their parents' presence, in uncontrolled surroundings, and to become intoxicated. Ullman also found that people of Jewish and Italian origins see alcohol as a neutral element of their everyday life; in addition, they do not have the high alcoholism rates that those of Irish and English origins experience.

Unlike Ullman's studies, however, recent findings suggest that an early onset rather than a later onset of drinking is negatively related to drinking levels for teenagers and young adults (Kandel, Yamaguchi, and Chen 1992). Problem-behavior theorists (Jessor and Jessor 1977) explain that early-onset drinking indicates a violation of the "age-grading" that marks adolescent development, just as delinquent and deviant behaviors do. Early engagement in these problematic behaviors indicates a proneness to develop troublesome behavior later. Following the principles of problem-behavior theory, alcohol and drug using behaviors in the adolescent stage follows noncompliance and aggressive behavior in early childhood (Steele et al. 1995).

A few studies have examined onset age of drinking in light of circumstantial factors associated with the first drinking experience. These studies have concluded that introduction of alcohol to teenagers in a controlled setting, with guidance, helps decrease negative impacts of alcohol habits later in their lives (Gonzalez 1983; Lo and Globetti 1991). One recent study delineated the process of how early onset generates eventual heavier drinking in young adults (Lo forthcoming). The results show that early-onset drinkers tend to associate with alcohol users and to develop more tolerance of high-quantity drinking, which makes them more likely to attain higher blood-alcohol levels when they drink during their college years.

While recent studies may cast doubt on Ullman's decades-old findings, the general validity of his main idea is unchallenged: Sociocultural differences determine the meanings alcohol has for individuals and shape how these individuals are introduced to alcohol, which in turn are important experiences for the development of the individual's drinking habits. Each family has its own way of socializing children, so the ethnicity of the family is not the only factor distinguishing alcohol's introduction to youngsters. Instead, family values and norms regarding alcohol use should be the target of investigation if further knowledge about teenage drinking is desired. Questions such as "What initiates early drinking?" and "How does early drinking start?" (Timofeeva and Perekrjostova 1990) are among those to examine in seeking a more comprehensive picture that the family plays in teenage drinking.

Other family factors that influence teen alcohol use involve family management practices such as parental monitoring, family rules, and sanctions (Steinberg, Fletcher, and Darling 1994; Peterson et al. 1995). Unfortunately, the effects of these practices on a teen's use has not yet received sophisticated study. Current research shows that parents tend to underestimate their own children's use of alcohol while overestimating its use among youth in general (Beck et al. 1995). Rather than assuming culpability for their children's misbehavior, they are more inclined to blame others such as unscrupulous adults, bars, the child's friends and their parents, or the media. Parents also seldom talk to their children about alcohol except in a proscriptive manner which increases its attraction as a symbol of deviance. Thus, when faced with peer pressures or drinking situations, the adolescent has few prescriptions to guide behavior.

Along with the family, another salient influence on how a young person uses alcohol is that of friends. As adolescents age from their preteen to late-teen years, peers become increasingly influential on a youth's drinking experiences (Margulies, Kessler, and Kandel 1977; Berkowitz and Perkins 1986). While adolescents spend more time with their peers, peer norms and values regarding alcohol use as being appropriate or "no big deal" progress to become these adolescents' own definitions and affect their attitudes and drinking behavior (Akers 1985; Lo 1995). In addition, in a competitive peer subculture, many youth desire to fit in and belong. Teenagers identify with their peers and look to their peers for sources of information that parents fail to provide, especially knowledge about illicit behavior.

Other Drugs

As is the case of alcohol use, both social control and differential association have been shown to be important factors in explaining other drug using behavior, including cigarettes and marijuana (Massey and Krohn 1986; White, Johnson, and Horwitz 1986; Bailey and Hubbard 1990). Social control is exerted through attachment with conventional significant others, involvement in conventional activities, commitment in future conventional goals, and engagement in conventional beliefs (Hirschi 1969). In the field of substance use, several social control factors such as religious attachment, parental attachment, and educational commitment have been shown to decrease drug use (Ensminger, Brown, and Kellam 1982; White, Johnson, and Horwitz 1986). Differential association of individuals who approve of and engage in substance use themselves is also shown to determine whether adolescents are involved in substance use (Akers 1985; Dupre et al. 1995). Many studies have found support on how significant others' permissive attitudes and consumption of substance increases adolescents' drug use

(Akers et al. 1979; Akers and Cochran 1985; White, Johnson, and Horwitz 1986).

Children tend to view their parents as role models for their own behavior, especially while they are younger. The presence of at least one parent with drinking problems does not just increase the chance of children's risky drinking behavior, but also their marijuana and other illicit drug use (Kandel and Andrews 1987; Orford and Velleman 1990). Parents' consumption of illegal drugs also increases the risk of children's substance use (Akers 1985). Parents' substance-using behavior, which indicates a permissive attitude toward substance use, is just one way of transferring to their children norms concerning drug use. The normative standards parents set for substance use, and parents' attitudes toward drug use, are also important in the development of children's own attitudes and behavior (Wilks, Callan, and Austin 1989). Of course, parental influences are not the only force existing in a family. Older siblings sometimes are the carriers of drugs and sources of approval of drug use (Needle et al. 1986).

Family plays an important role in adolescents' substance use. But parental/familial and peer supports are both important needs during adolescence (Maton and Zimmerman 1992). If peer influence is stronger than parental power, individuals are likely to associate more exclusively with peers and to be exposed to peers' substance-using behavior, assuming that individuals are more likely to choose friends who do not abstain (Wills and Vaughan 1989). The general notion is that individuals are influenced more and more by their peers as they grow from children to teenagers to young adults (Huba and Bentler 1980). The family's opinion becomes less significant in certain matters, especially drug use (Swadi and Zeitlin 1988). Kandel and her associates indicated specific risk factors for initiation in different types of drug use. Peer norms, as compared to parental norms, do show a more significant impact on an individual's drug use (Kandel et al. 1976). Peers in many situations are also sources of availability of different drugs (Lopez, Redondo, and Martin 1989). Numerous studies indicate that peers become the primary force affecting adolescents when substance use is the concern (Krohn et al. 1982; Needle et al. 1986; Ong 1989). However, family factors should also directly affect adolescents' association with particular peers, some of whom may expose adolescents to things like legal or illegal drugs (Aseltine 1995).

Even though alcohol is a legal drug in this society for adults, underage drinking is considered to be illegal. The involvement in alcohol use may signify a tendency for other deviant behavior among adolescents. Studies show that the legal drugs, alcohol and nicotine (cigarettes), are "gateway" drugs for illicit drug use such as marijuana and cocaine among youth (Kandel et al. 1976; Kandel and Logan 1984; Kandel and Yamaguchi 1993). In general, studies show that youth who are heavily involved with either alcohol or illegal drugs are also more apt to be involved in other delinquent acts (Wechsler and Thum 1973; McMurran and Hollin 1989). Some studies, for example, have shown a predictive power of early adolescent delinquent acts on later substance abuse and alcohol-related problems (Windle 1990). As the same process is applied to drinking behavior, onset age of delinquency and that of certain substance use is also an important predictor of later, more serious delinquent acts and substance abuse, respectively (Tolan and Thomas 1995).

Problem-behavior theorists (Jessor and Jessor 1975) suggest that various deviant behaviors are interrelated, and these behaviors are predicted by individuals' "perceived environmental system" and "personality system." "Perceived environmental system" refers to other support and approval of deviant behaviors; "personality system" is the individual's beliefs and attitudes about deviant behaviors. The interaction of personality-system variables with perceived environmental variables determines individuals' behavior, whether or not individuals engage in problem behaviors (Jessor, Donovan, and Costa 1986). Onset drinking, therefore, according to problem-behavior theorists (Jessor and Jessor 1977), influences the occurrence of other problematic behaviors as young people act to fulfill their perceptions of themselves as an adult and independent. Research shows that the onset age of drinking not only predicts adolescent alcohol abuse, but also teens' current substance-using behavior, including use of cigarettes and marijuana (Yu and Williford 1992). Of course, individual psychosocial factors, such as peer and parental supports and the presence of relatively tolerant attitudes, are main determinants of the occurrence of all problematic behaviors (Jessor 1976; Smith, Canter, and Robin 1989; Tolan and Thomas 1995).

Several researchers have tried to examine whether a single latent construct accounts for many different problem behaviors, including drinking, illicit drug use, and delinquent behavior. Some of these studies show support for the existence of a "deviant style" (Donovan, Jessor, and Costa 1988; Vingilis and Adlaf 1990); others indicate the relative independence of different problem behaviors (White 1987), while finding that a small variance of problem behaviors can be explained by a core, underlying construct (Smith, McCarthy, and Goldman 1995). Of course, the search for explanatory factors and social mechanisms generating different problem behaviors will take different directions, dependent upon which one of the above conditions is valid.

While an identical set of sociocultural and psychosocial factors may not predict and explain the variance of all problem behaviors, most of these factors do partially explain more than one deviant behavior because of the behaviors' highly correlated nature. For example, drinking is often associated with delinquency (McMurran 1991), even though knowledge of the relationship is still limited. Alcohol use is more similar to marijuana use than to hard drug use (Newcomb, Maddahian, and Bentler 1986). Many marijuana users are also shown to be problem drinkers and cigarette smokers (Jessor, Chase, and Donovan 1980; Welte and Barnes 1987; Ellickson and Hays 1991). Correlates of marijuana use are also predictors of problematic drinking and delinquency (Jessor, Chase, and Donovan 1980; Simons, Conger, and Whitbeck 1988). Heavy drinking and illegal drug use behavior may cause youngsters to commit crime, it may simply provide an excuse for delinquent acts, or it may be that the two problem behaviors are actually caused by additional factors. It is important to look further at all these different relationships in order to understand the dynamic better and to facilitate treatment programs.

Dynamic Processes Leading to Alcohol and Drug Using Behavior

As shown above, there has been a prodigious effort to understand the dynamics of teenage substance use. Most of these studies have investigated the correlates of teenage drinking and drug use, and the consequences of substance abuse. The results of these studies are valuable to our understanding of substance abuse. However, research of how these antecedent and consequent factors interact with each other is lacking. Our picture of why and how a teenager becomes a substance abuser is, therefore, incomplete.

Full investigation of a teenager's substance abuse must include a dynamic view starting with initial use. What are the circumstantial factors surrounding the first substance using experience? Do parents know and sanction the first drinking experience? What guidelines do they offer? Why and how do youth continue to drink and/or use other drugs? What family or peer factors contribute to heavy involvement with alcohol or drug? How is prior or current delinquent behavior related to substance use/abuse? What are the specific processes leading young people from initial alcohol and drug use to continual use and, finally, dysfunctional use of substance? What factors modify the process toward substance abuse? When answers to these type of questions are obtained perhaps our understanding of substance abuse will be more complete.

In order to gain a greater understanding of the social dynamics that underlie adolescent substance use, we employed a case study approach to elicit accounts of several circumstances related to this behavior. The data solicited here were demographic variables, childhood experiences, onset of substance use, first substance using experience, first intoxication experience, delinquent behavior history, parental control, parental substance using behavior, family structure, family disciplinary practices, peer influences, and school influences.

With the objectives in mind, the first author interviewed four teenagers who were referred to a counseling program by authorities in a midwestern county. These adolescents were notified by the counselor about our study and volunteered to participate. After they obtained parental consent, an interview was arranged. The interview took about two hours to complete. The teenagers received a $15 incentive for their participation. During the interviews, the respondents were asked some basic background questions and which drugs had been used in their lifetime. Based on this information, we organized our efforts around those factors shown in the literature to be associated with substance abuse, emphasizing the dynamic aspect of the behavior.

JIM: A CASE STUDY

Jim is a 16-year-old white male from a middle-class background. Both of his parents are employed. When interviewed, he was pretty sure that he was going to change because of the troubles he had caused. He was attending school regularly and trying to achieve better grades (his grade point average in the previous semester was less than .5). Even though he was still drinking "once a while," he said he had cut down on the amount, in his words, "Uh, I did, I sipped, you know, it really wasn't like when I got drunk, but yeah, I drank a little bit, yeah." For him a little bit meant four drinks per sitting, twice a week. Binge drinking is defined in the research literature as five or more drinks per sitting at least once in the last two weeks for males (Wechsler et al. 1994).

Jim began to drink when he was 11. He and his good friend were bored, found alcohol in the house and started drinking until both of them got very sick and began vomiting. His parents were sleeping upstairs when they "sneaked" that first drink and were never aware of it. Jim remembered the feeling while he was drinking and described it as a "buzz." The feeling made him talk more and feel more expansive or more than he was. He liked that feeling. But the later feeling was not exciting or pleasant. He and his friend told each other that they were not going to drink again.

However, Jim got drunk again in his backyard when three friends came to "hangout" and jump on the trampoline. He was 12 years old and his friends were about the same age or a couple of years older. He recalled the thought to drink came to him after they had been jumping for a while. He asked his neighbor who was over 21 years old to buy them beers and vodka. Jim consumed two shots of vodka and four cans of beer this time and described the feeling as pleasant until getting sick again. His mother found out this time and "flipped out." To his surprise, however, his mother did not say anything to him about the incident after he woke up the next day although he was grounded for a couple of days. His father never knew about the incident nor did his mother inform his friends' parents.

Jim did not plan to repeat the experience again but did so numerous times. His next experience was two year later at about age 14. At this age, drinking occasions became more frequent and intensive. He began to associate with friends a couple of years older than he was. In meeting these older peers, he described that his drinking became more frequent and heavy. He found that he could tolerate more alcohol without getting sick, and he continued to increase the quantity that he consumed. Before counseling, he drank pretty much every day—three "forties" in each episode. Jim said that he used to be able to get a buzz after two forties (about seven drinks), and then it was three within a four-hour period. Since he was still under age, he mostly drank at his friend's house. He described that he would drink until he got the "buzz." He liked the feeling.

Jim experienced several problems with his drinking. One serious act included being caught while driving someone else's car under the influence of alcohol.

He was jailed four times before counseling and spent two months in jail for one of the offenses. While drinking, he said he did not worry about being caught. He indicated some remorse about letting his family down, getting in fights, and having sex with people he did not want to—at least to begin with—as a result of drinking. He associated being bored and hanging out with neighbors with his drinking and getting drunk. In his words, "You can't find hardly nobody sober where I live, nobody. It's almost impossible."

Jim described his after-drinking behavior to be pretty "ordinary." Not many people except his mom could tell that he was drunk although in his words "she would never say anything." When Jim started to drink, the relationship between his father and mother was pretty strained. His father was not around much. Later, Jim's parents were divorced, and he lived with his mom. His mother, therefore, had to "deal with" Jim's drinking problems. His father, beyond threatening to tell Jim's probation officer about his drinking, never addressed Jim's drinking problem in any other way.

When asked about his attitudes toward alcohol use in general, Jim replied that young people should be prohibited by law to drink because they are not equipped to handle it. Moreover, they often use drinking as an excuse for misbehavior. However, Jim did not see anything wrong with alcohol use. In his words, "I did not think it was bad because my dad did it."

Jim described his father as an alcoholic, although his father had quit drinking. His father worked two jobs but often got drunk. He deserted the family when Jim was very young (about 9 or 10 years old). Contact thereafter between Jim and his father was rare. At the time of the interview, Jim's father had quit drinking and had remarried. Neither of Jim's stepparents drank, nor did his biological mother. She told him that drinking was no good. But according to Jim, "She never enforced nothing." There were no rules besides curfew. Jim associated problems at home with his drinking, until the time his mom committed him to a hospital for help. Despite having him committed, Jim still expressed affection for his mother. In Jim's words, "She is a really good lady, I love her a lot."

Along with drinking at the age of 12, Jim expressed a curiosity about other drugs and asked his parents about them. He related that his parents tried to scare him by saying that he would die if he smoked the wrong stuff, and he would have a "big" problem.

Jim seemed to limit his other drug use to an occasional use of marijuana. He did not enjoy its effects and felt guilty about using it. "I would feel paranoid and dirty, I never really like it." He used marijuana because his friends asked him, and he did not want to refuse. He never discussed his dislike or the drug's effects on him with his friends. This group of friends was different from the group of friends with whom he drank. Jim also said he avoided too much use of marijuana because it was detectable in the urine and therefore could cause problems with his probation.

Jim did not have too much to say about school because he did not go to school that much. He described himself as a poor student who cheated on almost all his tests. His GPA was extremely low. He had been suspended many times (fifteen or so), once for carrying a big rock to class. He explained that he brought the rock to school to protect himself from students who did not like him or his lifestyle. He stated his involvement in a number of fights was always because others picked on him or his friends. When asked to define "friend," he replied it was someone who did not steal his money. Jim, however, said he trusted no one.

Drinking was a major activity for Jim and his friends. Some of these friends drank everyday perhaps to escape boredom and to have something to do, a reason that Jim also gave. He heard his friends boast about alcohol enhancing opportunities toward the feeling for and the feeling of sex. These friends also had run-ins with the law although Jim expressed that they were luckier in this respect because he had more citations than the others.

Jim blamed his delinquent acts on alcohol. He admitted that he purposely damaged property belonging to other people, stole a car or car stereos, bought stolen properties to resell, threw rocks to start trouble, ran away from home after arguing with his mom, lied to buy alcohol or get into a movie, seriously hurt someone, threatened someone at school, got drunk in a public place, and broke into a building or a car. He believed that his drinking led to negative behavior because he forgot things when he got drunk and did not think about the consequences. He said he did not steal to buy alcohol but rather to secure money to buy other material things. So in a sense he was stealing to buy alcohol, because the odd jobs he claimed he had did not provide enough money to buy other things.

JUDY: A CASE STUDY OF MARIJUANA USE

Judy is a white 17-year-old high school senior, with a grade point average of 3.1 for the semester prior to her interview. She described her family's socio-economic status between the middle and upper strata. She regarded her family as being "better off" than those in her neighborhood. She got into trouble with the police after being stopped while driving with marijuana apparatus in her car. She was sentenced to sixteen hours of community service, three months probation, and counseling.

Judy's first experience with alcohol occurred around the age of 13, an experience she described as getting very drunk, getting caught, and being severely punished by her father. After that experience, she replied, she stopped using alcohol and rather began to smoke marijuana with older, 18-year-old friends from the neighborhood. Her first-time experience with marijuana was under a bridge with these older companions who urged her to try it. Up to that time, her only information about drugs was provided by a speaker invited to her school. She recalled little, if anything, about this school sponsored drug education effort. Although she knew her parents would object to drugs in general and her use of them in particular, she could not recall any discussion with her parents on this subject.

Judy's second experience with marijuana came two months after her initial use, this time in the home of one of her close friends. Judy acknowledged that she did not suffer any particular effect from her first-time smoking of the drug. She then was "taught" how to smoke marijuana much in the same way Becker explained in his classic article "Becoming a Marijuana User" (1953). This time she felt relaxed, tranquil, and "hungry" after smoking.

Judy continued using marijuana after this second occasion for about fourteen more times before she turned 17. She described her frequency of use as being about four to five times a month, usually one joint per occasion. She explained that she used marijuana when she was bored and the drug was available, which was almost any time in her neighborhood.

According to Judy, smoking marijuana made her friends more exciting because they laughed and were gregarious and talked a lot. She said she talked a great deal after she smoked if she was around close friends. She liked to have a good time and talk with friends, which marijuana enhanced. However, when she was "high" on marijuana she described her thinking as confused, followed by slowed reaction, and a feeling of sluggishness and laziness. She did not like these feelings. During one of her marijuana intoxication episodes she experienced a blackout—a situation that frightened her. Her grades also began to suffer, which she blamed on marijuana.

The police informed Judy's mother about her marijuana-related trouble; she got very angry and threatened her to not do it again. Judy's father did not know about the whole event. Judy and her father did not get along well. They yelled at each other so often that they just did not talk to each other much at all. However, the communication between them was better if her father was drinking. Judy described her father as a heavy drinker who forbade her to drink. Even though her father did not allow Judy to drink, he occasionally asked her to serve him a drink at home. There were few parental rules set for Judy at home except a curfew and requirement to do her homework. She was sanctioned once for a curfew violation—being grounded.

Judy did not think that marijuana should be illegal because it is a natural product made by God. She believed it should be a personal decision if people wish to use it or not. Her two close girl friends and her boyfriend also approved of the drug.

Judy said she was close to her mom and would talk with her concerning financial, social, or emotional support. However, at times she felt it easier to talk to one of her close female friends about boys, dating etc. Judy occasionally engaged in delinquent behavior. She admitted writing on the bathroom wall, lying about her age to buy cigarettes, cheating on school tests (almost every test), getting in fights in school, taking her mom's vehicle for a ride without her permission, and making obscene phone calls. Judy did not think she suffered from negative consequences of marijuana use. Many of her delinquent acts, according to her, occurred before she started using marijuana.

DAVID: A CASE OF MULTIPLE-DRUG USE

David is a 16-year-old white eleventh grader. He was employed part time in a fast food restaurant, working approximately thirty hours a week. David was sent to the counseling center for a number of misdemeanor charges including marijuana abuse, underage alcohol consumption, park violations—littering and being loud in the park after 11 o'clock—and disorderly conduct. He described that he was partying with a group of friends at a camp site in the summer. He denied using marijuana although his friends did. He admitted to alcohol use.

David began to smoke cigarettes when he was around 10 years old and continues to smoke. He usually smoked three cigarettes a day as a preteen. He was smoking about a pack a day at the time of the interview. David replied that his parents were more lenient toward his smoking than his drinking or using marijuana. In other words, they did not seem overly concerned about his current use of tobacco but were concerned about drinking and smoking marijuana. He started using marijuana when he was in sixth grade (12 years old). He first heard about marijuana from peers in his middle school who described its euphoric effects when they used it. His parents also talked about the drug then and described it in negative terms. They said they had used marijuana before as a result of peer pressure and that it was harmful to one's health. His parents also said that alcohol was bad too. His stepfather is an alcoholic but quit drinking right about the time he met David's mom (when David was about 2 years old).

David was offered marijuana by a friend and he liked the effect. He was "high" and felt like he could do whatever he wanted. From his initial use, he smoked marijuana almost every day—before school, after school, and before he went home at night. However, he did not use the drug alone but always with friends. He hid his marijuana use from his parents but his parents were suspicious because David came home "high" a few times. Eventually, his parents were pretty certain about his drug use and confronted him and David confessed. David continued to use marijuana for another two years, quitting when he was 15 years old. He said that a friend of his called him a pot head (the friend had just quit using marijuana), and he quit. He said that he used marijuana a couple of times after that. David continued that his marijuana use led to a series of delinquent acts, especially while he was in the seventh and eighth grades. He stole alcohol from stores, ran away from home, and stole goods from cars for resale.

David was in the seventh grade when he took his first drink. The alcohol was secured by an older person who agreed to buy it for him and his friends. After school, they went to a playground where they used marijuana and alcohol. David consumed two beers on this occasion, and said he felt drunk. He also indicated that he felt weak and uncoordinated. These effects were unpleasant and not very rewarding to him. However, he continued to drink at least once on the weekend. Eventually, his frequency of consuming alcohol was at least three times a week, usually the nights of the weekend. David said he usually consumed about twelve drinks per sitting each of these times, well into intoxication. These drinking episodes, unlike the first, were pleasant to David and gave him "something to do." He said his parents never suspected that he was drinking until he was reported to them by the police. He engaged in a number of techniques to avoid getting caught by his parents such as chewing gum, sneaking in the house at night, etc. He was grounded as a result of the police report. He replied that after this incident and several others, he felt his parents just gave up on him.

David reported using a variety of other drugs during this time such as acid, crack cocaine, and barbiturates or pain pills. He used acid about twenty times and enjoyed what it did to him and thought the hallucinations were "fun." He mixed crack and marijuana once and replied that it blunted the effects of the cocaine. He used the pain pills to reduce the "buzz" effects of alcohol.

David felt some guilt because his drug use was affecting his mother to whom he felt "close." However, he replied that he felt somewhat distant from his stepfather who, in David's words, "never did father and son things with him." There were some parental rules such as curfew hours and household chores with which to comply to earn an allowance. But as mentioned above, as David broke these rules, his parents "gave up on him," and cut his allowance to keep him from buying drugs. David, however, had other ways to make money and used it to obtain his drug supply.

David was ambivalent about whether marijuana should be legal or not. He said some people miss classes because of marijuana use, and that the drug is harmful to the brain. However, he also said that some people handle marijuana well and they can use it responsibly.

David's views toward alcohol were also inconsistent or ambiguous. He disapproved of underage drinking or at least said it should not be legal. However, he did not frown on parents allowing their children to drink in the home. He continued to drink, although underage, because he liked its effects and it was fun. His major concern was how to avoid getting caught.

David exhibited several problems in school. First his grades were average and he missed a number of classes. While in the seventh grade, he ran away from home a couple of times, vandalized buildings, and stole things. He managed to be promoted to the eighth grade anyway. His school employed security guards and installed a system to check on absenteeism. David then started going to school more often and his grades improved. David said that he liked school during this time because he could "hang out" with friends.

His delinquent behavior went back to the age of 10. He started by stealing cigarettes almost daily in order to impress his friends. He quit when caught by the store owner who threatened to call the police. David said that "cops don't scare me any more, however." His delinquency increased when he started to use marijuana at 14 years of age. To him, drinking did not "cause his delinquent acts but only made him have a "bad" attitude and want to pick fights. In the year prior to the interview, David threw eggs or toilet paper at someone's house a couple of times, was suspended from school about ten times, cheated on school tests "a couple of times," shoplifted small things from a store, took money from his mom's purse, engaged in disorderly conduct in public places, took his mom's car without her permission, was drunk in a public place "many times;" threatened other students, and got into gang fights.

JOHN: A CASE STUDY OF ALCOHOL AND MARIJUANA USE

John is a 16-year-old African American raised in what he called a "ghetto." He described his neighborhood as one where people did not "have means to meet their needs and did not control their children." John, however, described his mother as being good at clothing and feeding the family. At the time of the interview John was working full time as a cashier and cook at a local restaurant. John was sent to court while apprehended riding with an older lady who was driving a stolen car. He was put under house arrest awaiting trial. John violated his house arrest and was put on probation. His urine tested positive for marijuana during the probation which resulted in him being sent for counseling.

John's initial use of alcohol and marijuana was when he was 13 years old. He was offered both drugs by an older teen and an adult. John and his friend had seen these two older individuals using marijuana and alcohol for a time before John tried them. John and his friend shared a 22-ounce beer and smoked marijuana that day. His older friends taught him how to smoke to get high. He replied that the primary effect of this initial use was a feeling of being "stoned" or "high" accompanied by a body sensation which he characterized as shivering.

After this experience, he continued to use marijuana and alcohol. The second time he used marijuana, he described himself as being more sociable and outgoing. But he experienced obvious redding of the eyes, which led others to ask if he had used the drug. As a result, John learned how to hide his drug use by disguising his demeanor and appearance. John said that he was very good at hiding his use especially from his mother. He used alcohol once or twice a week, but he smoked marijuana every day. John said that he was a "little out of control" when he first started to smoke marijuana but soon learned how to manage or mask his behavior as time went on.

John was around people who smoked marijuana before his first use, including those he hung out with and his cousins. John's mother also was a marijuana user and a drinker. She used alcohol once every week or two weeks. She consumed about fifteen drinks in a typical drinking episode. According to John, his mother hid her marijuana smoking from the children at first. Then she smoked marijuana in front of the kids and told them she could do it because she was grown. John's mother, however, told John that it was not good for him to smoke marijuana. Actually, she did not know about his marijuana and alcohol use until later because of John's calculated impression management strategy.

John's mother and father were never married nor did they live together. John said that his father ignored him as a child. Thus, John did not want to have anything to do with his father as he grew older. When John was young, he stayed with his mother in his grandmother's house until the age of 8 when he and his mother moved to their own apartment. His mother supported the family by receiving welfare and money from her boyfriend. There had not been any shortage of food and clothes while John was growing up.

Curfew, cleaning up the porch, and taking turns with his brother washing dishes were John's household rules. John said that he would be grounded for violating these rules. However, he received less punishment and restrictions as he grew older. According to John, the curfew rule was not reasonable. Therefore, John sneaked out and back many times without his mother's knowledge. John said he usually did the chores, even though sometimes he did not finish them on time. John described that his mother did not punish him as much as she should.

John was a poor and disinterested student in school. He regarded going to school as going to a fashion show. John's punishment for poor grades consisted of his mother demanding more household chores from him. John believed that smoking marijuana led to his poor performance in school since he was more interested in getting high. However, John admitted that he never liked school. He said that he had a smart mouth, which teachers deplored. He and school never matched.

John approved of people using marijuana. John thought that marijuana was better than cigarette use, which may cause cancer. Marijuana should be legal. However, John believed that underage drinking was problematic. John preferred associating with more mature females from whom he could learn. These older female friends showed him how to dress and ways to manage his impression on others.

Before John was sent to the counseling center, he consumed about an ounce of marijuana per week and about six drinks per typical drinking episode (about two hours). He said that he used marijuana whenever he could get his hands on it. Sometimes John drank more. John described becoming angry and violent a few times after drinking. One time, he wanted to kill a guy after he consumed about ten drinks of hard liquor.

John engaged in a long list of delinquent acts since he started drinking and smoking marijuana. He reported that he damaged other people's property, rented cars for drug use, stole other people's property to resell, ran away from home, was put in jail, was sent to court, was put under house arrest, violated probation, lied to buy alcohol, shoplifted, attacked a police officer with an intention to kill him after his drinking, had sexual relations with someone to support marijuana use at the beginning of his marijuana use, sold crack cocaine and marijuana, cheated on school tests, threatened and hit other people such as teachers, was loud and unruly in public places, took a vehicle for a drive without the owner's permission, had sex with people who did not want to have sex, avoided paying for food after getting the food from a drive through, was drunk in public places, stole things, broke into houses for valuable things, skipped classes without an excuse, was suspended from school, and made obscene or harassing telephone calls.

DISCUSSION AND CONCLUSION

Each case illuminates and/or confirms several theoretical and empirical observations, including the symbolic interactionist perspective, reported in the field of alcohol and drug studies. The main emphasis of this research is that human actions are best understood in reference to the meanings that the actor attaches to his actions rather than to preexisting personal or social conditions (Vold and Bernard 1986). These meanings are sometimes derived by the individual, but more often they are obtained from personal interactions with significant others, an idea first espoused by Mead (1934) and formulated by Sutherland (1947) in his Differential Association Theory.

Similar to many alcohol and drug abusers, the four respondents began their drinking experience early in life. The parents, especially the mothers, were negative about alcohol. However, in some instances, the youth regarded their father figures as alcohol abusers and "distant" in their relationship with them. Some studies have found that the father's drinking is more influential than the mother's, especially for males (Barnes, Welte, and Dintcheff 1992). Beyond the admonition not to drink, these youth received little guidance about alcohol, its effects, or how to resist pressure to drink. Teenagers encounter numerous opportunities to drink or to use marijuana. The 1997 national survey by the University of Michigan asked high school students how difficult it was to obtain different drugs (Johnston, O'Malley, and Bachman 1997). The results show that almost 90 percent of seniors said that marijuana was either "fairly easy" or "very easy" to get. When parents forego giving guidance, peers become the source of information and/or pressure to abuse drugs. Teenagers are less likely to drink problematically if parents introduce them to alcohol or at least provide them with well-defined standards about alcohol use beyond the statement "don't." Youth want and need objective nonemotional and reasonable information about substances. Yet what they often receive in the home and/or in the school is biased, fear-provoking information that either entices risk taking behaviors or symbols of defiance.

Of these four youth, only Jim did not like marijuana. Judy, David, and John believe that marijuana use is acceptable behavior and used it on an occasional or regular basis during adolescence. They learned "how" to smoke and sense the effects of the drug from their peers as well as ways to hide their use from parents and others. As observed by Kaplan et al. (1986), adolescents became regular marijuana users because they like the feeling it gives them, because they believe it is acceptable, and because it is readily available. It is assumed that the increasing approval of marijuana use has triggered the escalation of use among adolescents during the final decade of the twentieth century.

Thornberry's interactional theory of delinquency (1987;1996), an extension of social control theory that is integrated with social learning variables partially explains these cases. In early and middle adolescence, parents are most influential on a child's values and commitment to school, or conversely, association with delinquent peers, delinquency and delinquent value development. Lax parental monitoring, parents' alcohol and drug abuse, the respondents' noncommitting attitudes toward school, and associating with friends who are excessive drinkers or marijuana users all contribute to the drinking problems and/or marijuana use found in each of these cases.

In most instances, these youth were engaging in minor delinquent acts at the time they had their first drink as early teenagers. The serious involvement in delinquent behavior such as fights and stealing became more visible as they became excessive alcohol or marijuana users. Drug abuse and delinquent acts, in turn, resulted in a drift from family, and closer association with their drug-using friends. Peers obviously played a major role in the drug-using behavior and delinquent acts of these four young people. The family and the school were not very effective in controlling their behavior.

General delinquent behavior and substance-using behavior appear to be closely associated. These four youngsters began their substance use and delinquent behavior during their early teen years. Peer influence played a major role in the lifestyle. Each respondent claimed that people in their neighborhoods used alcohol or drugs. In all four cases, parents did not or were not able to redirect the peer selection process for their children. When these four teenagers progressed into later adolescence, their parents become less influential, compared to their peers, in their commitment to conventional values, activities, and family.

Social processes lead teenagers to begin substance use and eventually to engage in abusive behavior. The social interaction with friends obviously enhanced delinquent values and drug using behavior, at least for these four teenagers. Failure in school and cheating behavior indicate low competence in the student role. The low performance may be partly compensated by satisfaction received from substance use, being with friends, and getting a high, as noted by Wills, Vaccaro, and McNamara (1992). The lack of parental guidance about drug and alcohol use may also explain why these youngsters developed evaluations of substance use based on their friends' definitions. Peer influences are strong and the continued association with friends who use drugs may drive these adolescents to get involved in the drugs again. These four teenagers never mentioned their parents' monitoring their friends and their whereabouts before and after they were in trouble. Thus, the lack of parental monitoring may explain these four teenagers' problem behaviors.

These four cases illuminate the validity of the symbolic interaction perspective. Since their early teens, these respondents had been exposed to tolerant attitudes toward deviant behavior and a lack of general parental support from at least one parent. In time, they developed relatively tolerant attitudes toward behaviors that included drinking and marijuana use. Each of these youth derived their meaning of substances through the modeling of a substance-abusing parent, usually a father, or from interaction with other youth who held similar beliefs about the act of using drugs. This finding corresponds to Sutherland's (1947) point that the learning of the meanings and motivations to use substances occurs within intimate personal groups. Moreover, these young people generally started to use and abuse alcohol and/or drugs early, as preteens, usually in the company of friends or older youth who either taught them the techniques of substance use or who, more importantly, provided them with the rationale and encouragement to engage in the behavior. Thus, in Sutherland's terms, these youths' association with deviant meanings of substances were of long and frequent duration. Studies show that youth who begin to use substances early in their development are more prone to experience a series of complications and problems as they grow older, even as adults. One explanation for this finding is that substances are often used to minimize some deficiency in a young person's developing self-concept for life situations or to maximize self-esteem and acceptance by his peers by using drugs to prove masculinity.

Most of these youth drank or used drugs as a rebellious act against a "nagging" or permissive parent or to "escape" from a boring routine. Each had more or less become alienated from their school and other conventional groups. Drugs transformed them and gave them status among their peers. David, for example, said that marijuana made him feel he could do anything. It also made it easier to overcome conventional standards and to engage in irresponsible, risk-taking or delinquent behaviors. As Jim stated, his drinking led to negative behavior because he forgot things when he got drunk and did not think about the consequences.

In time, although reluctantly, each of these youths acquiesced with society's definition of their behavior. Subsequently, at least on the surface, they accepted the meaning that others attached to their behavior and were making attempts to change.

REFERENCES

Akers, Ronald L. 1985. *Deviant Behavior: A Social Learning Approach*. 3rd. ed. Belmont, Calif.: Wadsworth Publishing Company.

Akers, Ronald L., and John K. Cochran. 1985. "Adolescent Marijuana Use: A Test of Three Theories of Deviant Behavior." *Deviant Behavior* 6: 323–346.

Akers, Ronald L., Marvin D. Krohn, Lonn Lanza-Kaduce, and Marcia J. Radosevich. 1979. "Social Learning and Deviant Behavior: A Specific Test of a General Theory." *American Sociological Review* 44: 635–655.

Arria, Amelia M., Ralph E. Tarter, and David H. Van Thiel. 1991. "The Effects of Alcohol Abuse on the Health of Adolescents." *Alcohol Health & Research World* 15: 52–57.

Aseltine, Robert H. 1995. "A Reconsideration of Parental and Peer Influences on Adolescent Deviance." *Journal of Health and Social Behavior* 36: 103–121.

Augustyn, Marycatherine, and Bruce G. Simons-Morton. 1995. "Adolescent Drinking and Driving: Etiology and Interpretation." *Journal of Drug Education* 25: 41–59.

Bailey, Susan L., and Robert L. Hubbard. 1990. "Developmental Variation in the Context of Marijuana Initiation among Adolescents." *Journal of Health and Social Behavior* 31: 58–70.

Bales, Robert Freed. 1946. "Cultural Differences in Rates of Alcoholism." *Quarterly Journal of Studies on Alcohol* 6: 480–499.

Barnes, Grace M., and John W. Welte. 1990. "Prediction of Adults' Drinking Patterns from the Drinking of their Parents." *Journal of Studies on Alcohol* 51: 523–527.

Barnes, Grace M., Michael P. Farrell, and Allen Cairns. 1986. "Parental Socialization Factors and Adolescent Drinking Behaviors." *Journal of Marriage and the Family* 48: 27–36.

Barnes, Grace M., John W. Welte, and Barbara Dintcheff. 1992. "Alcohol Misuse among College Students and Other Young Adults: Findings from a General Population Study in New York State." *The International Journal of the Addictions* 27: 917–934.

Beck, Kenneth H., Majorie Scaffa, Robert Swift, and Mia Ko. 1995. "A Survey of Parent Attitudes and Practices Regarding Underage Drinking." *Journal of Youth and Adolescence* 24: 315–334.

Becker, Howard S. 1953. "Becoming a Marijuana User." *American Journal of Sociology* 59: 235–242.

Berkowitz, Alan D., and H. Wesley Perkins. 1986. "Problem Drinking among College Students: A Review of Recent Research." *Journal of American College Health* 35: 21–28.

Chou, S. Patricia, and Roger P. Pickering. 1992. "Early Onset of Drinking as a Risk Factor for Lifetime Alcohol-Related Problems." *British Journal of Addiction* 87: 1199–1204.

Donovan, John E., Richard Jessor, and Frances M. Costa. 1988. "Syndrome of Problem Behavior in Adolescence: A Replication." *Journal of Consulting and Clinical Psychology* 56: 762–765.

Dupre, Deirdre, Norman Miller, Mark Gold, and Kathy Rospenda. 1995. "Initiation and Progression of Alcohol, Marijuana, and Cocaine Use among Adolescent Abusers." *The American Journal on Addictions* 4: 43–48.

Einstadter, Werner, and Stuart Henry. 1995. *Criminological Theory: An Analysis of Its Underlying Assumptions.* New York: Harcourt Brace.

Ellickson, Phyllis L., and Ron D. Hays. 1991. "Antecedents of Drinking among Young Adolescents with Different Alcohol Use Histories." *Journal of Studies on Alcohol* 52: 398–408.

Ensminger, Margaret E., C. Hendricks Brown, and Sheppard G. Kellam. 1982. "Sex Differences in Antecedents of Substance Use among Adolescents." *Journal of Social Issues* 38: 25–42.

Globetti, Gerald. 1967. "The Social Adjustment of High School Students and Problem Drinking." *Journal of Alcohol Education* 2: 21–29.

———. 1969. "The Use of Alcohol among High School Students in an Abstinence Setting." *Pacific Sociological Review* 12: 105–108.

Gonzalez, Gerardo M. 1983. "Time and Place of First Drinking Experience and Parental

Knowledge as Predictors of Alcohol Use and Misuse in College." *Journal of Alcohol and Drug Education* 28: 24–33.

Hanson, David J. 1973. "Social Norms and Drinking Behavior: Implications for Alcohol and Drug Education." *Journal of Alcohol and Drug Education* 65: 159–165.

Hartnagel, Timothy. 1996. "Cannabis Use and the Transition to Young Adulthood." *Journal of Youth and Adolescence* 25: 241–258.

Hirschi, Travis. 1969. *Causes of Delinquency.* Berkeley: University of California Press.

Huba, G. J., and P. M. Bentler. 1980. "The Role of Peer and Adult Models for Drug Taking at Different Stages in Adolescence." *Journal of Youth and Adolescence* 9: 449–465.

Humphrey, John A., and Jennifer Friedman. 1986. "The Onset of Drinking and Intoxication among University Students." *Journal of Studies on Alcohol* 47: 455–458.

Jessor, Richard. 1976. "Predicting Time of Onset of Marijuana Use: A Developmental Study of High School Youth." *Journal of Consulting and Clinical Psychology* 44: 125–134.

———. 1987. "Problem-Behavior Theory, Psychosocial Development, and Adolescent Problem Drinking." *British Journal of Addiction* 82: 331–342.

Jessor, Richard, James A. Chase, and John E. Donovan. 1980. "Psychosocial Correlates of Marijuana Use and Problem Drinking in a National Sample of Adolescents." *American Journal of Public Health* 70: 604–613.

Jessor, Richard, John E. Donovan, and Frances Costa. 1986. "Psychosocial Correlates of Marijuana Use in Adolescence and Young Adulthood: The Past as Prologue." *Alcohol, Drugs, and Driving* 2: 31–49.

Jessor, Richard, and Shirley L. Jessor. 1975. "Adolescent Development and the Onset of Drinking: A Longitudinal Study." *Journal of Studies on Alcohol* 36: 27–51.

———. 1977. *Problem Behavior and Psychosocial Development: A Longitudinal Study of Youth.* New York: Academic Press.

Johnston, Lloyd D., Patrick M O'Malley, and Jerald G. Bachman. 1997. *Drug Use among American Teens Show Some Signs of Leveling After a Long Rise.* Ann Arbor: The University of Michigan.

Kandel, Denise B., and Kenneth Andrews. 1987. "Processes of Adolescent Socialization by Parents and Peers." *The International Journal of the Addictions* 22: 319–342.

Kandel, Denise B., and John A. Logan. 1984. "Patterns of Drug Use from Adolescence to Young Adulthood: I. Periods of Risk for Initiation, Continued Use, and Discontinuation." *American Journal of Public Health* 74: 660–666.

Kandel, Denise B., Donald Treiman, Richard Faust, and Eric Single. 1976. "Adolescent Involvement in Legal and Illegal Drug Use: A Multiple Classification Analysis." *Social Forces* 55: 438–458.

Kandel, Denise, Kazuo Yamaguchi, and Kevin Chen. 1992. "Stages of Progression in Drug Involvement from Adolescence to Adulthood: Further Evidence for the Gateway Theory." *Journal of Studies on Alcohol* 53: 447–457.

Kandel, Denise, and Kazuo Yamaguchi. 1993. "From Beer to Crack: Developmental Patterns of Drug Involvement." *American Journal of Public Health* 83: 851–855.

Kaplan, Howard B., Steven S. Martin, Robert J. Johnson, and Cynthia A. Robbins. 1986. "Escalation of Marijuana Use: Application of a General Theory of Deviant Behavior." *Journal of Health and Social Behavior* 27: 44–61.

Kinney, Jean, and Gwen Leaton. 1983. *Loosening the Grip: A Handbook on Alcohol Information.* St. Louis, Ill.: The C. V. Mosby Co.

Krohn, Marvin D., Ronald L. Akers, Marcia J. Radosevich, and Lonn Lanza-Kaduce. 1982. "Norm Qualities and Adolescent Drinking and Drug Behavior: The Effects of Norm Quality and Reference Group on Using and Abusing Alcohol and Marijuana." *Journal of Drug Issues* 12: 343–359.

Lee, Gregory P., and Carlo C. DiClimente. 1985. "Age of Onset versus Duration of Problem Drinking on the Alcohol Use Inventory." *Journal of Studies on Alcohol* 46: 398–402.

Lo, Celia C., 1995. "Gender Differences in Collegiate Alcohol Use." *Journal of Drug Issues* 25: 817–836.

————. 2000. "The Impact of First Drinking and Differential Association on Collegiate Drinking." *Sociological Focus* 33: 265–280.

Lo, Celia C., and Gerald Globetti. 1991. "Parents Noticing Teenage Drinking: Evidence from College Freshmen." *Sociology and Social Research* 76: 20–28.

Lopez, Jose Manuel Otero, Lourdes Miron Redondo, and Angeles Luengo Martin. 1989. "Influence of Family and Peer Group on the Use of Drugs by Adolescents." *The International Journal of the Addictions* 24: 1065–1082.

Margulies, Rebecca Z., Ronald C. Kessler, and Denise B. Kandel. 1977. "A Longitudinal Study of Onset of Drinking among High-School Students." *Journal of Studies on Alcohol* 38: 897–912.

Massey, James L., and Marvin D., Krohn. 1986. "A Longitudinal Examination of an Integrated Social Process Model of Deviant Behavior." *Social Forces* 65:106–134.

Maton, Kenneth, I., and Marc A. Zimmerman. 1992. "Psychosocial Predictors of Substance Use among Urban Black Male Adolescents." *Drugs and Society* 6: 79–113.

McMurran, Mary. 1991. "Young Offenders and Alcohol-Related Crime: What Interventions Will Address the Issues?" *Journal of Adolescence* 14: 245–253.

McMurran, Mary, and Clive R. Hollin. 1989. "Drinking and Delinquency: Another Look at Young Offenders and Alcohol." *British Journal of Criminology* 29: 386–394.

Mead, George H. 1934. *Mind, Self and Society*. Edited, with an introduction, by Charles W. Morris. Chicago: University of Chicago Press.

Milgram, Gail Gleason. 1982. "Youthful Drinking: Past and Present." *Journal of Drug Education* 12: 289–308.

————. 1990. *The Facts About Drinking*. Mount Vernon, N.Y.: Consumers Union.

Needle, Richard, Hamilton McCubbin, Marc Wilson, Robert Reineck, Amnon Lazar, and Helen Mederer. 1986. "Interpersonal Influences in Adolescent Drug Use: The Role of Older Siblings, Parents, and Peers." *The International Journal of the Addictions* 21: 739–766.

Newcomb, Michael D., and Peter M. Bentler. 1989. *Consequence of Adolescent Drug Use: Impact on the Lives of Young Adults*. Newbury Park, Calif.: Sage.

Newcomb, Michael D., Ebrahim Maddahian, and Peter M. Bentler. 1986. "Risk Factors for Drug Use among Adolescents: Concurrent and Longitudinal Analysis." *American Journal of Public Health* 76: 525–531.

Ong, Teck-Hong. 1989. "Peers as Perceived by Drug Abusers in their Drug-Seeking Behavior." *British Journal of Addiction* 84: 631–637.

Orford, Jim, and Richard Velleman. 1990. "Offspring of Parents with Drinking Problems: Drinking and Drug-taking as Young Adults." *British Journal of Addiction* 85: 779–794.

Peterson, Peggy L., J. David Hawkins, Robert D. Abbott, Richard F. Catalano. 1995. "Disentangling the Effects of Parental Drinking, Family Management, and Parental Alcohol Norms on Current Drinking by Black and White Adolescents." In Gayle M. Boyd, Jan Howard, and Robert A. Zucker, eds., *Alcohol Problems among Adolescents: Current Directions in Prevention Research*, p. 33–57. Hillsdale, N.J.: Lawrence Erlbaum Associates.

Robins, Lee N., and Thomas R. Przybeck. 1985. "Age of Onset of Drug Use as a Factor in Drug and Other Disorders." In Coryl LaRue Jones and Robert J. Battjes, ed., *Etiology of Drug Abuse: Implications for Prevention*, pp. 178–192. Rockville, Md.: National Institute on Drug Abuse.

Samson, Herman H., Cindy O. Maxwell, and Teresa F. Doyle. 1989. "The Relation of Initial Alcohol Experiences to Current Alcohol Consumption in a College Population." *Journal of Studies on Alcohol* 50: 254–260.

Simons, Ronald, R. D. Conger, and Leslie B. Whitbeck. 1988. "A Multistage Social Learning Model of the Influences of Family and Peers Upon Adolescent Substance Abuse." *The Journal of Drug Issues* 18: 293–315.

Smith, Maurice B., William A. Canter, and Arthur L. Robin. 1989. "A Path Analysis of an Adolescent Drinking Behavior Model Derived from Problem Behavior Theory." *Journal of Studies on Alcohol* 50: 128–142.

Smith, Gregory T., Denis M. McCarthy, and Mark S. Goldman. 1995. "Self-Reported Drinking and Alcohol-Related Problems among Early Adolescents: Dimensionality and Validity over 24 Months." *Journal of Studies on Alcohol* 56: 383–394.

Steele, Ric G., Rex Forehand, Lisa Armistead, and Gene Brody. 1995. "Predicting Alcohol and Drug Use in Early Adulthood: The Role of Internalizing and Externalizing Behavior Problems in Early Adolescence." *American Journal of Orthopsychiatry* 65: 380–388.

Steinberg, Laurence, Anne Fletcher, and Nancy Darling. 1994. "Parental Monitoring and Peer Influences on Adolescent Substance Use." *Pediatrics* 93: 1060–1064.

Sutherland, Edwin H. 1947. *Principles of Criminology*. Philadelphia: J. B. Lippincott Company.

Swadi, Harith, and Harry Zeitlin. 1988. "Peer Influence and Adolescent Substance Abuse: A Promising Side?" *British Journal of Addiction* 83: 153–157.

Thornberry, Terence P. 1987. "Toward an Interaction Theory of Delinquency." *Criminology* 25: 863–891.

———. 1996. "Empirical Support for Interactional Theory: A Review of the Literature." In J. David Hawkins, ed., *Delinquency and Crime*, p. 198–235. New York: Cambridge University Press.

Timofeeva, A. S., and L. F. Perekrjostova. 1990. "Social-Psychological Aspects of Drinking by Youth and Young Adults." *Drugs and Society* 4: 31–37.

Tolan, Patrick H., and Peter Thomas. 1995. "The Implications of Age of Onset for Delinquency Risk II: Longitudinal Data." *Journal of Abnormal Child Psychology* 23: 157–181.

Ullman, Albert D. 1952. "The Psychological Mechanism of Alcohol Addiction." *Quarterly Journal of Studies on Alcohol* 13: 602–608.

———. 1953. "The First Drinking Experience of Addictive and of "Normal" Drinkers." *Quarterly Journal of Studies of Alcohol* 14: 181–191.

———. 1960. "Ethnic Differences in the First Drinking Experience." *Social Problems* 8: 45–56.

Vingilis, Evelyn, and Edward Adlaf. 1990. "The Structure of Problem Behavior among Ontario High School Students: A Confirmatory-Factor Analysis." *Health Education Research: Theory & Practice* 5: 151–160.

Vold, George B., and Thomas J. Bernard. 1986. *Theoretical Criminology.* 3rd ed. New York: Oxford University Press.

Wechsler, Henry, Andrea Davenport, George Dowdall, Barbara Moeykens, and Sonia Castillo. 1994. "Health and Behavioral Consequences of Binge Drinking in College." *JAMA* 272: 1672–1677.

Wechsler, Henry, and Mary McFadden. 1979. "Drinking among College Students in New England." *Journal of Studies on Alcohol* 40: 969–996.

Wechsler, Henry, and Denise Thum. 1973. "Teen-Age Drinking, Drug Use, and Social Correlates." *Quartery Journal of Studies on Alcohol* 34: 1220–1227.

Welte, John W., and Grace M. Barnes. 1987. "Alcohol Use among Adolescent Minority Groups." *Journal of Studies on Alcohol* 48: 329–336.

White, Helene Raskin. 1987. "Longitudinal Stability and Dimensional Structure of Problem Drinking in Adolescence." *Journal of Studies on Alcohol* 48: 541–550.

White, Helene Raskin, Valerie Johnson, and Allan Horwitz. 1986. "An Application of Three Deviance Theories to Adolescent Substance Use." *The International Journal of the Addictions* 21: 347–366.

Wilks, Jeffrey, Victor J. Callan, and Derek A. Austin. 1989. "Parent, Peer and Personal Determinants of Adolescent Drinking." *British Journal of Addiction* 84: 619–630.

Wills, Thomas A., Donato Vaccaro, Grace McNamara. 1992. "The Role of Life Events, Family Support, and Competence in Adolescent Substance Use: A Test of Vulnerability and Protective Factors." *American Journal of Community Psychology* 20: 349–374.

Wills, Thomas Ashby, and Roger Vaughan. 1989. "Social Support and Substance Use in Early Adolescence." *Journal of Behavioral Medicine* 12: 321–339.

Windle, Michael. 1990. "A Longitudinal Study of Antisocial Behaviors in Early Adolescence as Predictors of Late Adolescent Substance Use: Gender and Ethnic Group Differences." *Journal of Abnormal Psychology* 99: 86–91.

Windle, Michael, Carol Miller-Tutzauer, and Donna Domenico. 1992. "Alcohol Use, Suicidal Behavior, and Risky Activities among Adolescents." *Journal of Research on Adolescence* 2: 317–330.

Yu, Jiang, and William R. Williford. 1992. "The Age of Alcohol Onset and Alcohol, Cigarette, and Marijuana Use Patterns: An Analysis of Drug Use Progression of Young Adults in New York State." *The International Journal of the Addictions* 27: 1313–1323.

4

AIDS

Mary-Rose Mueller

INTRODUCTION

In June 1981, the federal agency charged with tracking and analyzing national trends in health and illness, the Centers for Disease Control and Prevention (CDC) issued the first report on the complex and puzzling condition we now know as the Acquired Immune Deficiency Syndrome, or AIDS. Since then, AIDS has come to be viewed as one of the most significant social and public health problems of our times. Between 1981 and 1996, more than 573,000 Americans have been diagnosed with AIDS (CDC 1997), and nearly one million more are believed to be infected with the causal agent of the disease, the human immunodeficiency virus (HIV). Despite recent advances made in the medical management of the condition, AIDS remains the leading cause of death among persons 25–44 years of age (CDC 1997).

Recognition of the enormity of the American AIDS epidemic has led to the mobilization of efforts among representatives from nearly every major social institution in this country, including government, law, medicine, science, education, and religion. Much social scientific analysis has focused on the actions of groups involved in shaping the public response to AIDS, and in particular on the activities of affected persons (Weitz 1991), AIDS activists (Altman 1987; Patton 1990; Epstein 1996) and policymakers (Panem 1988; Bayer 1989).

This chapter contributes to the growing literature on the response of medical professionals to the American AIDS epidemic (Bosk and Frader 1990; Epstein 1996; Mueller 1998). In so doing, it presents the case of a small group of clinicians caring for people with AIDS in the first decade of the crisis and their organized efforts to create both a new professional role, that of clinician researcher, and a new arena, or jurisdiction, of practice within the federal government's program of AIDS treatment research, that of the Community Program of Clinical Research for AIDS.

Recent scholarship in the sociology of professions attends to the ways in which occupational groups create, expand, and secure the boundaries of their work (cf. Abbott 1988; Bucher 1962; Halpern 1988; Scull 1993). While this scholarship is primarily concerned with competition between and among professionals, it seems to suggest that as professional groups seek to establish novel occupational roles and jurisdictions of practice they sometimes act in ways that differ, or deviate, from extant and structured patterns of work. For example, subgroups of professionals sometimes redefine and claim expertise over problems that had been under the purview of other occupational groups. One such example of this type of occurrence is when physicians renamed some childhood misbehaviors as the medical condition "hyperactivity" and replaced teachers as experts in the care of school-aged children's classroom comportment (Conrad and Schneider 1980). Scholarship further suggests that whether or not the deviant activities of professional groups result in the establishment of new occupational roles and practice niches depends on a variety of social, political, and professional factors.

The case presented here permits a view of one subgroup within the medical profession whose actions deviated from the normative structure of modern medical practice. The division of medical labor is stratified into three ideal typical organized work roles: physician administrators, physician researchers, and rank-and-file clinician practitioners (Freidson 1985).

Traditionally, physician administrators have held positions as chiefs of staff and heads of departments or programs, and have performed advisory functions such as scheduling and organizational oversight, within medical and academic service settings. More recently, however, some physician-administrators have carved out new managerial roles within corporate and governmental settings, and have taken on more formal authoritative control over the actions of their clinician-practitioner and medical-researcher colleagues (Freidson 1985; Montgomery 1990; 1992). Medical researchers usually work in academic medical centers. There, they are involved in the education and training of the next generation of medical doctors and, through scientific activities, they produce knowledge that forms the basis of medical practice in various facets of health, disease, and therapeutic management (Freidson 1985, 1987). Whereas physician administrators and medical researchers represent a small segment of the profession, the majority of doctors constitute the rank and file of the profession; this is the group most intensively engaged in the actual work or practice of medicine. These physician practitioners, or clinicians, work in a variety of settings, such as private offices and community health centers. Their primary role is to oversee the health care needs of patients through the application of knowledge of health, disease, and therapy that has been produced by medical researchers (Freidson 1985; 1988).

Obviously, there is some overlap in the work roles of these groups. For instance, some physician-administrators and medical researchers take care of patients, albeit on a far more limited basis than most clinicians do. Nevertheless, as Montgomery (1990) shows, some physician managers self-identify as "administrators" and not "practitioners"; it seems therefore likely that medical investigators would identify as "researchers" and not "clinicians." Role distinctions are important because they signify status differentials within the profession: physician-administrators and physician researchers are accorded higher status and deference than rank-and-file practitioners (Abbott 1981). In part because they do not have access to essential resources and infrastructural services, the majority of clinicians have little involvement in the actual planning, execution, and analyses of medical science. Those practitioners who do participate in medical research usually do so in a limited capacity. Rather than designing research studies, conducting laboratory or clinical experiments, and analyzing and disseminating research findings, as academic medical researchers do, the participation of clinicians in research is usually limited to enrolling patients in clinical studies that have been designed by and are under the direct control of medical investigators (cf. Kaluzny and Warnecke 1996). As we shall see, some community clinicians caring for people with AIDS deviated from these structured professional roles and practices in important ways. We shall also see that as a result of their actions, these practitioners created a new professional role, that of AIDS clinical investigator, and formed a new professional jurisdiction of practice, that of federally funded, community-based research for AIDS.

OVERVIEW OF THE AIDS RESEARCH FUNDING PROBLEM

By the mid-1980s, thousands of people had suffered and died with AIDS and a million more were predicted to be infected with the human immunodeficiency virus (Institute of Medicine 1986). The social and medical consequences of the AIDS epidemic had captured the attention of a small but influential group of policymakers, medical doctors, and persons with AIDS. Indeed, within the first few years of the appearance of AIDS, congressional hearings and governmental inquiries had revealed that federal appropriations for AIDS-related biomedical science in general, and for AIDS treatment research in particular, had been grossly inadequate. It had come to be recognized that because AIDS was a new and novel disease entity, a standardized approach to its therapeutic management had yet to be established. It was further recognized that to develop such a medical regime would require putting a range of drugs through the widely accepted scientific rigors of the clinical trial process to determine the benefits and harms of unknown and unproved anti-AIDS therapies. As a consequence of these and other factors, Congress increased the federal budget for AIDS in fiscal year 1986, and designated that some of the funds be accorded "to research and test treatments for AIDS" (U.S. Congress 1985, p. 392).

In 1986, medical administrators in the National Institute of Allergy and Infectious Disease (NIAID) established a program of AIDS treatment research. Fourteen of the nation's leading AIDS medical researchers, located in academic medical centers throughout the country, formed the core of NIAID's program, the AIDS Treatment Evaluation Units, or ATEUs (NIAID 1987).

From the outset, NIAID's program was fraught with problems. For example, the congressional allocation for treatment research, $100 million to be spent over five years, was viewed by interested groups as grossly inadequate to the task at hand. A congressional hearing was convened following the announcement of the establishment of the ATEUs. Representatives of the medical and AIDS advocacy community testified that NIAID's program represented an inequitable distribution of federal resources: ATEU contracts had been awarded primarily to academic medical centers located on the east and west coasts and, as a result, physicians and patients in other regions of the country did not have ready access to clinical trials. Perhaps more importantly, physicians and patients did not have access to the investigatory drugs that held the only hope for relief from the ravages of the disease.

In response to these comments, NIAID's Director, Dr. Anthony Fauci, informed congressional hearing members that funds in excess of allocated amounts would be needed to increase the number of ATEU centers as well as to enhance the availability of clinical trials to patients in geographically diverse areas of the nation (U.S. Congress 1986). In September 1986, Congress appropriated additional moneys for AIDS treatment research (Nussbaum 1990). Anthony Fauci used these additional funds to enhance the participation of medical researchers and academic center sites in NIAID's treatment research activities. Eventually, the expanded treatment research program was renamed the AIDS Clinical Trials Group or ACTG. Since then, federal allocations for AIDS treatment research has continued to increase. As a result, the number of ACTG sites and the range of ACTG activities has grown considerably (NIAID 1994).

The Rise of Community-based AIDS Research

From the early 1980s onward, clinicians and patients alike were frustrated with the dearth of scientifically grounded research on the benefits and harms of therapies for AIDS-related illnesses. It was during this time that an interest in conducting clinical trials for anti-AIDS agents in community-based settings arose among a subgroup of physicians and patients. As such, between 1984 and 1986, clinicians in New York and San Francisco implemented small-scale, community-based drug trials for AIDS; however, because they were unable to secure sufficient fiscal and organizational resources to support other clinical trial activities, their efforts to further advance the cause of community-based research were, for awhile, thwarted. Nevertheless, by the time NIAID's academic program had been launched and broadened in 1987, more than a dozen community-based organizations had been established throughout the country. This effort resulted in two distinctively different "models," or approaches, to community-based research for AIDS being instituted. The first model was developed by the Community Research Initiative (CRI) of New York, and the second was put into place by the County Community Consortium (CCC) of San Franscico (James 1989, p. 381).

The Community Research Initiative Model

Although CRI was constituted as a formal organization entity in 1987, its historical legacy is connected to the activities of key members of the then-existing AIDS Medical Foundation. This New York–based, nonprofit agency was organized in 1983 by Drs. Mathilde Krim and Joseph Sonnabend to raise and administer funds for AIDS-related research. Prior to the establishment of the Foundation Krim and Sonnabend had assumed highly visible positions on various facets of the AIDS epidemic. Krim, a laboratory scientist at Memorial Sloane-Kettering Institute for Cancer, had been a strong political advocate on behalf of federal sponsorship for biomedical research for cancer and AIDS. Sonnabend, a Greenwich Village clinician, had advanced controversial theories of the casual factors involved in AIDS (Nussbaum 1990).

In 1984, the AIDS Medical Foundation sponsored a small number of New York clinicians in what has come to be known as the nation's first nonacademic center, community-based clinical trial for AIDS: A small scale study of the safety and effectiveness of isoprinosine, an agent thought capable of stimulating the immune systems in HIV disorders (Krim 1993). Not only did the founders of the AIDS Medical Foundation believe that clinical trial research could be executed in nontraditional settings such as public clinics and private physicians' offices, they also believed that decisions about the conduct of clinical trials—drugs to be tested and methods of testing to be utilized—should not be left to the exclusive purview of medical doctors. The foundation constituted an Institutional Review Board, the legally mandated committee charged with overseeing the safety and ethics of biomedical research, with a variety of interested groups, including physicians, patients, ethicists, attorneys, and clerics (Nussbaum 1990). Shortly after the completion of the isoprinosine study, however, the AIDS Research Foundation folded and, as a result, community-based research languished for a time in New York. Nevertheless, Krim and Sonnabend were instrumental in persuading AIDS activist Michael Callen to use his influence as founder and president of the People With AIDS Coalition (PWAC) to sponsor a new community-based organization. In March 1987, the CRI was formally instituted (Nussbaum 1990).

From the outset, CRI was organized as a community-based, physician-patient driven alternative to NIAID's treatment research program. As one of CRI's founding members put it: "Dissatisfied with the National Institutes of Health

(NIH) approach to clinical trials of experimental drug treatment for AIDS and AIDS Related Complex (ARC), PWAC decided to take advantage of the pool of private physicians who were developing expertise in the treatment of AIDS and ARC" (Merton 1990, p. 503).

Indeed, CRI actively sought distinction from NIAID's program in several important respects. First, the Institutional Review Board would consist of medical and nonmedical personnel and be given full authority to determine and oversee all CRI-related activities. Second, CRI would test classes of drugs that had not been put into trial by NIAID researchers but had been of interest to the AIDS-affected community, like anti-infective agents and "naturalistic" remedies. Third, CRI would not necessarily adhere to the normative, or "gold standard," methods of conducting clinical trials used by academically oriented researchers. Rather, CRI would sponsor clinical trial protocols that were rooted in the practical concerns and real-life contingencies of the physicians who run them and the patients who participate in them. Fourth, CRI would target recruitment efforts to patient groups that had been underrepresented in NIAID trials, specifically intravenous drug users, people of color, women, and prisoners (Merton 1990). Fifth, CRI's research activities would be centralized in a single, free-standing facility because, unlike the "NIH approach [which] asks the patients to come to locations where the treatments are available," CRI's "approach takes the treatments to the patients" (Merton 1990, p. 503).

Over the next year, CRI's organizational structure was transformed, due in large measure to the financial backing of "the AIDS communities and from pharmaceutical companies willing to pay for clinical trials" (CRI 1989, p. 3). Though CRI was eventually extricated from the PWAC and organized as a licensed, not-for-profit corporation in the fall of 1988, it held firm to its commitment to involve people with AIDS in the activities of the organization. For example, CRI leaders instituted measures to educate the medical and nonmedical members of the Institutional Review Board in key components of clinical trial work, like drug selection processes, clinical trial methodologies, execution of clinical trial protocols, and the interpretation of trial data (Merton 1990). By February 1988, dozens of community physicians were participating in CRI-sponsored treatment studies. Thus, in part because of its organizational legacy and, in part because of its sponsorship by AIDS-affected groups, CRI was organized and structured in such a way as to sanction, at least in principle, the authority of both medical and nonmedical groups in the work and practice of treatment research for AIDS.

The County Community Consortium Model

The San Francisco model of community-based research originated in a manner that was decidedly distinctive from that of the CRI. It also had very different research-related concerns and very different organizational outcomes.

The impulse for what would later become known as the County Community

Consortium (CCC) occurred in early 1985, prior to the institutionalization of NIAID's treatment research program. At the behest of San Francisco mayor Dianne Feinsteinn, a meeting of the two groups of medical doctors involved in the medical care of Bay Area residents with AIDS was convened: clinicians from the private practice community and researchers from the University of California, San Francisco (UCSF). By then, it was apparent to Feinsteinn and others that the majority of AIDS-related medical care was being rendered at UCSF and San Francisco General Hospital. But it was also clear that because of the rising numbers of AIDS cases more physicians and hospitals in the greater Bay area would need to provide medical care area services as well. Moreover, because physician researchers at UCSF were engaged in state and pharmaceutically funded investigations of anti-AIDS drugs, it was believed that establishing links with private physicians would enhance referral of patients to the facility's research studies (James 1989; Abrams, personal communication 1992).

Community clinicians agreed to continued to meet and organize around AIDS-related treatment issues. Dr. Donald Abrams, a UCSF physician involved in AIDS-related research, was accorded the group's leadership role. Over time, the group was named the County Community Consortium and commenced meeting on a regular basis (Abrams, personal communication 1992).

Soon after the consortium's formation, clinicians expressed an interest in conducting clinical research studies from the vantage point of their own practice settings. According to Abrams, the consortium clinicians realized that they knew a great deal about caring for patients with AIDS (personal communication 1992). Thus, in the first half of 1986, consortium members designed a clinical trial to prevent recurrences of one of the most virulent opportunistic infections affecting AIDS sufferers, *Pneumocystis carinii pneumonia*. They also drafted a clinical research protocol for an observational, or natural history, study of patients with AIDS. At the time, however, the consortium was more of a concept than an operational organization. Because they were unable to secure substantial fiscal and administrative resources that would support their research efforts, the first two studies were not fully implemented nor completed. To assure the survival of the consortium, Abrams eventually sought and received funding from such private sources as the American Foundation for AIDS Research (AmFAR) and pharmaceutical manufacturers as well as public agencies, such as the University of California and NIAID (James 1989).

By 1988, the consortium had secured sufficient funds to begin to attend to its organizational goals and functions as a community research enterprise. Indeed, consortium membership had expanded to include about 125 Bay area clinicians (Abrams, quoted in James 1989, p. 286). While consortium physicians were aware of the CRI's patient participation model of organization, they were reluctant to institute similar organizational structure (Abrams, personal communication 1992). Eventually, however, consortium members established a new organizational structure, inclusive of an Executive Board and a Scientific Advisory Committee, composed of physicians and staff, and a Community Advisory Forum, composed of representatives of the AIDS-affected community. Within this arrangement, the Scientific Advisory Board was charged with overseeing all treatment research-related matters, and the Community Advisory Board was charged with facilitating communication between people with AIDS and consortium practitioners (Abrams, personal communication 1992; Community Research Initiative and County Community Consortium, 1989, p. 8).

By late 1988, the consortium had received external funding and had therefore been able to institute four clinical studies designed to evaluate the effectiveness of anti-AIDS agents. Unlike CRI, however, consortium studies were designed to be executed in the medical offices and practice settings of participant members (Abrams, personal communication 1992).

Thus, the idea for community-based research emerged as an alternative organizational form of NIAID's academically oriented program of AIDS treatment research, the AIDS Clinical Trials Group or ACTG. By the late-1980s, two models of community-based research had been established: the patient-physician collaborative model of the CRI and the more physician collaborative model of the CCC. Notwithstanding these differences, community-based research, as conceived in the context of the AIDS epidemic, was a nontraditional form of medical practice in which clinical and treatment investigations were to be planned by practicing clinicians and/or patients and executed outside of the normative organizational structure of academic medicine by clinicians in community or private practice settings.

Community Clinicians Take Action

Pneumocystis carinii pneumonia (PCP) is an infection of the air passages (bronchi) and air sacks (alveoli) of the lungs and is caused by a common, though usually dormant parasite, pneumocystis carinii (Andreoli et al. 1986). From the earliest years of the crisis, PCP was recognized as one of the most common AIDS-associated conditions. It was further known that although people with AIDS often survived the first episode of PCP, they were usually plagued with increasingly severe recurrences, requiring hospitalizations and expensive medical management. Recognition of the problem of PCP led some clinicians, researchers, and patient advocates to search for therapies to ameliorate its harmful, and sometimes fatal, outcome. Yet even by the mid-to late 1980s, there had not been a systematic and organized effort to institute large-scale, rigorously designed clinical trials of anti-PCP agents. As previously mentioned, the CCC had attempted to implement a locally based PCP trial, but they lacked the financial and administrative resources to do so.

In the absence of sound research data, a state of therapeutic anarchy existed with regard to the treatment and prophylaxis, or prevention, of PCP. Patients were demanding effective therapies and doctors were experimenting with a range of medical remedies. Indeed, this state of uncertainty was highlighted at a congressional hearing on the AIDS epidemic when Paul Popham, a representative of the AIDS-affected community, testified that, "the whole question of PCP and whether it should be treated prophylactically, if you talk to five different doctors you might get five different answers as to what we should be doing" (Committee on Government Operations 1986, p. 7). And even though the medical administrators and the medical researchers of NIAID's academic based clinical trial program had, in mid-1986, identified PCP prevention and treatment as one of its research priorities (NIAID 1986), it did not implement a PCP-related multiclinical trial for almost two years (NIAID 1988).

It was in this context of medical uncertainty and therapeutic anarchy that San Francisco's community-based clinicians launched a clinical study of PCP prophylaxis and treatment. In late 1987, the CCC had designed and initiated a trial of aerosolized (or inhaled) pentamidine with funds received from the pharmaceutical manufacturer, Lypomed, and from the University-wide Task Force on AIDS (University of California, San Francisco 1989). Shortly after the consortium's trial began, Lypomed awarded funds to the CRI to conduct a similarly designed trial (Community Research Initiative 1989). Although the trial was conducted under the auspices of these two community-based organizations, Lypomed assisted with the collection and analysis of data and, at the trial's completion, submitted the results of the study to the Food and Drug Administration (FDA) for evaluation and approval to market the drug (Arno and Feiden 1992).

In the spring of 1989, officials from the FDA approved aerosolized pentamidine (AP) for the prevention of PCP and granted Lypomed full marketing authority. The approval of AP was vitally important to the cause of clinicians and community-based research because it was the "first time in modern history [that] the lifeline of a new drug had been extended to patients solely on the basis of data gathered in a community setting" (Arno and Feidan 1992, p. 118). The FDA's approval of AP was important for another reason for it demonstrated that, at least under certain circumstances, clinicians were capable of designing and conducting clinical trial research. In 1990, members of the CCC published the results of their arm of the AP trial in the prestigious *New England Journal of Medicine* (Leoung et al 1990). Thus, the PCP investigation—the successful launching of the trial, the approval of AP by the FDA on the basis of data collected in community-based settings, and the publication of the study results— can be seen as an attempt by community clinicians to accomplish what social interactionists refer to as "a redefinition of the situation" (cf., Charon 1985) of AIDS treatment research from the exclusive domain of academic medical researchers to include the efforts of community-based clinicians as well.

DISCUSSION AND CONCLUSION

The clinical trial activities of community-based clinicians had not escaped the attention of interested policymakers, AIDS advocates, and NIAID physician-administrators. Indeed, discussions of AIDS treatment research held by NIAID officials, members of Congress, and panelists on the Presidential Commission on the Acquired Immune Deficiency Virus Epidemic throughout 1987 and 1988 invariably focused on the clinical trial efforts of clinicians. By then, it had become increasingly clear that people with AIDS were willing to participate in NIAID's clinical trial activities, but many were unable to do so. It was also clear that while women, minorities, and drug-infected persons with AIDS had been underrepresented in NIAID's clinical trials, clinicians in community-based settings had been able to enroll these groups into their studies. For example, in late 1987, Anthony Fauci convened a group of national medical research experts to review NIAID's academic center-based AIDS clinical trial program and asked them to make recommendations to strengthen its clinical trial capabilities and outreach to all AIDS-affected persons, including women and minority people. One of the suggestions offered by this Ad Hoc Advisory Group was that NIAID "should explore innovative opportunities for community-based providers to perform clinical research" (NIAID 1987, p. 9). At a hearing of the Presidential Commission, New York clinician and AIDS sufferer, Barry Gingell, urged that federal support be given to community research efforts because "[t]hese organizations represent large [and diverse] patient populations in all stages of HIV related disease who are generally eager to participate in clinical trials" (Presidential Commission 1988, p. 5). A report issued in the wake of a congressional hearing on AIDS drug development and research in mid-1988 called for, among other things, a "long-term commitment of resources to a community-based research program" (Committee on Government Operations 1988, p. 34).

By the end of 1988, community-based research was accorded further legitimacy. Anthony Fauci had launched plans to create a nonacademic clinician-focused program of research within NIAID's overall treatment research effort. In addition, congressional support of community-based research came in the form of the Health Omnibus Programs Extension Act of 1988. This act included a provision for the establishment of community-based evaluations of experimental therapies (U.S. Congressional Record 1988, p. 2304).

In the fall of 1989, Fauci announced that clinicians and their colleagues located in eighteen communities throughout the country would participate in NIAID's new and novel scientific enterprise, the Community Program for Clinical Research on AIDS (CPCRA). Among other duties, these doctors were to design and conduct clinical studies to evaluate the benefits and harms of untested therapies for AIDS. Anthony Fauci noted that the CPCRA broadened the federal response to the AIDS epidemic by bringing science to the community. Moreover, the CPCRA was a mechanism for engaging the expertise of medical doctors on the frontline of the epidemic in local clinics, drug addiction centers, private practices, and inner-city hospitals. The CPCRA was a mechanism to increase opportunities for patients to participate in federally sponsored clinical research (NIAID 1989).

This case study illustrates one of the responses to the American AIDS epidemic as it was launched by interested medical professionals during the first decade of the crisis. This case is special because it underscores, for the first time, the way in which the activities of a few clinicians led to a "redefinition of the situation" (i.e., Charon, 1985) of AIDS treatment research which, in turn, resulted in an alteration in the normative structure of medical practice.

That these interested clinicians organized to plan, design, and conduct clinical trials to test anti-AIDS agents symbolizes a rather novel occurrence in the history of modern medicine (Mueller 1995). The novelty of their actions stems in part from the barriers they had to overcome to incorporate research activities into the day-to-day exigencies of clinical practice. As mentioned above, early community-based clinical trial efforts of the CRI and the CCC faltered for lack of infrastructural and financial support. However, over time, these groups succeeded in securing the resources needed to incorporate clinical research into their community-based medical care practices. Moreover, they succeeded in not only completing the aerosolized pentamidine trial, but also enrolling patient groups in clinical trials for anti-AIDS agents that had previously been left out of NIAID's academic medical center program of research. These efforts served to affirm their legitimacy as clinical researchers. Indeed, the symbolic import of the actions of these professionals is apparent in the way in which community-based research was characterized when NIAID director Anthony Fauci announced the establishment of the new community program of AIDS research. "Through these new Community Programs for Clinical Research for AIDS, we can take advantage of the extraordinary expertise of doctors in private practice, in community clinics, and at large inner-city hospitals" (NIAID 1989, p. 1). Fauci also stressed the contribution of community-based research to the nation's AIDS medical science effort. "We expect these community programs to add substantially to the knowledge we are gaining from our [university-based AIDS] clinical trials programs" (NIAID 1989, p. 1).

This case study also illustrates the reaction of other groups to the deviant actions of community clinicians. As discussed, some policymakers, AIDS advocates, and NIAID physician-administrators came to recognize and endorse a role that community clinicians could play in augmenting the efforts already underway by medical researchers in NIAID's academic AIDS treatment research program, the AIDS Clinical Trials Group. As John Y. Killen, one of NIAID's key medical administrators involved in the AIDS treatment research put it:

We need both kinds of capabilities [academic and community] to get studies done. We need community participation because there are lots of questions in the realm of primary care that need to be addressed and that might not otherwise get addressed by academic centers. We need academic centers because we need high-tech capabilities for a lot of what we're doing . . . [like] sophisticated virology and immunology . . . which we need to do in some studies. And it's just not possible to pull that off in primary care settings. (Killen personal communication 1994)

Thus, the establishment of the CPCRA served not only to expand the boundaries of the federal government's program of AIDS treatment research, but perhaps more importantly, it served to establish a new jurisdictional arena of practice for CPCRA's clinician participants and thus expand the boundaries and structure of clinician-directed professional practice.

REFERENCES

Abbott, Andrew. 1981. "Status and Strain in the Professions." *American Journal of Sociology* 86: 819–835.

———. 1988. *The System of Professions: An Essay on the Division of Expert Labor.* Chicago: University of Chicago Press.

Abrams, Donald. 1992. Personal interview, June 11.

Altman, Dennis. 1987. *AIDS in the Mind of America.* New York: Anchor Books.

Andreoli, Thomas E., Charles C. J. Carpenter, Fred Plum, and Lloyd H. Smith. 1986. *Cecil Essentials of Medicine.* Philadelphia: W. B. Saunders Company.

Arno, Peter S., and Karyn L. Feiden. 1992. *Against the Odds: The Story of AIDS Drug Development, Politics, and Profits.* New York: Harper Collins Publishers.

Bayer, Ronald. 1989. *Private Acts, Social Consequences: AIDS and Politics of Public Health.* New York: The Free Press.

Bosk, Charles L., and Joel E. Frader. 1990. "AIDS and Its Impact on Medical Work: The Culture and Politics of the Shop Floor." *Milbank Quarterly* 68 (suppl. 2): 257–279.

Bucher, Rue. 1962. "Pathology: A Study of Social Movements within A Profession." *Social Problems* 10: 40–51.

Centers for Disease Prevention and Control. 1997. "Update: Trends in AIDS Incidence, Deaths, and Prevalence—United States, 1996." *Morbidity and Mortality Weekly Report* 46: 165–173.

Charon, Joel M. 1985. *Symbolic Interactionism: An Introduction, An Interpretation, An Integration.* 2nd ed. Englewood Cliffs, N. J.: Prentice-Hall, Inc.

Community Research Initiative. 1989. "Stage II Proposal in Response to RFP-NIH-AIDSP-89–11: Community Programs of Clinical Research on AIDS." Mimeo.

Community Research Initiative and County Community Consortium. 1989. "Organizing Community-Based Clinical Trials: Models for the AIDS Epidemic." July 7–9. Conference Proceedings Mimeo.

Conrad, Peter, and Joseph W. Schneider. 1980. *Deviance and Medicalization: From Badness to Sickness.* St. Louis: Mosby.

Epstein, Steven. 1996. *Impure Science: AIDS, Activism, and the Politics of Knowledge.* Berkeley: University of California Press.

Freidson, Eliot. 1985. "The Reorganization of the Medical Profession." *Medical Care Review* 42: 11–35.

———. 1987. "The Future of the Professions." *Journal of Dental Education* 53: 140–144.

———. 1988. *The Profession of Medicine: A Study of The Sociology of Applied Knowledge.* Chicago: University of Chicago Press.

Halpern, Sydney A. 1988. *American Pediatrics: The Social Dynamics of Professionalism, 1880–1980.* Berkeley: University of California Press.

Institute of Medicine. 1986. *Confronting AIDS: Directions for Public Health, Health Care, and Research.* Washington, D.C.: National Academy Press.

James, John S. 1989. *AIDS Treatment News: Volume I*. Berkeley: Celestial Press.

Kaluzny, Arnold D., Richard B. Warnecke, and Associates. 1996. *Managing a Health Care Alliance: Improving Community Cancer Care*. San Francisco: Jossey-Bass Publishers.

Killen, John Y. 1994. Personal Interview, January 28.

Krim, Mathilde. 1993. "Remarks for the National Research Staff Meeting of the American Foundation for AIDS Research." Mimeo.

Leoung, Gifford S., David W. Feigal, Bruce Montgomery, Kevin Corkery, Linda Wardlaw, Michael Adams, David Busch, Shelley Gordon, Mark A. Jacobson, Paul A. Volberding, Donald Abrams, and the San Francisco Country Community Consortium. 1990. "Aerosolized Pentamidine for Prophylaxis Against *Pneumocystis arinii* Pneumonia." *New England Journal of Medicine* 323: 769–775.

Merton, Vanessa. 1990. "Community-Based AIDS Research." *Evaluation Review* 14: 502–537.

Montgomery, Kathleen. 1990. "A Prospective Look at the Specialty of Medical Management." *Work and Occupations* 17: 178–198.

———. 1992. "Professional Dominance and the Threat of Corporatization." In Judith Levy, ed., *Current Research on Occupations and Professions*, vol. 7, pp. 221–240. Greenwich, Conn.: JAI Press.

Mueller, Mary-Rose. 1995. "Science in the Community: The Redistribution of Medical Authority in Federally Sponsored Treatment Research for AIDS." Ph.D. diss., University of California, San Diego.

———. 1998. "Professional Practice and Public Policy: The Case of Treatment Research for AIDS." *Research in Social Policy* 6: 119–136.

National Institute of Allergy and Infectious Diseases. 1986. "AIDS Treatment Evaluation Units Group Meeting." July 17 and 18. Mimeo.

———. 1987. "Report of AIDS Clinical Trials Advisory Group Meeting." December. Mimeo.

———. 1988. "Fourth AIDS Clinical Trial Group Meeting." October 6 and 7. Mimeo.

———. 1989. "Statement by Anthony Fauci, M.D." October 5. Mimeo.

———. 1994. "History of ACTG Obligations." November. Mimeo.

Nussbaum, Bruce. 1990. *Good Intentions: How Big Business and the Medical Establishment are Corrupting the Fight Against AIDS*. New York: Penguin Books.

Panem, Sandra. 1988. *The AIDS Bureaucracy*. Cambridge, Mass.: Harvard University Press.

Patton, Cindy. 1990. *Inventing AIDS*. New York: Routledge.

Presidential Commission on the Human Immunodeficiency Virus Epidemic. 1988. "Research Hearings: Basic Research Vaccine Development." February 18–19. Mimeo.

Scull, Andrew T. 1993. *The Most Solitary of Afflictions: Madness and Society in Britain, 1700–1900*. New Haven, Conn.: Yale University Press.

United States Congress. 1985. "Federal and Local Governments: Response to the AIDS Epidemic." *Hearings before a Subcommittee of the Committee on Government Operations*. Washington, D.C.: U.S. Government Printing Office.

———. 1986. "AIDS Drug Development and Related Issues." *Hearings before a Subcommittee of the Committee on Government Operations*, House of Representatives. Washington, D.C.: U.S. Government Printing Office.

———. 1988. "AIDS Drugs: Where Are They?" *Report of the Subcommittee of the*

Committee on Government Operations, House of Representatives. Washington, D.C.: U.S. Government Printing Office.

United States Congressional Record. 1988. "Public Law 199–607: Health Omnibus Programs Extension Act of 1988." Washington, D.C.: Government Printing Office.

University of California, San Francisco. 1989. "Stage II Proposal: Community Programs for Clinical Research on AIDS: RFP-NIH-NIAID-AIDSP-89–11." January 3. Mimeo.

Weitz, Rose. 1991. *Life With AIDS*. New Brunswick, N.J.: Rutgers University Press.

PART II

FAMILY ISSUES

Included in this section are five social problems that have gained considerable notoriety and become the basis for an extensive public discussion. This public discussion is consistent with the evolution of a social problem; when members of society recognize a problem, begin to publicly discuss the issues involved, and express a belief that something should be done to solve it, we witness the beginning of a social problem.

Although poverty, divorce, and spousal abuse received a great deal of attention and scrutiny during the 1960s, 1970s, and 1980s respectively, other social problems included in the family issues section are more recent discoveries. Babies having babies, issues relating to the nonpayment of child support, and homelessness are predominantly social problems of the 1990s. Each of these objective conditions existed previous to their discovery, but they took on a subjective interpretation during the final decade of the millennium.

This subjectivity factor is well illustrated in chapter 5 on teenage mothers contributed by Norman A. Dolch, Kelly E. Orr, and Julie Ezernack. The case studies of Mary, Tina, and Jamie constitute a composite picture of a social problem, the solution of which elicits strong sentiments from various groups. Teenage pregnancy is itself a problem when the teenager is incapable or unable to provide the human investment and financial resources essential to care for herself and the child. However, legal abortion, one solution to the pregnancy problem, also is very symbolic in that it attracts strong emotions and meaning from various organized groups. Thus, options to assist teenagers are available and the authors describe one such program. The authors' recognition of the conflicting perspectives and interpretations of the teenager's behavior and her assessment of self before and after pregnancy also blend well with the symbolic interaction explanation used for this case study. The teenagers respond first to the cultural meanings that surround teenage pregnancy and then to the reactions of significant others as they negotiated a satisfactory conclusion to their personal dilemma.

What currently is referred to as a social problem of epidemic proportion—spousal abuse/domestic violence—was "discovered" during the 1970s. This discovery is noteworthy since the controlling and abusive behavior involved represents what family analysts state has received social approval for thousands of years. Within this context, the power of the symbolic interactionist perspective is useful to our understanding of the domestic violence problem. A new social reality exists, but this reality would not have been possible without challenges to the traditional role of women that occurred throughout the twentieth century. This new reality includes an enlightened perception that a woman's potential should be acknowledged, a view that facilitated the passage of laws which currently protect women from the extraordinary influence men previously held over them.

Although women abuse and batter males, the domestic violence problem, as noted by Melanie L. Miller, is primarily a male phenomenon. In a recent publication Michele Harway and James M. O'Neil (1999) raise an important question: what causes men's violence against women? In the spousal abuse/domestic violence chapter Miller responds to this question. She notes that the recent challenges to traditional gender roles by members of the women's movement and the actions taken at the local level in support of abused and battered women deserve credit for bringing this problem into the public realm.

A discussion of the stages and causes of the domestic violence problem provides a foundation for understanding the complex process involving male dominance and the power and control strategies that are intended to limit the life chances of women. Such strategies, the responses to these strategies, and the commonalties of the domestic abuse problem are illustrated in the case studies of Gina and Dan, a professional, middle-class couple, and Susan and Lyle, a working-class couple of modest education and limited financial resources.

Although the divorce rate has steadily declined throughout the 1990s, the large number of divorces recorded each year (more than one million) and the dramatic decline in economic and social stability experienced by divorced women in particular qualify divorce and poverty as social problems. To many individuals, divorce represents one indicator of the breakdown of the American family. To others, however, divorce is viewed as a sign of the new freedoms women enjoy. Thus, the increased rate of divorce documented after World War II and, more recently, since 1973, is a strong social indicator of the changing role of women and their declaration of independence from a social and financial dependence upon males.

In chapter 7, three case studies offer a composite picture of the interactive effects of divorce and poverty. The experience of Jennifer, a high school drop-out, Rose, a middle-aged housewife, and Marcos, an unconventional father, bring to life the large amount of aggregate data offered throughout this chapter. This discussion is especially useful for understanding the nature of powerful social influences that affect human interaction and, as noted by Erving Goffman (1959), the frontstage and backstage negotiations that humans engage in. The resultant social order is constructed, deconstructed or altered, and finally reconstructed. Each stage of this process is based on divergent symbolic meanings.

N. Ree Wells' emphasis is on the economic, social, and psychological consequences of divorce. Although these consequences present a greater disadvantage for women and children, the consequences of a family broken by separation or divorce also affect the fathers, as noted in the case of Marcos.

In chapter 8 on deadbeat dads, the economic and legal consequences of court-ordered child support mandates are viewed from the perspective of the noncustodial father. The case study of Carlos, a victim of what Kimberly A. Folse identifies as a regressive system of child support, proposes that a much different reality lies outside the conventional wisdom. Negotiations between responsible fathers and the state skews heavily in favor of court-mandated expectations, but the subsequent reactions by both parties may, as Folse suggests, be counterproductive for all family members. Whether the author is correct in arguing that the legal arrangements mandated to ensure, to some extent, the financial security of children may be unfair, the question is: who should be responsible for the well-being of innocent children?

Homelessness, the final chapter in this section, represents a national problem that is, according to the authors, difficult to understand. The current homelessness problem differs from the past when homeless men who rode the rails and hitchhiked along the nation's roadways were identified as hobos and bums. Today an increasing number of individuals known to be without a stable residence or financial support include women and even entire families.

When the causes of homelessness became recognized and were redefined as societal rather than personal in nature, the problem was considered a national embarrassment about which something should be done. Programs to assist the homeless were created and city officials actively sought to work with advocates for the homeless. But during the 1990s the visible presence of homeless people began to generate a less benevolent reaction from the public.

As reported by Debra M. McCallum and John M. Bolland, in the early 1980s, the homelessness issue was transformed into a national problem that became well-represented on the national political agenda. But with the current emphasis on revitalization of the central portions of older urban cities and the large investments being funneled into such areas, the visibility of homeless people has become a problem. The public perception of the homeless has been redefined from that of benevolence and sympathy to one of impatience. This time the reaction involves the police rousting the homeless from their meager surroundings and the creation of city ordinances that are intended to control the homeless by prohibiting their presence at certain times of the day and at specific locations.

The authors make a distinction by differentiating the chronic homeless from the short-term homeless. This distinction is important for understanding the characteristics of the homeless problem and for the creation of viable policies to alleviate it. The well-documented case study of Sissy adds credence to this distinction.

Sissy's story contains all the basic elements of the symbolic interaction perspective as proposed by Jerome G. Manis and Bernard N. Meltzer (1978). She is not a complete retreatist or social drop-out, nor is she without goals or a sense of being. Rather the life process that Sissy experienced ranges from being a member of a well-to-do family with a controlling abusive father, a teenage runaway, an involvement in marriage and eventual motherhood, jail, prostitution, and subsequently street life as a mentally disturbed homeless individual. Sissy's symbolic world and her interpretations of that world lend depth to our understanding of a difficult social problem. Although incomplete, Sissy's rehabilitation is assisting her to forge a new set of symbols and meanings based on a much different perception and interpretation of the world, self, and her future role in society.

REFERENCES

Goffman, Erving. 1959. *The Presentation of Self in Everyday Life*. Garden City, N.Y.: Doubleday and Company.

Harway, Michele, and James M. O'Neil. 1999. *What Causes Men's Violence Against Women?* Thousand Oaks, Calif.: Sage Publications, Inc.

Manis, Jerome G., and Bernard N. Meltzer. 1978. *Symbolic Interaction: A Reader in Social Psychology*. Boston: Allyn and Bacon.

5

Teenage Mothers

Norman A. Dolch, Kelly E. Orr, and Julie Ezernack

INTRODUCTION

An astute analyst of American society, sociologist C. Wright Mills (1959), once observed that when personal troubles, such as teenage pregnancy, became recognized as widespread and problematic in society, they become a social problem. Teenage pregnancy is one example of the kind of social problem Mills wrote about.

Pregnant adolescent females are usually unmarried, experience difficulty completing high school, financially dependent, and emotionally unprepared for the responsibilities of motherhood. Irwin Garfinkel and Sara McLanahan (1986) reported that single, teenage mothers "are more likely to drop out of school, to give birth out of wedlock, to separate or divorce, and to be dependent on welfare" (pp. 1–2). While only 1 to 6 percent of the American population perceive teenage pregnancy as *the* most important problem facing the country (Gallup News Service 1999), the taxpayers' current yearly contribution to assist pregnant teenagers and their infants is estimated to be between $35 to $50 billion (Campaign For Our Children 1999).

OVERVIEW OF THE TEENAGE MOTHER PROBLEM

According to the National Center for Health Statistics, in 1986, teenage births reached their lowest point in fifty years with a recorded rate of 50.2 percent. However, by 1991, the rate of teenage pregnancy had increased to 62.1 percent and then declined to 54.7 percent in 1996 (Annie E. Casey Foundation 1997). In raw numbers, adolescent mothers accounted for slightly more than one million births in 1996, of which 78.6 percent were first births (Ventura et al. 1997). The reported birthrate for females ages 15 to 19 per 1,000 women during 1997 was 53.4 (Henshaw 1999).

That teenage pregnancy represents a serious social problem in the United States becomes obvious when comparing U.S. teenage birthrates with those recorded for other advanced countries (Park, Card, and Miller 1998, pp. 53–54). In 1990, the recorded U.S. teenage birthrate per 1,000 females ages 15 to 19 was sixty compared to thirty-three in the United Kingdom, twenty-six in Canada, nineteen in France, thirteen in Sweden, eight in the Netherlands, and four in Japan. In 1990, the average teenage birthrate for each of these six developed countries was 15.5 per 1,000 females ages 15 to 19, averaging 44.4 less births than in the United States.

The teenage birth problem appears to be equally distributed by race as suggested by Jane Park, Josefina Card, and Kathryn Miller (1998, pp. 53) who argue that the high U.S. teenage birthrate does not result from either disproportionately high parenthood or from the lower rate of abortion recorded for nonwhite teenagers. Obviously other factors must be involved. In the following, the essence of teenage pregnancy problem is captured in three case studies: Mary, who became pregnant and had an abortion; Tina, who discovered she was pregnant and planned to give her baby up for adoption, but decided to raise her baby as a single mom; and Jamie, who considered adoption but then decided to keep the infant and marry the child's father. These cases not only bring to life the statistics relating to teenage pregnancy, but they also raise several important issues pertaining to this problem.

THE CASE STUDIES

Mary: A Case Study of Low Self-Esteem

According to Mary, her journey toward pregnancy occurred when she was a freshman in high school. A group of girls who attended Mary's school and church youth group intentionally excluded her from their clique. Shunned by the girls, Mary turned to boys for acceptance because they gave her a great deal of attention. Mary was pleased by this attention, and their opinions began to take on important meaning for her.

Mary's self-concept suffered because of the rejection of the girls with whom she had a desire to establish friendship. But, as Mary stated, "Maybe the girls that I so desperately wanted to befriend were jealous of the attention I was getting. I started dating a very handsome senior that attended my school and church youth group." Erving Goffman posed that the "self" becomes an object "about which the actor wishes to foster an impression" (Meltzer, Petras, and Reynolds 1975, p. 69; Reynolds 1993, p. 99). Mary's sense of self and impression management are noted in the following: "Several of the girls in the clique had a crush on him, so tension mounted between me and the clique."

Mary reported her boyfriend was aware of this tension and he used it to his advantage. He began to boast about having sexual experiences with some of the girls in the clique. Mary was inexperienced in such matters, and she intended to remain a virgin until she married because of her belief in the Bible and its instructions. However, she eventually had sex with her boyfriend. According to a 1991 survey of high school students, Mary's boyfriend was similar to 76 percent of high school males in his first sexual encounter experience and she was one of the 66 percent of young females (Lauman et al. 1994, p. 322).

In 1995, the National Survey of Family Growth data indicated that most teenage girls reported using some form of birth control. The data further indicated that the less the age difference between the girl and her partner, the more likely she was to use some form of contraception (Moore and Driscoll 1997). In Mary's case, her boyfriend was three years older than she, and they seldom exercised such caution.

Mary initially justified having intercourse by persuading herself that she would one day marry her boyfriend, who she dated for a period of three years. Although her parents thought highly of her boyfriend, Mary characterized him as manipulative. She protested and resisted engaging in sexual intercourse, but Mary found herself giving in to his desires, often on the couch of her parents' home. Mary concealed from her parents the fact that she was having sex, and she began to perceive herself as a moral failure. She feared becoming pregnant, but rarely used birth control because her boyfriend was unwilling to do so.

By the end of her junior year of high school, Mary became attracted to a boy who formerly had attended public school but recently transferred to the private institution where Mary was a student. He had a James Dean manner about him, and he was quite different from her current boyfriend who had attended college in a different city during the previous two-year period. This absence provided Mary with an opportunity to get to know this new boy and, after a time, Mary broke up with her boyfriend and began to date the new boy. However, her parents disliked the young man because of his open rebelliousness. Mary, on the other hand, soon recognized her new boyfriend was similar to his predecessor, who she now viewed as being a hypocrite.

At this point in her life, Mary could no longer suppress her sexuality. Because Mary knew that most teenagers in her church youth group, like many of her classmates, were having sex, she began to consider many of these church members to be hypocrites. She also began to use alcohol and drugs at the beginning of her senior year; she usually was drunk when she had sex with her boyfriend. Although Mary suspected her parents knew of her alcohol drinking, use of drugs, and sexual behavior, they did nothing to stop this behavior. However, the parents complained and accused her boyfriend of being a culprit, an accusation which angered Mary who "felt affectionate toward him, almost sorry for the way that he was treated by those in my private school who thought they were better than him." The emotions reported by Mary resulted from physiological arousal (Rosenberg 1990). Such emotions lead to behavior such as making love.

Toward the end of her senior year Mary became pregnant. She felt as if her life was over: "Now, the truth would come out about my failure to live up to everyone's expectations, especially my parents'. I was supposed to attend college in the fall, and I could not imagine going to school pregnant. I resented my boyfriend for getting me pregnant, even though I had been a willing participant." Mary confided in a school friend who had terminated her own pregnancy by having an abortion. Mary and her friend confided in the friend's mother who, unaware of her daughter's own action, encouraged Mary to have an abortion. Although Mary believed abortion was murder, she was also ashamed of the fact she was pregnant, thereby overcoming her religious reservations.

Mary decided to go to an abortion clinic, where she had a positive pregnancy test. The clinic nurse encouraged Mary to have an abortion the next day; an appointment was scheduled, and Mary went to the clinic accompanied by her girlfriend and boyfriend. Compared to the number of women who were at the abortion clinic, some of whom appeared untroubled, even nonchalant, Mary was weepy and confused. Even when she was lying on the operating table, she remained reluctant to carry out the abortion. The doctor who performed the abortion smiled and cracked jokes, but Mary tried not to think about what was happening until the procedure was complete. Similar to 35 percent of all pregnant teenagers (Moore, Manlove, and Connon 1998, pp. 3–4), Mary had ended her pregnancy.

When Mary walked out of the clinic, she collapsed into the arms of her friend and boyfriend. She cried the entire day, convinced God would never forgive her. Mary's parents were out of town on the day of the procedure, and they never learned of Mary's abortion. Mary was adept at impression management. As Erving Goffman (1969) indicates, information is shared with or withheld from others so that these others will form the impression that we want them to have. The abortion ended Mary's pregnancy after which she broke up with her boyfriend. She graduated from high school and attended college.

What could have been done for a teenager like Mary? Perhaps a primary care program that teaches parenting skills, using computerized baby dolls, would have been helpful. The theory upon which such programs are based is that realistic experiences involving infant care will dispel whatever idealized notions teenagers have about parenthood, thereby motivating them not to become pregnant. This approach is consistent with the interactionist tradition, which places central emphasis on the thought process of individuals as it relates to their behavior.

Boys and girls enrolled in this program are provided a doll for three to seven days. The doll is anatomically correct, race appropriate, and computerized. The computer determines the time the "baby" requires diaper changing, feeding, and holding. Just like a human infant, the doll awakens at night for feeding and diaper change. The teenager is required to respond as a parent would to the needs of an infant. The teenagers must take the doll with them everywhere or make arrangements for child care. Those who attend school must take the doll with them or place it in the care of a responsible individual. Teenagers quickly learn that child care is a twenty-four-hour-a-day responsibility. The computerized doll not only acts like a real baby but it also records life-threatening events such as if the baby cries and is not responded to, or if the baby is hit or dropped.

Program participants engage in a variety of activities that emphasize the serious responsibilities of parenthood. One such activity is shopping, an exercise that demonstrates the considerable cost for items such as diapers and baby food. The teenager's parents also receive guidance and instruction, but they are requested to refrain from becoming involved in the care of the "baby" and they are urged not to take responsibility for the doll. Most teenagers who complete the program indicate they are not yet ready to care for a baby, and they do not desire to become pregnant prior to adulthood (Space and Wood 1998). If Mary had participated in such a program, perhaps she would not have become pregnant.

Tina: A Case Study of a Pregnant Teenager

Tina initially made contact with a center when she was six months pregnant. Her pregnancy was very unsettling to her inasmuch as parenthood would jeopardize her future plans. Also fearful that she would lose the respect of her family and friends, Tina did not inform anyone of her pregnancy.

Tina's fear of "losing respect" suggests an awareness of social norms regarding teenage pregnancy. Christopher Jencks (1993, pp. 189–190) identified three such norms regarding the birth of children. First, it is expected that women will postpone giving birth until they are at least 20 years old. Having children earlier interferes with the educational training which, since the 1970s, is viewed as crucial to being a productive, self-sufficient adult. Second, people should not have children out-of-wedlock unless they can support their offspring. Finally, if adults should not have children until their twenties, then children should not be conceiving children. These norms foster the present view of teenage pregnancy as a social problem. Tina's concern with maintaining the "respect" of family and friends indicates an awareness of these social norms.

Despite her reluctance to deal with pregnancy, Tina realized that she had not gained much weight and she began to worry about the baby's health. She not only had the desire to see a doctor, she also wanted someone to assist her in making the best decision concerning the baby. According to Larry Reynolds (1993, p. 68), Tina has become the object of her own actions, through the self-indication process, a process during which one confronts the world by carrying on a mental conversation, making self-indications regarding what should or should not be done, and then responding. Tina's "self" becomes an object, and meaning is conferred upon herself. In this case, Tina accepts her pregnancy and desires to have a healthy baby, indicating, according to Reynolds (1993, p. 68), that human action is constructed or built up, instead of merely being released. "Human social life is a communicative process, not just between persons but also in terms of an internal dialogue of assessing and conferring meanings on objects."

Tina found pregnancy clinics advertised in the phone book and knew that she could find help. Although she was uncertain what to do about her pregnancy when she spoke with a counselor, she confirmed her fears. Tina knew she would be confronted with a tremendous challenge as a single parent; she also knew the father of the baby could not be counted upon for financial and/or moral support. Being a single parent was not going to be easy. In addition, motherhood would interfere with her education, which had been, and still was, an important part of her life. Although she planned to finish high school and then attend college, having a baby could postpone or even permanently damage these plans. She knew many other girls who dropped out of school and then went to work to support their babies. How could she find a job that would provide for her child? Her mother would approve of any decision that Tina made, but how would other members of her family react? Tina weighed each of these matters while attempting to arrive at a final decision.

The interaction of emotions Tina experienced is analogous to the experiences of the single parent reported by David Maines (1983). According to Maines, emotions alter or at least influence the negotiated order or the way in which an individual such as Tina defines a situation and presents herself to someone such as a counselor.

After receiving information and advice, Tina decided to place her baby for adoption. When she learned of Tina's pregnancy, Tina's mother thought she would choose adoption, but she also wanted her daughter to make the decision. The mother knew this was a difficult time for Tina, and she remained supportive throughout Tina's pregnancy.

Tina received information about the adoption procedures and was in the process of choosing an adoptive family when she went into labor. No families suitable to Tina were available prior to the baby's birth, but she was so certain the baby would be adopted that she had not chosen a name. Because the counselor's office was closed for the weekend, Tina was unable to reach a program representative when the baby was born. Although Tina decided to take her baby home, she did not intend to keep the infant. The hospital provided samples of baby supplies and family members, visiting the new mother of the first time, brought other baby items to assist her. Then, having the opportunity to spend time with her baby at home along with other members of her family, Tina decided to keep the male infant.

Does this change in Tina's thinking indicate that normative expectations influence behavior? From the interactionist perspective, a change in meaning creates a change in social relationship. The real question, according to Reynolds (1993, p. 164), is how social structure can be conceptualized as social interaction. Perhaps the best explanation for the effect of normative expectations is the fact that only about 5 percent of teenagers actually give their babies up for adoption. Yes, Tina changed her mind, but she followed the norm. We should also consider her awareness and initial concern about her pregnancy as we evaluate how Tina responded to these normative expectations.

One might also inquire why she engaged in sexual behavior in the first place if she was aware of normative expectations; that is, of the social norm to refrain from being sexually active. The Health and Social Life survey conducted in 1992 reported that 80 percent of the respondents believed teenage sex was always or almost always wrong. However, based on a 1991 survey of high school students, 76 percent of young males and 66 percent of young females experienced first intercourse by the time they had reached the senior year of high school. Males who desired to have intercourse reported that their primary reason had been curiosity, whereas, for females, this desire was based on affection for their partners.

Most teenagers do not use contraceptives for first intercourse, which places them at risk not only for pregnancy but for sexually transmitted diseases (Lauman et al. 1994, p. 332). Tina's behavior mirrors that of her peers. She falls within typical sexual behavior patterns for teenagers in general, and these obviously co-exist with clear expectations that one should not get pregnant. However, Tina did become pregnant and she dealt with this pregnancy by responding to the situation. Moreover, the positive response of family members supported the normative expectation, suggesting this aspect of American life may not be as limited as some commentators would have us believe.

Conceptualizing social structure as unfolding social interaction is challenging, but the solution for preventing teenage pregnancy is not a simple matter. Tina acquaints us with a type of intervention for teenage pregnancy known as tertiary or acute intervention, which is designed to assist the person to manage the experience. The center used by Tina offers a wide range of services, including pregnancy tests, prenatal care, and childbirth preparation classes. For women who desire to place a child for adoption at birth, the center offers such a program. As a part of this program much of the information gathered from prospective adoptive parents is shared with the birth mother, who is allowed to choose which family may adopt the infant. Working along with the family selected, birth mothers also decide how much personal information is to be shared and how much contact with the adopted child will be allowed. The program staff assisted Tina in thinking through her options, and they provided the emotional support necessary for her to talk about the pregnancy with family members. They also placed Tina in touch with another service that provided a nutritious food program for pregnant women.

Jamie: A Case Study of a Married Parent

Jamie made contact with a pregnancy center when she was seven to eight months pregnant. Jamie was depressed, and she did not think she would be able to handle motherhood at the young age of 19. Jamie's intersubjective experience was between her and her boyfriend, Chris. The two had not been dating for very long, and Jamie was worried that their relationship was incapable of handling the stress and strain brought on by parenthood.

According to the interactionist perspective, humans act because they are capable of viewing the situation from the perspective of the other person. Cooperation occurs when

(a) each acting individual ascertains the intention of acts of others, and then (b) makes his own responses on the basis of that interpretation. What this means is that, in order for human beings to cooperate, there must be present some sort of mechanism whereby each acting individual: (a) can come to understand the lines of action of others, and (b) can guide his own behavior to fit in with those lines of action. (Meltzer 1964, p. 12)

Jamie and Chris cooperated. Both the mother and father wanted their baby to have a stable, two-parent home, so Jamie moved in with Chris. Chris planned to take care of Jamie and the baby; Jamie was still uncertain of the decision that had to be made. When she informed Chris she was contemplating placement of the baby for adoption, he was supportive. Both individuals had the desire to do the right thing, and they made a commitment to support each other. After much thought, the decision was made to place the baby for adoption.

Although Jamie and Chris considered adoption a private matter, it was important to them to have an open adoption. Thus, they selected a program that allowed the birth parents to have contact with the child after adoption. Chris and Jamie viewed the program staff as understanding and supportive, helping them sort out many of the pros and cons involved in the adoption process.

Since Jamie was close to giving birth when she sought assistance, she and Chris selected an adoptive family during their first visit. They met the family, and Jamie put together a basket of items for the baby. She also attended group meetings, some of which proved to be helpful in coping with the idea of giving up the baby.

However, at the time she went into labor Jamie began to have doubts about placing the baby for adoption. Chris also began having doubts about allowing the adoption to take place, and he informed both families of his uncertainty regarding the impending adoption. When the baby was born, the decision to keep him was final. Jamie and Chris said they "woke up" when they both realized they were ready to take on the responsibilities of parenthood.

Joseph Schneider and Peter Conrad (1980, p. 42) suggest three strategies exist to control the flow of information between deviants and normals: selective concealment, therapeutic disclosure, and preventive disclosure. The doubt expressed by Jamie and Chris might have been a combination of therapeutic disclosure, talking about their concerns with family members, preventive disclosure, and talking about their concerns with family members while seeking support for an uncertain action. In this instance, the young parents-to-be were unsure about placing the baby for adoption; because of this uncertainty they were encouraged by family members to keep the child. Jamie and Chris renegotiated a discreditable attribute (having a baby) into a more favorable event within in the hospital maternity ward, a ward populated by family members.

Jamie and Chris were planning to marry within a few months of their interview. Chris is employed as an automobile salesman, while Jamie is planning to attend college in the hope of establishing a career in the medical field. This young couple is getting on with life. But, what if they were in need of further assistance for their new baby?

Rehabilitative interventions are designed to restore people to useful, productive lives through education and therapy (Freeman, Jones, and Zucker 1999, p. 564). One such program is designed around three objectives: to teach teenage mothers parenting skills thereby reducing the risk of child neglect and abuse; to encourage mothers to continue their education in order to become self-sufficient citizens; and to encourage teenage mothers to avoid another unplanned pregnancy. This assistance program assigns home visitors who personally call on the mother every two weeks beginning when the infant is taken home from the hospital and continuing until the child reaches 3 years of age. Incentives to encourage participation in the program, such as diapers and baby care products, are offered. The professionals also teach young mothers the importance of things such as keeping appointments, having the baby inoculated, and ensuring appropriate infant care. Home visitors also explore general issues such as the family's ability to pay bills in a timely manner.

DISCUSSION AND CONCLUSION

Mary, Tina, and Jamie illustrate well the nature of the youthful pregnancy problem in that many teenage mothers lack appropriate parenting skills and experience difficulty finishing their education, thus leaving both mother and child at risk. These three individuals did continue with their educational plans, but this is not the norm with most teenage mothers. Adolescent parents (and their children) who remain unmarried and are high school dropouts are more likely to live in poverty ten years after giving birth than are mothers who marry and/or graduate, according to the Annie E. Casey Foundation (1997, p. 13). Mary's solution to her pregnancy was to have an abortion procedure performed, a decision which allowed her to attend college, while Tina was scheduled to graduate from high school at the time the interview was conducted. However, marriage was not in Tina's immediate future. Jamie, on the other hand, plans to marry and pursue a career in a health-related field.

The majority of sexually active adolescents use some form of contraception; those who fail to do so risk teenage pregnancy and disease. Mary, Tina, and Jamie failed to use contraception and became pregnant. For the pregnant teenager, preventive programs exist which respond to their needs. With prevention as its focus, the baby doll parenting program is useful. Some programs respond to parenting needs while others are rehabilitative in nature.

Because of the large number of factors affecting pregnant adolescents, it is impossible to predict the behavior of any one adolescent. In each of the three cases reported, the teenagers exhibited an awareness of the social norms pertaining to sexual behavior; norms which prohibit teenagers from engaging in such activities. But the relationship between emotion and behavior is strong, and this relationship represents one reason teenage girls engage in sex. That is, they feel affection for their partner or they have a need to fulfill. Such emotions influence the way situations are defined.

For Tina and Jamie, in particular, we observe the important correspondence between kinship and the teenagers' decisions to parent as opposed to placing the infant for adoption. This decision extends beyond parental approval. Both Tina and Jamie were concerned about the reactions of relatives in their extended families to their decision to either parent or give up their baby for adoption. Tina and Jamie valued the opinions of other family members, and these opinions influenced their behavior. From Mary's view, her perception of self corresponded to that held by individuals whose opinion she valued, such as the girls who formed the high school clique. What is especially clear in evaluating Mary's case is the interactionist explanation for understanding teenage mothers and their attachment of meaning to objects, including self.

Jamie's case illustrates a cooperative effort based on the situation in which she and her boyfriend were involved. Jamie and Chris were able to manage information and to redefine a discreditable situation (having a child out of wedlock) by deciding to keep the baby. Tina's behavior is consistent with the pattern of teenage motherhood; 95 percent of all teenage mothers choose to keep their child. Tina's concerns were eliminated when family members embraced her motherhood.

In sum, self-concept, impression management, and definitions of the situation show how people mentally process their social environment and then take action. In Mary's case, her self-concept suffered because of rejection by an important clique of girls. Mary's "self" became an object about which she attempted to foster an impression. At this time she began dating a handsome senior. She concealed from her parents the fact that she was having sexual relations as well as the abortion which she had after becoming pregnant; therefore, the parents and others would form an impression of her which Mary wanted them to have. Tina's case further illustrates some of these same points.

Tina was fearful that she would lose the respect of her family because of the pregnancy. Tina realized that she had to take some action regarding her pregnancy and established contact with the center. In Tina's case, Reynolds (1993, p. 88) would maintain that she had become the object of her own actions through the self-indication process, a process during which one confronts the world by carrying on a mental conversation, making self-indications about possible actions, and then responding.

The final case, Jamie, centers on her worries regarding the relationship with Chris, the boyfriend who impregnated her. Once again, mental processes lead to action and Jamie sought assistance through an adoption agency. While saying they planned to give the baby up for adoption, Jamie and Chris also engaged in therapeutic and preventive disclosure during discussions held with members of their families which, in turn, led to the decision to keep their baby. The reality of the situation was redefined.

Finally, each case study contributes to our understanding of how self-concept, impression management, and a definition of the situation enter into a process through which people mentally evaluate their social environment and then take action. In this instance, that action was taken by teenage girls in response to their pregnancy.

REFERENCES

Annie E. Casey Foundation. 1997. *KIDS COUNT Data Book: 1997*. Baltimore: Annie E. Casey Foundation.

Campaign For Our Children. 1999. *Facts, Figures, Statistics: Costs*. Retrieved December 22 <http://www.cfoc.org/statscost.html>.

Freeman, Howard E., Wyatt C. Jones, and Lynne G. Zucker. 1979. *Problems: A Social Policy Perspective*. 3rd ed. Chicago: Rand McNally.

Gallup News Service. 1999. "Gallup Poll Trends—'Most Important Problem.' " Retrieved December 22 <http://www.gallup.com/poll/trends/ptproblem.asp>.

Garfinkel, Irwin, and Sara McLanahan. 1986. *Single Mothers and Their Children*. Washington, D.C.: The Urban Institute.

Goffman, Erving. 1969. *Strategic Interaction*. New York: Ballantine.

Henshaw, Stanley. 1999. *Special Report: U.S. Teenage Pregnancy Statistics With Comparative Statistics for Women Aged 20–24*. Retrieved December 22 <http://www.agi-usa.org/pubs/teen_preg_sr_0699>.

Jencks, Christopher. 1993. *Rethinking Social Policy: Race, Poverty, and the Underclass*. New York: HarperTrade.

Lauman, Edward O., John H. Gagon, Robert T. Michael, and Stuart Michaels. 1994. *The Social Organization of Sexuality: Sexual Practices in the United States*. Chicago: The University of Chicago Press.

Maines, David R. 1983. "In Search of Mesostructure: Studies in the Negotiated Order." *Urban Life* 11: 267–279.

Meltzer, Bernard N. 1964. *The Social Psychology of George Herbert Mead*. Kalamazoo: Center for Sociological Research, Western Michigan University.

Meltzer, Bernard N., John W. Petras, and Larry Reynolds. 1975. *Symbolic Interactionism: Genesis, Varieties and Criticism*. London: Routledge & Kegan Paul.

Mills, C. Wright 1959. *The Sociological Imagination*. New York: Oxford University Press.

Moore, Kristin A., and Ann Driscoll. 1997. "Partners, Predators, Peers, Protectors: Males and Teen Pregnancy." Paper available from Child Trends, Inc., Washington, D.C.: <www.childtrends.org/partner3.htm>.

Moore, Kristin A., Jennifer Manlove, and Lauren Connon. 1998. "Repeat Teen Births." Presented at an AEI Video Conference on "Preventing Second Births to Teenage Mothers: Demonstration Findings." Washington, D.C.: Child Trends, Inc.

Park, M. Jane, Josefina J. Card, and Kathryn L. Miller. 1998. *Just The Facts: What*

Science Has Found Out About Teenage Sexuality and Pregnancy in the U.S. Los Altos, Calif.: Sociometrics Corporation.

Reynolds, Larry T. 1993. *Interactionism: Exposition and Critique.* 3rd ed. Dix Hills, N.Y.: General Hall.

Rosenberg, Morris. 1990. "Reflexivity and Emotions." *Social Psychology Quarterly* 53: 3–12.

Schneider, Joseph, and Peter Conrad. 1980. "In the Closet with Illness: Epilepsy, Stigma Potential and Informational Control." *Social Problems* 28: 32–44.

Space, Marc, and Carolyne Wood. 1998. "Adolescent Pregnancy Strategies to Encourage the Delay of Early Parenthood Adolescents." Paper presented at the National Conference on Education, American Association of School Administrators, San Diego, Calif., February.

Ventura, Stephanie J., Kimberly D. Peters, J. A. Martin, and Jeffrey D. Mauer. 1997. "Births and Deaths in the United States, 1996." *Monthly Vital Statistics Report,* 46(1), supp. 2. Hyattsville, Md.: National Center for Health Statistics.

6

Spousal Abuse/Domestic Violence

Melanie L. Miller

INTRODUCTION

What was once a problem to be discussed only behind closed doors, has in recent years been referred to as an "epidemic." What is this epidemic that is occurring in 20 to 30 percent of families across America (Stark and Flitcraft 1988)? It is most frequently referred to as spousal abuse or domestic violence.

A ground-breaking national survey on family violence was conducted in 1980 by sociologists Murray Strauss, Richard Gelles, and Suzanne Steinmetz, finding that one in four wives and one in three husbands thought that hitting one's spouse was a necessary and normal part of being married. The supporting statistics gathered since that early study continue to be startling. According to the FBI statistics, a woman is beaten in this country every fifteen seconds. The National Victim Center estimates that two to four million American women are battered each year by their male partners. Domestic violence, unfortunately, does not stop with battering one's partner. The U.S. Department of Justice reported that in 1994, approximately 31 percent of female victims of homicide were murdered by their husbands, ex-husbands, or boyfriends. Over six million children are assaulted each year (Strauss 1990).

OVERVIEW OF THE DOMESTIC VIOLENCE PROBLEM

Historically, violence against women has been accepted and approved of by societies for thousands of years. Many examples can be given. Many Christian sects of white Western European cultures existed with a patriarchal family structure that viewed women as the sinful successors of Eve. This patriarchal authority was based on male control over women's productive capacity and over her person. Women were first the property of their fathers and then their husbands. Patriarchal cultures believed in the service role of women and the rigid sex roles of the traditional family.

Roman law gave the husband sovereign authority over his wife. This authority granted the husband the powers of life and death and unrestrained physical chastisement of his wife and other family members.

Battering was upheld by legal and moral codes. A modified version of patriarchal law was incorporated into English common law. Under this law, a husband had the right to use force to ensure that his wife performed her wifely duties including consummation of the marriage, fidelity, and general obedience of his wishes. In 1768, William Blackstone detailed a husband's right to chastise his wife in order to enforce obedience. The established criteria was called the "rule of thumb," allowing him to beat his wife with an instrument or a rod no bigger or thicker than his thumb (Schechter 1982).

The husband's right to chastise his wife was upheld by the U.S. Supreme Court in Mississippi in 1824. It was not until 1871 that wife beating was actually declared illegal in two states, Alabama and Massachusetts (Steinmetz 1971).

Despite changes in the law as early as 1871, for decades battering continued to be viewed as primarily a family problem, with no public outcry. Only with the growth of the women's movement in the latter part of the twentieth century has the plight of battered women been brought into public awareness. In 1975, Women's Advocates, the first American shelter for battered women was opened in St. Paul, Minnesota (Stark and Flitcraft 1996).

Domestic Violence: A Contemporary Social Problem

As is noted above, domestic violence has, for centuries, been viewed as a familial problem, rather than a social issue. In the mid-1970s, Murray Strauss and Richard Gelles began documenting some of the social causes of violence in the family. Around this same time, feminists began studying the history of rape as a means for men to control women. It was also in 1975 that Lenore Walker, who at that time was affiliated with the Rutgers University Medical School, began to examine the psychology of battered women as victims. It was from her examination of hundreds of case studies of battered women that Walker coined the term "battered woman syndrome" and began to identify a pattern of behavior referred to as the cycle of violence. This cycle has provided one of the most widely referenced theoretical frameworks offering insight into this phenomenon (Walker 1979).

As domestic violence has become a problem of interest to many, we have come to define it in similar ways. One commonly accepted definition of domestic violence might be that domestic violence involves a continuum of behaviors ranging from degrading remarks to cruel jokes and may involve punches and kicks, false imprisonment, sexual abuse, maiming assaults, and even homicide. If left unchecked, domestic violence increases in frequency and severity. Victims of domestic violence suffer all forms of abuse, with many of them reporting that the emotional and verbal abuse is as destructive as the physical abuse.

In her book, *The Battered Woman* (1979), Lenore Walker describes a cycle of violence that focuses on physical violence in an abusive relationship and includes three stages:

1. The tension building stage—tension builds over a series of small occurrences such as the wife serving a meal that the husband does not like, the household chores not being completed or asking him for money. This stage may last minutes or weeks or months.

2. The battering incident—this stage involves the release of the pent-up tension in the form of violent behavior. She may become the object of punching, kicking, shoving, choking, slamming against a wall, or threats of the use of weapons or their actual use.

3. The honeymoon stage—this third phase occurs after the beating when the batterer feels guilty for his behavior. He is sorry and often very loving. He assures her that this will never happen again. She wants to believe him and to believe that he will change. It is during this stage that most reconciliations take place.

It should be noted that there is no way to estimate how long any one stage will last. There also are cases that do not follow this cycle and cases when the honeymoon stage has been known to never exist or to stop at some point. If a case does not fit this pattern it does not mean that the woman is not being abused.

Underlying Causes of Battering

According to the Duluth Abuse Intervention Project (one of the oldest programs in the country providing counseling to batterers), battering is based on the man's desire to maintain power and control. To do this he will isolate his partner, intimidate her, emotionally, economically and sexually abuse her, and threaten her. The weapon that he most commonly uses to back up all of these methods of controlling her is violence. In battering relationships, the women are always controlled, not always physically beaten (Resko 1989).

Why Do They Stay?

Perhaps one of the most difficult things for people to understand about domestic violence is why a woman stays in this type of relationship. There are usually many complex reasons, but the most obvious is the amount of control the male has gained over her through the various tactics used. Additional considerations for why she stays relate to fear, economic dependency, children, religious beliefs, and embarrassment.

GINA AND DAN: A CASE STUDY

The first case study provides insight into many of the historical misconceptions regarding the influence of class, status, and family background on battering. It also illustrates the stages identified in Walker's cycle of violence as many of the types of abuse identified in the definition of the problem.

Gina met Dan shortly after graduating from college. Gina had completed a degree in public relations and was working with an advertising firm when she was asked to develop an ad campaign for Dan's law firm. Gina was very comfortable working with attorneys as her father had a successful law practice for many years prior to becoming a judge.

Dan, the son of a prominent physician, had moved up fast in his law practice. After being with the firm for only three years, he had already been made a full partner. Gina found Dan to be intelligent, ambitious, and very charming. After a couple of meetings, Dan and Gina began dating. One of Gina's co-workers mentioned to Gina that she had heard a rumor that Dan hit his last girlfriend. Gina was concerned about this at first but when she confronted Dan about it, he explained that it only happened once when he had been drinking too much and that his girlfriend had been flirting with another man. Gina accepted this explanation and did not give the incident further thought.

It was not long before Gina and Dan were inseparable. Dan spent Thanksgiving with Gina's family and immediately won them over—even Gina's father liked Dan. After a six month whirlwind romance, they were married. The first couple of months were wonderful. Gina had never had such an exciting social life. Dan's business required that they spend a great deal of time entertaining clients and making business contacts. Gina was incredibly happy and acclimated quickly to the fast-paced social schedule.

One evening, Dan and Gina were to meet a prospective client and his wife for drinks before attending a concert. Gina had planned to meet Dan at home by 6:00 P.M. to change clothes, and they would then meet the other couple across town at 7:00 P.M. Gina was completing a project at work and was late leaving. She arrived at home around 6:30 P.M. When Gina arrived home, Dan was frantically pacing the floor. She apologized for being late and explained that she would still have plenty of time to change. Dan had a look in his eyes that Gina had never seen. He accused her of staying at work late because she was having an affair. She tried explaining what happened, but Dan's anger continued to escalate. He called her a slut and a whore and accused her of purposefully trying to seduce other men by the way she dressed. At one point, he became so enraged that he grabbed her by the shoulders, shook her frantically and then shoved her against a wall. She slumped to the floor crying uncontrollably. Suddenly Dan's demeanor changed. He came over, helped her up, and began to apologize. Gina thought he was going to cry. Dan assured Gina that this would never happen again but that he just loved her so much that he could not stand the thought of any other men looking at her. Gina had not realized just how much Dan did love her until now. He was so remorseful that she genuinely felt sorry for him. Later that evening, as Gina was getting ready for bed, she noticed the bruises on her arms. For the next several days, she felt terrible that she had not been more sensitive to Dan and had not known how much reassurance he needed about her love for him. Gina had never been around anyone with a temper like Dan's so she was not sure how to handle it. She decided she would be extra careful not to say anything that would make him jealous.

For the next two or three weeks, Dan was the perfect husband. He sent flowers to Gina at work at least once a week and bought her an expensive diamond bracelet she had been admiring. Several months went by before there was another incident of violence. Although Dan was not physically abusive for a while, he became increasingly critical of Gina. He seemed to be criticizing constantly her clothing, her hair, her cooking, even her friends. The couple of times that she had invited friends over, he had acted so rude that they stopped coming around much after that.

Gina's closest family member was her sister but she was over 300 miles away, and Gina often felt that Dan was all she had. She had tried to describe to her sister how Dan could be so charming one minute and so critical and possessive the next. Her sister said he sounded like a real "Jekyl and Hyde." Gina had never thought of him that way, but it was so true. It seemed that the more Gina confronted Dan, the more agitated he would become. Gina attempted to anticipate Dan's needs before he became upset, but often found that she was not successful. If only she were a better wife, she kept thinking, Dan would not get so angry with her.

Dan's law practice was growing rapidly, and the couple was doing very well financially, but Dan seemed under constant pressure. He worked long hours and their social life centered entirely around his work. At Dan's urging, Gina quit her job to be more available for wining and dining Dan's clients. She focused all her energy on Dan and helping him build his firm.

Gina noticed that Dan had begun to drink more often as the demands from his work seemed to increase. She knew he was under a lot of pressure to make the business succeed so she often excused his behavior by telling herself that it was the stress. Dan began to check up on her, insisting that Gina call before going somewhere and when she arrived home. Dan also would call several times during the day demanding to know where she was at all times. It seemed that the more involved Gina became in Dan's life and the more she tried to please him, his expectations became greater and greater. It seemed she could never do enough.

One evening Dan was out with his business partners at a Christmas party. Gina had come down with the flu and was unable to attend the event. She could hear the tension in Dan's voice when she called to tell him that she just did not feel up to it. Gina was in bed when Dan came home, slamming doors and knocking things over as he came through the house. He had been drinking but was not drunk. He came into the bedroom and tried to force Gina to have sex. Initially, she tried to fight him off and pushed him away, even hitting him a couple of times, but it was no use. Her protest only made him angrier. He pulled her off the bed, on the floor, slapping her hard across the face and kicking her in the side before he proceeded to rape her. Gina does not remember how long she lay on the floor after that. The next morning she looked in the mirror to see a huge bruise on the side of her face. Every time she moved, she was in excruciating pain.

As soon as Dan saw her, he began to cry. He was so apologetic over what he had done that she almost felt worse for him than for herself. Once again, he promised Gina that nothing like this would ever happen again—that he had had too much to drink and had been upset that she could not attend the party. Dan again begged her to forgive him. Gina was very quiet. She didn't know if she could forgive him this time. This incident had really scared her. Yet, she felt somewhat guilty for not being there when he needed her. Maybe this was partly her fault too, she kept thinking.

Gina was very confused and decided to visit her sister for a few days hoping to sort things out. She made arrangements for a flight that same evening and left Dan a note informing him that she needed time alone to think things through. When Gina arrived, her sister seemed shocked by her appearance. The bruise on her face was still fresh, and Gina had a hard time even walking without wincing in pain. At first, she told her sister she had fallen down some stairs, but her sister could see right through that. Eventually Gina told her sister about the fight with Dan and that he had pushed her. She could not, however, bring herself to tell her sister that he had forced her to have sex or that this was not the first incident. Gina was just too humiliated to tell anyone, even her sister, the whole story. Her sister insisted on taking her to a doctor. The examination revealed that three of her ribs were broken.

Even though Gina had not told Dan where she was going, it did not take long for him to figure it out. By the second day of her visit, he was calling about once an hour, begging her to come home. He sent her flowers and repeatedly reassured her that it would never happen again. He promised to do whatever she wanted if she would come home. At first, she told Dan that she needed more time to think about things. This just made him angry and when she did not agree to come home right away, he threatened to come and get her. He told her that if he had to come after her, she would really be sorry and so would her sister for letting her stay there. Gina was not sure what he meant but did not want him coming there and making a scene. She finally told Dan that the only way she would return was if he would go with her for counseling, which he promised to do. Gina returned home with the assurance that they would find a counselor and go together. Dan did in fact go with her to see a counselor on two occasions. But after the second visit, he decided that counseling was a waste of his time. Gina went back home now, and things seemed better so he refused to go again.

Shortly after this incident Gina found out she was pregnant. She was excited but also a little nervous about how Dan would react to the news. They had not really talked about having children but Gina hoped that this might be just what their relationship needed. Having a baby might soften Dan and help him not be so up tight about everything. When she told Dan the news, initially he seemed thrilled. Unfortunately, this enthusiasm did not last long.

During the pregnancy the physical violence that had previously been sporadic became much more frequent. Gina began to feel that Dan was jealous of her being pregnant and even of the baby itself. She stopped objecting to Dan forcing her to have sex—it was easier just to go along. She became very depressed during the pregnancy as she was fearful that the beatings would cause damage to the baby. She left Dan again shortly before the delivery and stayed away a couple of weeks this time. Dan told her how badly he wanted to be there when their baby was born and that if she did not come back, he would kill himself. He had never sounded this desperate before. Gina was afraid that he might actually do it, and then her child would not have a father. So, reluctantly, she went back.

For a few weeks prior to the birth and a couple of weeks after their daughter Meagan was born, Dan seemed like his old self again. He was very loving and caring. Gina thought that maybe she was right. Perhaps becoming a father had changed Dan. He seemed to adore Meagan.

While the actual beatings did seem to decrease, within a couple of weeks, he was once again forcing her to have sex, despite her protests that her doctor had advised her not to have sex for six weeks after giving birth.

When Meagan was about six months old, Dan came home late from work and immediately became enraged that Gina had not finished preparing dinner and complained that the house was in disarray. Gina tried to explain how fussy the baby had been all day and that she had not been able to get much done, but Dan would not listen. Dan's screaming awoke Meagan and she began to cry. Gina got her back to sleep and laid her down in the nursery. She then walked outside, hoping that if she was out of sight Dan would calm down. Instead he followed her into the garage and continued his outburst, telling her what a terrible wife and mother she was and that she couldn't do anything right. When she tried to calm him down, Dan shoved her into the wall, cutting her head on the corner of a shelf. Gina was so upset that she did not even realize that she was bleeding. Suddenly Dan picked up a tool laying on his workbench in the garage and threw it at the window. The window shattered. Gina never knew who called them but within a few seconds, two police cars pulled up in front of their house. As the officers approached, Dan's demeanor changed almost instantly. When one of the officers questioned Dan regarding what had happened, he explained that Gina had been trying to get a can of paint from a shelf in the garage and had fallen. He had come out of the house to see if she was okay when he realized she had cut herself. Gina looked at him but did not say a word. The second officer then took Gina inside and asked her what happened while the first officer stayed outside with Dan and questioned him further. This time, Gina told the officer the truth about what had happened. She was scared and did not want to keep covering up the truth.

The officer told Gina that they were going to arrest Dan for domestic violence assault, but that he would probably make bond within a few hours. He suggested that Dan would probably be very agitated when he got out of jail and asked if she and the baby had a safe place where they could stay. Gina's nearest relative was six hours away and her sister's house would be the first place Dan would look. She also was afraid to travel alone with Meagan. The officer told her about a domestic violence shelter where she and Meagan would be safe. Gina decided that this was the best option. She packed a few things and an officer assisted her in getting into the shelter. In the meantime, Dan was arrested and charged with assault.

While at the shelter, Gina had an opportunity to meet other women who were in similar situations and to talk with many of them. She also had time to talk to a counselor and to learn more about domestic violence. The more Gina talked with the other women at the shelter, she began to realize that she was not responsible for Dan's behavior. Gina felt a huge sense of relief when she began to understand that this was not her fault. She also began to carefully evaluate what she wanted for her life and for Meagan. She had also learned a lot about the effects of domestic violence on children. While she had always known that the tension was not good for Meagan to be exposed to, she had never realized the effects that continuing to live in this environment could have on her child. This was probably the strongest factor in Gina's decision to secure a protection order and, ultimately, to divorce Dan.

The only contact that Gina had with Dan over the next few weeks was when she saw him at the hearing on the assault charges. Having been found guilty and ordered by the judge to complete a treatment program for domestic violence batterers, Dan tried to convince Gina that this counseling would be just what he needed and that they could be happy again. He promised he would complete the program and that the battering could never happen again. This time, however, Gina did not go back. She had decided that even if the counseling did help Dan she could not live with him anymore nor risk having her daughter affected by the violence. The staff at the shelter supported Gina through the legal proceedings, helping her obtain the restraining order and the divorce.

Gina knew that her sister had begun to sense that something more was wrong. She had always been too ashamed to tell her parents about her situation. Initially she did not tell them because she believed her inadequacy as a wife was causing Dan to beat her. After a while, she was just too embarrassed and she kept hoping that things would change. As she began to gain a clearer understanding of what was really happening in their relationship, it became clear to her that Dan's behavior was not her fault. At that point Gina was able to admit to her family what had been going on in her marriage. Initially family members found it difficult to believe that Dan could have done the things Gina claimed. He had always been so charming and attentive when they had spent time with him. But as more of the story unraveled, her parents realized that Gina was telling the truth. They offered to help her and Meagan financially until they could get on their feet. Gina decided to move closer to her family and, with the support of her parents and her sister, she relocated and began divorce proceedings.

Gina continues to attend a support group for battered women in the city where she now lives. Dan was given supervised visitation with Meagan, but he does not spend very much time with her. Gina has heard that he has a new girlfriend and that they are making wedding plans.

SUSAN AND LYLE: A CASE STUDY

The second case study illustrated a very different situation from the first. Both individuals in this relationship have limited education and fewer financial resources. In this case, the victim experienced family violence as a child and then married a man who was socialized to exert power and control over his partner. This case also clearly demonstrates the impact that isolation from a support system and the involvement of children can have on a victim remaining in an abusive relationship.

Susan only completed the eleventh grade in high school. She ran away the summer after her eleventh grade year and married Lyle when she was only 17. Getting married seemed like the only thing to do at the time. She had grown up in a home where her father was very abusive to her mother, herself, and her two brothers. She was ready to get away from all that.

Lyle had completed high school a couple of years prior and had a job at a meat processing plant. Susan was sure she could find a job with no problem so they ran away and got married. Lyle's family owned some land about twenty miles from town so Lyle and Susan bought a mobile home and moved it to the property.

Susan became pregnant almost immediately, and Lyle decided he did not want her to work if they were starting a family. They only owned the one car that Lyle used to go to work every day, leaving Susan home alone. They had been married only a short time before Susan realized that Lyle had a problem with alcohol. He did not drink much during the week but, on the weekends, the consumption was almost constant. When Lyle was drinking, Susan noted that his personality changed entirely. She described him as a "mean" drunk. It was during these drinking binges that the beatings first started. After a while, Susan noticed that it did not matter if Lyle was drinking or not; the beatings continued. At one point, Susan commented to Lyle that she thought he was going to be different from her father. Belligerently, he informed her that it was his "God given right to beat her, if that's what it took to keep her in line." He also told her that women were put on earth to have babies and to take care of their husbands.

By the time Susan was 25, she had four children: Jason—7, Katie—5, Matt—

3, and Lisa—2. They still only had one car so Susan rarely left their home. The nearest grocery store was ten miles away and Lyle usually did the shopping on his way home. Susan only saw her family a couple of times a year even though they lived within sixty miles. They had stopped coming to see her after a weekend visit when Lyle was drinking; Lyle became especially agitated with one of Susan's brothers and pulled a knife on him. The brother was unharmed, but after that none of her family would come and visit.

At one point, Susan had called her mom and talked to her about Lyle's abusive behavior. Her mom asked Susan what she had done to make him so mad. She then told Susan that she had "made her bed, now she had to lie in it". After that, Susan stopped talking to her family about Lyle's abusive behavior. She remembered that her mom had lived with similar behavior all these years and wondered if this was just how all marriages were. She didn't know of any that were any different.

Lyle had never hit the children when they were young although he frequently yelled at them over insignificant things. When their oldest son, Jason, was 10 years old, he received a watch for Christmas. He had worn it and played with it most of Christmas Day. About mid-afternoon Jason realized that he had put the watch down somewhere and could not find it. He asked everyone if they had seen his watch. When he asked his father, Lyle flew into a rage, ranting about the watch and threatening to make Jason sleep outside if he was unable to find it. Susan, Jason, and the other siblings looked everywhere for the watch. Just before dark, Lyle took Jason out on the porch and told him to stay there until he came and got him, that he was going to teach him a lesson. The temperature was dropping and Jason only had on a light jacket. One of his younger sisters slipped some food out to him around dinner time. Later in the evening, a concerned Susan also went out to check on him. Lyle saw her outside and became enraged, shoving Susan down the porch steps and punching and kicking her. He then gathered the other three children from inside and shoved them out the door, locking it behind them. Susan and the children began to walk through the woods. It was almost a mile to the nearest house.

The neighbor called the police but, when the police arrived, Susan told them that she had accidentally fallen down the stairs. The officer did not believe Susan and encouraged her to tell him what really happened so he could arrest Lyle. Susan refused. She did not want Lyle to go to jail, she just wanted the beating to stop. The officer also told her about a shelter where she and her children could spend the night, which Susan agreed to do. Susan only stayed at the shelter a couple of nights. The children wanted to go home, and she was afraid to stay any longer. Susan did not want Lyle to become angrier, so the family returned home.

After they arrived, Lyle appeared to be sorry for what had happened. Although he did not apologize, he had cleaned up around the yard and had found Jason's watch. Things seemed calm for a while. The beatings did not seem to come as often although Lyle was still verbally very abusive. He also was very tough on the children. As the children grew older he was especially hard on the boys. Spankings seemed to turn into beatings. Susan knew Lyle disciplined the children too harshly, but she was afraid that if she said anything it would make matters even worse.

By now Susan had become almost totally isolated from anyone outside her family. Since she never had access to the car, she rarely left the house. Indeed, Susan had become totally dependent on Lyle for all her needs. He would often tell her that he was all she ever needed and that he was the only one who had ever really cared about her.

When Katie was 12, she began attending junior high school and taking physical education. One day as she changed clothes for class, the teacher noticed bruises and old scars on her back. The scars had the imprint of the plug of an electrical cord. Katie's teacher called her aside and questioned her about it. Katie told her that it was from her father hitting her. Katie's teacher reported the information to the Child Protective Services division, and they sent a worker to the school to interview all the children. The following afternoon a social worker, accompanied by the sheriff, came out to the house. Lyle was not home from work at the time. The social worker told Susan of the complaint and that while they were completing the investigation she and the children must leave and go to a safe place or the children would be taken into protective custody. This news frightened Susan terribly. Her children were all she had at this point, and she could not risk losing them. The worker offered to take the children back to the domestic violence shelter they were in before. Susan knew that this time they may not be coming back.

Shortly after arriving at the shelter, Susan became very depressed. She had been so isolated that it was difficult for her to adjust to living with other people. She also found it overwhelming to be filling out so many forms for everything. It had been a long time since she had really been responsible for handling such things. Even grocery shopping was difficult at first. Susan almost went back to Lyle several times but she knew that if she did, her children would be placed into foster care. She could not bear the thought of that. Slowly, she began to realize that if she wanted to keep the children, she had to find a way to make it without Lyle. She knew she could not continue to let him hurt them even if she was allowed to return.

The children were all attending school now so she had the days free to take care of business matters. She applied for public assistance, for housing, and began looking for a job. Since she had not completed high school and had no marketable job skills, employment opportunities were limited, but Susan eventually found a job waiting tables. The shelter offered GED classes, which she began attending during time off from work.

The children were attending new schools and the adjustment to a new place to live and a new school had not been easy. There were still times when one of them would beg her to go back home and would cry for their Dad. These were the hardest times for Susan to handle, but she knew she could not give in.

It also seemed that there were other roadblocks at every turn—finding an attorney to assist with the divorce, a long waiting list for public housing, no car, and limited public transportation. However, Susan was determined to get through this difficult period.

Five years after leaving Lyle, Susan has a small apartment and continues to work as a waitress. She makes good money on tips and has flexible hours. She has made new friends as have her children, who are now doing well in school although there are still occasional behavior problems. Susan completed the GED and will soon graduate from junior college with a degree in nursing.

DISCUSSION AND CONCLUSION

The above case studies involve distinctly different families yet strongly symbolize the commonalties found in most domestic violence cases. In both situations, it is clear that power and control provide the basis for the battering behavior. In each case control is maintained through verbal and emotional abuse; isolation from friends, family, and work; economic control; intimidation; threats; and violence. The victims stay, even after the violence begins, because of fear, lack of resources and support, and the children.

Patterns, previously discussed in the cycle of violence, can be identified in each case study, with the violence increasing in frequency and severity, a honeymoon period in which the batterer seems remorseful and the violence decreases coupled with promises of changed behavior. In both cases, the victims leave the relationship and return on more than one occasion due to the desire to believe that a change has indeed occurred.

These cases clearly illustrate the role that power and control play in domestic violence relationships and commonalities that are evident even in families with very diverse backgrounds.

Over the years since the first studies of domestic violence began, an enormous body of literature on the problem has evolved and the response to battered women has developed into an international network of services. Legislative advocacy has resulted in significant strengthening of laws, both at the state and federal levels, that have provided for additional protection as well as services. Two short decades ago, domestic violence as a family problem was largely invisible; it is now recognized as one of the most pervasive social problems of our time.

As we look at the progress made in addressing the problem of domestic violence toward the end of the twentieth century, we are aware that there is much that remains to be done. The following ideas are offered for consideration as we move into the next era of addressing this problem:

1. Domestic violence is a serious social problem and warrants further research, especially in the area that examines new theoretical frameworks and the linkages of domestic violence to other social problems.

2. Coordinated community response teams that join together law enforcement, prosecutors, victim advocates, and the court system must continue to expand.

3. Services for women and children impacted by domestic violence should continue to be provided with a focus on safety but also a strong emphasis on empowerment.

4. Effective identification, assessment, and intervention tools must be refined for use in a variety of settings, especially within the medical community where many battered women seek help but are not identified.

5. Prevention programs must be increased and offered to both males and females beginning in elementary school and continuing through college.

6. Men must become more involved at all levels in taking responsibility for speaking out against, and for ending, men's violence against women as well as other forms of sexual inequality.

7. Society must examine and challenge, at every level, the institutions and practices that breed and foster sexual inequality.

The impact of domestic violence on the family is well documented and can manifest itself in a variety of related problems such as child abuse, alcohol and drug addition, depression, suicide, homelessness, truancy, incest, and rape. This problem has been identified as one of the few social problems that impacts almost every institution in our society—from businesses, courts, and prisons to emergency rooms, public health clinics, and schools.

It is now recognized that the underlying cause of individual cases of domestic violence are rooted in issues of male power and control. We must also acknowledge that there is a greater social context that allows such violence to continue, one of discriminatory systems and institutional practices of sexual inequality. Although tremendous strides have been made in the area of domestic violence over the last couple of decades, this progress is not enough to provide a safety net that allows women a means of escaping a relationship in which the male exerts all of the power and control. It is essential that a cultural climate be created that allows women to share power with men.

REFERENCES

Brinegar, Jerry. 1992. *Breaking Free from Domestic Violence*. Minneapolis, Minn.: CompCare Publishers.

Gelles, Richard, and Murray A. Strauss. 1988. *Intimate Violence: The Causes and Consequences of Abuse in the American Family*. New York: Simon & Schuster.

Resko, Beth. *Training Manual for Domestic Violence Counselors and Advocates*. Harrisburg: Pennsylvania Coalition Against Domestic Violence.

Schechter, Susan. 1982. *Women and Male Violence*. Boston: South End Press.

Stark, Evan, and Anne Flitcraft. 1988. "Violence Among Intimates: An Epidemiological Review." In V. N. Hasselt, A. S. Morrison, M. Bellack, and V. N. Hersen, eds. *Handbook of Family Violence*, pp. 292–317. New York: Plenum.

————1996. *Women At Risk: Domestic Violence and Women's Health.* Thousand Oaks, Calif.: Sage Publications.

Steinmetz, Susan K. 1971. *Family Violence, Past, Present, Future.* Newark: University of Delaware.

Strauss, Murray A. 1990. "2001: Preparing Families for the Future." *National Council on Family Relations Presidential Report,* p. 26.

Strauss, Murray A., Richard Gelles, and Susan Steinmetz. 1980. *Behind Closed Doors: A Survey of Family Violence in America.* New York: Doubleday.

Walker, Lenore. 1979. *The Battered Woman.* New York: Harper & Row.

7

Divorce and Poverty

N. Ree Wells

INTRODUCTION

Children's bedtime stories often end with "and they lived happily ever after." Yet, contrary to the cultural ideals of marital bliss and permanence, many marriages are not satisfying and many do not endure. Regardless of the lifelong commitment implied in the traditional wedding vows, "until death do us part," over one million married couples in the U.S. are divorced each year.

Still, we are a society of people who highly value the institution of marriage. In fact, one of the most consistent aspects of family life in the United States has been the high rate of marriage (Appelbaum and Chambliss 1997). The vast majority of adults in the United States, around 90 percent, will marry at least once (Macionis 1997). Various agents of socialization, including parents, peers, teachers, religious leaders, and the media teach children traditional gender roles in anticipation of marriage and, eventually, a family. Little girls are taught the symbolic importance of their wedding day and of a white dress, while little boys are encouraged to acquire the skills necessary to get a good job that will support their families. Adolescents engage in a series of dating rituals that assist in mate selection. Young adults are encouraged to make a marriage commitment if they fall in love and want a sexual relationship. Is it a surprise that most young adults report a desire to marry at some point in their lives?

A marital relationship between a husband and a wife is the classic example of the smallest of all social groups, the dyad. Marriage is also classified as a primary group, characterized by intimacy and cooperation. Unlike larger secondary groups, a dyad can be destroyed by the loss of a single member (Simmel

1950). Therefore, the thought of termination hangs over a dyadic relationship perhaps more than any other type of relationship (Schaefer and Lamm 1998). Although most of us marry, we have also become a society of people who often exercise the option to divorce. The negative social stigma attached to divorce has lessened considerably with its increasing frequency.

The prevalence of divorce, coupled with the severity of its social, psychological, and economic consequences, make divorce a significant contemporary social problem. Divorce may be the appropriate choice under the circumstances of an unhappy or abusive marriage. However, the economic consequences associated with divorce may be severe. For example, the income of single-parent families plummets by more than one-third within several months after separation or divorce (Cherlin 1990). Thus, marital dissolution frequently leads to an unintended or latent dysfunction (Merton 1968): poverty for divorced women and their children.

This chapter is organized around the case studies of three individuals who have experienced divorce and its negative consequences: Jennifer, a young mother of two who dropped out of high school in order to get married; Rose, a middle-aged housewife who is facing divorce with few marketable skills; and Marcos, a rather unconventional father who sought custody of his children after divorce. Each of these cases will be examined from the symbolic interactionist perspective; this is a theoretical framework based on the assumption that society is the product of the interactions of individuals. This approach is especially interested in the shared understandings of everyday behavior and how social forces shape interaction (Schaefer and Lamm 1998).

First, the chapter will examine divorce rates and some of the social causes of divorce. Then, it will explore poverty rates and some of the social factors associated with poverty. Data on the frequency of divorce and the feminization of poverty provide an empirical context for the three case studies and discussion of the economic consequences of divorce. Each of the case studies, in turn, will illustrate the interplay between divorce and poverty.

OVERVIEW OF THE DIVORCE PROBLEM

The United States has one of the highest divorce rates in the world. In 1993, for example, the U.S. divorce rate was "almost twice as high as [that of] Canada, four times as high as [that of] Japan, and ten times as high as [that of] Italy" (Macionis 1997, p. 471). By the beginning of this decade, researchers had noted a slight decrease in our annual divorce rates (Appelbaum and Chambliss 1997).[1] Still, in 1995, nearly 1.2 million couples experienced divorce, while nearly 2.3 million couples were married that year (National Center for Health Statistics 1996). This translates to 6,400 marriages and 3,200 divorces on a typical day.

Although marriage and divorce statistics seem relatively straightforward, they can be difficult to interpret (Schaefer and Lamm 1998). Recent data show that one divorce is granted for every two marriages that occur in the United States each year. For example, for every 100 marriages performed in 1996, 50 divorces were granted (National Center for Health Statistics 1997). This type of statistical comparison has led to the popular, but incorrect, assumption that one-half of all new marriages will end in divorce. However, such comparisons do not take into account the millions of marriages established prior to each year.

The divorce rate is typically measured as the number of final divorce decrees granted under civil law per 1,000 mid-year population (Soroka and Bryjak 1995). This allows for comparisons over time, as well as cross-cultural comparisons. For example, in 1955, the U.S. divorce rate was 2.2 per 1,000 people, whereas the divorce rate in the early 1990s was 4.6 per 1,000 people (Macionis 1997). Examining the number of divorces in a given year per 1,000 married women of ages 15 to 44, however, may provide a more accurate picture of divorce among newer marriages (Schaefer and Lamm 1998). Using this approach we find that the number of divorces per 1,000 married women who are less than 45 years old nearly tripled between 1965 and 1975, and has remained relatively stable since. An age-adjusted divorce rate demonstrates that there were nearly 40 divorces for every 1,000 younger married women in 1996 (p. 397). This approach documents that less than one-half of all marriages end in divorce.

Causes of Divorce

Why is divorce so frequent in the United States? Both societal-level influences and interpersonal factors contribute to the high rate of divorce.

Societal-level influences. A country's level of modernization is strongly associated with increasing rates of divorce; generally, the higher the level of economic development, the higher the rates of divorce (Soroka and Bryjak 1995).[2] Secularization and industrialization also have contributed to the rising U.S. divorce rate. With the increased secularization of society, most people no longer consider divorce a sin (p. 319). Industrialization led to a reduction in the extended family and the predominance of the nuclear family. The nuclear form, however, isolates many wives and husbands from the stabilizing influences of a network of close relatives. Changes in the U.S. economy have occurred, and most married men are not paid a "family wage" now. This, coupled with changes in traditional gender roles for women, has led to a larger proportion of dual-earner families. With both partners working, today's marriages are particularly stressful. Further, spouses who are working outside the home are exposed to new people, some of whom may seem more attractive than their current spouse.

Values are cultural standards of what is good or desirable. For example, most people value romantic love and see it as the foundation of marriage (Macionis 1997). Further, many young people considering marriage believe that their love for each other will be larger than any interpersonal problems that may arise. Yet romantic love often subsides and this loss leads some people to seek a new relationship. The value of individualism is rising, and many people seem to be more concerned with personal happiness than with their family's well-being

(p. 471). According to Bellah et al., (1985, p. 90), "divorce as a solution to an unhappy marriage, even a marriage with young children, is far more acceptable today than ever before." If a person grows unhappy with his/her current relationship, we tend to believe that person has a right, if not an obligation, to leave the relationship.

Norms are the expectations or rules that govern social behaviors. Although divorce deviates from the norms of marriage, it no longer carries the powerful negative stigma it once did, especially for women. As people experience the divorces of family members, friends, and acquaintances, as well as role models portrayed in the media, divorce has become more acceptable, regardless of the reason. For example, in a recent public opinion poll, about one-half of all Americans favored divorce as a solution for a marriage that "isn't working out." only one-third of the respondents opposed divorce under such circumstances (Appelbaum and Chambliss 1997, p. 401). Divorce may be more prevalent now because the formal sanctions against it have lessened and divorce is simply easier to accomplish today than it was before no-fault divorces. Even so, nearly half of people in the United States believe that divorce is perhaps too easy to obtain (Macionis 1997).

One of the most salient social influences on the divorce rate is the rate of women's labor force participation. Generally, the higher the rate of married women's labor force participation, the higher the rate of divorce (Beeghley 1996). Historical analysis reveals that as the percentage of women in the labor force rose—from 5 percent in 1890 to 59 percent in 1990—the proportion of divorces to marriages each year also rose—from 10 percent in 1890 to 48 percent in 1970 (p. 232). Thus, the long-term increase in the divorce rate is tied to women's economic independence, which is generated by paid employment.

Although women who are not employed often have access to the resources of their husbands or families, they rarely have control over those resources (Beeghley 1996). Working women tend to have some control over finances and are more likely to initiate divorce. According to Beeghley, "a relatively high proportion of women will end their marriages simply because they enjoy a modicum of economic independence"; furthermore, some men seek a divorce, "simply because they have fewer economic obligations to their wives" (p. 232). Although this argument has merit, it also oversimplifies the case. There is no single or simple explanation for divorce: Multiple social and interpersonal factors contribute to the high divorce rate in the United States.

Interpersonal factors. Certain sociodemographic factors are important predictors of divorce and thus may be considered relevant to intervention strategies for reducing the number of divorces. Those at highest risk of divorce include young spouses, who have yet to mature emotionally, and people who marry after a brief courtship, especially those who have not experienced their spouses in a variety of situations (Macionis 1997). Strategies to reduce the potential for later divorce may include waiting to be married until one's twenties and longer engagements. Young couples who marry in response to an unexpected pregnancy are also at higher risk of divorce, as are partners who have alcohol- or drug-abuse problems (p. 472). Community resources, such as sex education and family planning programs, as well as alcohol- and drug-addiction counseling, may be helpful in lessening the effects of those risk factors. Couples from the lower social classes or others who have financial strains are at higher risk of divorce (p. 472). In fact, "poor couples are twice as likely to divorce as more affluent couples" (Eitzen and Baca Zinn 1997, p. 209). Familial ties also influence the probability of divorce; if your kin (or friends) disapprove of the marriage, divorce is more likely than for couples with approval.

On the other hand, there is an inverse relationship between religiosity and divorce: The more religious the couple, the less likely they are to divorce (Macionis 1997). As one popular saying goes, "The couple that prays together, stays together." However, couples with different religious faiths are more likely to divorce than those who share similar religious beliefs (Schaefer and Lamm 1998). Since social researchers have identified many of the correlates or risks associated with divorce, intervention strategies may be incorporated to reduce these risks, and consequently, the overall number of people who experience the negative consequences of divorce.

OVERVIEW OF THE POVERTY PROBLEM

In 1993, the poverty rate was 15.1 percent and 39.3 million people were officially classified as poor (Eitzen and Baca Zinn 1997). Since then, the U.S. economy has slowly expanded and the poverty rate has fallen slightly. By 1996, 13.7 percent of the U.S. population, or 36.5 million people, were living at or below the official level of poverty (U.S. Bureau of the Census 1997). The poverty level is set by the Social Security Administration, based on a formula of the minimal amount of money required for subsistence. For example, the average poverty threshold for a family of four in 1996 was $16,036. However, critics claim that this type of measure is arbitrary and underestimates the true extent of poverty (Eitzen and Baca Zinn 1997). Further, it does not consider the relative poverty experienced by millions of people who have earnings just above the poverty threshold.

Correlates of Poverty

Poverty is not randomly distributed across the population. A number of socio-demographic characteristics, including age, marital status, race and gender, are associated with poverty.

Age and Poverty. Children in the United States bear a heavy burden of poverty; although the nation's poverty rate was 15.1 percent in 1993, the poverty rate for children under age 18 that year was nearly 23 percent (Eitzen and Baca Zinn 1997). Thus, nearly one in four children was living in poverty. Another way to measure children's poverty is to ask, "Of all poor people in the U.S., what percent are children?" The answer is nearly 40 percent (Macionis 1997). Either way, children in the United States are disproportionately poor.

The poverty problem is exacerbated for children of divorced or single parents. Nearly one-half of all children in female-headed households live in poverty (Farley 1998). Some families are female-headed because the mother never married the father of her child(ren); others because of marital disruption. Of all children in female-headed households, most (two-thirds) have parents who are separated or divorced and only one-third have parents who never married (p. 325). According to Farley, "the single biggest risk factor for poverty is living in a family with a female householder and no husband present" (p. 208). This assertion is significant because 85 percent of children in single-parent households live with their mothers (Renzetti and Curran 1998). Also, the number of single-parent families has increased, from 13 percent of families with dependent children in 1970 to 31 percent of such families in 1995 (U.S. Bureau of Census 1996).

Family Composition and Poverty. In the years between 1960 and 1990, a discernable change in the composition of poor families occurred. Single women headed only 25 percent of all poor households in 1960; the majority of poor families had both husbands and wives in the home (Macionis 1997). By the early 1990s, however, the proportion of poor households headed by a woman had more than doubled to 52 percent; now more than half of all poor families are female-headed (Beeghley 1996). Another way to measure the relationship between family composition and poverty is to ask, "Of all single-parent families headed by women, what percent are poor?" The poverty rate for single female-headed families in 1993 was 46 percent; this is considerably higher than the poverty rate for two-parent families (8 percent), or for single male-headed families (22 percent) (p. 99).

Women who head households bear the brunt of poverty (Eitzen and Baca Zinn 1997). Most women who head households are employed and 85 percent of these workers are full-time (Renzetti and Curran 1995). And yet, the median income in 1993 for females who head households and work full time and year-round was less than $16,848 per year (p. 274). According to Renzetti and Curran, "it is not difficult to see how employment is hardly a safeguard against poverty for women raising children alone, nor is it surprising that the inadequacy of their wages make welfare benefits more appealing than jobs to some women who head households" (p. 274).

The Feminization of Poverty. Women are overrepresented among the country's poor. Of all poor people in the United States over the age of 18, 62.3 percent are women (Macionis 1997). The trend by which women represent an increasing proportion of the poor is called the feminization of poverty. The combined effects of traditional gender role socialization, sexism, occupational segregation by sex, and institutionalized discrimination, have exacerbated the earnings gap between women and men (Anderson 1997). The female-to-male earnings ratio reached a new high in 1996 for persons working full time and year-round; the real median earnings for women were $23,710, which represented about 74 percent of the median earnings of $34,144 for men (U.S. Bureau of the Census 1997). Because of the earnings gap, most women are not as financially secure as are most men. Women's financial situations become even more precarious after marital disruption.

Race and Poverty. Whites comprise nearly 80 percent of the U.S. population (Beeghley 1997); however, only 12 percent of the white population is poor (Etizen and Baca Zinn 1997). In contrast, blacks comprise 12 percent of the U.S. population, and over 33 percent of all blacks are poor (p. 187). Although most poor people are white (nearly two-thirds), blacks are disproportionately overrepresented among the poor.

As previously indicated, the overall poverty rate of female-headed households is 46 percent. If we consider the race of those households, the figures are even more noteworthy: in 1993, 67.2 percent of black and 70.3 percent of Hispanic female-headed families were officially poor (Renzetti and Curran 1995). Thus, the economic plight of single-parent families is much worse for racial-ethnic minorities. Anderson (1997, p. 14) suggests in order to understand more fully women's place in society, we must consider a "matrix of domination" whereby a person's race, social class, marital status, and gender combine to influence her life chances. For example, "Women of color who head households have the same economic problems as white women who are in the same situation, plus the added burdens of institutional racism" (Eitzen and Baca Zinn 1997, p. 371). Integrating work and family is a balancing act for all employed mothers, but the ability to do so varies by social class and marital status (Anderson 1997). For example, divorced women are more likely than married women to experience higher levels of role overload and role conflict. The multiple demands of child rearing and labor force participation tend to be less stressful for middle-class women than for impoverished women.

THE PROBLEMS OF DIVORCE AND POVERTY

Marriage is, in part, an economic union. Generally, two incomes are better than one and women often experience an increase in financial status through marriage. On the other hand, women nearly always suffer a considerable loss of income and decrease in their standard of living when their marriages end. In fact, many divorced women become impoverished, if only temporarily (Beeghley 1996). A change in social class position that occurs during a person's lifetime is called intragenerational social mobility: this movement may be either upward or downward (p. 48). The following case study illustrates social mobility, as well as the association between divorce and poverty.

JENNIFER: A CASE STUDY

Jennifer and Jason were childhood sweethearts who met when Jennifer, a junior, became a cheerleader. Jason was a senior and a member of the football team when they began to date. The couple became part of the popular crowd at school and other students envied their prestige across the campus. The high school was located in a city of about 100,000 people and bordered two neighborhoods: Eastside was middle class and Longview was working class. Jason's family owned a home in Eastside and enjoyed the benefits of affluence: his father was successful in insurance sales and his mother was a full-time homemaker. Jennifer's family rented a house in Longview. Although Jennifer's parents both worked—her father as a restaurant cook and her mother as a secretary—they could not afford any of the luxuries that Jason's family took for granted. Still, both sets of parents initially seemed supportive of the teenagers' dating relationship. Even so, Jennifer's parents interpreted their relationship as serious and as an avenue for upward mobility, while Jason's parents saw it as a youthful learning experience.

Jennifer and Jason were the epitome of youthful vitality on the one hand, and traditional gender roles on the other. During their interactions, Jennifer usually deferred to Jason's opinions and he, in turn, frequently demonstrated his dominant, yet protective, role over her. As their relationship became increasingly intimate, Jason became more insistent on sexual intercourse. This pressure was fueled by the frequent stories of premarital sexual activity among his peers. By early spring, the couple began having unprotected intercourse. Within a couple of months, Jennifer was pregnant.

The couple informed their parents when Jennifer was nine weeks pregnant. A conflict of values arose, which may have been predicted, based on the social class differences (Beeghley 1996). Jason's family insisted on an abortion and offered to pay for it. Jennifer's parents opposed abortion, suggested the couple should be married, and offered to pay for a simple wedding. Jennifer and Jason decided to get married. They rented an efficiency apartment and began their married lives with Jennifer three months pregnant. Although Jason had graduated from high school by that point and was currently working, his parents planned for him to start college that fall. Because of his new family obligations, however, Jason felt pressured to postpone college and informed his boss that he would continue to work full time. Jennifer started her senior year that fall; after all, there were numerous pregnant teens in the high school, and the baby was not due until February. Yet, Jennifer's goal of finishing high school was never realized.

After the birth of Megan, Jennifer's life was filled with childcare. Jennifer's parents were helpful, but they could not offer financial assistance. Jason's parents, who had refused to attend the wedding, remained distant to Jennifer and rarely saw their new granddaughter. Within a few months, the flow of visiting family and friends slowed to a trickle.

By each evening when Jason returned home from work, Jennifer was exhausted. Further, since she received little assistance from Jason with the housekeeping chores or child-rearing tasks, she began to feel resentful. Though Jason usually responded to her specific requests for help, he did so reluctantly. Like many men in our society, Jason was uncomfortable caring for the baby in the ways that Jennifer seemed to enjoy. He became jealous of the attention Jennifer gave Megan and was disturbed by the dampening effect on their sexual relationship. Many evenings he would coerce Jennifer into intercourse, even though she was not interested. Although they used a diaphragm for birth control, Jennifer became pregnant by the time she stopped breast-feeding Megan. When she told Jason, he became angry, accusing her of getting pregnant "on purpose." Since they were already in a struggle to make ends meet, he began working overtime to cover expenses. Jennifer also altered her behavior, giving Jason more attention in the evenings. The marriage seemed to be moving in a positive direction, especially after prenatal tests confirmed that the fetus was male. Jason's image of parenthood was playing ball with a son; he became more supportive of Jennifer during this pregnancy.

As a newborn, their second child, Michael, was often sick with colic and the nights without sleep wore on the young couple. Jennifer became irritated and less tolerant of Jason's passivity around the house. He often responded to her complaints by leaving the apartment angry, yelling that he was going out to have "a drink with the guys" from work. This pattern created a cycle of frustration. After an argument one night, Jason did not come home. The next morning, Jennifer became worried, and after calling the hospital and the police station, she reluctantly called Jason's parents. They informed Jennifer that Jason had returned home and would seek a divorce.

Three months later: "It wasn't supposed to turn out this way," thought Jennifer, sitting for the first time in the welfare office. She felt exhausted—physically and emotionally—caring for her two young children: Megan, a daughter of 3 years, and Michael, 14 months. It was a large, noisy room, filled with other women attending to their unruly children. She completed the form documenting her need for public assistance, took a number from the dispenser, and collapsed in an uncomfortable chair. The woman sitting next to her complained that she had been waiting over two hours for her interview with a social worker. Jennifer closed her eyes, fighting back the tears. Just then, Michael lunged out of her hands and hit his jaw on the back of her chair, letting out a blood-curdling scream. As she struggled to comfort him, Megan began crying, too, and Jennifer noticed that most eyes in the room had turned her way. Yet, no one moved to help her. She felt a wave of anger rush over her and thought, "This mess is all Jason's fault."

Jennifer felt embarrassed when she met the social worker. During their interview, she provided an "account" to legitimize her current situation: "If their father had kept his promises to me, we wouldn't be here." The social worker was not moved emotionally; she'd heard worse. Jennifer did not see herself as a "welfare mother" and was struggling to counter the label. And yet she needed public assistance and felt it was the only way for her to remain responsible for the children. After the meeting, as she stepped out of the welfare office and into the fresh air, she felt relieved for the first time in weeks; she had been approved for Aid to Families with Dependent Children (AFDC), Medicaid, and Food

Stamps. Even so, Jennifer was depressed about her situation: she was only 20 years old, a high school drop-out, and, for the past three months, a single mother. Although her husband, Jason, never said he did not love her anymore, she felt unloved. Jason simply refused to play the roles associated with marriage and the family; he had envisioned himself a college-bound bachelor and never wanted the obligations of being a husband and father. Divorce and poverty are Jennifer's reality now.

The Presentation of Self

One of the more fascinating approaches to studying everyday life from the symbolic interaction perspective was developed by Erving Goffman (1959). According to Goffman we learn to create distinctive appearances in order to satisfy various audiences, through a process that involves managing the impressions that others have of us. Thus, a set of interactions can be seen in terms of a theatrical performance that can be understood through "dramaturgical" analysis. We can apply such analysis to the last scene in Jennifer's case study. For example, the waiting room represents the frontstage, where Jennifer and the other clients encounter a receptionist, who acts as gatekeeper to the organization. The furniture in the waiting area is sparse and uncomfortable and there are no accommodations for mothers present with children. The social worker's office constitutes the back region of the setting, with a computer on a messy desk and book shelves covered with printouts. It is not nearly so noisy as it was in the waiting room. Most of the agency's decisions are made here; such decisions will effect the ability of recipients like Jennifer to survive financially.

One type of impression management, called face-work, is often essential to continued social interactions (Schaefer and Lamm 1998). If a person experiences embarrassment or some form of rejection, face-saving behavior is often initiated. This may explain some of Jennifer's behaviors at the welfare office. For example, she felt compelled to provide the social worker an account of what led her to these particular circumstances; from Jennifer's perspective, her husband abandoned her and the children. She did not initiate the divorce, nor did she invite such harsh economic consequences.

According to Becker (1963), there is no inherently deviant act; rather, "deviant behavior is behavior that people so label" (p. 9). Jennifer was very concerned that applying for public assistance not be construed as what may be called "deviant" behavior. The labeling perspective emphasizes how a person who deviates from a social norm, such as financial independence or marriage, comes to be labeled and whether she or he decides to accept that label. It is clear that Jennifer, originally from the working class, understands the negative stigma attached to receiving welfare and to being divorced.

Public Assistance

Like Jennifer, most poor women with children do not have the human capital or work skills to obtain paid employment that would pull them out of poverty

(Eitzen and Baca Zinn 1997). And since most poor women with children are either not employed, or are employed at minimum-wage jobs, nearly two-thirds must turn to government assistance (p. 284). Although public assistance is a necessary "safety net" for millions of people, it has recently been identified in the perpetuation of the cycle of poverty (Beeghley 1996, p. 106).[3] Paradoxically, public assistance programs help poor families survive, but recipients must remain poor in order to remain eligible for benefits. Clearly programs such as AFDC, Medicaid and Food Stamps alleviate some of the problems of living associated with poverty. Because the penalties for obtaining employment are so severe for mothers on welfare, the cycle of poverty persists.

To further understand some of the constraints of poverty, we will explore the relationship between minimum wage and public assistance. In 1997, the minimum wage was increased to $5.15 per hour. At this rate, a person who works full time and year-round would only earn about $9,500 (Renzetti and Curran 1998). If this worker were the sole source of support for herself and one child, their family income would be below the 1997 poverty line. Single young mothers like Jennifer do not have many options. They may increase their human capital (education level or marketable skills) and find a decent-paying job, necessitating adequate and affordable day care (Beeghley 1996) or they may find a new husband who can afford to support them, which is not an option for most mothers on public assistance.

Farley (1998) asserts that, "The economic situation of female-headed families would be far less difficult if women were simply paid at the same rate for their work as men are, and if day care and health care were publicly funded, as they are in nearly all other industrialized countries" (p. 211). Although child care is a major expense for many U.S. families, the financial burden of care is disproportionate: single and poor mothers "generally pay less in absolute dollars, but they spend a relatively greater share of their family income on child care than other families" (Bayfield and Hofferth 1995, p. 159).[4] A mother working at a low-wage job uses most of her income for this single expense (Farley 1998). In most states, people who are employed are not eligible for Medicaid, which means that workers must pay for all medical care expenses. How can poor women afford to take a job, when the costs of day care and medical care are so high? Under the constraints of Jennifer's situation, would her decision to remain on welfare, and not seek paid employment, be a rational one?

Economic Consequences of Divorce

One need not be a social scientist to realize that divorce can result in both short-term and long-term psychological, social, and economic suffering for all concerned. These hardships, coupled with the fact that divorce is widespread in modern societies, make this a social problem of major proportions (Soroka and Bryjak 1995, p. 321).

As Jennifer's case shows, there are potential consequences for all family members touched by divorce. Although some of the consequences are psychological or involve social adjustments, much of the following discussion focuses on the economic consequences of divorce, especially for women and their children.

Policymakers and researchers have focused considerable attention on the economic consequences of divorce over the past two decades (Peterson 1996a). Several concerns have highlighted this interest, including the fact that the number of people affected by divorce has increased dramatically and "the economic well-being of women and children after divorce has become a significant problem" (p. 528). As new reforms were introduced across the country, such as no-fault divorce legislation, and new guidelines were established for dividing property, assigning custody of children, and awarding alimony, key stakeholders became increasingly interested in evaluating their effect (p. 528).

According to Berger and Luckmann (1966), social reality is literally constructed through social interactions. Furthermore, our definitions and perceptions of each situation shape reality. And yet, for every social interaction, there are at least two perspectives—one for each of the participants. For example, Jesse Bernard (1972) studied the dynamics of interaction within contemporary marriages. She found that husbands and wives applied different meanings or interpretations to the same situations, and labeled her findings his marriage and her marriage. In other words, the couples had one marriage, but separate experiences and accounts of that shared reality. Likewise, divorce often creates a different set of experiences for women and for men, the economic consequences of which may be referred to as his divorce and her divorce.

Divorce settlements. Scholars have begun to document the differential economic consequences of divorce for men and women (Peterson 1996a). Generally, women more often than men have difficulty obtaining equitable divorce settlements (Beeghley 1996). Of particular concern are alimony, child support, and the division of shared property. For example, partly as a result of no-fault divorce settlements, women and children typically must move out of the family home and into less expensive rental housing. "Adding to the financial difficulties women and children face is the fact that in dividing marital property, the courts usually consider only tangible assets, such as the family's home, car(s), and furniture. Given that most divorcing couples have mortgages and other debts, by the time the bills are paid, there may be little left to divide. The equal division of property often forces the sale of the family home" (Renzetti and Curran 1998, p. 407). Since women earn less income on average than do men, female-headed households are further disadvantaged.

No-fault divorce laws have reduced the amount of both alimony and child support paid by divorced men to their former wives (Renzetti and Curran 1998). According to Farley (1998), courts are awarding alimony much less frequently, since women are more often able to take care of themselves financially. Even when alimony is awarded, the average annual payment is only about $4,000 (p. 323). Alimony is awarded in less than 14 percent of divorce cases and is received in less than 7 percent (Anderson 1997).

Child custody and child support. The issues of physical custody and financial support of children are concerns for more than half of all divorcing couples (Macionis 1977). Before the Industrial Revolution, fathers were usually awarded legal custody of their children, who were considered property. There was a dramatic shift in custody decisions in favor of mothers by the turn of the twentieth century (Lindgren and Taub 1993). More recently, social norms have shifted toward joint custody, with an arrangement for dividing the child's time between the homes of both parents. Clearly, this arrangement has the advantage that children maintain contact with both parents. Extreme difficulties, however, may arise with parents who live in different communities (or states) or with parents who do not get along (Macionis 1997).

Because fathers typically earn more income than mothers do and mothers usually secure custody of the children, the financial well-being of the children depends upon the father's making child-support payments. The lack of adequate and consistent child support contributes to the economic plight of divorced mothers. In 1995, courts awarded child support in only 54 percent of all divorce cases (Macionis 1997). Thus, nearly one-half of the children who were legally entitled to child support each year received no payment or only partial payments (p. 473).

In many cases, fathers do not pay what they have been ordered to pay. Further, two-thirds of fathers stop paying court-ordered child support within two years (Beeghley 1996). Federal legislation has recently mandated that employers withhold money from the earnings of parents who fail to pay court-ordered child support. This mandate targets the nearly 2.5 million deadbeat dads in the United States who choose not to support their offspring (Macionis 1997, p. 437). According to Farley (1998), child support is actually paid in full in only half of the cases in which it was awarded and the average amount of child support actually paid is only $2,700 per year. This widespread pattern of nonsupport results in an easier recovery for divorced men from the financial strains of divorce, leaving their former wives and children in a financial position worse than when the family was intact.

Changes in per capita income. Most married women in the United States are employed, and the rate of labor force participation has been even higher for married women with children than for those without. Only 53.2 percent of married women without children under 18 were in the labor force in 1996; however, 63.5 percent of married women with children under age 6 were working that year, as were 70.2 percent of those with children under age 18 (Farley 1998). Thus, the pattern suggests that most mothers work out of economic necessity. Many married women who were not in the labor force prior to their divorce find that they must seek paid employment afterwards. Thus, the average personal income for divorced women actually increases; however, because they lose their ex-husband's income, most face a significant reduction in their per capita income (Smock 1994). In contrast, few men experience job changes upon marital disruption; thus, their personal income is generally not affected by divorce and their per capita income actually increases (p. 250).

In her influential book *The Divorce Revolution*, Weitzman (1985) concludes that California's no-fault divorce laws have exacerbated a major social problem, namely a gap in the standard of living between divorced women and men. Ironically, divorce raises the standard of living of most men, who no longer support their ex-wives and children. Peterson (1996a) notes that women's standard of living declines by an average of about 27 percent after divorce, whereas men's rises by about 10 percent. This 40 percent difference in the postdivorce standards of living between women and men illustrates an important distinction between her divorce and his divorce.

The economic consequences of divorce and women's experiences of those consequences vary by stage in the lifecycle. In other words, some issues are unique to younger divorced women with children; other issues are more relevant to older women whose marriages end after the children have left the nest.

Younger divorced women. The customary practice of assigning mothers child custody after divorce places them at a distinct disadvantage with regard to per capita and total family income. This is especially true for younger divorced women, whose postdisruption, per capita income averages between 55 percent and 66 percent of their ex-husband's income (Smock 1994). In other words, younger divorced men earn between one-third and one-half more than their ex-wives, and yet these wives usually have physical custody of, and primary financial responsibility for, their children.

According to Smock (1994, p. 258), women's postdivorce economic disadvantage stems, either directly or indirectly, from their responsibilities toward their children. For the young adults in her sample, childless women who divorced fared about as well as men; however, divorced mothers were at a distinct disadvantage (p. 258). Women's traditional role as primary child caretaker before marital disruption reduces their ability to develop human capital, such as further education or valued work skills. This was evidenced in Jennifer dropping out of high school at the time of her first pregnancy and failing to complete the formal education necessary for most employment. Further, tasks associated with taking care of children cut into working women's job commitment (e.g., if the children are sick, mothers take more time off work than do fathers) and job tenure (e.g., mothers tend to have fewer years invested in their occupations than do fathers).

Older divorced women. Women who experience divorce later in the life cycle have the additional burden of social norms and laws that systematically disadvantage older women. For example, with regard to Social Security benefits, "a divorced woman receives half of her former husband's benefits if they had been married at least 10 years" (Eitzen and Baca Zinn 1997, p. 132). In other words, if divorce occurs before ten years, the ex-wife receives nothing. Further, most health and/or life insurance coverage for wives stops under their husband's policies when they are divorced or widowed (p. 437). In order to understand some of the issues unique to older women who divorce, consider the following case study.

ROSE: A CASE STUDY

Although Rose took some college courses in her early twenties, she never trained for a specific field, nor did she graduate. Like most of her girlfriends, she saw college as the avenue to meet a husband. She met Kyle during her first semester in college, and they were married by Christmas that year. Rose became a full-time housewife and Kyle landed a full-time job. The couple set up a small home and decided to start a family. The traditional gender roles of wife and mother were both time-consuming and fulfilling to Rose. However, hers wasn't a storybook ending. After being married to Kyle for twenty-nine years, Rose was recently separated.

Rose is now 53 years old and has two grown children (ages 27 and 23) from her marriage. In the month following the college graduation of their youngest daughter, Kyle admitted to having a nearly two-year affair with his secretary, Melissa. He moved into Melissa's apartment and filed for a divorce in order to marry this younger woman. In addition to feelings of betrayal and anger over Kyle's deception and infidelity, Rose is also now faced with serious financial concerns.

Rose has worked part time and seasonally for the past decade as a salesperson in a department store in order to earn extra money for the children's needs. Although she earns a little more than minimum wage, her take-home pay is less than $5,000 per year. Kyle is in industrial sales and earns around $37,000 annually. Since they recently put their youngest child through college, Rose and Kyle had only a small savings account (about $4,000) and considerable credit card debt (about $16,000) at the time of their separation. Although Kyle has continued to pay the house mortgage over the past few months, he insists on selling the family home, which has about $30,000 total equity. He wants to use his half of the equity as down payment on a home for his new fiancée. Rose calculated that if she were forced to sell the family home, her share of the equity would be spent the first year on moving expenses and setting up an apartment. Although she currently has too many assets to qualify for public assistance, Rose will be eligible within the next year or so if her employment status doesn't improve. She laments, "All those years of marriage, and I'll soon have nothing to show for it."

Rose has managed to cover her automobile payments and the monthly utilities, but she is without enough income to pay all of her current bills. In the past three months since the separation, Rose has spent all of her earnings and most of her savings for daily living expenses. Although her children are sympathetic to her situation, and feel betrayed by their father as well, neither of them is in a financial position to provide Rose much help. Also, she had to secure a divorce lawyer whose retainer was nearly $1,000. Since Rose and Kyle live in a no-fault divorce state, she cannot file for divorce on grounds of desertion. Her lawyer has warned her not to expect a large alimony, even though they were married for nearly three decades and she raised their two children. She is worried about her finances and her future. Rose is still twelve years away from the age at which she could access Social Security benefits. She has had trouble sleeping and a recent trip to the physician's office verified a stomach ulcer. Although she is still covered by Kyle's company policy, her coverage will be cancelled with the formal divorce decree and her part-time job does not provide health insurance benefits.

Although she has continued to work at the department store, her boss is not able to schedule additional hours for her at this time. Trying to be proactive, she applied for several full-time sales positions in local businesses, but none of the personnel managers have called her back for a second interview. Many people in Rose's age-cohort have experienced prejudice and discrimination in the workplace and in the labor market. Ageism, combined with sexism, makes for difficult job hunting for women like Rose. Divorce and poverty seem inevitable. Under these circumstances, Rose asks her closest friend, "What can I do to stay out of poverty?"

Nonverbal Communication: Couple Identity

Interactionists recognize nonverbal communication as a form of social behavior (Schaefer and Lamm 1998). For example, for years Rose avoided prolonged eye contact with men, lest they think she is available. Because she valued her marital status, she wanted to avoid any behavior that might stimulate interest in her sexually. Now she recalls the numerous times that Kyle had avoided eye contact with her, as well as most physical touching, in the months before he left the marriage. Also important to interactionists are symbolic gestures, such as wearing a wedding band. During her most recent job interview, Rose casually rubbed her left ring finger with her thumb, until she realized that she no longer wears a wedding ring. That awareness startled her, as it would have had she lost the ring. She soon remembered she had lost the relationship.

Over time, partners in a marriage develop a "couple identity" (Renzetti and Curran 1998, p. 394). In other words, each person's self-concept is influenced by the daily interactions that they, as a married couple, share with one another and with others; these interactions change how both people see themselves and how others see them. Further, a couple's identity changes over the course of a marriage as they adapt to new situations, such as the birth of a child. For nearly three decades, Rose's self-perception has been determined largely by her positions as wife and mother, and it is difficult for her to embrace the loss of those familiar roles.

Blumer (1969) posited that instead of merely reacting to each other's actions, we interpret each other's actions. Accordingly, "people's actions derive from their interpretations of what goes on around them, and much of this interpretation is learned through interacting with others" (Renzetti and Curran 1998, p. 18). Our responses to another person are based, in large part, on the meanings we attach to the other's behavior. These meanings often reflect the norms and values of the dominant culture (Schaefer and Lamm 1998). From Rose's point of view, Kyle broke their marriage vows and should be held financially responsible for his deviance. Rose feels resentment over the social, psychological, and economic changes forced upon her by Kyle's actions. Also, she feels stuck in a pattern of reacting to Kyle's extramarital affair and his decision to divorce her. Kyle, on the other hand, is behaving in a way that excludes much consideration of his first marriage; he is currently focused on future plans to marry Melissa. He was not particularly happy in his first marriage, and although he never wanted to hurt Rose, he was determined to make the changes necessary to be with his new partner.

The traditional norms of marriage have been changing in recent decades, and as support for such norms weakens, more people feel free to violate them and will be less likely to receive serious negative sanctions for doing so (Schaefer and Lamm 1998). Although it does not appear that Kyle has experienced negative sanctions for his actions, Rose's lawyer will likely intervene and insist on a level of economic support. Further, Kyle will need to negotiate the reactions of his two children, who are currently more sympathetic to their mother.

Second marriages. In part because the social norms for marriage are so prevalent, many people choose to marry again after divorce. Overall, 80 percent of people who divorce marry again, most within five years of the divorce (Macionis 1997). This has created a pattern of serial monogamy, whereby long-term, but not lifelong, marriages are formed. Second marriage patterns vary by gender: about two-thirds of divorced women and three-fourths of divorced men eventually marry again (Schaefer and Lamm 1998).[5] In the previous case, for example, Kyle was headed toward a second marriage before his first one, with Rose, was legally over. Divorced women are less likely to date than are their ex-husbands, given women's typical custody of children. Thus, many divorced mothers find it difficult to have much of a social life outside of their family obligations (Arendell 1992).

Recent estimates suggest that nearly half of all marriages are second marriages for at least one partner (Macionis 1997). Although the high rate of second marriages may be interpreted as an endorsement for the institution of marriage, second marriages pose new challenges, especially when children are present. Unfortunately, many second marriages also end in divorce, as the divorce rate for second marriages is slightly higher than for first marriages (Farley 1998). This may be due, in part, to the additional stressors of dealing with ex-spouses and blending households of children from two sets of parents.

Psychological consequences. In addition to the previously discussed issues of physical custody and financial support of children whose parents experience marital dissolution, there are psychological consequences for the children, as well as for the divorcing parents. Studies have shown mixed results with regard to the long-term consequences of divorce on children. Some have shown that children from mother-only families, when compared to those from two-parent families, have poorer academic achievements and lower attendance at school, are more likely to marry early, to have children early, and to divorce (Eitzen and Baca Zinn 1997). Since women mostly head single-parent families, a common explanation for the problems experienced by these children has been that the absence of a male adult is detrimental to children's development (p. 371). Clearly, the absence of one parent makes coping with parenting more difficult. However, at least one scholar has argued, "It seems likely that the most detrimental aspect of the absence of fathers from one-parent families headed by women is not the lack of a male presence but the lack of a male income" (Cherlin 1981, p. 81). Again, single mothers and their children are much more likely to live in poverty than are single fathers—with or without custody.

Divorced women who state that leaving the marriage ended a physically and/ or emotionally abusive situation have also reported positive psychological consequences (Anderson 1997). Theoretically, this may reduce the intergenerational transmission of violence, since exposure of children to violent episodes between the parents lessens after divorce. Further, some women note improved relationships with their children following a divorce (p. 159).

Divorced fathers. With regard to family and emotional ties, men generally fare worse than women do after divorce. Separated and divorced mothers are more likely than fathers to maintain existing social ties because of the children and these patterns keep most women home-centered (Gerstel 1988). For most men, separation and divorce are more likely to reproduce the character of young bachelorhood (Anderson 1997). This is a likely scenario for Jason, from Jennifer's case study. All divorced fathers, of course, do not desire a pattern of returning to bachelorhood. Many divorced men did not initiate their divorces.

Some divorced fathers experience discrimination as a result of the social norms surrounding child custody and support. These concerns may be highlighted with a short case study.

MARCOS: A CASE STUDY

Marcos' parents immigrated to the United States from Brazil in the 1950s. He grew up with his family in upstate New York. Marcos met his wife, Monica, while attending an art institute; he was studying abstract painting and she was studying modern dance. She was the most beautiful and graceful woman Marcos had ever seen; he was the most creative and gentle man Monica had ever met. They fell in love, nearly at first sight, soon married and had two daughters, Georgia and Imogene. As a couple, Marcos and Monica lived outside typical social conventions. For example, they were an interethnic couple: Marcos was of mixed Portuguese and Afro-Brazilian ancestry and Monica was African American. Further, their religious affiliations differed: Like most of his ancestors, Marcos was Catholic; Monica, who grew up in Atlanta, was Southern Baptist. Even their careers and work schedules were unusual. For example, Monica was gone for extended periods of time, touring with a national dance troupe. Since Marcos worked at home in his studio as a freelance painter, he took care of the children before and after school. He also enjoyed cooking, so meals in the evening were joyful. By the time the girls were 9 and 11 years old, he had taught them how to shop, to cook, and to keep the apartment clean, as those were never interests for Monica. Marcos regularly took them to art receptions and museums in the evenings and encouraged their creative interests. From the beginning of their relationship, Marcos and Monica had trouble meeting financial obligations. Even so, their somewhat unconventional household ran smoothly, if on a limited budget.

There were recent signs of Monica's unhappiness with the marriage. Although she was attracted initially by Marcos' gentle nature, later she found that he did not fit her image of a traditional or masculine man. For example, he didn't earn a steady income, as she did. Further, unlike Monica, he was not athletic and was, in fact, somewhat overweight; this was probably associated with his hobby of cooking. After a three-week tour, Monica returned home and, without prior warning, asked Marcos for a divorce. He tried to change her mind, to no avail. She became angry and threatened to fight for full custody of their children. Marcos became frightened, because he knew how nasty custody battles could get. Later, Marcos agreed with the judge's decision to grant him joint custody with Monica; however, he did not understand why he was only allowed to keep the girls during the weeks Monica traveled and, otherwise, on alternate weekends.

Although Marcos kept the same apartment, his routine with the girls was severely altered and he became depressed. This affected his ability to work and with lower productivity, his income decreased. He could not pay all of his bills and his self-esteem was negatively affected; since he was not providing for his family, he began to feel like a failure. Because he missed two consecutive child support payments, Monica threatened to stop his visitation rights. It seemed as if Marcos was on a downward spiral, when he was offered a two-year contract at a local museum. Although the work would be commercial rather than artistic, Marcos accepted it for the sake of his daughters. Upon hearing of his new position and steady income, Monica informally agreed to allow the girls to spend three nights with Marcos every week.

DISCUSSION AND CONCLUSION

According to Charles Horton Cooley's looking-glass self (1964), the self is the product of our social interactions with other people. How we view ourselves is influenced by our impressions of how others perceive us. This involves a three-phase process through which we develop our self-concept: first by imagining how we present ourselves to others; then, by imagining how others evaluate us; and finally, by developing a sense of self as a result of these impressions. Marcos' inability to earn a family wage negatively affected Monica's image of him as a good provider and, in turn, his self-esteem suffered. His low self-esteem was further exacerbated by Monica's decision to divorce. After the job offer, Marcos was pleased, in part, because he knew it was significant in elevating Monica's perception of him as a man and as a father. Although Monica's impression of Marcos is important to him, so is the impression of the art community. Especially since the new job offer, Marcos is reminded that a large part of his self-image, as well as self-worth, is tied to his status as an artist.

Negotiations, or the attempts to reach agreement with others concerning an objective, underlie much of our social behavior (Schaefer and Lamm 1998). Marcos' case illustrates how the social order is continually being constructed and altered through interpersonal negotiations. An example of a failed negotiation, from Marcos' perspective, occurred the night Monica asked for a divorce. Although he pleaded with her to reconsider, she did not. Another round of negotiations took place in the courtroom, after which a judge decided on a divorce settlement, physical custody of the girls, and child support. Monica threatened to renegotiate the settlement when Marcos fell behind on child support payments. Last, a subtler example of negotiation occurred after Marcos' job offer, when Monica informally allowed him more frequent contact with their children.

A few sociological observations can be made about Marcos' case. First, some men are more oriented toward parenting than others are, and would do as good a job fathering their children as their ex-wives would do mothering them, if not better. As gender roles become more androgynous, this may become more prevalent. Second, traditional custody arrangements limit the contact that most divorced fathers have with their children. Like many men, Marcos initially was granted very limited visitation rights; this also limits the influence that fathers have on their children. Thus, limited visitations may lead to a decrease in fathers' emotional and financial commitments to their children. Finally, some legal arrangements, when influenced by traditional gender role stereotypes, may simply be unfair. Even though Marcos had primary responsibility for the girls' care prior to the divorce, Monica, like most divorced mothers, was granted physical custody after the divorce.

Most married people who get divorced often try to get on with their lives as quickly as possible. Although the negative stigma associated with divorce has lessened, some stigma remains. Thus, the process of divorced people reestablishing normal behaviors takes place in a social context that strongly encourages marriage. Further, the process is exacerbated by the social, psychological, and economic consequences of divorce.

The focus of this chapter has been the economic consequences of divorce. Although it is generally not intentional, poverty may be seen as a latent dysfunction of divorce. Even so, the economic consequences of divorce are not evenly distributed among spouses: ex-wives generally have a more difficult time than ex-husbands do obtaining equitable divorce settlements; the implementation of no-fault divorce laws has exacerbated this pattern. Further, mothers are granted physical custody more frequently than are fathers, and many fathers do not consistently honor court-ordered child support agreements. This, coupled with the fact that women earn, on the average, less than their male counterparts, places divorced women and their children at a distinct disadvantage.

Since many of the interpersonal factors that influence divorce are known, intervention strategies may be incorporated to reduce these risks, and consequently, the overall number of people who experience downward social mobility, poverty, and other negative consequences of divorce. However, we must consider the structural or societal-level influences on divorce outcomes, as well. Peterson's (1996b) recent analysis illustrates that "there is a significant gender gap in the economic consequences of divorce, [and] that this gap results in financial hardships for many divorced women and their children" (p. 539). Such a difference in the economic consequences of divorce for men and women "is unconscionable for a legal system and a society committed to fairness, justice and equality" (Weitzman 1996, p. 538). Thus, legal reform and changes in public policy will be necessary to correct this inequity.

NOTES

1. This decrease may be attributed, in part, to the graying of the U.S. population and the fact that most divorces occur in the earlier years of marriage (Appelbaum and Chambliss 1997).

2. However, one exception to this trend is Japan, where divorce is still considered disgraceful, especially for women (Soroka and Bryjak 1995).

3. According to Beeghley (1996, pp. 106), a "vicious cycle of poverty" occurs because the economic situation of the poor combines with other aspects of life in "a reciprocal cause-and-effect way that produces persistent poverty."

4. A recent study of child care costs for over seven million employed women with children under age 15 showed the typical amount spent per week was $54 (Brayfield and Hofferth 1995).

5. It has been suggested that men are more likely to marry again than women are because they derive greater benefits from marriage (Macionis 1997).

REFERENCES

Anderson, Margaret L. 1997. *Thinking about Women: Sociological Perspectives on Sex and Gender*. 4th ed. Boston: Allyn & Bacon.

Arendell, Terry. 1992. "After Divorce: Investigations into Father Absence." *Gender & Society* 6: 562–586.

Appelbaum, Richard P., and William J. Chambliss. 1997. *Sociology*. New York: Addison-Wesley Educational Publishers Inc.

Becker, Howard S. 1963. *The Outsiders: Studies in the Sociology of Deviance*. New York: Free Press.

Beeghley, Leonard. 1996. *The Structure of Social Stratification in the United States*. Boston: Allyn and Bacon.

Bellah, Robert S., Richard Madsen, William M. Sullivan, Ann Swidler, and Steven M.

Tipton. 1985. *Habits of the Heart: Individualism and Commitment in American Life*. New York: Harper & Row.

Berger, Peter L., and Thomas Luckmann. 1966. *The Social Construction of Reality: A Treatise in the Sociology of Knowledge*. Garden City, N.Y.: Anchor Books.

Bernard, Jesse. 1972. *The Future of Marriage*. New York: Bantam.

Blumer, Herbert. 1969. *Symbolic Interactionism: Perspective and Method*. Englewood Cliffs, N.J.: Prentice-Hall.

Brayfield, April, and Sandra L. Hofferth. 1995. "Balancing the Family Budget: Differences in Child Care Expenditures by Race/Ethnicity, Economic Status, and Family Structure." *Social Science Quarterly* 76: 158–177.

Cherlin, Andrew. 1981 (1990, rev. ed.). *Marriage, Divorce and Remarriage*. Cambridge, Mass.: Harvard University Press.

Cooley, Charles Horton. 1964 [1902]. *Human Nature and the Social Order*. New York: Schocken Books.

Eitzen, D. Stanley, and Maxine Baca Zinn. 1997. *Social Problems*. 7th ed. Boston: Allyn & Bacon.

Farley, John E. 1998. *Sociology*. 4th ed. Englewood Cliffs, N.J.: Prentice-Hall.

Gerstel, Naomi. 1988. "Divorce, Gender and Social Integration." *Gender & Society* 2: 343–367.

Goffman, Erving. 1959. *The Presentation of Self in Everyday Life*. Garden City, N.Y.: Anchor Books.

Lindgren, J. R., and N. Taub. 1993. *The Law of Sex Discrimination*. Minneapolis: West Publishing Company.

Macionis, John J. 1997. *Sociology*. Upper Saddle River, N.J.: Prentice-Hall.

Merton, Robert K. 1968. *Social Theory and Social Structure*. New York: Free Press.

National Center for Health Statistics. 1996. "Births, Marriages, Divorces, and Deaths for November 1995." *Monthly Vital Statistics Report* 44 (May): 11.

———. 1997. "Births, Marriages, Divorces, and Deaths for August 1996." *Monthly Vital Statistics Report* 45 (March): 1–18.

Peterson, Richard R. 1996a. "A Re-evaluation of the Economic Consequences of Divorce." *American Sociological Review* 61: 528–536.

———. 1996b. "Statistical Errors, Faulty Conclusions, Misguided Policy: Reply to Weitzman." *American Sociological Review* 61: 539–540.

Renzetti, Claire M., and Daniel J. Curran. 1995. *Women, Men, and Society*. Boston: Allyn and Bacon.

———. 1998. *Living Sociology*. Boston: Allyn and Bacon.

Schaefer, Richard T., and Robert P. Lamm. 1998. *Sociology*. New York: McGraw-Hill.

Simmel, Georg. 1950. *Sociology of Georg Simmel*. Translated by K. Wolff. Glencoe, Ill.: Free Press.

Soroka, Michael P., and George J. Bryjak. 1995. *Social Problems: A World at Risk*. Boston: Allyn & Bacon.

Smock, Pamela J. 1994. "Gender and the Short-run Economic Consequences of Marital Disruption." *Social Forces*, 73: 243–62.

U.S. Department of Commerce, Bureau of the Census. 1996. *Statistical Abstract of the United States*. Washington, D.C.: U.S. Government Printing Office.

———. 1997. "Poverty in the United States, 1996." *Current Population Reports: Consumer Income, Report P60–198*. Washington, D.C.: U.S. Government Printing Office. <http://www.census.gov>.

Weitzman, Lenore J. 1985. *The Divorce Revolution: The Unexpected Social and Economic Consequences for Women and Children in America*. New York: Free Press.

———. 1996. "The Economic Consequences of Divorce are Still Unequal: Comment on Peterson." *American Sociological Review*. 61: 537–538.

8

Child Support/Deadbeat Dads

Kimberly A. Folse

Don't Scarr [sic] Fathers Away . . .

—Anonymous Deadbeat Dad

INTRODUCTION

Each year billions of child support dollars are transferred from nonresident to custodial parents. About 2.8 million children are entitled to receive child support, but three out of ten parents who owe child support pay nothing. While the number of dollars collected increases each year, the current shortfall in child support payments is estimated to be $10.5 billion dollars or about 37 percent of what is owed. According to a 1996 report to Congress entitled *Child Support Enforcement: 20th Annual Report* (DHHS 1996, p. 3), about 25 percent of fathers who owe child support pay nothing.

During 1995, more than $10.8 billion in child support payments was collected from noncustodial parents. Over the next ten years, the goal is to increase child support collections by $24 billion (DHHS 1996). This growth in collections results from increasing governmental involvement by first establishing orders for child support and, second, through the passage of laws to enforce these orders.

Child support enforcement legislation was first initiated in 1950 under the aegis of the social security program. Then, in 1975, the Child Support Enforcement program (CSE) was established to enforce the previous child support initiative. Since that time Congress has passed additional legislation intended to increase the enforcement power of CSE and to establish standards and procedures for the collection of child support. Individual states, following federal guidelines, establish their own laws for collecting from the responsible noncustodial parent. For example, in an effort to ensure payment is regular and timely, CSE agencies are entitled to invoke automatic wage withholding, call for revocation of professional and personal drivers' licenses, and report fathers to credit bureaus should they fall behind in their child support payments.

One important piece of welfare reform legislation, the Personal Responsibility and Work Opportunity Reconciliation Act of 1996 (P.L. 104–193), addresses child support enforcement laws. Enforcement is a key factor in reducing state and federal welfare expenditures. According to the Secretary of Health and Human Resources, stricter enforcement of child support is expected to result in $4.2 billion in welfare savings. One portion of the target population is low-income fathers of children who are most likely to receive welfare assistance.

By definition, a deadbeat is one who fails to fulfill a contractual obligation. Thus, the assumption pertaining to a deadbeat is that the responsible party is capable of meeting the financial obligation but chooses not to do so. Deadbeats are thought to be lazy, irresponsible, or belligerent parents who try to avoid paying thousands of dollars in back child support by fleeing from state to state or by refusing to work to avoid paying higher child support.

Compelling public pressures indicate that any parent, if not paying regular child support, should be considered a deadbeat. The deadbeat parent is a term used to identify those who fail to meet their court-mandated child support payments. However, deadbeat dad is a more familiar term because fathers comprise the majority of child support enforcement cases, and the concept has gained considerable notoriety within the recent past. Well-to-do professionals are targeted by government agencies but, until recently, many low-income individuals who desire to support their children but are unable to do so have been the primary focus of these collection efforts. The question that guides the analysis of this social problem is: Can low-income fathers pay the child support mandated by the court? This chapter will focus on such fathers who, because of their financial circumstances, are at risk of being labeled a deadbeat.

OVERVIEW OF THE PROBLEM OF DEADBEAT DADS

Noncustodial and nonresident fathers are disproportionately young, nonwhite, unmarried at the time of the child's birth, and poorly educated. They earn about 33 percent less than a resident father; approximately 20 percent are estimated to earn less than $6,000 annually. Twenty percent experience problems with drugs and alcohol (Garfinkel, McLanahan, and Hanson 1998) and many have served jail time. This symbolic stigma creates a barrier to their finding a decent paying job which would enhance their ability to pay child support. Low-income parents who experience difficulty in meeting their financial obligation are at greater risk of falling into the deadbeat parent category.

During the 1960s, the number of families seeking welfare increased substantially because of the rising number of single-parent households. These families, due either to separation, divorce, or never-married mothers, created tremendous pressure on state welfare programs, but it was the never-married mothers who created the greatest financial burden. Between 1960 and 1975, the number of children under the age of 18 years living with a mother who had never been married increased 427 percent (Bureau of the Census 1997a). Shifting the responsibility of financial support from the state to responsible fathers is the primary goal of the Child Support Enforcement program.

Absence of legal enforcement mechanisms in the early years of the program made the identification and collection of child support difficult. To enhance enforcement efforts, Congress passed several major pieces of legislation. During the 1980s, two legislative acts enhanced state efforts to enforce support from non-resident parents. The Child Support Enforcement Amendments of 1984 (P.L. 98–378) established the mechanism for collecting support such as information-gathering techniques for identifying and establishing paternity, guidelines for setting child support orders, collecting support through the withholding and garnisheeing of wages, intercepting tax refunds, revocation of driver's and trade licenses, reporting to credit bureaus, property seizure, denial of passports and, ultimately, the imposition of jail time for nonsupport. The Family Support Act of 1988 (P.L. 100–485) placed a stronger emphasis on establishing paternity for children born out of wedlock, thereby increasing the percentage of identified fathers and facilitating the establishment of an increasing number of child support orders.

In 1996, child support enforcement was a major component of welfare legislation. Passage of the Personal Responsibility and Work Opportunity Reconciliation Act of 1996 (P.L. 104–193) abolished the Aid to Families with Dependent Children (AFDC) public assistance program and replaced it with Temporary Assistance to Needy Families (TANF). It also created a strong interagency relationship between Federal assistance funds and the states' compliance with federal child support guidelines. Under the new law, states are required to increase the percentage of paternity established and to increase collections from parents whose children are on public assistance—even ordering fathers who owe support into work activities—or jeopardize their share of Federal funds.

Although a delinquent obligor can be charged with either civil or criminal contempt, most states have statutes making nonsupport a criminal offense. However, in 1998, Congress passed the 1998 Deadbeat Parents Punishment Act (P.L. 105–187). Parents who refuse to provide support for their children, who owe more than $5,000, and who travel across state or country lines with the intent to evade child support payments or, who owe in excess of $10,000, and remain (willfully) unpaid for a period of two years, can be charged with a federal felony.

Proving willful nonsupport is critical in establishing a parent is a deadbeat. Although the elements of criminal abandonment or nonsupport vary from state to state, typical elements include desertion, nonsupport, a culpable state of mind, and the ability to provide support. Establishing culpability depends on agency ability to establish that the obligor's mental state is one of deliberate or perverse design of neglect, malice, or intentional or deliberate breach of duty of support (*Burris v. State*, 382 NE2nd 963 [Ind. App. 1978]). On the other hand, it is up to the obligor to prove that non-support was not willful or excusable. Ability to pay is determined according to the defendant's ability to earn as determined by the court. The lack of means is not a supportable defense (Reynolds 1986, pp. 131–134).

In the case study that follows the special qualities of the social-interactionist paradigm are used to explore the meaning actors attach to behavior, including their own. By viewing the father's behavior from this perspective, it is possible to gain an understanding of the special circumstances affecting the decision of whether or not to pay child support. The purpose of this case analysis is to provide one plausible explanation for the nonpayment of child support as viewed from the father's perspective.

Peter Berger and Thomas Luckmann (1967) observe that social interaction is influenced by attaching names to events and things. Thus, one who is labeled a deadbeat will experience the negative social consequences attached to that label. Within this context, nonpayment of child support has meaning both for the person who fails to pay and for those who expect him to do so. The perspective of such forms of deviant behavior, offered by Pfuhl and Henry (1993), is useful for the analysis of this social problem. "Basically deviance refers to behaviors and attributes that people define as problematic. The basis of such definitions rests on the definer's interests, which are felt to be jeopardized or threatened in some way by these acts or conditions" (p. 23). Fathers' rule-breaking behavior, from the social constructionist perspective, is assumed to be a matter of choice. But for low-income fathers paying child support is perceived as the problem. Although nonpayment or even partial payment is considered by some fathers to be a viable alternative for adapting to this situation, the state views nonpayment as jeopardizing the well-being of children.

The goal of the welfare legislation of 1996 is to transfer responsibility for the support of children from the state to parents, and more particularly to the responsible father. Those who fail to fulfill this financial obligation to their children can be classified into three distinct groups. The first group is comprised of fathers whose children receive benefits from the Temporary Assistance to Needy Families (TANF) program. TANF and CSE programs work together; women who receive welfare must cooperate with CSE program officials by identifying the father(s) of their children. Those unwilling to do so risk losing their welfare benefits. Group one fathers remain in this program until their child reaches legal age and until any outstanding child support payment is paid in full, including any interest that was added to the balance. Group one fathers are the least financially well-off.

The second group of fathers, a combined low- to high-income group, are so clustered because the mothers of their children use locator services to find them, the mothers seek to establish support orders, or mothers seek assistance for enforcing extant support orders. New CSE cases and collection increases are usually derived from this low- to high-income group.

The final group of fathers, not part of the CSE caseload, have support orders but through the use of lawyers are successful in avoiding involvement in the CSE program. These fathers are generally the most financially secure. The composition of this third group of fathers is due, in large part, to the legal process. Fathers who demonstrate good cause, have a written agreement that their wages will not be garnisheed, or have established that the court order need not be administered through the CSE program can make their payments privately. Such private payments are not tracked by the CSE program.

Although deadbeat fathers can be identified from among all three groups, most are likely to be members of the first two groups. The following case will focus on fathers whose low yearly income level place them at risk of failing to fulfill their court-mandated financial obligation to their children. The case represents a composite of low-income fathers who owe child support. The data are drawn from a statewide survey of noncustodial parents (n=477), of whom 185 fathers had an annual income of $20,000 or less. Eighty percent of the fathers earned $10,000 or less per year at the time the data were gathered.

Hispanic fathers are disproportionately represented in this low-income group (Folse 1997). Comprising 27.6 percent of the Texas population, Hispanics are disproportional in the sample in that they represent 54 percent of the child support enforcement cases for the counties studied. In this regard, this state caseload is similar to other jurisdictions where low-income minority parents comprise the majority of nonpaying parents (see, for example, Bartfeld and Meyer 1993; Garasky 1997). Overrepresentation of minorities in child support enforcement cases is also reflective of a nationwide pattern involving welfare recipients (Bureau of the Census 1997b, Table 745).

CARLOS: A CASE STUDY

As an unskilled worker Carlos earns approximately $10,000 a year. Last year he had one place of employment; the year prior he worked for two companies. Believing his child support order is too high, Carlos views the CSE program as unfair. Although willing to support his children, Carlos' lack of a steady income affects his ability to pay. His child was on welfare previously; thus part of the debt Carlos owes is based on a repayment to the state for past benefits received. Carlos further claims the child's mother is negligent in that she does not spend what support money is paid in a manner that directly benefits his child.

In addition to the $140 per month support obligation, Carlos is required to pay an additional $25 each month for the money owed in arrears. This amount is formidable given that Carlos remarried and is supporting another child from his current wife's previous relationship. Required by law to inform his employer about the court order, the support money is withheld from Carlos' paycheck. Based on the support state guidelines (*Vernon's Texas Codes* 1994), the amount deducted is approximately 17 percent of his gross income. Nevertheless, should Carlos be two months delinquent, this debt is reported to national credit bureaus, thereby establishing this debt as a part of his credit record. If the delinquency should be three months or more, up to 65 percent of his earnings can be garnisheed.

The CSE assists mothers in filing federal and state tax refund intercept papers that allow any tax returns to be sent directly to the CSE. However, such action will not likely benefit the child because the state will apply whatever amount is recovered to the father's arrears balance. If Carlos were to seek financial relief through filing bankruptcy, the child support obligation remains a nondischargable debt. Should Carlos decide to leave the state to avoid this financial obligation, failure to pay for a one-year period will result in a federal felony offense being charged against him. Carlos' picture and the amount of child support owed also could be displayed on a post office poster or on the Internet.

The reasons for nonpayment of child support can be established in the circumstances in which the parent is involved. From the symbolic interaction perspective, behavior is viewed as a rationally determined outcome based on an assessment of one's environment. Economic factors are perhaps the most critical in establishing this decision. The question germane to this case study is: how can a low-income father pay? Two plausible explanations for why low-income fathers are unable to meet their support obligation are presented, both of which are economic in nature. A third explanation, new family formation, is presented as an additional factor for why fathers fail to pay child support.

A Regressive System of Child Support

According to the June 1997 *Child Support Report*, the poorest noncustodial fathers pay an average 28 percent of their income for child support. The average obligated father, on the other hand, pays approximately 15 percent of his income for such support. It is obvious that child support is regressive. Elaine Sorensen (1996: 5) notes that a large number of delinquent fathers have incomes low enough to meet the standard for food stamp eligibility. If present policies are intended to ensure that fathers pay support, Sorensen argues, the problems of low-income fathers must be addressed as a special case.

Low-income fathers, especially those unmarried at the time their children are born, are least likely to pay support (Bartfeld and Meyer 1993). What increases compliance, according to Bartfeld and Meyer, is an increase in income. Increasing the level of income at two times the single-person poverty level significantly increases compliance. When income reaches three times the single person poverty level, compliance increases to 87 percent.

Job skills are also related to income level. Without such skills many fathers have little potential for enhancing their income to a level sufficient to support themselves and their children. One North Carolina study (Haskins 1988) supports this contention. Ron Haskins concludes that low-income fathers earned approximately 60 percent of the U.S. worker average and one-half of the delinquent fathers experienced unemployment sometime during the preceding two years.

However, it is likely that fathers' economic and personal circumstance will change over time. Indeed, it is this assumption which serves as the basis for establishing the base upon which the child support order is determined. Fathers' incomes are expected to increase over time, especially among the youngest fathers. However, the income level for fathers such as Carlos often decline. In the following verbatim statements the difficulty of this situation is demonstrated. According to one father,

I've been paying little at a time 'cause I have no job I've been trying to pay 25 to 50 a month when I do side jobs but at least I try some people don't even pay anything. I have to pay anymore sure I'll pay back pay as soon as I get money on the side jobs or if I get a full time job. I have been laid-off since May of this year. When I was working I was only making $192.00 every 2 weeks. Which is $389.00 every month, and I had to pay $240.00 for 2 orders of child support because I have 2 girls with two different mothers and it was very hard to make it with only $149.00 every month.

The plight of yet another low-income father further demonstrates this problem. "The only problem with my child support, is when there is a lay-off, or I lose my job, and I have to catch up with my support. I know that my child have to dress and eat. But it is not like she will starve. I think that I should be at least be excused for the time that I am unemployed." Such comments point to the obvious. Irregular employment and low wages are not conducive to making regular child support payments.

When child support orders are established, the father's income level is documented based either on existing employment or on potential employment determined on the basis of the father's past work history. Future unemployment is not a consideration, although extreme financial hardships are known to develop. As indicated by the first father, more than 60 percent of his income is paid out for child support. However, the law allows for up to 65 percent of a person's earnings to be garnisheed. In such circumstances the father is left with little, making it almost impossible to be self-supporting.

Adjustment for changed economic circumstances is not an option for such fathers. Even if they are unemployed, fathers are required to maintain the payments at the level ordered and to make such payments on time. Only after a period of thirty-six months beyond the initial court order will the CSE agree to review a case, but only if requested to do so by either parent. In the meantime, balances accrue as does the interest on these balances. Low-income fathers like Carlos also are more aggressively pursued and prosecuted than are other better-positioned fathers who avoid making their payments (Thompson 1994).

Being part of the CSE program does affect how fathers view the system, and low-income fathers generally cite the program as being unfair to men. As one father stated: "I have nothing against paying child support cuz I love my son. . . . I just wish there were more laws for [because] the paying father always needs an attorney and I can't afford it."

Individuals who are more financially well-off than Carlos are known to fare much better. For example, despite a 1995 Executive Order that requires government agencies to withhold the wages of federal employees, a 1997 Department of Health and Human Services report revealed that contractors, doctors, and medical researchers employed in federal programs owed a total of $21.5 million in unpaid child support (Meckler 1997).

New Family Formation

Despite a separation, divorce, or death of a partner, most adults create new family situations (Coleman and Ganong 1991). Carlos is no exception; he has a second family. Such new family formations are acknowledged by the CSE in some states, but adjustments in support payments are generally negligible. It is not unusual that one child in the newly formed family is from yet another union, and that child may not be the beneficiary of child support paid from the responsible father. Janet Seltzer (1991) found that when the noncustodial parent creates a new family, he diverts attention to the new family and child support decreases, as does visitation. Martha Hill (1984), on the other hand, reported that new family formation actually increases the probability of payment, except when the mother of the child remarries, at which time payments cease. According to Hill's assessment, Carlos is just as likely to be in compliance as is a father who remains single. Nevertheless, responsibility for two families represents a financial challenge, as is suggested in the following statement. "I am remarried with three small girl's. I only make about $800.00 a month. It takes's all the money I have to support my family and pay bills & feed & buy diapers. I make less than $10,000 a year and live from paycheck to paycheck."

Deadbeat Dads

When a noncustodial parent falls three months behind in payment, he is considered a deadbeat dad. Although the CSE is moving away from this descriptive identifier, these fathers are informally identified as deadbeats and the legal system views them as such. Such forms of rule-breaking behavior can be explained in two ways: (1) people are compelled to engage in unacceptable behavior, and (2) deviant behavior arises as a consequence of choice, decision, judgment, reason, and motive (Pfuhl and Henry 1993, p. 49). The utility of viewing the nonpayment of child support problem from the social construction of reality perspective lies in establishing a link between instructional structure and individual situations which account for deviant behavior (Heimer and Matsueda 1994; Heimer 1995).

The label deadbeat does not establish why a father is delinquent but merely that he is delinquent. Although the public may not be interested in explanations, Carlos' failure to comply is not consistent with the definition of deadbeat who is able to meet the conditions of the contract but chooses not to do so. Rather, the father cannot meet the financial obligation and is, therefore, delinquent. Despite this conceptual difference, both types of rule-breakers are identified as deadbeat.

In light of legal and social consequences, factors other than financial may influence one to withhold child support. Pfuhl and Henry (1993, p. 60) offer some insight: Peoples' definitions of their circumstances help inform their actions. Although nonpayment may result from personal choice, the economic circumstances are an important factor in the father's decision to withhold child support, as does his view of the fairness factor. Within this context, it is noteworthy that analysts for the Institute for Research on Poverty found that even if all noncustodial Hispanic parents paid child support as required, the Hispanic poverty gap would be reduced by a mere 2 percent (Garfinkel, Meyer, and Sandefur 1992).

DISCUSSION AND CONCLUSION

Efforts to curb government spending on family assistance programs requires that an increased emphasis be placed on lower income parents. As the case of Carlos illustrates, low-income fathers are most at risk of being labeled deadbeat because of their precarious financial situation. Earning $10,000 to $20,000 a year, these fathers represent the working poor who are subject to periodic unemployment. They also lack the educational and trade skills that could enhance their earning potential.

For fathers like Carlos, the choice of nonpayment is not intended to cause harm or to deprive the children involved, but results in large part from self-interest; that is, his economic survival. Nonpayment, then, symbolizes a personal perception of, and adaptation to, current circumstances. From the perspective of the state, nonpayment represents a form of deviance that has been transformed into a social problem. Such definitions are important for these establish the boundaries of socially acceptable behavior. The state's emphasis is on the monetary obligation, but an acceptable standard of living also is an important issue. Society views the choice of nonpayment as jeopardizing the well-being of children.

Efforts to control the child support problem will undoubtedly lead to the identification of more deadbeat dads. However, if enforcement efforts continue to focus on low-income fathers such as Carlos, it is unlikely enforcement and compliance will make a difference in the lives of the children affected or that the savings in public funds will be substantial.

Perhaps the question most germane to this social problem should be: what characteristics do these noncustodial parents have in common? The available data suggest that fathers who fulfill their child support obligation are able to do so because they have sufficient income above their basic survival needs. The relationship appears clear: as income increases above the poverty level, child support compliance also increases.

The deadbeat label is a consequence of a structural arrangement which influences the meaning society attributes to fathers whose failure to pay is defined as a form of selfishness that is motivated by a desire to cause hardship for their children. Although economic hardship characterizes the lives of low-income fathers such as Carlos, the CSE program is structured in a way that enhances the probability of failure. Given the economic circumstances of low-income fathers, it is unlikely that the Department of Health and Human Resources will reach the goals of reducing welfare expenditure by $4.2 billion through increased enforcement alone. Indeed, if support payment is to be encouraged among the working poor, it is in the best interest of policy makers not to "scarr" fathers away from their responsibilities. Rather, a social policy which encourages people to make positive choices is imperative to the ultimate success of the child support program.

The federal government's pressure to establish paternity, create more orders, and enhance collection efforts to collect more child support will continue to intensify enforcement efforts. Although more middle-income parents will come under scrutiny, lower-income parents will continue to be the target of these efforts because this portion of the American population contains the majority of out-of-wedlock births and the primary welfare base.

Two recent enforcement mechanisms focus particular attention on tracking parents who owe child support. Both focus on the workplace. The first is a mandate requiring federal agencies to do a better job of identifying employees who owe child support. The second is the implementation of a nationwide new-hire database. Under this law every business is required to report all new employees to a state child support agency which, in turn, will report this information to the Federal Office of Child Support Enforcement. The intent of the law is to track parents who cross state lines to avoid paying support; the reality is the new law will facilitate tracking and the location of any parent who owes child support.

REFERENCES

Bartfeld, Judith, and Daniel L. Meyer. 1993. *Are There Really Deadbeat Dads? The Relationship Between Ability to Pay, Enforcement, and Compliance in Non-Marital Child Support Cases. Discussion Paper* # 994–93. Institute for Research on Poverty. University of Wisconsin-Madison.

Berger, Peter, and Thomas Luckmann. 1967. *The Social Construction of Reality*. Garden City, N.Y.: Anchor Books.

Bureau of the Census. 1997a. *Current Population Reports, Series P-20–506. "Marital Status and Living Arrangements: March 1997* (Update). CH-5. Washington, D.C.: " U.S. Government Printing Office. <http://www.census.gov/population/socidemo/ms-la/tabch-5 txt>.

———. 1997b. *Statistical Abstract of the United States: 1997.* Washington, D.C.: U.S. Government Printing Office.

Child Support Report 14, No. 5. 1997, June. Washington, D.C.: Department of Health and Human Services.

Coleman, Marylin, and Lawrence H. Ganong. 1991. "Remarriage and Stepfamily Research in the 1980s: Increased Interest in an Old Family Form." In A. Booth, ed., *Contemporary Families: Looking Forward, Looking Back,* pp. 192–207. Minneapolis: National Council on Family Relations.

DHHS. 1996. *Child Support Enforcement: 20th Annual Report to Congress.* Washington, D.C.: Department of Health and Human Services.

Folse, Kimberly A. 1997. "Hispanic Fathers and the Child Support Enforcement Experience." *Journal of Multicultural Social Work* 6: 139–158.

Garasky, Steven. 1997. "User Fees and Family Policy: Attempts to Recover Costs for State Provided Child Support Enforcement Services." *Politics and Society* 25: 100–108.

Garfinkel, Irwin, Sara S. McLanahan, and Thomas L. Hanson. 1998. "A Patchwork Portrait of Nonresident Fathers." In Irwin Garfinkel, Sara McLanahan, Daniel Meyer, and Judith Seltzer, eds., *Fathers Under Fire: The Revolution in Child Support Enforcement,* pp. 31–60. New York: Russell Sage Foundation.

Garfinkel, Irwin, Daniel R. Meyer, and Gary D. Sandefur. 1992. "The Effects of Alternative Child Support Systems on Blacks, Hispanics, and Non-Hispanic Whites." *Social Service Review* 66: 505–523.

Haskins, Ron. 1988. "Child Support: A Father's View." In Alfred J. Kahn and Sheila B. Kamerman, eds., *Child Support: From Debt Collection to Social Policy,* pp. 306–327. Newbury Park, Calif.: Sage.

Heimer, Karen. 1995. "Gender, Race, and the Pathways to Delinquency: An Interactionist Explanation." In J. Hagan and R. D. Peterson, eds., *Crime and Inequality,* pp. 140–173. Stanford: Stanford University Press.

Heimer, Karen, and Ross L. Matsueda. 1994. "Role-taking, Role-Commitment and Delinquency: A Theory of Differential Social Control." *American Sociological Review* 59: 365–90.

Hill, Martha. 1984. *PSID Analysis of Matched Pairs of Ex-Spouses: The Relation of Economic Resources and New Family Obligations to Child Support Payment.* Ann Arbor: University of Michigan, Institute for Social Research.

Meckler, Lynn. 1997, September 14. "Agency Called Lax in Child Support." *Austin American Statesman,* p. A29.

Pfuhl, Erdwin H., and Stuart Henry. 1993. *The Deviance Process.* 3rd. ed. New York: Aldine de Gruyter.

Reynolds, Mark R., ed. 1986. *Essentials for Attorneys in Child Support Enforcement.* Washington, D.C.: U.S. Department of Health and Human Resources.

Seltzer, Janet. 1991. "Relationships Between Fathers and Children Who Live Apart: The Father's Role After Separation." *Journal of Marriage and Family* 53: 79–102.

Sorensen, Elaine. 1996. "Low-Income Noncustodial Fathers." *Child Support Report* 18: 5.

Thompson, Ross. 1994. "The Role of the Father After Divorce." *The Future of Children* 4: 210–235.

Vernon's Texas Codes Annotated. 1994. Vol. 2. St. Paul, Minn.: West Publishing.

9

Homelessness

Debra M. McCallum and John M. Bolland

INTRODUCTION

Mobile, a city of 202,000 people, is the second largest in Alabama. Like other cities located on the coast, Mobile has a long and glamorous (although in some minds, checkered) history. The influence of the early French settlement is everywhere. The population is largely Catholic (an aberration in the predominantly Protestant South). The streets in the old downtown section of the city bear French or Catholic names (Dauphin Street, Conception Street, St. Emanuel Street), and the downtown park is named Bienville Square. Like its more famous neighbor located 100 miles to the west, Mobile celebrates Mardi Gras, and much of the city literally closes down for several days to enjoy it thoroughly. Mardi Gras occurs at the time when the azaleas are beginning to bloom, producing a riot of color in the parks and yards of the old mansions that line Dauphin Street and Government Street in the near downtown area. Mobile, called the Azalea City, capitalizes on its botanical beauty by hosting an Azalea Run each year and naming an Azalea Maid each week.

Like other cities in the United States, the appealing qualities of Mobile mask inner-city problems. Houses in two of its most historical downtown areas—Fort Conde and Detante Square—are boarded up and deteriorating, ravaged by weather and neglect. The commercial area of downtown was largely abandoned by merchants during the 1970s, and by the early 1990s entire blocks of storefronts stood empty or boarded up. Some parts of downtown are making a comeback, thanks in part to a new convention center and investment in a number of downtown restaurants. But much of the downtown remains empty. Several close-in neighborhoods are riddled with abandoned homes and businesses as well, and drugs and crime have become endemic in these areas. And there is homelessness.

OVERVIEW OF THE PROBLEM: HOMELESSNESS IN NATIONAL AND LOCAL PERSPECTIVE

Homelessness is perhaps one of the nation's most difficult social problems, at least partially because it is so visible. The homeless are seemingly everywhere: on the streets in alleys and doorways; under bridges; in parks; and in shelters of all types. But does the prominence of a population necessarily correspond to the size of that population? This question has generated considerable debate, and it is far from settled today.

Former Governor Mario Cuomo, reporting for the 1983 Governors' Conference, described any attempt to enumerate the homeless as "counting the uncountable" (quoted in Rossi 1989, p. 47). The truth in this statement has been supported by numerous attempts to estimate the size of the homeless population. The late Mitch Snyder, a homeless advocate and founder of the CCNV shelter in Washington, D.C., placed the figure at a million in the late 1970s. However, he derived this estimate in a rather unscientific manner: "We got on the phone, we made a lot of calls, we talked to a lot of people" (interview with Ted Koppel, quoted in Jencks 1994, p. 2). Snyder went on to say that this estimate "has no meaning, no value." But it has considerable political value, and based on this estimate homelessness found its way onto the national political agenda, where it has stayed ever since. Perhaps as a way of ensuring that it remained there, subsequent estimates by homeless advocates were even higher, reaching between two and three million (Hombs and Snyder 1982). The Reagan administration, embarrassed by the magnitude of these estimates, asked the Department of Housing and Urban Development to derive its own estimate; its study, which was based on an equally flawed methodology, concluded that there were only between 250,000 and 350,000 homeless people in the United States (U.S. Department of Housing and Urban Development, 1984).

Since then, some of the rhetoric has died down, and most current estimates of homelessness (see Burt 1992, for a review) hover between 500,000 and 750,000 on any given night. However, when these figures are aggregated over the course of a year (or a lifetime), they suggest a much larger problem. A national telephone survey (Link et al. 1995) reveals that 7.4 percent of adults report that they have been literally homeless at some point during their lives, and 4.6 percent report being homeless at some point during the previous five years. This produces estimates that 13.5 million adult residents of the United States have directly experienced homelessness, and that 5.7 million have been homeless in the recent past.

On any given night, Mobile has between 400 and 500 people who are literally homeless (i.e., who spend the night on the streets or in shelters, group homes, treatment programs, and short-term motels). Over the course of a year, between 3,300 and 3,600 people are literally homeless in Mobile (Bolland and McCallum 1995). Thus, a small but significant segment of Mobile's population (1.5 percent) is literally homeless during the course of a year. None of these figures include either the near homeless (i.e., those who are hanging onto their housing by the skin of their teeth) or people who are living doubled-up with family or friends; although no one knows exactly the magnitude of this population, many estimate that it is considerably larger than the number of literal homeless.

The magnitude of these statistics, both nationally and locally, is guaranteed to keep the issue of homelessness from slipping into obscurity. But it is useful to consider how popular conceptions of homelessness have changed over the decades. The homeless have been a prominent part of the American landscape for over a century. In the early years, the homeless were largely viewed as winos and bums, riding the rails from city to city or settling into the skid row area that was a part of every large city. Despite these negative images of the homeless, they were largely viewed as harmless eccentrics or "characters" (see Mitchell 1992, for a sympathetic portrayal of several homeless people living in New York's Bowery during the early years of this century). But with the expansion of homelessness during the 1970s, the numbers simply became too large to treat them as harmless eccentrics; rather, their alcohol consumption, their increasing drug use, their increasingly aggressive panhandling, and their increasingly evident mental illness made them something to fear when their numbers were large, and many people began to avoid areas where homeless people congregated.

The causes of homelessness were changing during this period as well. In contrast to substance abuse and personal choice, which were the primary causes of homelessness for their predecessors, many of the new homeless were casualties of a changing economic system (e.g., Blau 1992) that saw high unemployment and the loss of many well-paid jobs. Now, many more people were at risk of becoming homeless; and one of the most often cited statistics held that the typical American family was only two paychecks away from becoming homeless (Gorder 1988). Thus, in popular conception, the causes of homelessness became societal rather than personal and it was much easier for the general population to look upon the homeless sympathetically. In our study of homelessness in Mobile, we found that 28 percent of adult respondents in a telephone survey reported that at some point in their lives they worried about becoming homeless (Bolland and McCallum 1995). This same emphasis on societal causes of homelessness allowed homeless advocates to downplay the importance of personal characteristics as a cause of homelessness, and many of them argued that alcohol and drug abuse occurred after rather than before the onset of homelessness for most homeless people (Baum and Burnes 1993).

The causes of homelessness and the progression of homelessness are much more complex, however, than any of these popular conceptions would suggest. In fact, if homelessness were simply a result of economic restructuring, it could be solved through the creation of jobs. However, the creation of new jobs during the economic recovery of the 1990s did little to alleviate homelessness. To understand why, we must differentiate between the chronic homeless and the short-term homeless. The short-term homeless are largely casualties of a changing economic system; and through vocational retraining, or help finding a job, or even short-term financial support, they are able to get back on their feet. Those who are chronically homeless are the victims of inadequate personal resources, inadequate coping skills, learned helplessness, long-term alcohol or substance abuse, or mental illness. They will not easily escape homelessness, despite programs and support services designed to help them. During the 1990s, these were the homeless people the public saw, and with whom the public largely lost patience.

In Mobile, the chronically homeless congregated primarily in the downtown area and several of the near-in neighborhoods, forming their own social group. This is the area where services for the homeless are located—Salvation Army, Waterfront Mission, Loaves and Fishes Soup Kitchen, Catholic Social Services, the Health Department, and others. The downtown area is located adjacent to the railroad yard, and homeless people riding the rails into Mobile found the downtown area convenient to their stop. It was also an area of vacant buildings, providing convenient shelter for homeless individuals. And finally, there were very few people in the downtown area to complain about the homeless and they were seldom rousted by the police.

With efforts to revitalize downtown, the homeless became an unwelcome fixture on the city's downtown streets and parks. Police became more aggressive in attempting to control the homeless, particularly when they congregated in the downtown parks or panhandled visitors. Some of the new investors in downtown suggested that homeless services should be moved. During the summers, homeless people were banned from Bienville Square during lunchtime. Several years ago, they were evicted from under a bridge in the downtown area where a number of them lived. These efforts to crack down on homelessness reflected the growing view that the chronic homeless were not among the "deserving poor," and mirrored get-tough policies in cities around the country (Stoner 1995). So far, these strategies have done little to reduce homelessness, or to make the chronic homeless less visible.

If a solution is to be found—in Mobile or elsewhere—it must reflect the special circumstances and needs of the homeless. It must take seriously the emphasis of the symbolic interactionists on understanding things from the perspective of the actor, in this case, the homeless individuals. Yet, the homeless are among the least understood segments of the population. Despite the visibility of homelessness in general, individual homeless persons live their lives in such a way as to make them fit into their surroundings—to blend in with the azaleas, as it were, in Mobile. The ability to become invisible is a highly adaptive quality, one necessary for their survival; but it makes homeless people, and homelessness in general, difficult to understand.

At the same time that these get-tough strategies were being implemented, community leaders in the city of Mobile made a commitment to engage in a study of homelessness in the city, to determine the range of needs, and to develop plans for coordinating services and meeting these needs. As part of this study (Bolland and McCallum 1995), we interviewed numerous homeless individuals, social service providers, community leaders, and members of the general population. In the following pages, we will tell the story of the homeless in Mobile by concentrating on the life of one person, a woman we call Sissy. Her story contains elements of all of the stereotypes that one typically associates with homelessness—mental illness, drug and alcohol abuse, and disaffiliation. Her story also includes some surprises that might help us better understand homelessness and why it is such a difficult social problem to solve.

SISSY: A CASE STUDY

We first met Sissy during our 1994–95 study of homelessness in Mobile, and we revisited her in December 1996. When we interviewed Sissy in 1996, she was not homeless; rather, she was in a relationship and living with her boyfriend in a small apartment. She was not working at the time, but was trying to gather her emotional resources and cope with her life one day at a time. The self she developed as a mentally ill homeless woman was struggling to identify a meaningful and manageable role in her current situation.

In presenting the results of our research on homelessness, talking with students and colleagues, and working with communities, we found that many of the questions and concerns about homelessness revolve around the three central issues of past, present, and future. Therefore, we will tell Sissy's story by addressing these three questions: How did you get here? What is it like to be homeless? What does the future hold? These questions bear strong resemblance to the three research objectives promoted by Blumer: "to gain a picture of the inner and private experiences of the individual that seem to constitute the background for the emergence and existence of a given form of conduct; . . . to show the nature of the individual's subjective slant on life; . . . to throw light on the life and operation of the imaginative process" (in Schmidt 1937, p. 194).

How Did You Get Here?

Variations on this question include: Why are you homeless? How did a nice girl like you end up in a place like this? Possibly underlying these is the personally relevant question, could it happen to me? When we asked the question, "How did you get here?" we wanted to know the reasons or causes for a person's homelessness as well as the path that was followed to that point. So it was as much a why question as a how question. We were seeking both the chronological and the motivational answer. The information we received to such a question was complex, often distorted by tricks of memory, intervening events, and reconstructions of the past.

For Sissy the beginning of the chronology was simple—she ran away at the age of 15, got on a bus, and hit the streets of San Diego. She was only gone a month that first time, but it set the stage for repeated episodes of homelessness, of turning to the streets when family and personal circumstances were unbearable. Sissy managed to find herself in unbearable circumstances numerous times; thus the motivational issue emerged—why did she keep getting into such circumstances? For that, we must go back further than the first homeless episode.

Sissy described her family as well-to-do, with her parents' careers being more important than spending time with the children. She recalled her biological father as alcoholic and abusive and has memories of him screaming, hollering, and beating everyone. Her mother left that man, then struggled to raise the three children. She eventually married a man who was out of town quite a bit. Sissy's biological father continued to try to win back the mother, stalking her whenever he was in town. One night when Sissy was 9 years old, her mother had to work and was apprehensive because the father was back in town. In fear and desperation, she locked the three children in the house, gave Sissy, who was the oldest, a gun, and told her if her father came in to shoot him. Fortunately, for all involved, the father did not appear that night. However, the social reality revealed by this memory sets the stage for the meanings Sissy attached through the interpretative process (Blumer 1969) to her later relationships. As Sissy got older, her mother started drinking excessively and became abusive toward the children herself. By the age of 15, Sissy said she began running away just to find something better. Her first trip to the streets of San Diego seemed like fun during the day, but the nights of fear and loneliness were not so fun. A church group found her on the street and gave her enough money to get back home.

Like many other homeless people, the onset of homelessness for Sissy was not an event so much as a process. Sissy was able to identify her first time on the streets and, for her, this represents demarcation in her life. Even so, Sissy left home and returned several times before severing her ties to her stable, housed environment for good. For the typical homeless person, the onset of homelessness is rather fuzzy, and like Sissy there may be a series of episodes which reflect varying degrees of housing instability. Did the process begin, for example, when he ran away for a weekend and stayed with a friend? Or was it the time his stepfather beat him up, and he spent three days in the woods behind his home; or when he was put out by his mother for using drugs, and he slept in his car for ten days before finding an apartment? Or was it the time he drove to Atlanta to find a job, ran out of money, and had to stay in a shelter for a week? At what point does a person cross the line from being between homes to being homeless? And when do self-indications shift to defining the self as a homeless person, or defining one's community as other homeless people? Without a clear marker for the onset of homelessness, it is difficult to determine the causes of homelessness, and therein lies much of the difficulty in understanding the problem.

When Sissy returned home from her first experience on the streets, she felt things were acceptable for a while, but then the situation started to get bad again. For her, it was most difficult to watch her younger brother and sister being abused by a mother who was, in Sissy's view, schizophrenic and alcoholic. Sissy felt powerless to affect this situation. She was fearful that telling the authorities about the abuse would lead to the loss of her siblings and recalled a police officer telling her, "They will break you kids up, if you say anything." So the three children developed a conspiracy of silence, depending on each other, and convincing themselves that they could handle it. "We couldn't let anyone know, or we would lose each other." She did apparently run away several more times, however, as did the other children. "Once I started running away, that made it easier for the others to run away. I hate that I became a role model for running away." Sissy's childhood experience was not unusual in comparison to other homeless women. Nearly 43 percent of the homeless women we interviewed in Mobile indicated that their childhood memories were mostly unhappy, and only one in four indicated having a happy childhood.

At 19, Sissy married "for security," and quickly became pregnant. The marriage "didn't work out, then I was on the streets with my daughter." Looking back on the marriage, she says she did not realize then that she was battling mental illness the whole time. Since that time, she was diagnosed with manic-depression.

After a period of being on the streets, Sissy entered into a relationship with a smooth-talking boyfriend, who knew "how to make you feel good, how to make you feel pretty." So although he was "on the run" and "into crime," she and her daughter stayed with the "soothsayer," crossing the country several times on the run with him. Sissy finally ended up in jail, and the daughter went to live with her father. But some months later, when Sissy was released, the father gave the child back to Sissy.

Sissy struggled to be a good mother and take care of her daughter, but without support from the father or other family members, and without marketable skills or financial resources, she found herself stealing and engaging in prostitution to provide enough food. In time, Sissy voluntarily gave her 3-year-old child to foster care, after she saw the child panhandling, mimicking what she had seen Sissy do. Although she got her daughter back for a short while, Sissy was unable to create a stable life for herself and the child. She danced in nightclubs, turned tricks, and looked for day jobs. Sissy eventually lost her daughter permanently when desperation and mental illness led Sissy to attempt suicide. At that point, the father was given custody of the child. Sissy was 23 years old, and says of that time, "A woman without her child feels hopeless; there is nothing to live for. I didn't care any more. I just rambled from place to place for about three years. I realize it was the best thing for my daughter. I didn't realize at the time how messed up I was." In her rambling, which took her all over the country, Sissy landed on the streets of Mobile.

Based on Mead's notion of the formation of self through socialization (1934), Sissy had by this time become a full member in the society of the homeless, and she developed a self that held the values and exhibited the behavior of that group. The fact that the values and behavior of this group often clash with those of the larger society, leads to the labeling of the group as deviant (Becker 1963). But deviance, in common parlance, suggests a motivational quality that leads to behavior outside of societal norms. In Sissy's case, and in the case of many homeless people, these behaviors are adaptive, allowing them to survive in a hostile environment.

What Is It Like to Be Homeless?

Variations of this question or underlying questions might be: How do you spend your days and nights? How do you manage to get enough to eat? Where do you stay? Should I be afraid of you or other homeless people? What is your view of the world? More fundamentally, can we connect at all—do we have anything in common on a day to day basis? In terms of symbolic interactionism, we might be asking, are there any symbols or meanings that we share? We approached these questions by asking Sissy about a series of topics, all of which related in one way or another to the social interactions of everyday life among the homeless.

Relationships—Romance and friendship. Women on the streets are very vulnerable, and so they look for someone to offer a semblance of safety. In Sissy's words, "You stay on the street until you find a guy to take care of you for a while. You're not thinking about the long term; you're looking for protection. Nine times out of ten, they're going to abuse you. I've been abused and raped so much; but I was raised that way, and I just assumed it would happen." Fifty-six percent of the females we interviewed reported that they had been assaulted physically during the past year; many of these were, no doubt, sexually related, leading to the conclusion that any woman who spends time on the streets runs the risk of rape. The assault figures suggest that Sissy's experience, while personally traumatic, was not unusual for a homeless woman.

Sissy had been through numerous relationships with men. There was the abusive husband shortly after she came to Mobile, who was sending her out to get drugs, especially marijuana. Later she was "staying with someone who beat me up. I was the enabler. I was addicted to this role. I thought that was love." But the abuse became more than she could handle, and she grew frightened that he would kill her. After fourteen beatings, and encouragement from a mental health outreach worker, she went to the police and to a shelter for abused women. When she left the shelter and returned to her apartment, he stalked and threatened her for several weeks, and then he finally left town.

Friendships on the street are tenuous, and built more around physical than emotional needs. Thirty-eight percent of homeless women in Mobile reported that they had no close friends, and another 34 percent reported that they had only one or two close friends. At one time, Sissy thought she was different.

When I had [a] motor cycle wreck, the homeless came to visit, brought me food. It felt real good to have these friends. Then when I had my breakdown, and I needed someone else, I didn't have as many friends as I thought. It was my illusion that they were my friends, but there weren't too many people around to help. It's a barter system. They will give you things or give you help, but they expect you to give to them later. Rarely have I found someone who was doing something just for me.

Many of the homeless people we talked with, in fact, used the term "associates" rather than "friends" to describe the people they spent time with. Stack (1974) reported similar utilitarian relationships within a low-income housed population she studied. Residents of the neighborhood regularly shared what they had with each other; but this was motivated more by a need to obligate them to return the favor at some future point rather than genuine concern for the well-being of the other person.

Contributing to the difficulty of friendships among the homeless is the fact that homelessness is largely a male-oriented subculture, with the women viewed as objects. Sissy described the competition for women this way:

There are not as many women as men, and when a female comes into the circle, there's a game going on. Everyone's playing for the same ticket. You might even feel treasured at first, and think, "Oh, everyone's being so nice." Well, they're being nice because they're all bidding on that woman. She's property, and he can say, "I'm looking after her." A woman can become a man's old lady in a day, and then all transactions go through him.

Although women might be cared for by men, there also are feelings of resentment on both sides of these relationships:

Men think women have it made. They don't understand how much we have to give away every time—and it's part of our soul. They don't realize we have it harder. They even resent that women get to go first at some of the social agencies. But there are more services for men than women. And on the street, if you're going to help out a man, you're not going to say, "well you have to go to bed with me before I'm going to feed you." Men don't realize. They're angry. Most of them have bad relationships, divorces; so they're having their issues with women anyway.

Prostitution. Fully one-quarter of the women we interviewed in Mobile indicated that they had sold sex as a means of getting money while they were homeless—and given the sensitivity of the question, we expected that the real figure was considerably higher. In addition to money, a homeless woman may exchange a sexual relationship for other necessities. These relationships can be characterized as "survival sex." Sissy regularly turned to prostitution as a means of meeting her needs for shelter, food, and security. Sometimes it would earn her a place to stay, or food to eat, or someone would protect her and treat her like a mistress, finding food for her, protecting her from other men, and sharing whatever he had. Some of the time these relationships were dangerous, abusive, and dysfunctional. "The pain, sometimes is all that you have left, so you allow yourself to experience it. You don't know why you're doing it, but it's all you're comfortable with."

Condoms were rarely used because some men would refuse to use one or just would not deal with a woman who wanted them to use a condom, and others would not pay as much if a condom was used. The immediate needs for shelter, food, or security often outweighed this concern. "You have to make a decision, what's more important at that time?" Did Sissy ever worry about getting AIDS? "That wasn't really a consideration. It was just part of the game." The lack of concern about contracting HIV is alarming, since the HIV infection rate among homeless people had been nearly twice that within the general population (Raba et al. 1990).

Drugs and alcohol. Sissy did not use drugs as an adolescent. Drugs came much later and were a direct result of living on the streets. She said, "Running away is an escape. Drugs is the next level, escaping in your mind. Others offer it, saying it will make you feel better. Especially men use it to control women." She started using drugs in her late twenties, but they were never a big motivation for her. They were, however, always available, and she tended to use whatever her current boyfriend or husband was using. She added, "When you're stoned, that may be the only time you feel comfortable talking about things."

While illegal drugs and alcohol did not seem to play a big role in Sissy's life, substance abuse is a major problem for many homeless people. Among the homeless we interviewed in Mobile, 70 percent of males and 50 percent of females indicated they currently abused drugs or alcohol, while nearly 90 percent of males and 60 percent of females reported having problems with substance abuse at some time in their lives.

Mental illness. Sissy recalled that she had heard voices all through her life. But it wasn't until the suicide attempt, leading to the loss of her daughter, that she underwent assessment and received a diagnosis of manic depression. At that time, she did not cooperate with therapy. After several years in Mobile, the mental health outreach workers were able to get Sissy into a treatment program which included monitoring and medications, allowing her to become stabilized. Unfortunately, a disastrous trip to visit her family resulted in a total mental breakdown. For some time she was lost on the streets of San Diego, sleeping in a dumpster, and suffering from abuse, confusion, seizures, and hallucinations. She said she tried to get help from some of the social services, but she could not handle the paperwork. "I was in a long-term manic phase. I could think grand thoughts, but I couldn't remember my last name. My self was lost in there." Social workers finally determined her identity and returned her to Mobile.

Upon her return, she continued to be completely confused and felt abandoned by her friends and the mental health and social workers who had helped her in the past. In reality, they were trying to help her, but in her confused state of mind she rejected their help. One of these social workers recalled; "Sissy came back to the streets; she linked up with some crack users and let herself be sexually abused. I went looking for her, and when I found her, she just told me to get lost." Sissy picked up the story here, "No one did anything until she stepped in with a court committal. Seeing me out there like that, dirty, without clothes, being raped. My clothes were ripped off, and I didn't even realize I was naked." Gaining a court committal to force a mentally ill person to enter a treatment program is always difficult and unpleasant; and yet, for Sissy, this was clearly the right thing to do at that time, and she recognized it. Again, the social worker remembers, "I was so sad. She had come a long way. I knew that wasn't her, and I wasn't going to let her stay that way. I did feel frustration—a feeling of "here we go again." We work with people for a while, and they seem to be doing well; then something happens."

Over the years of treatment, Sissy reported that she would take her medication regularly for a while, and would become stabilized, "I'd be doing good, and then I thought I didn't need it and would go off. During manic stages, you think you can do anything."

In popular conception, mental illness accounts for much of homelessness. Perhaps this derives from the belief that only those who are mentally ill would stay on the streets. Perhaps it is due to a few memorable encounters with obviously mentally ill homeless people. Or perhaps it is due to the rise in homelessness that appeared to follow the de-institutionalization of the mentally ill in the 1960s and early 1970s, although the cause and effect relationship of these two events has been debunked by the National Institute for Mental Health (Blau 1992). The perceived problems created by mentally ill homeless people are sufficiently great that 87 percent of respondents in a telephone survey of Mobile residents felt that mentally ill homeless people should be sent to hospitals against their will, if necessary. The reality is that nationally, about one-third of homeless people suffer from mental illness. Among the female homeless we interviewed in Mobile, 41 percent indicated that they had been treated for an emotional problem, and 15 percent had been hospitalized for emotional problems. However, approximately 80 percent of females we interviewed appeared to be depressed clinically. Forty percent of the female homeless reported that they had attempted to commit suicide, nearly half of these during periods when they were homeless. Sissy tried to commit suicide seven times.

Identities. In our talks with homeless people we found that many used multiple identities, and they might relate different stories on different occasions when we met them. In fact, they exhibited a rather extensive system of impression management (Goffman 1959). We saw the front region of their stage, where they played out a script to manage the impression formed by the audience. Depending upon the circumstances, the desired impression would change. One of the problems for the homeless is that they might have little opportunity for a safe backstage or back region where they can relax and be themselves. Might they sometimes get lost in which person they are, no longer knowing which is the mask and which is the self? Sissy thought this could happen. "I believe we do get lost. A different person takes over. Especially the women. Different people expect you to be a different kind of person, so it comes as part of survival. You can be street tough or sweet and helpless. Men, too, build up the macho act, then they have to do it."

Meeting basic needs. Mobile had a number of agencies and organizations that offered a wide range of services to the homeless. They covered many of the basic necessities, including food, clothing, and overnight shelter. They also provided health care, mental health care, and some treatment options for substance abuse. These services were not always enough, however; and they were not always utilized by the chronically homeless for a variety of reasons. When homeless people come together under a bridge or in a park, do they share what they have with each other, or do they tend to hoard what they get? According to Sissy:

I would say first they are testing you. They want to see if you're going to share with them. So it's not automatic; you could get depleted or real used that way, where they just come to you when you have something. But if they see you will share, then they'll share with you. It's not automatic. But, most of the homeless I've met, if they have food, you have food. I never saw anyone who wouldn't feed another one. Of course, if they've been robbed a bunch of times, they get a bitter feeling and just take care of themselves.

One way that people get what they need or want is to "hustle" it by making up stories. We had seen and heard about many hustles in our interviews with homeless people. We asked Sissy's opinion: Do most street people have some kind of hustle going on?

They have to. Nine times out of ten, they do. I don't mean everyone's dishonest. I didn't steal or rob, but I panhandled, and diverted the truth to get a little finances. I felt because I asked for it, that was better than taking it. Everyone has their own little policy. You have to in order to survive. You're out there and you're on your own. Once you start hustling, it's hard to get out of that mode, hard to even talk to anyone without saying, "I need this; I'm hungry." Sometimes the story they spin becomes another personality, it becomes them, and they forget they started out just trying to get something to eat. You watch others at first. It's hard the first time you ask for money for food. But going hungry for a couple of days gives you the incentive to ask for food or money. Then once you start manipulating, it's very hard to get out of it. It's like designing another personality. And you are judged by how good your hustle is. I wasn't proud of it, but I knew it was that, or I would have to sell myself. Asking someone for money, spinning a little tale, was a lot better than the alternative.

In this brief passage, we saw many of the critical elements of symbolic interactionism. Sissy referred clearly again to the self presentation and impression management issues raised by Goffman (1959), the development of self and socialization process discussed by Mead (1934), and the shared or common group understandings presented by Blumer (1969).

Sissy, the street social worker. Sissy loved to help people in need; she believed it was part of her own dependency problems, that she needed to feel needed. She called herself a street social worker, although she did not get paid for this work.

It helps me to help someone else who is where I was. I know what they're going through. My role models were the social workers who came and helped me. I started by listening to people, and I found that I knew about things that they needed. So I started taking them to the social workers. Mainly I would try to help the homeless mentally ill, because I'm bipolar. For example, I might meet someone at McDonalds, and just talk with him and buy him a cup of coffee; then I would take him to the Catholic sisters [Catholic Social Services] for a change of clothes, then some place where he could take a shower. Sometimes it would take a while, maybe a month, because he wouldn't feel comfortable in these places. I would stay with him through everything. I call this the incubator stage.

She also worked with a number of women, who she said would go with her because "I had been out there; they knew I wasn't judging them." Women, she said, were harder to reach because their self-esteem was gone. For men, the sources of mental illness tended to be Vietnam experiences or drugs; for women it was abuse, molestation, and rape. "I couldn't believe how many women were like me, who went through mental illness because of abuse they couldn't tell anyone about."

Sissy's orientation toward her street social work, and her genuine concern for other people, was reflected in an incident that occurred shortly after our survey of Mobile's homeless population. Sissy was walking in the downtown area when she happened on an elderly homeless woman known universally among the homeless population as Mamma. Mamma was lying under a tree, listless, obviously not feeling well. Sissy asked if there was anything she could do to help, and Mamma asked Sissy to let her have the sweater she was wearing—a new sweater, it turned out, that Sissy had just bought from the thrift store. Without giving it a thought, Sissy took off the sweater and gave it to Mamma. Then, she walked to Catholic Social Services to see if they could provide some assistance for Mamma. Within a few days, an outreach worker had made contact with Mamma and helped her get admitted to a hospital, where she was diagnosed with cervical cancer, and where she died shortly thereafter. Sissy helped make the funeral arrangements and found a burial dress for Mamma.

One of the workers in a social service agency describes Sissy's work this way: She is good on the streets. She sees what people need, and she knows how to help. She sometimes brings them in here for help. She's very needy herself, and she gets her needs met by taking care of others. It's not really a healthy situation for her. She gets involved with others, and then loses her balance. I suspect she was seriously abused, and it's difficult to get over that. Plus she's missing the strength of a supportive community. Just think of what she could do, if she didn't carry all that pain and background with her, what a gift she could be giving. There are people she has helped who are alive today because of her.

Organizing the homeless to help themselves. Sissy joined several other homeless individuals, turning their desire to help others into an organization designed to allow the homeless to help themselves. Sissy was doing fairly well at this time—she was receiving counseling, had friends, and had found a purpose. The group was given a building to use as a shelter, and they began painting and fixing it up. "I was around people I was used to. We started taking in others. It was the homeless doing it for themselves. Hope sprang up on the streets among the homeless." The organization (Mobile Union Chapter of the Homeless, MUCH) seemed to prosper for a time, gaining some respect among others who served the homeless, but then it appeared to spiral out of control. There were rumors of fights, cuttings, beatings, drug dealing, and prostitution in the shelter, and Sissy confirmed that many of the rumors were true. Others involved in MUCH recall that these activities were taking place outside the building where they had little control, but were not occurring inside the shelter. Still MUCH was blamed for the bad behavior. In Sissy's view, "The clients had taken over the staff; there was no discipline, no distinction between clients and staff. The respect was gone. We can't be our own police. There has to be someone else being the bad guy, because they [the clients] will say, "I remember when you did this," or "Why are you telling me what to do, when you have the same problem yourself?"

In other words, there was no legitimate authority afforded to the staff, and their own past or present behavior undermined the respect they needed to maintain control. Similarly, when trying to form an organizational structure: "There were too many chiefs and not enough indians. No one wanted to be an indian, everybody wanted a position. Everyone wanted to call back to their family and say, "I'm this," whatever their position was. And every time their picture was in the paper, that was something they were proud of." Again we are reminded of Goffman's ideas about presentation of self and the importance of creating a viable role for the self within the social organization. Sissy continued:

See, all of us had these great gifts, but because we weren't over our thing, our problem, and didn't get counseling on our thing, we never resolved our own issues. Remember one of the ideas was to take us apart and give us business training or give us organizational training. We all needed to be pulled away from there and get counseling and get training and then be brought back in.

Unfortunately this training never happened. MUCH was finally evicted from the space it had been occupying, and the people in the organization dispersed. To Sissy and the other primary organizers, this was a crushing failure. Sissy described her own stress and frustration:

All of us were feeling good for giving and getting something done, and all of us grew from it. But I think when it got pulled from underneath us, and all the rumors came on us, no one saw the good things that were happening—like the group therapy room we had which was doing some good, or the guy we had who was going to help with GED classes, or the people who were helped off the street and nurtured and helped the best way we could—those thing weren't seen. All they heard were the bad things—the police were over there, there were drugs, there was drinking, it was dirty.

I had totally put everything into being over there; that was my whole life stream. I thought, if this succeeds, I'm going to be all right. That's why I put so much into it. That was me on the line. This was our dream, and it was actually going to happen. When I realized we were failing and nothing was working, then it was me failing; it was because I didn't do something. To me, it was always on my back.

Obviously, Sissy was profoundly affected by the failure of MUCH. According to her memory, the other organizers were equally disappointed:

When all the bad stuff fell down, all the dreams and all the hopes, we felt crushed, we felt the city looked down on us and made us a laughing stock. You put yourself on the line. You have to understand that most people in the homeless situation are not putting themselves on the line, and since other people were doing it, and they saw the success, they were putting their talents on the line and trying it. Then when it failed, it gave them even more reason to say, "Oh, I'm never going to make it." Everyone put themselves on the line and wanted to believe this was our last shot at being somebody. When it crashed, I think all of us kind of died a little bit.

In this reaction to failure we see glimpses of the "looking-glass self" described by Cooley (1922), in which feelings about the self result from how we imagine others to be judging us. The people who organized MUCH felt badly, partly because of the way they imagined the rest of the city was looking at them. This was less of a problem when they were clearly flouting the norms of general society, but once they decided to enter that game, the judgment of a wider range of others became important.

Episodes of home and homelessness. During her years in Mobile, Sissy had been on and off the streets a number of times. Many of the men with whom she had relationships had apartments, and so she lived with them for periods of time. Because she was eligible for some government assistance, she also had income that allowed her to pay for her own apartment at times. During one such time, after she had left an abusive husband, and had an apartment herself, she said she missed the people on the streets and started bringing them home with her. "I felt I belonged out there. It was the only place I felt I belonged. I realized I was addicted to living on the edge, living in danger." This feeling was heightened during her manic episodes. "I definitely got onto the street more when I was manic. You can't keep a manic person in the house. On the streets there's no one over you, and there are no rules. But it is stressful." Mead (1934, p. 162) argued that "one has to be a member of a community to be a self." Even with an apartment, Sissy remained a member of the homeless community, strongly socialized into that group, and demonstrating what Lemert (1967) called "career deviance," being locked into a deviant subgroup and finding it difficult to lead a normal life.

Is religion important to you? Responding like 75 percent of the homeless we interviewed, Sissy indicated that religion was very important to her. She struggled to merge her understanding of a loving God with her generally negative view of her self.

Yes [religion is important to me]. Well, not religion, but knowing that God loves me, that there's forgiveness. I don't have that for myself. I want to know that God does love me and may be the only one who will love me unconditionally. Some of the things I went through, I wouldn't be alive unless God was looking after me. I could have been murdered or killed so many times. I believe God has looked after me. Sometimes I believe maybe I don't deserve forgiveness, that maybe I'm not worthy; but I know that's not right. I want to come to the point where I can see me the way He sees me.

What Does the Future Hold?

Variations and underlying questions: Where do you go from here? Can you do any better than this? What do you want out of life? If society helped, would you and others get off the streets? In other words, is it a good investment of my time, money, and energy to help you?

Most homeless people we met wanted something better for themselves. In our interviews, 90 percent of homeless people said they wanted a job and 90 percent said they wanted their own place to live. Furthermore, most of them believed they could and would achieve something better for themselves. Sometimes these beliefs were unrealistic. For example, in our survey, nearly 80 percent said they thought that within a year they would have a job and a place of their own to stay; this in spite of the fact that the average length of time since they last had a place of their own was thirty-five months. Sissy, however, was wise and had learned to be realistic in her expectations. In her tentative optimism, she said;

I don't know [where I go from here]. But I believe I have enough built up in me, I believe if I got in the right atmosphere, with the right counseling, and the right structure, I could make it go a little bit farther. But I'm not going to expect that from myself. I think the first thing I can do is take one day at a time and let people know my limitations. I want to do something. The only way I can get well is to get back [into things]. But this time, I need someone monitoring me and helping me along. Probably for the first time in my life I'm being real honest and not embarrassed to say I need help. I'm not as strong as I thought I was. And that might be more growth than thinking you can do it all. You know, being strong for everyone else, that doesn't put you in jeopardy. But starting to work on yourself, saying, "I made this mistake," or "I don't know what to do," or "I don't have the strength to do this," is probably more growth than anything else I could do. It's scary, letting down my barriers. Someone could come in and get to me. For the first time in my life, I'm laying it all out. It takes a lot of courage to put all my barriers down and express my real emotions. . . . I'm being more honest with myself than I've ever been. Maybe I can grow from there. But I'm not going to build myself up—the grandiose manic thing—oh, I can handle it all. Moderation, balance is probably a word I've never had. I don't know what balance is; I don't know what normal is.

Sissy understood that her hold on her current lifestyle and relatively healthy mental state was quite fragile. She was prepared to make positive steps, but she was always wary of what could bring her down. Sissy was working hard to redefine some of the meanings in her life and to build a self that understands its limits.

For other homeless individuals, too, past patterns would indicate that many will have a difficult time maintaining stability for long lengths of time. Evidence also indicates, however, that like Sissy, they will have periods of time when they have jobs and places to live. Then something will happen to throw that delicate balance off, and they will either slip or escape back to the streets.

Advice for those who want to help the homeless. Sissy had worked with a number of social service agencies, both in her own quest to meet her needs and in trying to help other homeless people. Her own subjective viewpoint on how to be of the best help can be informative to those willing to listen.

Most of the people on the street, even though they brag, or blame other people, they feel that they've failed, and this life is all they deserve. They don't deserve clean clothes. Even the women, they don't keep themselves up any more, they don't fix their hair, that's all gone. They feel they can't accomplish anything. I believe if they could ever get to the point where they actually completed one act that was something they wanted to do, even a GED, that would give them a milestone, a goal. But it would have to take nurturing that confidence. People say, "just give them a job." It takes somebody to say, "no, I think you can do it," and even farther than that, people who get into helping the homeless don't realize [what to expect] or set themselves up. When I did fall, a lot of people who had been helping me, didn't deal with it very well.[1] You have to realize these people are going to fall, and get them ready so that they can fall. People say, "Oh, you're going to get this job, and you're going to do good," and that's it. If you ever mess up, you'll lose it. They have to be in an atmosphere where they are allowed to make a mistake, allowed to show it, but get back up and try again. But no one was there to say that to me—"try it again."

Sissy believed that most of the counselors and services that help the homeless were truly trying to be helpful, but they were looking for quick fixes, instant recoveries, and no backward steps. As she said, "Our success is their success; when we fall, they feel they've failed." This perception affected Sissy's description of feelings about her own failure and what it would take to work toward recovery:

I didn't want to disappoint anyone else, so I said, "I can do this," and "I can do that;" and then when I did fall, I just totally pulled away because I was ashamed and they weren't ready for it. I needed them to say, "This can happen, Sissy; just get back up and try the best you can." I pulled away and went into my own little capsule and got depressed, and I've been that way for about two years now.

I would like to break out of that, but it would have to be in an atmosphere where they knew, and I would be able to say, "I can't handle this right now," instead of saying, "We want you to come in at this time, and this time, and this time, and this time," or "You were supposed to be here; where were you?" They have to understand that a bipolar or manic, we have our bad days or bad weeks. Not to say that inspiring us isn't good, not letting us go back into our shell; but if we have to, we have to. That's why it's hard for us to find a job. Or it's like they want me to go to college, and I want to; I want all this, but I hate to get myself all built up that I'm going to handle it, and then I'm going to have a bad day.

Sissy understood the self-fulfilling nature of some of her negative expectations, and likewise, she understood her inability to completely control them. She knew that other homeless people suffered similar problems.

I don't believe in self-destructive behavior, but it's there because it's always been there; and I feel like that's what I deserve. And the guilt—like I said about all the women who have been molested and all the people that have been abused, they feel like—well, no one's ever told them, "It's not your fault."

Maybe the social workers should just be helping people bear what they have to get through, making it a little bit easier on them on their journey, giving them a little more confidence, having a special moment with you, a smile, a meal. Most have this journey, this goal or thing they're going to overcome one day. Their dream is to see their child, have their wife back or their job back; whatever it is, it's always out there, stewing in them. You might not be able to spare them all the pain, but it might be for one moment their pain is spared.

Sissy thought one of the best ways to help was to bring people together who have similar problems. When she learned of her bipolar mental illness, she found it to be very helpful to meet other people who had the same difficulty, but she believed it was equally helpful for other issues, such as someone who had been raped or molested.

Just knowing other people are going through it, and that they understand. That is probably the biggest peace you could have, because you don't feel so strange. That's one of the biggest gifts you could have. That's why I wanted people going through the same things to help each other. You can't find it from someone from suburbia. But, they have it, too; they go through the same things, too; we don't have the market on pain. Everyone goes through these things. Knowing other people go through them, having someone say, "I know what that feels like," I didn't feel so odd anymore, and I thought, "Maybe I'm all right; maybe this hasn't been all me."

Social services workers sometimes expect too much, setting unrealistic goals; and sometimes they expect too little, wanting to do everything for homeless people and not allowing them to make their own decisions.

They have to let us go, too, like kids. They should help us to a point, then realize the rest is up to us. We have to make our own mistakes. It's easy to say, "I don't want you to make a mistake, so I'm going to walk this way with you." Then they plot little roads, "this will be good for you," and don't ask what you want to do, and don't get ready for the fact that you might have other ideas about things. They may set goals and expectations that the homeless person can't achieve. Maybe your only expectation for the day is to find a good meal. They want you to do this, this, this, and this. Let them start from little things they want to do and know they can achieve, and then add things on at their pace. Most social workers and social services are putting expectations within their time limit—"you've got to go on my wavelength, march to my tune." That's what a lot of services have wrong, you have to march to their tune, instead of, "What do you think you could handle right now?" and then go in levels.

Sissy seemed to be expressing an idea presented by Goffman (1961) in his analysis of institutions. He found, for example, that inmates invented numerous strategies to preserve their selfhood within the strict confines of the institution. While conforming in many important ways, the inmates made a number of "secondary adjustments" to circumvent certain rules or maintain some idiosyncracy to avoid completing stripping away the old self. Goffman says, "Our sense of being a person can come from being drawn into a wider social unit; our sense of selfhood can rise through the little ways we resist the pull" (p. 320). All too often, social services set up arbitrary rules and require lockstep conformity to norms, without giving the homeless person enough flexibility to maintain the old self while developing new social meanings.

DISCUSSION AND CONCLUSION

Obviously Sissy was incredibly reflective and had spent much time in therapy, which had given her insights and understanding about herself that not all homeless people (or nonhomeless people, for that matter) have. She understood a great deal about the cycles of behavior and circumstance that she had experienced, and in sharing her insights she shed light on similar cycles experienced by many homeless individuals. In closing our interview with Sissy, we wondered how she would assess her life, and so we asked her the questions we will all ask ourselves at some point.

1. What things would you do differently, if you had it to do all over again?
   "I'd make different choices to get off the merry-go-round. I wish I could have had the skills to have a stable life."
2. What are you most proud of in your life?
   I'm proud of giving love when there wasn't much given to me, of reaching out to

people and taking a chance. Somebody came back and said I helped them because of my kindness or because I took time with them. Even though I've messed up, and I get mad at myself, I have these little treasures of when people came back and said this. I've had compassion; I'm proud of knowing that I took the time to do that without looking for something for myself.

This assessment revealed the depth of our common humanity with Sissy. We all experience the merry-go-round pace of life and sometimes wish our choices had been different; and we, too, can be most proud of the times we have touched another's life and made his or her journey a little easier.

NOTE

1. This reaction is similar to that of a group of nurses studied by Glaser and Strauss (1965). They found that nurses caring for terminally-ill patients developed various strategies for avoiding the later stages of dying because they defined the death scene as upsetting. Sissy experienced a withdrawing of her support systems just at the time she was failing to meet their expectations.

REFERENCES

Baum, Alice S., and Donald W. Burnes. 1993. *A Nation in Denial: The Truth About Homelessness.* Boulder, Colo.: Westview.

Becker, Howard S. 1963. *Outsiders: Studies in the Sociology of Deviance.* New York: Free Press.

Blau, Joel. 1992. *The Visible Poor: Homelessness in the United States.* New York: Oxford University Press.

Blumer, Herbert. 1969. *Symbolic Interactionism: Perspective and Method.* Englewood Cliffs, N.J.: Prentice-Hall, Inc.

Bolland, John M., and Debra M. McCallum. 1995. "The Magnitude and Demographics of Homelessness in Mobile, Alabama." Unpublished Report, Institute for Social Science Research, University of Alabama.

Burt, Martha R. 1992. *Over the Edge: The Growth of Homelessness in the 1980s.* New York: Russell Sage.

Cooley, Charles H. 1922. *Human Nature and the Social Order.* New York: Charles Scribner's Sons.

Glaser, Barney G., and Anselm L. Strauss. 1965. *Awareness of Dying.* Chicago: Aldine.

Goffman, Erving. 1961. *Asylums: Essays on the Social Situation of Mental Patients and Other Inmates.* New York: Doubleday.

Goffman, Erving. 1959. *The Presentation of Self in Everyday Life.* Garden City, N.Y.: Doubleday.

Gorder, C. 1988. *Homeless! Without Address in America.* Tempe, Ariz.: Bluebird.

Hombs, Mary Ellen, and Mitch Snyder. 1982. *Homelessness in America: A Forced March to Nowhere.* Washington, D.C.: Community on Creative Nonviolence.

Jencks, Christopher. 1994. *The Homeless.* Cambridge, Mass.: Harvard University Press.

Lemert, Edwin, ed. 1967. *Human Deviance, Social Problems and Social Control.* Englewood Cliffs, N.J.: Prentice-Hall.

Link, Burce, Jo Phelan, Michaeline Bresnahan, Ann Stueve, Robert Moore, and Ezra Susser. 1995. "Lifetime and Five-Year Prevalence of Homelessness in the United States: New Evidence on an Old Debate." *American Journal of Orthopsychiatry* 65: 347–354.

Mead, George H. 1934. *Mind, Self, and Society* Chicago: University of Chicago Press.

Mitchell, Joseph. 1992. *Up in the Old Hotel*. New York: Pantheon.

Raba, John M., Joseph Herman, Robin Avery, Ramon A. Torres, Stacy Kiyasu, Robert Prentice, Jo Ann Staats, and Philip W. Brickner. 1990. "Homelessness and AIDS." In Philip W. Brickner, Linda Keen Scharer, Barbara A. Conanan, Marianne Savarese, and Brian C. Scanlan, eds., *Under the Safety Net: The Health and Social Welfare of the Homeless in the United States*, pp. 215–233. New York: Norton.

Rossi, Peter H. 1989. *Down and Out in America: The Origins of Homelessness*. Chicago: University of Chicago Press.

Schmidt, Emerson P., ed. 1937. *Man and Society*. Englewood Cliffs, N.J.: Prentice-Hall.

Stack, Carol. 1974. *All Our Kin: Strategies for Survival in a Black Community*. New York: Harper & Row.

Stoner, Madeleine R. 1995. *The Civil Rights of Homeless People: Law, Social Policy, and Social Work Practice*. New York: Aldine de Gruyter.

U.S. Department of Housing and Urban Development. 1984. *A Report to the Secretary on the Homeless and Emergency Shelters*. Office of Policy Development and Research, Washington D.C.

PART III

BEHAVIOR BEYOND
THE BOUNDARIES

This section includes aspects of the subjective and the traditional objective approaches to understanding social problems. The title, behavior beyond the boundaries, is suggestive of the traditional objective response to social problems. At first glance the objective approach seems reasonable since all societies have normative cultural proscriptions which prohibit behavior that jeopardizes or threatens human life and property. Such is the nature of an evolutionary transition from the "eye for an eye" and "tooth for a tooth" tribal mentality to the creation of a system of criminal and civil law that is characteristic of advanced societies. On the other hand, the subjective view of interactionism advances the view that widespread agreement may not exist on other issues.

Long ago, Emile Durkheim wrote in *The Rules of Sociological Method* that a certain amount of crime in advanced civilized society is normal; crime is expected to occur, and a certain level of crime is even tolerated. As societies grow in size and complexity, so too does the amount of crime. Emile Durkheim utilized the functionalist theoretical paradigm to argue that a certain amount of crime and other forms of extraordinary behavior are functional for society in that crime and other nonconforming behavior assist in establishing the boundaries of acceptable behavior. On occasion, these boundaries change. That is, behavior occurs and members of the community elect to either react to, or ignore, it. However, certain types of behavior are not expected nor are they acceptable or tolerated by most adult citizens. Indeed, as illustrated in the chapters included in this section, these behaviors not only violate the public trust, but each is against the law. Within this context, certain behavior can be considered as beyond the boundaries of social tolerance and acceptance.

Howard S. Becker, a proponent of the symbolic interaction perspective, wrote:

When a rule is enforced, the person who is supposed to have broken it may be seen as a special kind of person, one who cannot be trusted to live by the rules agreed on by the group. He is regarded as an outsider. But the person who is thus labeled an outsider may have a different view of the matter. He may not accept the rule by which he is being judged and may not regard those who judge him as either competent or legitimately entitled to do so. Hence a second meaning of the term emerges: the rulebreaker may feel his judges are outsiders. (1973, pp. 1–2)

Rules, such as normative proscriptions and laws (codified mores) exist in all societies. Some rules are archaic and their violation does not illicit much if any public attention or official reaction. However, other rules illicit severe sanction no matter how advanced the society in question may be.

Sexual harassment is illegal and the definition of what constitutes sexual harassment appears clear enough. But, as Beverly E. Thorn demonstrates, interpretation of sexual harassment laws is not straightforward. In the first chapter of this section, the author guides the reader through a process of human interaction, a process through which people distinguish between the perceptions males and females hold regarding sex roles and the work-related role. The sometimes difficult task of establishing the boundaries of sexual harassment is, as noted in the case study of Lisa, a matter of interpretation.

Although the signs, symbols, and overt behavior may appear explicit enough from one perspective, the impressions and meanings can differ dramatically because, as Howard S. Becker notes in the quote cited above, others "may have a different view of the matter." The early resolution of the court case, the quid pro quo or "he said/she said" status of Lisa's case, was contaminated by an extralegal factor that symbolized to others that Lisa may not be who they thought she was. This conflicting set of symbols (legal and extralegal) and their meaning, according to Thorn, also placed Lisa at risk when she was cast into the outsider category. The label affixed to Lisa was that of a mentally unstable individual who overreacted to what others thought was the harmless behavior of a male co-worker. That Lisa perceived the unwanted attention from her co-worker as sexual harassment was overshadowed by a public perception of her stigma. This socially recognized stigma also had an affect on her physical, social, and psychological well-being in that it interfered with her ability to respond to the needs of her daughter and to cope with the arduous legal process she had initiated.

The U.S. system of justice is based on an adversary system that is predicated on the premise that members of the judiciary are engaged in the search for truth. In theory, the most important thing is not whether one side wins or loses; what is important is that the truth is discovered. In reality, however, it does matter whether one wins or loses a court case. Within this context, the composition of the jury often is an important factor to this final determination.

Prosecutors, as well as law firms, hire experts trained in the art of selecting jury members who may have a greater probability of being partial to their side of the argument. That this kind of decision making enters into the negotiated process of justice may not seem important to some observers. However, to those whose liberty is at risk or for whom damages are sought this issue is significant. The prospect of having jury members who may be supportive of one side or the other is considered a critical factor.

Voir dire when used as a preemptory challenge based on one's race, age, gender, or social status is against the law. As noted by Larry D. Hall and Audwin Anderson, equal protection under the law means that no person shall be denied the right to serve as a jury member unless an individual's prejudice or bias can be demonstrated. The right of the accused to have an impartial trial by a jury of peers, as guaranteed by the Sixth Amendment, is at risk when voir dire preemptory challenges are employed to inappropriately skew the balance of this selection process.

Exclusion of minorities from participating as jurors has a long legacy in the American judicial system. However, it was not until 1965 that the Supreme of the United States ruled in *Swain v. Alabama* that excluding minorities from jury duty is unconstitutional. Later, the Swain ruling was refined in *Batson v. Kentucky*, a case heard in 1986. Currently the Batson ruling serves as the case law precedent against which challenges to intentional race-specific exclusion are based.

The two case studies, one criminal and one civil, are illustrative of the fine line that distinguishes this race neutral issue. The issue becomes even more complex given the potential negative consequences for the accused when race-based preemptory strikes occur. To infer intent and meaning of attorney actions when explanations for race neutral exclusion appear inadequate is a significant matter for all Americans but especially for the men and women who are entrusted with the task of ensuring that a legal process intended to ensure social justice will prevail.

As noted by Erving Goffman (1963, pp. 41–104), when one's entire self is not readily apparent, this person may engage in information control strategies to avoid whatever social penalties would apply should their spoiled identity become known. The issue, according to Goffman (1969), is impression management or the concealment of undisclosed discrediting information about self. In chapter 12, Thomas C. Calhoun and Greg S. Weaver discuss one form of male prostitution, namely street hustling, and the learning process through which male street hustlers pass. In this discussion, the authors document reasons why male street hustlers conceal their involvement from others who do not participate in the trade. The reader is given an insider's view of the hustlers' rationalization of their behavior and the reasons they manage a social identity and protect their self-image as nonhomosexual. Maintaining this image of self is important to male street hustlers and the authors discuss strategies male prostitutes engage in to avoid detection by legal authorities as well as friends and relatives.

Although learning to protect one's social image, sense of self, and manage one's true identity represent significant challenges in the everyday experiences of street hustlers, it is also important they be able to communicate why they are on the street. As Calhoun and Weaver observe, the street hustler avoids the communication of stigma symbols or signs that may draw attention to their debasing identity discrepancy. There exist various strategies for managing one's discredited identity, and the authors of this chapter draw upon the lexicon of their subjects to illustrate Goffman's point. In what is often graphic language, the subjects discuss such strategies and they also relate their perceptions of other street hustlers and their clients.

Contrary to popular myth, career criminals are few in number but they commit a disproportionate amount of crime. Also known as habitual criminals, career criminals are somewhat unique since they continue their legal activity well into adulthood. Although most people who commit crime during early adolescence and young adulthood enter into a maturation phase during which they assume the responsibilities expected of adults, career criminals defy this convention by continuing to engage in illicit activity.

In chapter 13, Ronald E. Jones offers a review and critique of the scholarly efforts to explain criminality. Of particular interest is the symbolic interaction perspective of deviant behavior, a general rubric under which the crime problem is subsumed.

The career criminal case study is a unique composite of twelve habitual offenders who at the time they were interviewed had spent an average of 20.5 years of their average 49.5 age under incarceration. The focus of this chapter is on the adoptive means career criminals use in negotiating with representatives of the criminal justice system—the police, the court, and corrections—in order to maintain their sense of being rather than accept the assigned social label as low-level career criminal. For each processing phase, the respondents speak of topics that many citizens consider to be public issues. Gun control is one example of symbolic importance to career criminals who, because of their public persona, are forced to live among dangerous others who share a similar social liability.

Perhaps the most insightful aspect of this chapter is the authors' attention to a myriad of issues, events, and procedures that career criminals must consider as they negotiate their way either as a member of the free world or as inmate. Because of changes in the law, court rulings, due process procedures, and the even the sociodemographic characteristics of the police and correctional staff, career criminals are forced to adopt new survival mechanisms to cope with these components of the criminal justice system. The resultant social order is unfair from the perspective of these career criminals because it places them at a disadvantage in the negotiated process upon which their psychic and social survival is based.

The final two chapters on mass murder and serial murder represent the most reprehensible and heinous forms of behavior. Civil society bears no tolerance for this kind of behavior and no cost is considered too great to bring to justice perpetrators who cross this boundary of social tolerance.

Mass murder, the topic of chapter 14, is a shocking, sensational event. It is shocking because many people are affected; mass murder is sensational because, as noted by Thomas A. Petee, Kathy G. Padgett and Thomas S. York the news media plays a role in characterizing the event in sensationalist terms. Although people seek answers for why mass murder occurs, such answers are not easily created. This problem is exacerbated when, in the words of the authors, "the stereotypical representation of mass murders . . . gives a somewhat distorted view of this phenomenon."

Contrary to public impression, most mass murders occur because the perpetrator is prompted to kill by identifiable motives. Moreover, most mass murderers do not fit the mass media–inspired stereotype of someone who is insane or mentally ill who has "run amok," gone "ballistic," is "going postal," is paranoid, manic depressive, deranged or disgruntled, or is motivated by anger and revenge. However, the framing of the mass murder event by the mass media accentuates the purpose expressed by publishing magnet William Randolph Hearst who long ago advocated the idea that sensational news maintains the interest of the audience. Such framing also shapes public attitudes and perceptions. In essence, the mass media is not only instrumental in constructing a social problem, but it serves as a filter through which only certain images deemed newsworthy flow and upon which the public perception is based. By characterizing only a small proportion of mass murderers using certain descriptors that dramatize aberrations and other unusual aspects of a specific event, the news media distorts reality. This distortion is not without motivation or intent because the descriptions of such events also serve to support other agenda such as gun control arguments.

The case study of Joseph Wesbecker is one example of the kind of event used to construct what the authors contend is factual but which inaccurately frames social reality. Although the public is encouraged to accept the media's characterization of the mass murder problem as representative, the authors use two other case studies to deconstruct this popular image of mass murderers. This deconstructed reality is no less interesting and compelling; it is also a more accurate portrayal of social reality. This reality, as suggested by the authors, is not as sensational as that portrayed by the mass media. But, mass murder that occurs as the result of domestic violence precipitated by jealousy or during the commission of another felony such as robbery or burglary is no less of a social problem.

Suspected serial murders create fear in the community and pose a particularly difficult problem for law enforcement. In the final chapter, James A. Sparks draws upon interviews, letters, and various documents to create a case study of one of history's most prolific serial killers, John Wayne Gacy. The study portrays a social process through which Gacy passed, a process that included normal adolescent and early adult patterns as well as extraordinary behavior. The author provides an informed discussion of a man whose life included positive reinforcements from his mother as well as negative reinforcements from his father. The influence of his father was later to hold significant meaning in defining Gacy's perception of, and justification for, killing males with whom he had sex.

What can be described as a fairly normal upbringing that included some of the typical behavior and parental reactions characteristic of midwestern blue-collar working-class families, John Wayne had an early introduction to sexual activity including being abused by an adult male. By young adulthood, Gacy began to exhibit a tendency toward the bizarre sexual orientation that would later characterize his life; he engaged in extraordinary criminal activities to express his sexuality.

John Wayne Gacy may defy description, but the case study of a hedonistic lust killer serves as a signal to society. As Gacy grew older his sexual behavior became more extraordinary and ultimately criminal. Although he attempted to fulfill a role as a normal member of society, Gacy's vision of self and certain other members of society and his homosexual denial syndrome were ultimately framed by ideas embraced by his father and the society in which he grew up. That is, men were expected to act as men and do as men are expected to do. For a time at least, John Wayne Gacy displayed skill at presenting to the public a self that was not what he appeared to be. As the author of this chapter makes clear, Gacy rejected the societal label of serial killer. His denial is based on a desire to be accepted as a whole person and not as the bad guy portrayed in the media and official documents.

REFERENCES

Becker, Howard S. 1963. *Outsiders: Studies in the Sociology of Deviance.* New York: The Free Press.
Goffman, Erving. 1963. *Stigma: Notes on the Management of Spoiled Identity.* Englewood Cliffs, N.J.: Prentice-Hall.
———. 1969. *Strategic Interaction.* Philadelphia.: University of Pennsylvania Press.
Manis, Jerome G., and Bernard N. Meltzer. 1978. *Symbolic Interaction: A Reader in Social Psychology.* Boston: Allyn and Bacon.

10

Sexual Harassment

Beverly E. Thorn

INTRODUCTION

"I don't want to get anyone in trouble, I just want it to stop." These are probably the most common words uttered by a victim of sexual harassment, when she finally comes to someone for help with the situation. Those two short sentences symbolize a part of the dynamics inherent in the interplay between the harasser and the victim of sexual harassment. The victim (also referred to as the *target* of sexual harassment) often seems to be overly concerned with the welfare of the perpetrator, to the point that she may have put off complaining for fear it would get the harasser in trouble. The victim also may have forestalled a complaint hoping that if she simply ignored the inappropriate behavior, the harasser would get the message and leave her alone.

"It was just a little pat on the butt." "Women who dress like that have to expect a reaction from a red-blooded man." "Women can't expect to waltz into this business without paying some kind of dues." These are all-too-common rejoinders made by sexual harassers, and as such, represent common explanations for, or theories of, this kind of sexual exploitation. The harasser (also referred to as the *perpetrator* of sexual harassment) most frequently denies the severity of his actions, minimizes their impact, or places the blame for the behavior on the target instead of himself.

Theoretical models that have been used commonly in an attempt to explain the phenomenon of sexual harassment stress the contribution of society's reinforcement of stereotypic sex roles in and out of the workplace. Cultural enforcement of sex roles is argued to promote aggressiveness and domineering sexual behaviors in males and passivity and acquiescence in females (Tangri, Burt, and Johnson 1982). Stereotypic assumptions about men and women are that the sex drive is stronger biologically for men than for women, and thus, to some extent, less controllable. Also, it is assumed that men and women naturally are attracted to each other, thus both sexes voluntarily participate in sexually oriented behavior in any mixed-gender situation. These sex role stereotypes are carried over to the workplace and an individual's expectations of another's sex role are confused with his or her expectations of the individuals work role (Popovich and Licata 1987). Such culturally defined (and reinforced) sex role stereotypes are thought to promote gender inequality and contribute to the patriarchal system in which men are the dominant group (Paludi 1990). It is also thought that institutions provide an organizational structure that makes sexual harassment possible by hierarchy, climate, and specific authority relations. Since most women are in subordinate positions in work settings, culturally defined sex role expectations and workplace authority put males in a "two up" position (Loy and Stewart 1984).

It has been implied, but not stated directly, that women are more frequent victims of sexual harassment than are men. Although this is the case (about 10 percent of yearly Equal Employment Opportunity Commission (EEOC) claims are from men, whereas approximately 90 percent are from women), it is important to note that men are recipients of unwanted sexual attention. Both men and women can be perpetrators of sexual harassment, although the harasser is more typically male. It is thought by some that, as women gain increasing status in organizations, sexual harassment by women will increase.

In the following pages, I will illustrate the dynamics of the sexually harassing relationship. I will do so by the use of a case study that takes the perspective of the actor, in this case, the target of sexual harassment. The chapter begins by defining the term "sexual harassment." Next, an overview of the national problem of sexual harassment, both within the workplace and within academia, is provided. I will thereafter move into specific case study material and finish with implications based upon the material covered in the chapter.

The Problem of Defining Sexual Harassment

One dilemma in reviewing the scope of the problem of sexual harassment is the definition of the term. There is no universally accepted, clear and concise definition of sexual harassment (Foulis and McCabe 1997); organizations are responsible for the development of their own policies on sexual harassment, including a definition of the term. Despite the fact that definitions of the term are often ambiguous and susceptible to a variety of interpretations, sexual harassment is illegal. The EEOC has published the most widely disseminated definition of sexual harassment, from which many companies and universities adapt their own definitions and policies. According to the EEOC, sexual harassment is defined as:

Unwelcome sexual advances, requests for sexual favors, and other verbal or physical conduct of a sexual nature which constitute harassment when: Submission to such conduct is made either explicitly or implicitly a term or condition of an individual's employment; Submission to or rejection of such conduct by an individual is used as the basis for employment decisions affecting such individual; or such conduct has the purpose or effect of unreasonably interfering with an individual's work performance or creating an intimidating, hostile, or offensive working environment. (U.S. Equal Employment Opportunity Commission 1980, p. 25024)

In the Sex Discrimination Act of 1984, the Australian Human Rights and Equal Opportunity Commission defined sexual harassment as "any unwanted or uninvited sexual behavior which is offensive, embarrassing, intimidating, or humiliating. It has nothing to do with mutual attraction or friendship" (as cited in Foulis and McCabe 1997, p. 773).

Quid Pro Quo Sexual Harassment

Literally, the term means "this for that." This type of sexual harassment involves a tangible threat or a promise of a benefit to the target conditional upon the target's acceptance of the harasser's sexual advances. Examples include: promise of a higher grade or a promotion in exchange for "a date," or, the threat of being fired if one does not submit to the harasser's advances. Often, in cases alleging sexual harassment, the target alleges that he or she was terminated wrongfully after refusing a supervisor's sexual gesture or after complaining within the company. In such cases, retaliatory behavior is also considered quid pro quo sexual harassment. It is possible to successfully claim quid pro quo sexual harassment based upon a one-time event, provided it involves a tangible threat or promise of benefit to the target (i.e., sexual coercion or sexual bribery). Sexist remarks and seductive behavior are not considered quid pro quo sexual harassment, unless one's job is in some way made conditional upon submission to these behaviors.

Hostile Environment Sexual Harassment

Unwelcome sexual attention that creates an intimidating workplace or interferes with an employee's job performance is considered hostile environment sexual harassment. For hostile environment sexual harassment, the behavior must be repeated and pervasive so that it pollutes the workplace and creates an untenable working environment for a particular person because of her or his gender or for an entire gender. Examples of hostile environment sexual harassment include: pervasive display of pornographic material in a predominantly male workplace; repeated negative comments about women's ability for a particular job; or repeated, unwelcome, sexual or sexist jokes. Sexist remarks and unwanted seductive behavior, if repeated and pervasive, can be construed as hostile environment sexual harassment.

Consensual Relationships

Although not often considered sexual harassment per se, one area of increasing concern and litigation is the supposed consensual relationship between a subordinate (most frequently an employee or student) and a superordinate (most frequently, a supervisor or teacher). When the relationship goes sour, subsequent behavior may lead to a claim of sexual harassment. Often, the complainant will cite job-related retaliation against him or her following the termination of the consensual relationship. Since the employee or student is under the direct supervision (and influence) of the supervisor, the subordinate is at risk for such retaliation. The superordinate is then in the difficult position of trying to demonstrate that objective and impartial judgment was used in the negative evaluation of an employee after a failed romantic relationship with the employee. Often, the employer may have overlooked poor job performance while the relationship was ongoing, but then takes issue with the misbehavior postrelationship. If employer behavior toward the employee is deemed retaliatory in nature after a failed consensual relationship, a claim of quid pro quo sexual harassment is made. The retaliatory behavior validates that employment status of the subordinate was indeed conditional upon submission to the superordinate's advances.

In academic research studies, an operational definition of sexual harassment is often used. One such frequently used definition of sexual harassment is from Till (1980), who asserts that sexual harassment is essentially composed of five categories of behavior: (1) Gender Harassment: generalized sexist remarks or behavior; (2) Seductive Behavior: inappropriate and offensive, but essentially sanction-free sexual advances; (3) Sexual Bribery: solicitation of sexual activity or other sex-linked behavior by promise of rewards; (4) Sexual Coercion: coercion of sexual activity by threat of punishment; and (5) Sexual Imposition: kissing, fondling, grabbing, or assaulting a person.

A problem associated with defining sexual harassment is that different people view different behaviors as constituting or not constituting sexual harassment. There is general agreement that acts of sexual bribery and sexual coercion constitute sexual harassment. However, women are more likely than men to view gender harassment, seductive behavior, and nonassault forms of sexual imposition (e.g., kissing) as sexual harassment, indicating that women are more likely to classify more subtle behavior as sexual harassment (Fitzgerald and Ormerond 1991). Assaultive sexual imposition (e.g., rape) is not considered sexual harassment by either men or women.

OVERVIEW OF THE PROBLEM: INCIDENCE OF SEXUAL HARASSMENT IN THE WORKPLACE AND ACADEMIA

The problem of sexual harassment in the workplace first gained the attention of academics, legal scholars, and the general public with the 1979 publication of Catherine MacKinnon's now classic *Sexual Harassment of Working Women*. However, among those who debate issues relating to civility, the decade of the 1990s can be noted for its focus on inappropriate sexual conduct. Perhaps the initial focal point for this dialogue was the Clarence Thomas–Anita Hill congressional hearings that opened up the discussion about sexual harassment while encouraging the victims of harassment to speak out about their experiences (Anonymous 1997).

Since 1991, public awareness of the issue of sexual harassment has been raised, first by the Anita Hill/Clarence Thomas hearings. Since that time, the public has been inundated with highly visible cases alleging sexual harassment. In 1992, Senator Brock Adams dropped his bid for a second term after eight women accused him of sexual harassment. In July 1992, navy secretary H. Lawrence Garrett resigned over his handling of the 1991 "Tailhook" convention sexual harassment scandal in Las Vegas. In the mid-1990s the highest ranked noncommissioned U.S. Army officer was court martialed under military procedures for sexual misconduct with female subordinates. He was reduced in rank and forced to retire. And, in 1996, Major General Larry G. Smith was alleged to have made unwanted sexual advances to a female subordinate. The woman, now Lt. General Claudia J. Kennedy, withheld reporting this behavior until the fall of 1999 when Smith was to be appointed to the sensitive position of deputy inspector general, a post to which charges of sexual harassment are reported. Major General Smith's promotion was reversed in early 2000, and the future of his military career was uncertain.

In 1993, Senator Bob Packwood received heavy public pressure to resign as a result of sexual harassment complaints from over twenty-nine female employees. Ultimately, two years later, he resigned just hours after the Senate Ethics Committee voted unanimously to expel him from the Senate for sexual and official misconduct. The President of the United States, William Jefferson Clinton, was a defendant in a civil sexual harassment case brought by Paula Jones. Jones alleges that while she was employed by Clinton when he was Governor of Arkansas, he requested sexual favors and on one occasion allegedly exposed himself to her in a hotel room. In a landmark decision, the U.S. Supreme Court upheld the right of Ms. Jones to pursue the case even while Mr. Clinton is president, a case Ms. Jones ultimately lost when the charges were dismissed in 1998. However, as the two-time president's tenure came to a close he faced disbarment procedures in the Arkansas Supreme Court's Committee on Professional Conduct charged with contempt of court for giving misleading statements while under oath regarding his sexual relationship with White House intern

Monica Lewinsky. The same federal Judge Susan Webber Wright, who had dismissed the Paula Jones sexual harassment lawsuit, also fined him $90,000.

Perhaps related to the increase in public awareness of the problem of sexual harassment, EEOC complaints have steadily increased, with 3,456 in 1990, and 5,594 in 1992. Although it is believed that only 10 to 20 percent of victims report sexual harassment experiences to someone in authority (Welsh 2000), the EEOC total workload for the FY 1992–FY 1999 period, including sexual harassment charges transferred to EEOC from Fair Employment Practice Agencies, are even more impressive, and these data show a steady increase through 1997. In 1992, a total of 10,532 sexual harassment discrimination charges were filed, including 9.1 percent filed by males. By 1995, the total number of charges increased to 15,549 with 9.9 percent filed by males. As the millennium drew to a close, the numbers continued to be high: 1996—15,342 (10.0 percent male); 1997—15,889 (11.6 percent male); 1998—15,618 (12.9 percent male); and 1999—15,222 (12.1 percent male) respectively (U.S. Equal Employment Opportunity Commission 2000).

Reported frequencies of sexual harassment vary depending upon the definition of the behavior. In employment settings, several large-scale studies have supported the hypothesis that sexual harassment is a pandemic problem. In 1980, 1987, and 1994, the U.S. Merit Systems Protection Board (U.S. MSPB) surveyed federal employees regarding their experiences of being sexually harassed in the workplace. The 1980 survey included over 23,000 employees and asked them about their personal experiences of being sexually harassed in the workplace at some point during the preceding two-year period. Forty-two percent of the women and 15 percent of the men surveyed reported being the target of sexual harassment during this period. A survey of a similar magnitude was conducted in California (Gutek 1981) and 53 percent of the women surveyed reported that they had experienced at least one incident of sexual harassment during their working careers. In the 1994 U.S. MSPB survey, 44 percent of the women and 19 percent of the men surveyed identified themselves as recipients of uninvited and unwanted sexual attention. These statistics are similar to the 1980 and 1987 U.S. MSPB survey results.

Data collected from college and university samples suggest that the problem of sexual harassment in higher education is also widespread. Although reported frequencies of sexual harassment vary, a reliable estimate is that between 20 and 30 percent of undergraduate women have been the recipient of unwanted seductive behavior, sexual bribery/coercion, or sexual imposition from a male professor or instructor at some point during their four years of college. If the definition of sexual harassment is expanded to include sexist remarks or other forms of gender harassment, the incidence rate among undergraduate women rises to 70 percent (Adams, Kottke, and Padgitt 1983; Lott, Reilly, and Howard 1982). Unlike the workplace, where targets of sexual harassment are usually the younger of the workforce, in higher education graduate students rather than undergraduate students are more likely to be the targets of sexual harassment.

In one survey of graduate student women, 60 percent of them reported exposure to some type of gender harassment by male faculty, and 22 percent were asked out on dates by their professors (Lott, Reilly, and Howard. 1982).

Given the above statistics, it is obvious that sexual harassment remains a critically important problem in today's society. Evidently, individuals are disregarding federal statutes, increasingly strict company policies, and university standards. What then drives the behavior, and how does the dynamic interplay between target and perpetrator help to explain the continued problem of sexual harassment? The following pages will attempt to answer these and other questions by concentrating on the story of one central target of sexual harassment—Lisa. To illustrate other points, I will include relevant data from other sources in the case (company investigations, co-worker depositions, and testimony from the defense).

LISA: A CASE STUDY

I interviewed Lisa because she was the plaintiff in a civil sexual harassment case, and I had been hired by her attorney as an expert witness for the plaintiff. As a clinical psychologist with expertise in the area of sexual exploitation, I have been hired by attorneys representing plaintiffs, and in some cases, alleged perpetrators of sexual harassment. For six years, I also served as the Sexual Harassment Officer for a College of Arts & Sciences, investigating cases and providing counseling options where appropriate. Interviewing the complainant is a common and critical first step in trying to understand what has happened, how it happened, and what needs to be done about it.

Lisa began the interview by stating, "If you could've seen me a year ago, you wouldn't believe you were talking to the same person." She was quick to state that following her termination at the company where the sexual harassment took place, she was "a nervous wreck." She couldn't eat, weighed only 103 pounds, couldn't sleep, cried at the drop of a hat, and was constantly sick. "If I wasn't throwing up, I had diarrhea." Since this time, she stated, she has been getting progressively better and better, despite the stress of litigation.

At the time of the interview, Lisa was 34 and divorced from, but living with, her second husband. Her second husband was a recovering alcoholic and was verbally abusive when drinking. He had been physically violent toward Lisa "only" one time, during which he broke her nose. Lisa's first marriage, at the age of 18, was physically abusive and ended in divorce. She had a daughter from the first marriage who was 16 at the time of the interview. Lisa had a history of sexual abuse by an uncle. When she was 8 to 9 years old, the 18-year-old uncle would baby sit, lock her in the washroom, lay on top of her and masturbate until ejaculating on her. He never attempted to penetrate her vaginally, but frequently "stuck his hands down my pants." Lisa's father was physically abusive toward her and her siblings. Historical experiences (in this case, previous sexual exploitation) influence interpretations of interactions in later relationships (Blumer 1969). In Lisa's case, her previous sexual abuse may have influenced her to be hypersensitive to later behaviors that were potentially exploitative. On the other hand, it is possible that early experience with sexual and physical abuse created a "learned helplessness" style of coping whereby Lisa was less likely to stand up for herself, even in the face of exploitation.

Lisa completed high school and received on-the-job training as a bookkeeping clerk. Prior to becoming a bookkeeper, Lisa had worked at various restaurants. She had been employed as a bookkeeper for three years prior to coming to the company where the harassment occurred. She reported having always received good evaluations in her positions. She did not have a history of job termination, with the most recent exception of being terminated by the present company, and, when she was in high school, being terminated from a restaurant for arguing with a co-worker. Targets of sexual harassment are usually women with relatively little power within the organization or culturally. Trainees or those low in organizational positions, nonwhite, and young women are frequent victims of sexual harassment. Targets of sexual harassment are more heavily concentrated in low-income occupations and single or divorced—often, the sole supporter of the family (Center for Women's Policy Studies 1981).

Since the company where she worked was a large one, bookkeeping was split into several "teams," which included three accountants and several bookkeepers, as well as general clerical staff. Lisa's team was comprised of two male accountants and one female accountant. Although the accountants headed their team of workers, the chain of command in the company did not specifically endow the accountants with supervisory responsibility over the bookkeepers and clerical staff. Instead, there was a head administrative accountant (a department head) who was in charge of all three working teams and also responsible for evaluation of all employees in the accounting department.

One of the accountants on Lisa's team, Jeff, had a reputation for flirting and making suggestive remarks to the clerical staff and bookkeepers. He was also known for telling sexual jokes to small groups of people gathered at break areas. Some of the other workers weren't interested in his jokes, but none appeared offended by them. Another worker acknowledged that Jeff's behavior was somewhat different from the professional demeanor of the others, but explained away the behavior by saying, "He's just that way—he doesn't really mean anything by it." "Jeff is a really friendly guy, especially to women, but he's harmless." Jeff displayed flirtatious behavior toward women, but not indiscriminately; the female accountant on his team (his true equal, in terms of job status) was not a recipient of his "friendly" gestures. Jeff was 47 at the time the complaint against him was lodged. Married, somewhat overweight, and not particularly good-looking, he hardly fit the "Casanova" stereotype.

In a study by Gutek (1985), she found that most harassers were co-workers who were older than their target, married, below average in physical appearance, and were reported to behave in a generally harassing manner toward women. Although it is debatable whether Jeff's behavior was generally harassing toward women, he had been "friendly" toward a number of female co-workers, particularly those who were not of equal status.

Lisa stated that Jeff began harassing her after she had been with the company two and one-half years, and that the harassment lasted for five years before she "went public." The unwanted behavior began gradually; at first, Jeff simply complimented her when she wore something he liked. Lisa reported that being complimented was a nice event for her, and she didn't mind it at all. Looking retrospectively, though, she recalled that the way he complimented her was often more personalized than the way other co-workers might compliment her manner of dress. Instead of simply saying, "That's a nice dress," he would state, "Now, that's a good dress for you. The colors bring out the pink in your skin, and the cut of the dress is the kind I like." Gradually, his compliments became even more personal—a critique of her choice of clothes as they related to his personal taste: "Now, Lisa, you know I don't care for purple, why did you choose to wear that today?" A turning point, in her mind, was when Jeff began commenting on the way she was built. A rather petite woman with somewhat large breasts, Lisa took care not to wear clothing that made her look "top heavy." Jeff began commenting, rather directly, when an outfit accentuated her breasts and finally, he began making direct comments about her build independent of her outfit. She recalled the gradual shift of her feelings about his remarks from being pleased at first, to feeling a bit uncertain about his motivations for a compliment, to feeling exposed and "dirty," and finally, being nauseated on the day he told her that she was "built like a brick shit house."

Note that nowhere in the description of her feelings was outrage, anger, or even irritation at Jeff. Targets of sexual harassment are much more likely to blame themselves for the unwanted behavior than to hold the perpetrator responsible for his behavior. Lisa was indeed similar to many targets of sexual harassment in that she assumed if Jeff was behaving inappropriately toward her, it must be something she was doing to incite him. She illustrated this attitude by stating during the interview, "I'm a good Christian woman and I have never 'messed around.' I didn't understand why Jeff was saying these things to me, but I decided it must be my fault. After all, he wasn't being this way with the other women." As noted by Symbolic Interaction Theory, in the course of their interactions, persons (in this case, the target and the perpetrator of sexual harassment) develop meanings and symbols regarding their interactions (Stryker and Statham 1985). In this case, Lisa was making meaningful (albeit inaccurate) interpretations about her behavior based upon Jeff's response toward her.

Part of the interplay between target and perpetrator of sexual harassment is that the target is generally passive, is likely dependent upon what others think about her, and tends to attribute negative events in her life to something that she did to cause them. Thus, targets of sexual harassment, like other victims, often make an internal causal attribution to the negative events which befall them (Fiske and Taylor 1991). While this type of target does not incite or cause the sexual harassment, her passivity may contribute to its continuation. The perpetrator of sexual harassment, on the other hand, most typically takes undue credit for positive things that happen in his life, but ascribes blame to others for negative events. Whether he consciously chooses his victims or not, the best targets are those who have characteristics similar to those described above. It may be that women with little power within the organizational structure are the most likely to be passive, dependent, and negatively self-evaluative.

Many targets of sexual harassment are convinced that they are the only ones who are experiencing or have experienced unwanted sexual attention from the perpetrator. In reality, the perpetrator has often behaved in a similar manner toward other women, although they too have kept silent. It is sometimes the case that when a sexual harassment case is litigated, a handful (or more) of women come forward and "confess" that they too were harassed by the perpetrator.

That Lisa felt responsible for Jeff's behavior made her less willing to talk to anyone about it, including her husband, Rob. He was an alcoholic and Lisa stated that Rob was verbally abusive to her when he was drinking. Telling him about Jeff "would just give him more ammunition," so she kept it to herself. Even later, when Lisa was referred to a psychologist for treatment because of frequent unexplainable medical complaints, she did not tell the psychologist about Jeff's behavior. "It wasn't the only bad thing happening in my life, but it was a bad thing that I felt dirty and ashamed about. I chose to talk about the other bad things in my life."

Shortly after Jeff began commenting directly on Lisa's body, he began to touch her. At first, it was a casual hand on the shoulder or arm around the neck. She had seen Jeff do this with other people (including male co-workers), and no one seemed bothered by it. But, to her knowledge, Jeff wasn't commenting on anyone else's body. Lisa felt, as many targets of sexual harassment do, that if she kept a "low profile," he would eventually get bored and leave her alone. She began dressing in neutral colors and got some baggy sweaters to wear over her clothes around the office. She avoided Jeff's office whenever possible, but she did have to work with him and thus was forced to go to his office on occasion. To her horror, one day when she entered his office, Jeff shut the door, grabbed her, and nibbled on her neck. Reflexively, she scolded him. "Jeff, you are sick! You're a married man, and you're supposed to be a Christian!" Jeff seemed delighted by her reaction, laughed, and said, "I knew I could finally get a rise out of you! Will you relax? You are such a prude for such a good-looking broad! I'm not trying to go to bed with you, I'm just trying to loosen you up, for God's sake!" Then he opened the door, laughed some more, and swatted her on the buttocks as she left his office.

Sexual harassment is not a problem of uncontrollable sexual desire, but rather involves the inappropriate use of power. Often, the harasser does not even seem to want sexual relations with the target. Both men and women agree that power is a factor in sexual harassment (Beauvais 1986; Lott, Reilly, and Howard 1982).

After this incident, Lisa never went into Jeff's office alone. She entered only when her friend, and Jeff's clerical assistant, Joan, was in the office or willing to go with her. Lisa finally told Joan what had happened. Joan's response was typical of many co-workers who learn of sexually inappropriate behavior at the office. "Lisa, he's just doing that because he knows it upsets you. Jeff is a corny, harmless, nerd. When you get upset, it probably turns him on, so quit reacting. It's up to you to handle this guy." Now it wasn't just Lisa telling herself that she was accountable—her friend was also assigning responsibility to Lisa for Jeff's conduct. Lisa was more certain than ever that she was to blame and that telling anyone else would be a mistake. So, she suffered in silence and continued to avoid Jeff. Lisa also related that landing the job with this company had been "the job," and she was fearful of losing it if she made any complaints about Jeff's behavior. After all, he was an accountant and she was merely a book-keeping clerk.

One question many people have about victims of sexual harassment is why they do not report the behavior immediately. As we see from Lisa's case, the reasons are manifold. First, often the inappropriate behavior is gradual and not clearly objectionable until a certain point. At that juncture, the target often feels that she has been condoning the behavior by saying nothing and therefore is partly to blame. She also looks around and sees no one else being offended, or treated the same way, so she feels as if she must either be extremely sensitive, or encouraging the behavior in some way. Either way, she feels badly about herself and to "go public" is to risk widespread scrutiny and criticism. Targets of sexual harassment will often confide in a co-worker or confidante. The co-worker is unlikely to be well informed about harassment and may therefore inadvertently contribute to the problem by implying that the perpetrator's be-havior is the responsibility of the target. The support system of many targets of sexual harassment is typically limited and imperfect at best. That Lisa's husband was abusing alcohol and verbally abusive to Lisa contributed to her perceived sense of isolation regarding the problem and reluctance to talk about it. Finally, Lisa, as others, didn't want to get anyone in trouble. After all, maybe she was to blame. Certainly, it seemed, she was being overly sensitive to a co-worker seen by others as a "harmless nerd."

A few other incidents marked the extent of the severity of Jeff's behavior. Once, when Lisa was walking down the hall at lunch time, Jeff came along, "scooped me up, and twirled me around the hall." This he did in front of other co-workers, who seemed nonplused or mildly amused. Certainly, no one ap-peared appalled except Lisa. Another time, again in front of other co-workers, Jeff kissed Lisa on the lips and then laughed gaily. Lisa burst into tears and ran out of the lunchroom. Before Joan followed her out, Joan remonstrated Jeff, saying, "Why don't you leave her alone? Can't you see you're getting under her skin?" Jeff again laughed and stated, "I take it as my personal duty to loosen that woman up! What's the matter today, Joan—a bad time of the month for you?"

Later that day, Joan told Lisa that Jeff had kissed other women in the office and that while no one complained, it didn't seem to be highly prized by the recipient either. It was as if people were tolerating "marginally" inappropriate behavior or explaining it away rather than confronting it directly. Joan now felt drawn into the conflict, and she was nervous about it because she was Jeff's assistant. Joan felt that he behaved coolly toward her the rest of the week and merit raise decisions were coming up.

Let us pause with Lisa's story to examine in detail the nature of the inappropriate behavior exhibited by Jeff. Recall from earlier in the chapter that whether or not a behavior is deemed to constitute sexual harassment depends upon who is defining the behavior. According to Till's (1980) categorization of sexually harassing behaviors, Jeff's behavior includes gender harassment, seductive behavior, and nonassaultive sexual imposition. Note that none of these behaviors would constitute quid pro quo sexual harassment and would therefore fall under the category of possible hostile environment sexual harassment.

Regarding gender harassment, Jeff exhibited the following: the telling of sexual jokes; making personal remarks about Lisa's physical appearance, particularly "critiquing" her build; and asking Joan if it was "the wrong time of the month." Generalized sexist remarks can be explicitly hostile (e.g., "she's a bitch"), but in Jeff's case, the remarks were indirectly aggressive. Indirect aggression can give the illusion of a compliment or a neutral remark, but the recipient almost always feels put down or vilified in some way. Sexist remarks are conscious acts of direct or indirect aggression and serve to attempt to put the recipient in her place (i.e., beneath the perpetrator).

Jeff's "compliments" toward Lisa, particularly regarding her body and manner of dress, are an example of seductive behavior. Sometimes, seductive behavior is clearly courting behavior (i.e., aimed at getting the recipient to go out with or have a sexual relationship with the harasser). The behaviors Jeff exhibited seemed to be more to get a rise out of Lisa, rather than to get her to be interested in a romantic relationship with him. Unlike sexual bribery and sexual coercion, seductive behaviors do not carry with them the promise of reward for compliance or the threat of punishment for refusal. But, seductive behaviors deemed to be sexually harassing are unwanted, and they usually continue, even in the face of feedback from the recipient that she does not appreciate the seduction.

The last category of sexually harassing behaviors that Jeff evidenced was that of nonassaultive sexual imposition. Touching Lisa, nuzzling her neck, picking her up, and finally, kissing her are all physical sexual behaviors. Some readers might characterize some of Jeff's physical sexual behaviors as assaultive sexual imposition, although this usually implies forced sexual contact, such as rape.

Note that the three categories of sexually harassing behavior evidenced by Jeff are considered the more subtle of the categories of sexual harassment (Till 1980), and those around which there is the most disagreement, particularly between males and females. Since none of the behaviors involved bribery or coercion, they would not constitute quid pro quo sexual harassment. However, if repeated and pervasive enough to pollute the workplace and create an untenable working environment, these types of inappropriate behaviors might contribute to an allegation of hostile environment sexual harassment.

Getting back to Lisa's story, during the fifth and final year of Lisa's sexual harassment by Jeff, he was promoted to head the accounting department. Now, Jeff was explicitly in charge of evaluating all employees in this department, including Lisa. Jeff's inappropriate behavior toward Lisa tapered off, but in Lisa's mind, he began scrutinizing her behavior and not the behavior of others. One aspect of Lisa's work performance that was not exemplary was her frequent consultation with the company physician. Lisa had a myriad of somatic complaints and often visited the physician two to three times per week. To do this, she had to take some time off from work even though his office was in the same building. Her previous supervisor had been quite understanding about her needs, but Jeff seemed inflexible and suspicious of her motives. For the first time in her adult life, she received an unfavorable job evaluation. Lisa began to worry that Jeff was trying to build a case against her in order to fire her. She felt that Jeff was doing this because he "didn't want me around now that he was department head and couldn't afford any little black clouds over his head." The unfavorable job evaluation was thought by Lisa (and her attorney) to be evidence of retaliation against Lisa for not going along with his remarks and behavior. Thus, the claim of retaliation was made, which brings into play the allegation of quid pro quo sexual harassment. One month after Jeff's promotion, Lisa filed a complaint against Jeff with the company as well as with the Equal Employment Opportunity Commission. Both Jeff and Lisa were assigned administrative (paid) leaves of absence during the week-long company investigation. Certain behaviors exhibited by Jeff were validated by witnesses (i.e., sexual joke telling, kissing female co-workers, kissing Lisa, picking Lisa up and twirling her) and other behaviors were not verified for lack of witnesses (e.g., personal comments regarding Lisa's body, nibbling her neck, and swatting her buttocks).

In most sexual harassment cases, at least some behaviors alleged to have occurred do not have the benefit of witnesses or other validating evidence. Many investigations begin with a he said/she said scenario; the investigator must ferret out the truth, sometimes in the absence of proof. Many observers assume that an investigation will be biased toward the target of the sexual harassment. Others assume that the company is out to protect itself, unwilling to admit guilt unless absolutely necessary, and will therefore invalidate anything but established fact. My experience is that it depends upon the investigator. It is possible to immediately discount all disputed allegations (he said/she said), but it is also possible to keep asking, to ask in different ways, and to ask at multiple times. Not infrequently, one or the other's story will begin to break down on continued questioning. For example, when Jeff was asked if he ever nibbled on Lisa's neck, he flatly denied this behavior. "In fact," he stated, "I've never so much as closed the door to my office when she's been in there." Although no one saw Jeff nibble Lisa's neck, his assistant had indeed seen him close the door behind Lisa. Thus, Jeff's story begins to erode, even without the benefit of direct evidence regarding neck nuzzling.

In a written summary of the company investigation, Jeff's behavior was deemed "unprofessional, inappropriate, and unacceptable," but "not so severe or pervasive as to meet the legal definition of sexual harassment." These conclusions were based, in part, upon the company's interpretations of confirmed incidents. For example, they stated that "the kiss was not a passionate kiss." Other behaviors that allegedly occurred but had no witnesses (e.g., the incident in Jeff's office where he nibbled her neck and patted her buttocks) were dismissed as unverifiable. Jeff was demoted from his supervisory position without loss of pay, and both Jeff and Lisa were instructed to return to work. The company made the decision to keep the previous accounting teams intact; thus, Lisa was faced with continuing interaction with Jeff on a daily basis.

One of the most difficult things for Lisa in the aftermath of the complaint was her treatment by co-workers. Although no one ever said anything to her face, co-workers were now cool and aloof to her. Lisa's friend, Joan, reported that co-workers now described Lisa as "a gold digger," "childish," "crazy," "nuts," "doesn't want to work," and "selfish." Joan was shocked at co-workers' damnation of Lisa, even though she herself had initially ascribed responsibility for "handling Jeff" to Lisa. Joan eventually found another job because the aftermath of the harassment had polluted the working environment for her.

Although Lisa attempted to work in the department for the next several weeks, both she and her psychologist agreed that the situation was untenable, and she requested that Jeff be transferred. Instead, the company offered Lisa several other jobs within the company, all for decreased pay, and none for which she was trained. One of the jobs was night shift work and another involved working a swing shift. She refused these jobs and refused to continue working in the accounting department. Eventually, the company fired her "due to lack of employment for which she was qualified." In the deposition, the company representative justified the termination by stating that Lisa was not coming to work and they "could not pay her indefinitely." The plaintiff's attorney argued that the termination was a wrongful dismissal and retaliatory toward Lisa for filing the sexual harassment claim. The plaintiffs therefore claimed quid pro quo sexual harassment as well as hostile environment sexual harassment.

Although Lisa stated that she was experiencing ongoing emotional and physical problems during the time of the harassment, she stated that when she was terminated, she "lay in bed for weeks." She reported that she lost all her self-confidence and had a difficult time recovering from the impact of being terminated.

Lisa's daughter, Amy, experienced difficulty after Lisa was terminated. Financial difficulties notwithstanding, Lisa stated that the biggest hardship from being harassed and terminated was its impact on her daughter. Lisa found it difficult to explain to her daughter or anyone else why, if she was the victim, she was the one ultimately terminated. It made her question once again her own role in the harassment. Lisa's daughter, Amy, experienced frequent crying spells, often saying things like, "when am I gonna get my Mamma back?" . . . "Mamma, when are you going to do something with your life?" . . . "Mamma, you're the only one I have and when you're sick, I don't have anybody." Amy's feelings were common fallout experienced by loved ones of victims of sexual harassment.

After more than a year had passed since Lisa was terminated, she reported that she was getting progressively better. Her visits to physicians were less frequent, though she was still seeing her psychologist regularly, and she had gotten several temporary jobs through an employment service. Nevertheless, several collection agencies were in frequent contact about unpaid bills. Lisa was afraid that the publicity surrounding the civil case could jeopardize her chances of retaining a permanent job as a bookkeeper. She also felt guilty when she did not tell prospective employers about the pending litigation.

DISCUSSION AND CONCLUSION

For a moment, put yourself in the position of a co-worker who has witnessed some, but not all, of Jeff's behaviors toward Lisa. Are these behaviors really sexual harassment? After all, Jeff wasn't Lisa's boss, and he didn't require her to have intercourse in order to keep her job. He didn't even intend to have sex with her! Isn't this what we really mean when we use the term sexual harassment? Jeff's behavior didn't seem to bother other women, or at least they knew how to handle him. Lisa had always been kind of sensitive and up-tight; should Jeff be punished just because Lisa could not tolerate a bit of spicy behavior from a co-worker? And how about other co-workers? Lisa's complaint had really created havoc in the company: new policies, training programs, and lots of divisiveness. No wonder other co-workers were calling Lisa "selfish" and a "gold digger."

Imagine yourself as a potential employer and consider the prospect of hiring Lisa as a new employee. You had heard that something had happened at the company where Lisa used to work. She has told you that she will gladly provide references from other former employers, but she is uncomfortable providing references from the most recent employer. Then you hear she has filed a sexual harassment lawsuit. Despite her experience as a bookkeeper, why should you take a risk of hiring someone who might be a "loose cannon?" After all, there are other qualified applicants, maybe not with as much experience, but certainly qualified.

Now, imagine yourself a juror in this case. Is Lisa telling the truth, or is she exaggerating Jeff's behavior in order to win a settlement? Would a typical woman be offended by Jeff's behavior or was Lisa exquisitely sensitive? Was Jeff guilty of sexual harassment? What type? Quid pro quo, hostile environment, or both? Did the company handle the complaint appropriately? Did their termination of Lisa constitute retaliation and quid pro quo sexual harassment or were they justified in their actions? You're the juror. You decide.

For the record, prior to jury trial, the case was dismissed from federal court by the judge in an action called a Summary Judgment. One important issue complicating the testimony of the plaintiff was her history of emotional disorder, including previous psychiatric hospitalization. Plaintiff's attorneys argue that a preexisting psychiatric condition could make a victim more vulnerable to even relatively minor stress, causing extreme psychological damage (the "eggshell" theory, Binder 1992). Defense attorneys, on the other hand, argued that their client is not responsible for the preexisting psychological condition of the plaintiff. Regardless of which side of the fence one is on, previous psychiatric illnesses, in particular, may elicit behavior that makes the witness a less credible source in the eyes of the judge or jury. In Lisa's case, psychiatric records verified a history of difficulty with interpersonal relationships, perhaps raising questions about Lisa's ability to perceive other's intentions. Additionally, the day Lisa lodged her complaint with the company regarding Jeff's behavior, she made superficial cuts in her wrists at work. This type of impulsive and dramatic behavior, while a genuine plea for help, can be interpreted as an overreaction and thus further confirmation of instability (and therefore question credibility) on the part of the plaintiff. When the alleged sexual harassment behaviors are mostly unverifiable and boil down to a he said/she said standoff, issues of witness credibility become extremely important. The case went to trial in the state courts.

REFERENCES

Adams, Jean W., Janet L. Kottke, and Janet S. Padgitt. 1983. "Sexual Harassment of University Students." *Journal of College Student Personnel* 24: 284–490.

Anonymous. 1997. "Inappropriate Sexual Conduct Named Top Risk of the 90s." *The Internal Auditor* 54:14–15.

Beauvais, Kathleen. 1986. "Workshops to Combat Sexual Harassment: A Case Study of Changing Attitudes." *Signs: Journal of Women in Culture and Society* 12: 130–145.

Binder, Renee. 1992. "Sexual Harassment: Issues for Forensic Psychiatrists." *Bulletin of the American Academy of Psychiatry Law* 20: 409–418.

Blumer, Herbert. 1969. *Symbolic Interactionism: Perspective and Method*. Englewood Cliffs, N.J.: Prentice-Hall.

Center for Women's Policy Studies. 1981. *Harassment and Discrimination in Employment*. Washington, D.C.

Fiske, Susan T., and Shelley E. Taylor. 1991. *Attribution Theory: Social Cognition*. New York: McGraw-Hill.

Fitzgerald, Louise F., and Alayne J. Ormerond. 1991. "Perceptions of Sexual Harassment: The Influence of Gender and Academic Context." *Psychology of Women Quarterly* 15: 281–294.

Foulis, Danielle, and Marita P. McCabe. 1997. "Sexual Harassment: Factors Affecting Attitudes and Perceptions." *Sex Roles* 37: 773–798.

Gutek, Barbara A. 1981. "Experiences of Sexual Harassment: Results From a Representative Survey." Paper presented at the meeting of the American Psychological Association. Los Angeles, Calif., August.

———. 1985. *Sex and the Workplace*. San Francisco: Jossey-Bass.

Lott, Bernice, Mary Ellen Reilly, and Dale R. Howard. 1982. "Sexual Assault and Harassment: A Campus Community Case Study." *Signs* 8: 296–319.

Loy, Pamela Hewitt, and Lea P. Stewart. 1984. "The Extent and Effects of the Sexual Harassment of Working Women." *Sociological Focus* 17: 31–43.

MacKinnon, Catherine A. 1979. *Sexual Harassment of Working Women: A Case Study of Sex Discrimination*. New Haven, Conn.: Yale University Press.

Paludi, Michelle Antoinette, ed. 1990. *Ivory Power: Sexual Harassment on Campus*. Albany: SUNY Press.

Popovich, Paula M., and Betty Jo Licata. 1987. "A Role Model Approach to Sexual Harassment." *Journal of Management* 13: 149–161.

Stryker, Sheldon, and Anne Statham. 1985. "Symbolic Interaction and Role Theory." In Lindzey Gardner and Elliot Aronson, eds., *Handbook of Social Psychology*, 3rd ed., pp. 311–377. New York: Random House.

Tangri, Sandra S., Martha R. Burt, and, Leanor B. Johnson. 1982. "Sexual Harassment at Work: Three Explanatory Models." *Journal of Social Issues* 38: 33–54.

Till, Frank. 1980. *Sexual Harassment: A Report on the Sexual Harassment of Students*. Washington, D.C.: National Advisory Council on Women's Educational Programs.

U.S. Equal Employment Opportunity Commission. 1980. "Discrimination Because of Sex under Title VII of the 1964 Civil Rights Act as Amended: Adoption of Interim Guidelines—Sexual Harassment." *Federal Register* 45: 25024–25025.

———. 2000. "Sexual Harassment Charges EEOC and FEPAs Combined: FY 1992–FY 1999." January 12. <http://eeoc.gov/stats/harass.html>.

U.S. Merit Systems Protection Board. 1981. *Sexual Harassment of Federal Workers: Is it A Problem?* Washington, D.C.: U.S. Government Printing Office.

———. 1988. *Sexual Harassment in the Federal Government: An Update*. Washington, D.C.: U.S. Government Printing Office.

———. 1994. *Sexual Harassment in the Department of Justice: Results of a Study by the U.S. Merit Systems Protection Board Conducted for the Department of Justice*. Washington, D.C.: U.S. Government Printing Office.

Welsh, Sandy. 2000. "The Multidimentional Nature of Sexual Harassment: An Empirical Analysis of Women's Sexual Harassment Complaints." *Violence Against Women* 6: 118–141.

11

Equal Protection and Racial Exclusion

Larry D. Hall and Audwin L. Anderson

INTRODUCTION

The Sixth Amendment to the Constitution of the United States guarantees that any person tried for a crime has the right to a trial heard by an impartial jury. Potential jurors are selected randomly to represent the community at large. To insure impartiality, potential jurors can be removed by the trial judge if they have personal knowledge of the victim, defendant, or important witnesses; if they have already reached a decision pertaining to the defendant's guilt or innocence; or if they are considered unsuitable to serve. In addition, opposing attorneys are allowed to question potential jurors, or venire members, during voir dire to determine whether biases exist, which may prevent them from acting in a fair and impartial manner. Attorneys also use the information gathered during voir dire to remove venire members they believe may favor the opposing side. This is accomplished through the use of peremptory challenges.

The rationale upon which the peremptory challenge is based is that if attorneys from both sides strike or remove potential jurors they believe may favor the opposing side, the remaining jurors will be without bias. Unfortunately, in the American legal system, attorneys often attempt to use peremptory challenges to select a jury that is favorable to their client. As one example, in the past prosecutors frequently removed most or all minority group members from venire pools when prosecuting a minority defendant if they thought minority jurors would vote for acquittal.

OVERVIEW OF THE JURY SELECTION PROBLEM

The wholesale removal of minorities from jury pools through peremptory challenges was first challenged in 1965 by Robert Swain, an African American, who had been convicted of an interracial rape in the state of Alabama. An all-white jury was selected for the Swain trial after the six African Americans in his jury pool were struck by the prosecutor. In *Swain v. Alabama* 1965 it was argued that use of peremptory challenges to remove all African Americans from the jury violated the Equal Protection Clause of the Fourteenth Amendment. Swain further protested that through the use of peremptory challenges no African American had been allowed to serve on a trial jury in his county of residence during the preceding thirteen years.

The U.S. Supreme Court ruled that the removal of all African Americans from Swain's jury did not violate the Equal Protection Clause. However, the removal of minority venire members in every case tried by one specific prosecutor—regardless of the race of either the victim or the race of the defendant, or the nature of the case—did indeed constitute systematic discrimination, a violation of the Equal Protection Clause.

Because the "total exclusion of minorities" required under *Swain* is difficult to prove, a large percentage of minority venire members continue to be excluded from jury pools, resulting in primarily white or all-white juries, especially when minority defendants were tried from 1965 through 1986 (Hall and Anderson 1996). In 1986, Robert Batson, an African American, was convicted of burglary by an all-white jury. All four African American in Batson's jury pool were struck by peremptory challenge. On challenge, the U.S. Supreme Court ruled (*Batson v. Kentucky* 1986) that it was a violation of the Equal Protection Clause to use peremptory challenges to strike intentionally African Americans from a single jury.

Under Batson, the defendant has to establish prima facie that a juror was removed intentionally for racial reasons. If the judge decides that a prima facie case has been established, then the striking attorney is required to provide a race-neutral explanation for doing so. Then, provided the residing judge accepts the peremptory challenge as race-neutral, the trial proceeds. However, if the judge decides the strike is racially based, the venire member is placed back on the jury or an entirely new jury panel is selected prior to any evidence being presented.

Challenges based on the *Batson* decision are often denied by the trial judge whereupon the case may be appealed to the higher Appellate Court. To uphold a *Batson* challenge, the Appellate Court must conclude that the decision of the trial judge was "clearly erroneous."

Implementation of Batson

Although the procedures described above appear straightforward, the use of race-based strikes remains a reality in the American judicial system. Because the U.S. Supreme Court did not explicitly define that which constitutes either a race-neutral or a race-based peremptory challenge, it remains for the lower court to identify the characteristics. In so doing, the courts can focus on the proportion of strikes used to remove minorities, whether or not nonminorities with the same attributes, socioeconomic backgrounds, or attitudes also were struck, or the failure on the part of the striking attorneys to make meaningful inquiries during voir dire.

An objection based on the *Batson* decision is raised easily. Similarly, it is a relatively simple matter for the striking attorney to defend the strike of a minority as being race-neutral. The only guidelines provided are that the reasons for the strike be related to the specific case and that the strikes are not obvious in their racist orientation. If an attorney provides a reason that is even tangential in its relationship to the case or the strikes are based on questions that were asked during voir dire, the *Batson* challenge is generally overturned. Indeed, less than 16 percent of *Batson* challenges succeed.

In an attempt to understand the dynamics of how the peremptory challenge is employed we analyze two cases. In the following, we examine the interactions that occur during the jury striking phase of two cases, one criminal case and one civil case.

J. L. NEAL: A CRIMINAL CASE STUDY

In 1996, an African American male defendant charged with robbery and murder made a claim that the prosecutor violated *Batson* by using peremptory strikes to remove five minority venire members from the jury because of their race or ethnic origin. The state used four of its fourteen peremptory strikes to remove four of the six blacks from the jury (D. L., A. M., B. S., and C. S.) and a fifth peremptory strike to remove an Hispanic (M.S.). Without ruling whether a *Batson* prima facie case had been made, the trial court required the state prosecutor to explain the reasons for striking the five minority venire members. The prosecutor offered what he argued were race neutral reasons for the strikes.

While there exist many different perspectives and views for interpreting the real meaning and intent of peremptory strikes, the ultimate arbiter is the judge or, if the case is appealed, the Appellate Court. In the following we examine the symbolic process of such challenges to, and defense of, the peremptory strikes of minorities as it developed during a criminal trial and, later, before the Appellate Court.

Striking of the Criminal Jury

The first African American venire member struck by the prosecutor was a female, D. L. During voir dire (questioning) the defense attorney inquired of

D. L. if she had heard about the case under consideration. Responding she had not, the prosecutor asked no further questions. He then proceeded to strike D. L. A *Batson* objection was raised by the defense at which time the trial judge required the prosecutor to explain this strike.

The prosecutor offered the following: D. L. had a very weak personality relative to the questions asked by the state. She vacillated back and forth when questions were posed by the defense attorney as well as those entered by the state. The prosecutor further argued that the nature of this case required a person of strong personality. The lack of a strong personality constituted a race neutral reason.

The trial court found the explanation provided was a "sufficiently race free reason for the strike" and that the state did not intentionally exclude all blacks from the jury. However, upon appeal, the State Court of Criminal Appeals reversed the decision of the trial judge, remanding the case for retrial. The Appellate Court concluded the prosecutor asked no voir dire questions of D. L. and that D. L. answered the defense attorney's questions without undue vacillation. In the majority opinion the Court wrote: "From this exchange and the record as a whole as well, we see no indication that D. L. vacillated back and forth as the prosecutor alleged. Furthermore, the prosecutor indicated that D. L. had been questioned by the State. However, there is no evidence in the record that the State questioned D. L. at any time" (*Neal* 1996).

A second African American juror, A. M., was struck by the prosecutor. When challenged, the prosecutor offered as his reason that the individual stricken was a "real, real young black male" who was not well educated. Furthermore, the prosecutor stated this young man had difficulty understanding concepts when inquiries were posed by state and the defense attorney. Since this case would be complicated, involving the insanity defense, the prosecutor argued that A. M. would not make a good juror.

The trial judge accepted as race-neutral the justifications offered for striking A. M. The State Court of Criminal Appeals, however, did not reach a similar conclusion:

Upon examination of the record, we find that A. M. was not even questioned by the State and there is no evidence that A. M. had difficulty understanding any "concepts" as the State contends . . . In each of these two instances (D. L. and A. M.), the State alleged that part of its reasoning for striking these veniremembers stemmed from questions asked of these jurors by the State. The record reveals that the State did not specifically address any questions to either of these veniremembers (D. L. or A. M.). An examination of the voir dire questioning shows a complete lack of meaningful questions directed to black venire persons and related to the reasons given for striking them. A prosecutor's failure to engage African-American prospective jurors in more than desultory voir dire, or indeed to ask them any questions at all, before striking them peremptorily, is one factor supporting an inference that the challenge is in fact based on group bias . . . The allegations made by the state with regard to its reasons for striking D. L. and A. M. are not only wholly without support in the record, but are directly contradicted by it. Therefore, we are compelled to conclude that the explanations advanced by the State for its challenges of these veniremembers represent no more than a pretext for racial discrimination (*Neal v. State* 1996).

Explaining a third strike of an African American the prosecutor stated C. S. was an extremely young black female. The prosecutor further noted that C. S. appeared to hold little knowledge of the proceedings during voir dire and, therefore, he did not believe she was capable of understanding the complicated nature of the case. Again, the trial court judge found this explanation to be race-neutral.

The prosecutor did not question C. S. during voir dire. But the following exchanges between C. S. and the attorney for the defense did take place. C. S. nodded affirmatively to a question by the defense attorney that she had lived in the local area for three years. She responded to a question that she had heard about the present case when it happened, but she had not paid much attention to it. C. S. further stated she read about the case in the local newspaper, but had not heard or observed anything through other news media sources.

Upon further questioning, C. S. did not recall any newspaper stories pertaining to the arrestee nor was she aware this particular criminal case was scheduled for trial. Furthermore, C. S. indicated she had not discussed the case with anyone. Finally, in response to the defense attorney's questions, C. S. stated she was in support of the death penalty in certain instances and that she would have no trouble considering mental defect or insanity as a defense if offered by a defendant.

The State Court of Criminal Appeals concluded the individual voir dire of C. S. was more extensive than for either D. L. or A. M. However, the Court also questioned the state's explanation. The state merely explained that the notes as documented for this particular venire member were "limited" and that it was thought she would be unable to "grasp the complicated nature of this case."

In reality, the state's reasons for this strike were neither clear nor specific. In fact, the state failed to quesiton C. S. at all. From the voir dire examination of C. S., it appears she would have been a juror supportive of the state because she was in favor of the death penalty, and she knew little about this case. The state's reasons for striking C. S. may have been sufficient had C. S. been the only venire member removed based on a presumption of difficulty in understanding the complexity of this case. However, in light of the state's deficient explanations for striking D. L. and A. M., the Court concluded the reason offered for striking C. S. also was inadequate. In this instance, the Appellate Court's conclusion was that the state failed to meet its obligation to provide adequate nonracial reasons for striking these three venire members. Thus, the trial courts' decision was reversed, and the case was remanded for a new trial.

This trial typifies how peremptory challenges continue to be used in racially discriminatory ways. As is evident, trial judges do accept sham and/or pretextual excuses as providing race-neutral explanations for peremptory strikes.

The atypical aspect of the jury striking in the *Neal* case is that the racial neutrality of the peremptory challenges were weak and defended ineptly by the prosecutor. The Court of Criminal Appeals found clear error based on the blatant, flagrant racist use of peremptory strikes. Although the prosecutor repeatedly stated the strikes were based on responses to questions posed to minority venire members during voir dire, the reasons given were exposed as a sham and pretext by the voir dire record. The prosecutor had not questioned these potential jurors. In addition, by employing the word "black" in describing the strikes, the prosecutor actually cast attention on the racial nature of these strikes.

In a more typical case, the striking attorney would have perhaps offered race-neutral reasons that are both plausible and without contradiction by the trial record. Acceptable race-neutral reasons would include striking minorities because they are similar in age to the litigants or perhaps a witness for the litigant. Such reasons are related to the case and are without direct contradiction as noted within the trial transcript.

An adversarial system of justice is characterized by conflicting goals, objectives, and interest. Opposing attorneys desire to prevail for their client or on behalf of the people, while the judge desires to conduct a fair and efficient procedure of adjudication. At the same time, important constitutional principles often are in conflict, as expressed through the Sixth Amendment's guarantee to an impartial jury and use of peremptory challenges. On the other hand, the Fourteenth Amendment provides equal protection for all people.

The procedure for selecting a jury represents a symbolic process during which key concepts communicate important meanings. Under *Batson* case law, the court prohibits the practice of intentionally striking venire members because of race. Although difficult to assess intent accurately through observing the striking patterns used or the reasons attorneys provide in support of their strikes, the above described case demonstrates race continues to be used as an important criterion.

The theory of peremptory challenges can deteriorate quickly in instances of race-based strikes. If it is assumed that jurors are more likely to convict persons of races different from their own, then it is possible to use peremptory challenges to remove most if not all minority jurors. Such assumptions are often made by attorneys who do not have sufficient time to conduct lengthy voir dires to ascertain whether or not personal bias exists. Judges encourage attorneys to move the process along.

What is the intent behind the strike of a minority venire member from a jury panel? Are the courts capable of determining the purpose or intent of an attorney selecting a jury? The social theorist Max Weber (1946) observed more than one hundred years ago that to understand adequately human behavior it is necessary to penetrate to the subjective level of interpretation and to establish the meaning specific actions hold for individual actors. Weber's orientation is appropriate to our purpose.

Attorneys are required to use peremptory challenges to seat an impartial jury. In reality, lawyers attend seminars and workshops that explain how the peremptory challenge can be employed to obtain the opposite effect. Rather than impartial juries, lawyers prefer to seat juries favorable to their position. Their intention, of course, is to gain an edge through selecting a jury that will assist them in winning the case for their client. So, if attorneys strike a minority juror to gain what they perceive will be a strategic trial advantage, does this constitute racial intent or merely the intent to slant the jury in their favor? What is the primary intent of the peremptory strike?

Understanding the meaning behind the symbolic words uttered by attorneys when presenting their "race-neutral" reasons is made more difficult when other theories of symbolic interactionism are considered. George H. Mead (1954), for example, explained that people (in this case attorneys) are social actors who, aware their behavior is being observed and monitored (especially by judges), imagine how others perceive their actions and mentally rehearse alternate courses of action, often choosing a course of action that appears acceptable to their audience. In the arena of jury selection, this social audience includes the trial judge and possibly the Appellate Court. Therefore, attorneys who wish to strike minority jurors are cognizant of a need to convince the court that their strikes are made to select an unbiased jury and that the reasons offered are defensible according to the specific case.

Erving Goffman (1959) labeled such behavior "impression management" or behavior that is designed to convince others that certain images or information is true, regardless of the reality. Thus, attorneys engage in impression management strategies in an attempt to convince the court that the striking of minorities is based on considerations other than race. Sometimes such impression management is successful, as with the trial court judge who presided at the *Neal* case. The prosecutor's impression management was not successful with the Court of Criminal Appeals, however.

Goffman's ideas certainly appear to be relevant to the process being described. To further demonstrate how effective they can be, we examine a civil malpractice case, a case in which this kind of impression management is perhaps even more evident.

LILLIAN OLSEN: A CIVIL CASE STUDY

Lillian V. Olsen, a woman who was disabled as a result of a surgical procedure, brought a medical malpractice suit against the surgeon, the assisting nurse, and the hospital where the procedure took place. Defense attorneys, representing the doctor, the nurse, and the hospital, used five of their nine peremptory challenges during the jury selection procedure to remove five of the six African Americans from the venire pool of potential jurors. Plaintiff argued that such strikes were race-based and, therefore, a *Batson* violation had occurred. The defense's contended that all five strikes were based on factors other than race.

According to the defense, venire member R. T. was struck because he was on disability and the plaintiff was claiming disability. The defense also argued that R. T. was approximately the same age as the plaintiff. Also, one of the defendants, a physician, did not like R. T.'s demeanor and reactions to certain voir dire questions. These were all reasons thought to justify the use of a peremptory strike. The plaintiff, on the other hand, claimed that by combining disability, age, and demeanor, three suspect excuses were used to conceal racial intent. Plaintiff further claimed no record of voir dire questions on any of these issues were included in the court transcript.

The defense attorneys defended their strike of R. T., arguing he was removed because his disability might influence him sympathetically with the plight of the disabled plaintiff. At the State Supreme Court level, the ruling was that R. T. was the only individual who was struck because of a disability and this in fact constituted a race-neutral reason.

The defense argued that a second African American venire member, D. H., was removed because serving on a jury that would deal with evidence involving blood, needles, and surgery presented a problem for him. However, despite his discomfort with these topics, D. H. indicated he could conform to the law, the evidence, and any instructions from the judge. The defense asked no questions of D. H. during voir dire, but their claim that inquiries about the problem with blood, needles, and surgery was unnecessary since D. H. offered this information on three separate occasions. D. H. also stated he did not like going to a doctor. Because this was a medical malpractice case brought by a plaintiff claiming permanent disability due to negligence during surgery, the defense believed the strike of D. H. to be justified. The plaintiff attorneys argued that because of four previous strikes of minorities, the striking of D. H. was suspect.

The State Supreme Court ruled that the case was indeed about blood and needles and that venire member D. H. had stated he would have a problem with the testimony. Therefore, the strike was not based on race but on juror aversion to elements of the trial.

A third venire member, R. B., was struck for two reasons. The first was based on unemployment status. The second reason was based on R. B.'s failure to acknowledge at the moment the defense requested jurors nod their heads if they would agree not to reach a decision until they had heard the facts pertaining to the case as well as the judge's instructions pertaining to application of the law.

No voir dire questions were asked of either R. B. or of H. H., a white venire member, who also was unemployed. The plaintiffs' attorney argued that unemployment can be race-neutral and that such status held no "rational relation to the case." Furthermore, venire member H. H. had no job listed, was white, and was not struck. This the plaintiffs contended was disparate treatment.

Defendant lawyers stated R. B. was struck because of her demeanor, failure to follow along in an approving manner during defense attorney's questioning of the venire, and her unemployment status. There was no evidence of discrimination, according to yet another defense attorney who observed and later testified regarding R. B.'s demeanor. The trial court judge accepted the explanation offered by the defense, concluding that the demeanor of the second defense attorney and his/her telling the truth should represent the standard for determining whether or not peremptory strikes were race-neutral.

The court record did not indicate the race of venire member H. H. According to the defense, H. H. did not display a poor or hostile reaction, and the defendants ran out of strikes before they could remove him. The State Supreme Court ruled that the defense also struck a white venire member solely because he was unemployed. The primary reason for striking juror R. B. was R. B.'s demeanor. Thus, a clear error had not occurred.

The defense attorneys argued that V. N. and B. C., African American females, were removed from the jury because they were relatively young and held low-paying, unskilled positions. For these reasons they would be very similar to the plaintiff's daughters and nieces who could be called as witnesses in the case.

Plaintiff's attorneys argued that V. N. and B. C. were not asked about their age during voir dire. Plaintiff further stated the defense argument that the occupations held by the two venire members were low-paid and unskilled might appear contrived because many court cases involve testimony being taken from witnesses of similar status. Thus, age could be used in most cases. Still, no statement of a clear, specific, and legitimate reason for the strikes related to the case in a nondiscriminatory manner. No inquiry was made into specific employment in order to determine bias or to relate employment to the facts and issues of the case. Furthermore, plaintiff attorneys contended that disparate treatment was suggested because five unskilled white venire members were not struck.

Defendant counsel countered that the plaintiff, Lillian Olsen, had three daughters and two nieces with knowledge of the case and each were expected to testify. All relatives were generally young and most held unskilled positions. Thus, V. N., and B. C. were struck because their ages and occupations were similar to those of Olsen's daughters and nieces.

The plaintiffs countered that one daughter was a Certified Respiratory Therapist, not an unskilled or a poorly paid position. The defense argued that V. N. and B. C. were struck because of their similarity to family members identified with the plaintiffs. Therefore, there was no need to inquire about their age, which was apparent from appearance. Thus, questions were not required to meet a *Batson* challenge.

Disparate treatment is not a relevant issue since they were struck for their similarity to witnesses for the plaintiff. Furthermore, no evidence existed that the five venire members who were not removed were young, unskilled, or held low-paying jobs. There was no evidence in the record to indicate that the five white unskilled workers were young. The state Supreme Court opinion, based on the record, was that no white venire members were both young and unskilled, leading to a decision that no obvious court error had occurred. Both the trial judge and the State Supreme Court sided with the defense ruling that the peremptory strikes were not motivated by "racial intent." The State Supreme Court also found no clear error in the ruling that the strikes were race-neutral.

In most cases it is not easy for a trial judge or the Appellate Court to determine whether peremptory strikes are race-neutral or are in fact based on racial intent or purpose. The more aware the striking attorney is of the important audiences, namely the trial judge and the Appellate Courts, the better prepared the attorney will be in justifying the peremptory strikes as race-neutral. A creative or well prepared attorney will manage successfully the impression that the minority venire members were removed for reasons relating to the case and not to ethnic or racial characteristic.

Since subjective intent of the striking is unknown, the tendency among trial judges is to accept the reasons given as race-neutral, provided these arguments are reasonable. If attorneys can relate the strike to an important case element or establish that a particular type juror would more likely be partial, the probability that judges will accept such strikes as race-neutral is enhanced. Similarly, Appellate Court judges are unlikely to identify *Batson* lower court rulings as erroneous because the court room presence of trial court judges provides ample opportunity to view the total proceeding.

While difficult to determine racial motive or intent, the failure of prosecutors or attorneys to link satisfactorily peremptory strikes to the case or related issues of juror bias can lead the judge to rule in favor of a *Batson* violation. However, the peremptory challenges relating to the *Olsen* civil case were defended effectively by the defense attorneys. Several strikes were defended strongly. In other instances, the links were not as clear or specific.

DISCUSSION AND CONCLUSION

Two cases, one criminal and the other civil, illustrate several key points pertaining to the use of the peremptory challenge to achieve a certain racial composition during the jury selection process. Courts are only able to observe what social actors, in this instance striking attorneys, actually do, and then interpret the symbolic representations offered in the form of race-neutral explanations. It is impossible to ascertain the precise intent of striking attorneys during this jury selection process given the limited information available. This problem is further complicated by the fact that the intended selection of a favorable jury may result in discriminatory action against potential minorities.

Therefore, the intent must be inferred from attorneys' actions and their explanations when a strike is challenged as being biased racially. Since attorneys are aware that the courts monitor strikes to prevent race-base challenges, they often attempt to manage certain impressions in order to preclude the legal inference that their peremptory challenges are race-based. They do so by offering believable explanations the court will accept as race-neutral. Thus, an attorney can strike anyone they desire, including members of racial minorities, if they can offer an appropriated symbolic justification.

The following typology can be applied to both the *Neal* and *Olsen* cases; it may apply to other *Batson* cases as well. First, some peremptory challenges are obvious in being flagrantly race-based. The strikes of D. L. and A. M. in the

Neal case illustrate this kind of strike. Defending the strike of D. L., an African American female, the prosecutor stated she had a weak personality. However, the court record indicated that the prosecutor had not asked any questions of D. L. Similarly, the prosecutor struck A. M., a "real, real young black male," who was not very well educated. The prosecutor argued this juror would not be able to understand a complicated case involving the insanity defense plea.

While the trial court accepted the above reasons as race-free, the Appellate Court opinion was that these explanations were pretextual. Although the prosecutor could have inquired further into personality strength and the level of understanding, he chose not to do so. That the voir dire transcript contradicted the prosecutor's assertions provided direct evidence that the reasons cited represent a sham.

A second category or typology of *Batson* arguments are those that can reasonably be defended. Such explanations serve as plausible explanations for the actions taken. In such instances, the striking attorney may not have articulated a clear, specific, and nondiscriminatory reason to counter the challenge. However, the trial court generally accepts these explanations as race-neutral, provided the opposing counsel and the court record do not expose clearly these arguments as race-based. Similarly, the Appellate Courts may be reluctant to overturn the decisions of trial court judges. The strike of venire member, R. B., an African American female, because she was unemployed and did not nod her head in agreement illustrate this type of strike. The peremptory challenges used against V. N. and V. C., both African American females, because they were relatively young, held lower-paying jobs, and were similar in age to witnesses for the plaintiff, also fall into this category.

The third and final category of race-neutral defenses consists of explanations that pose a clear and specific reason relating to the particular case under consideration which is obviously nondiscriminatory. These strikes are, or appear to be, race-neutral. The striking of R. T., an African American male, is one example. R. T.'s disability could result in a jury being partial toward Olsen's claim of medical malpractice.

Racial discrimination through the use of peremptory challenges to remove minorities from jury service continues to be a problem in the American legal system. As is evident in the two cases discussed, minorities often are removed from jury panels through the use of weak or pretextual explanations. The court has no effective mechanism under *Batson* to appropriately infer or to ascertain strikes that are in fact race-based. Thus, the *Batson* ruling has not successfully eliminated racial discrimination in jury selection as intended. Under *Batson*, the courts can only infer racial intent if striking attorneys are blatant and obvious. Intelligent, resourceful, or creative attorneys continue to strike potential minority jurors using symbolic defenses that are interpreted as being race-neutral.

REFERENCES

Blumer, Herbert. 1969. *Symbolic Interactionism*. Englewood Cliffs, N.J.: Prentice-Hall.
Brand, Jeffrey S. 1994. "The Supreme Court, Equal Protection, and Jury Selection: Denying That Race Still Matters." 1994 *Wisconsin Law Review*, 512–629.
Goffman, Erving. 1959. *The Presentation of Self in Everyday Life*. Garden City, N.Y.: Doubleday Anchor Books.
Hall, Larry D., and Audwin Anderson. 1996. "Swain as a Case of Indirect Institutional Discrimination." *Sociological Spectrum* 16:263–286.
Mead, George H. 1934. *Mind, Self, and Society*. Chicago: University of Chicago Press.
Melilli, Kenneth J. 1996 "Batson in Practice: What We Have Learned about Batson and Peremptory Challenges." *Notre Dame Law Review* 71, no. 3: 447–503.
Raphaell, Michael J., and Edward J. Ungvarsky. 1993. "Excuses, Excuses, Neutral Explanations Under Batson v. Kentucky." *University of Michigan Journal of Law Reform* 27, no. 1: 229.
U.S. Constitution, Fourteenth Amendment.
U.S. Constitution, Sixth Amendment.
Weber, Max. 1964. *The Theory of Social and Economic Organization*. Translated by A. M. Henderson and Talcott Parsons. New York: The Free Press.

CASES CITED

Batson v. Kentucky, 1986, 476 U.S. 79

Ex parte *Bird*, 1991, 594 So. 2d 676

Ex parte *Branch*, 1987, 526 So. 2d 609

Hernandez v. New York, 1991, 500 U.S. 352

J. E. B. v. Alabama, 1994, 511 U.S. 127

Maddox v. State, 1997, CR-93–1208, Alabama Court of Criminal Appeals

Neal v. State, 1996, CR-93–1208, Alabama Court of Criminal Appeals

Olsen v. Rich, 1996, 653 So. 2d 993

Powers v. Ohio, 1991, 499 U.S. 400

Swain v. Alabama, 1965, 380 U.S. 202

Whitus v. Georgia, 1967, 385 U.S. 545

12

Male Prostitution

Thomas C. Calhoun and Greg S. Weaver

INTRODUCTION

Questions posed by sociologists often relate to the reasons why people behave the way they do, the motives that cause individuals to pursue one line of action rather than another, and the subjective meanings people attribute to their behavior. Perhaps more important, sociologists attempt to ascertain whether personal decisions are affected by one's understanding of how others, including those who engage in similar behavior, perceive their behavior.

The meanings attributed to behavior are relative to the time, situation, and place in which the behavior occurs and is affected by others who engage in similar activities as well as the perception held by the larger audience. For these reasons some forms of behavior may be more resistant to changing perceptions than other less threatening forms. For example, forty years ago cigarette smoking was quite acceptable. However, as scientific evidence regarding the harmful effects associated with smoking became known, a redefinition of smoking behavior emerged. No longer is smoking a generally socially acceptable behavior, and various government agencies currently attempt to curtail the use of tobacco, especially among teenagers.

Another example of changing perceptions of behavior is the role Mothers Against Drunk Drivers (MADD) has had. MADD is the organization that assisted in creating a new social meaning for those who drive under the influence of alcohol and other drugs. No longer are drinking and driving deemed to be acceptable behavior because of the now widely recognized fact that even small amounts of alcohol can reduce one's ability to operate a motor vehicle safely.

The public and legal perceptions of the drunk driver are now directed to the stigmatization of this behavior. The result is a reduced percent of blood alcohol level in establishing the legal definition of intoxication from .10 percent to .08 percent. For youthful drivers, a group responsible for the highest proportion of alcohol-related vehicular deaths, a zero tolerance for drinking and driving exists, and they will lose their privileges to operate a motor vehicle if found to have even a trace of alcohol in their blood (Thio 1998). At issue is the social reevaluation of acceptable and unacceptable behavior. The subject matter of this chapter, homosexuality and male prostitution are no exception.

OVERVIEW OF THE SOCIAL PROBLEM: MALE PROSTITUTION

American society remains restrictive about the role homosexuals can play. It is the social ambiguity and legal proscriptions associated with homosexuality that cause many individuals to conceal their involvement lest they fall victim to a stigmatized status. Of consequence, however, is the fact that even though homosexuals continue to experience problems in the workplace, in the area of housing, and in qualifying to receive work-related benefits most people take for granted, this form of sexual expression continues. For these reasons, this social problem is worthy of inquiry.

Male homosexual prostitution can be classified as the punk, drag prostitute, brothel prostitute, kept boy, call boy, bar hustler, and the street hustler (see, for example, Ross 1959; Ginsburg 1967; Caukins and Coombs 1976; Coleman 1989; and Calhoun 1992). A status hierarchy is known to exist among male homosexual prostitutes, with the kept boy accorded the highest ranking (Caukins and Coombs 1976) and the street hustler being accorded the lowest status (Ross 1959). However, among those who engage in sexual relations with multiple male clients, the call boy has a high status because he works through an agency that negotiates meetings between male prostitutes and homosexual clients. On the other hand, the low-status street hustler is visible and more likely to draw attention from law enforcement officials.

Although it is not known how many young males engage in homosexual prostitution, Kinsey, Pomeroy, and Martin (1948) suggest that their number is not much smaller than that of female heterosexual prostitutes. However, many young males drift in and out of prostitution, making futile any attempt to identify their exact number. Although male homosexual prostitutes have varied socioeconomic backgrounds, the majority are from the lower and working class, have limited education, and live in disorganized families (Reiss 1961; Ginsburg 1967; and Calhoun 1988). Thomas Calhoun (1992) notes that young males become involved in homosexual prostitution by way of two routes, namely peer introduction and situation discovery. Elsewhere, Calhoun and Weaver (1996) discuss the costs and benefits that young prostituting males encounter. Fear of arrest and contracting a sexually transmitted disease are two of the cost/liabilities identified, whereas control of work schedule, easy access to drugs and alcohol, and money represent important benefits associated with male homosexual prostitution.

The meanings attributed to male homosexual prostitution are explored using attribution theory as a compliment to the symbolic interactionist perspective. Both theoretical perspectives are based on the assumption that people act in a rational manner (Stryker and Gottlieb 1981). In attempting to identify how deviant identities are managed, the "why of attitude development" and the "how of management of identity" are evaluated as important to the process in which street hustlers deal with perceptions of self and others, including male homosexual prostitutes and their johns. Through assessing the words of young street hustlers to illuminate what Mills (1940) referred to as a "vocabulary of motive," we attempt to demonstrate why identity management is important to concealing their homosexual behavior from family, friends, and the authorities.

Rosenberg's (1979) discussion of the self concept is appropriate for understanding why street hustlers strive to maintain a nonhomosexual identity. According to Rosenberg, self involves "an object of perception and reflection, including the emotional responses to that perception and reflection. It is a product of 'self-objectification,' requiring the individual to stand outside himself and to react to himself as a detached object of observation" (p. 8).

Attitudinal differences are central to attribution theory (Heider 1980), a theory that focuses on the cause of behavior. Rationalizing one's behavior and developing negative attitudes toward others, the fundamental attribution error, emphasizes personal characteristics to explain the behavior of certain individuals while situation factors are emphasized to justify one's own behavior.

Fundamental to this process is how the subjects' attribution reinforces their positive self-image. It will be shown that male prostitutes hold different attitudes pertaining to their homosexual activities compared to their view of clients. This difference is important in understanding how male homosexual hustlers manage their identities and avoid the social stigma attributed to this behavior.

According to Rosenberg (1979), the self is shaped according to four principles: reflected appraisals,[1] social comparison,[2] self-attribution, and psychological centrality. The first three of these principles are used to facilitate our understanding of male homosexual street hustlers. In the following section we illustrate how young males maintain their sense of self as nonhomosexual, and we identify the techniques used to ensure that their deviant street hustling activities do not result in their being labeled as discredited persons. In presenting this case, we attempt to show that male prostitutes employ various means to conceal their involvement in homosexual activities while projecting to others an image of self as nonhomosexual.

MALE PROSTITUTION: A CASE STUDY

Male prostitutes attempt to avoid the stigma associated with homosexuality by rationalizing their behavior as nonsexual and by evoking negative images of their clients' sexuality (Reiss 1961; Boyer 1989; Salamon 1989; Brown and Minichiello 1995). This case study[3] explores how male prostitutes justify their participation in homosexual activities despite their professed "true" sexual orientations and the negative attitudes of homosexual customers.

Some observers argue that street hustlers are homosexuals who have yet to accept their true sexual identities (e.g., Coombs 1974), while others (e.g., Reiss 1961) contend that street hustlers are self-declared heterosexuals who so define themselves because they are capable of separating their perceptions of self from the job-related requirements. To address this issue, when male prostitutes were asked to identify their sexual orientations, twelve hustlers defined themselves as either *straight only* or *straight and bisexual*. The following statements are in reaction to this question.

I ain't gay. I just let them suck me and that's for the money. I think of myself as a woman lover and not a man lover. (Boo)

You sell your dick and that's it. I see that as straight and if a hustler does more than that he might be gay. (Mink)

I see my self as straight. Well I let guys go down on me. I guess I'd have to say that I'm bisexual more toward the straight side. (Mitch)

If you are bisexual you like men and women. I have to be "bi" if I am going to let a faggot suck my dick. (Bill)

I'm straight. I love the hell out of pussy. (Glenn)

If you let a dude suck you, you're bisexual. If I was a faggot I wouldn't have gotten my old lady pregnant. (Kenny)

The self concept emerges through social interactions with significant others who inculcate the values and attitudes deemed to be appropriate for male behavior. As these young men developed, they compared themselves first to other family males, such as father and brother, and later with peer and other reference group members. By adopting the attitudes and values learned from others as their own, these young males viewed their behavior through the perceptual lens of important others. James stated: "I always heard my uncles sitting around and saying they hated a faggot, they hated this and they hated that. At first I thought I don't want a gay around me. I just don't like them." Henry's statement lends some additional support for our contention that significant others play important roles in shaping the attitudes and perceptions we have of homosexuality and homosexuals. He stated: "I've heard so many different stories from so many different people about the gay community that I would later find out to be wrong."

Street hustlers internalize the norms appropriate to their environment and in so doing they initially view themselves as heterosexual. Later, however, those male hustlers who perceive themselves as straight do so because of their ability to separate perception of self from the act of prostitution. Boasting of their appreciation for the female gender and a preference for sex with women, hustlers limit the type of sexual acts they willingly engage in with other males. Such boundaries allow street hustlers to maintain this perception of self as nonhomosexual. It is this image that the hustler strives to project through avoiding disclosure of his hustling activities.

Perception of Other Hustlers' Sexuality

Whereas seventeen of the eighteen hustlers defined themselves as straight and/or bisexual, they appear to be less willing to give other hustlers the benefit of the doubt regarding their motivations for involvement in prostitution. Sixteen individuals reported their perceptions of other hustlers' sexuality: straight (five), straight and bisexual (three), and bisexual (three). The remaining responses included such statements as "some (are) gay but act straight" or the respondent refused to label other hustlers.

You never know. 'Cause mostly a fag won't tell you nothing like that. They'll tell you no, you ask him. What we do was our business. (Mink—straight)

Most of them are straight. I didn't say all of them. 'Cause they will only go so far. You know like I would. Just let them suck me. (Mike C.—straight)

Some of them I'd say are gay. They act straight but I believe some hustlers will suck dick and get fucked. (Speed—straight)

I'm just not capable of making that decision. If I ever had to or if I ever wanted to, but I have never been one to put nothing like that on nobody. I really couldn't put a tag on them. (Henry—Bisexual)

Hustlers' Perceptions of Tricks

These hustlers view sexuality on a continuum with one's location determined by one or more of the following three factors: (1) the sexual acts one engages in, (2) the sexual role one performs, and (3) a preference for heterosexual sex. Provided hustlers limit the nature of the sex acts they engage in and maintain their stated preference for women, this self-image is protected without compromise. In short, although engaging in sexual behavior with homosexuals, the street prostitute maintains he is not homosexual.

However, most hustlers define their clients as gay. In the following statements this perception of their tricks is captured.

You automatically know that if a guy picks you up that he ain't gonna be straight. You say to yourself, this guy is wanting to suck a dick. (Mink—straight)

Some of them is "bi," none of them is straight. I ain't never met none that is straight. (Boo—straight)

Some of them are gay, some straight, and some of them are "bi." Some of them is all the way queer. (Ron—bisexual)

Identity Management

Erving Goffman (1963) argues the self is composed of two identities, namely a *personal identity*, the person we think we are, and a *social identity*, the person we project to others. When the two identities are compatible, the individual's sense-of-self corresponds well with the perception held by others. However, should these perceptions be discordant, then the individual's sense-of-self is threatened. In an attempt to maintain compatibility between the personal and social identities, hustlers devise strategies to reduce the possibility that others will learn of their involvement in discredited behavior. This is accomplished by *passing*, or the "management of undisclosed discrediting information about self" (Goffman 1963, p. 42), and by *covering*, the "effort to keep the stigma from looming large" (p. 102).

Four techniques of information control, according to Goffman, are used to pass or cover involvement in discrediting behavior. Using these techniques, the individual is able to conceal his activity thereby maintaining an economic identity separate from the normal self. First, the individual can *conceal* symbolic signs associated with stigma. For example, a street prostitute can avoid dressing in a suspicious manner or avoid displaying a bandanna in the hip pocket. Second, the individual can use *disidentifiers*. Thus, a street hustler may comment often about the beauty of a female or make disparaging remarks about homosexuals. Third, the individual can *present* signs of "their stigmatized failing as signs of another attribute, one that is less significantly a stigma" (Goffman 1963, p. 94). In this case, the street hustler may attribute his homosexual behavior as a result of his experience as an abused child. Fourth, the individual can *divide* his world into two groups, the first of which includes a large number of people whom the deviant tells nothing, while the second, smaller group of people, the individual tells all and relies on them for help. For example, the street hustler reveals some aspects of his self with many people. However, he will restrict discussion of his homosexuality to only a small group of people, namely those in the "life."

Covering and Passing

Erving Goffman (1963, p. 102) states the individual's objective in covering and passing is to reduce tension and to deflect attention from involvement in discredited behavior. The hustler is always concerned while working the street. Because prostitution is illegal in most jurisdictions, he risks arrest as well as social rejection if discovered. Four strategies are used by street hustlers to cover involvement in prostitution. The first strategy is to ask a potential trick if he is a cop. By asking this question, the chance of being arrested is reduced greatly. Thus, by ascertaining whether the potential client is in fact a police officer, the hustler protects himself by avoiding disclosure. The following two statements highlight this avoidance tactic:

It's a law that requires that he cannot say he is not a policeman if he is. (Mitch)

Are you a cop? That's the first question I ask. If they say no, you know it's alright. But if they say yes, you run like hell. (James)

Second, the hustler may refrain from standing in any one location for an extended period of time.

If the cops see you standing still, they're gonna know something. If they just see you walking they can't prove nothing. (Mike C.)

They [police] always stop me when I was standing still and tell me I was loitering or something. (Bill)

However, hustlers differ in their opinion as to whether walking or standing in one position is preferable. To some, walking reduces the chance of police detection of their purpose while also increasing their chance of being identified by and negotiating with a potential trick. Responding to this issue, Bill stated: "if you are standing around in a crowd they won't pick you up because they think that you are a gang or something. Cause if you are walking by yourself, they'll think 'he's cool' and pick you up." Should suspicion be aroused, the hustler can always justify his presence given that many legitimate businesses operate in the gay district.

The third strategy used to avoid detection is abstaining from use of standardized dress. An individual may pass or cover by restricting or concealing symbolic attire. In some cities male homosexual prostitutes wear a handkerchief in their back pocket. Depending on its color or location, the handkerchief symbolizes the individual's preference for a particular kind of sex act. Absence of a symbolic wardrobe allows the hustler the freedom to operate in a cruise area while making it more challenging for law enforcement and others to conclude he is a prostitute.

The fourth and final strategy for covering is the frequency these youngsters are on the streets, as noted in the following:

I go down there and get a little spending money and go on home. I don't like to stay down there too much. (Bill)

I normally just trick once and go home. (Glenn)

Probably about three times a week, sometimes four. I really don't hustle all the time. (David)

Two additional reasons may explain why hustlers infrequently prostitute. The first is that the less time one spends on "the block," the less likely one will be identified as being involved in homosexual prostitution. The second reason is that male prostitutes often earn sufficient money from a few tricks to enable them to purchase the amount of marijuana and alcohol needed. Most hustlers indicate they turn a single trick on a given night, and they generally do not return to the cruise area.

Sexual Limitations

Hustlers willingly provide more traditional heterosexual services, thereby adding some support for Hoffman's (1972) assertion that the street hustler perceives himself as heterosexual yet willingly participates in homosexual activities. Negotiations between the hustler and the trick are complex, suggesting that hustlers place some limitation on the type of sex acts they perform willingly. Acceptable sexual acts generally are limited to oral-genital and anal-genital contact, with the hustler acting in the active or insertor role. James, who perceives himself as bisexual, stated: "I went out on a trick with Mike and that will be my last, cause I don't like Mike. When we went out on that trick he did me dirty. He said 'I ain't a doing this, I ain't a doing that.' It made me so mad I will never trick with him again. I am usually a one man stand."

According to Reiss (1961), there are sexual roles that identify one as a homosexual and those that do not. It appears that the sex acts requested are inconsistent with Mike's concept of self. Thus, another question germane to this case study is what sexual acts are perceived as homosexual? Although these hustlers participate in homosexual activity, only certain sexual acts appear to be compatible with their nonhomosexual identity. As one hustler stated: "they have asked me if I would suck their dick. I say no, I wouldn't do that, couldn't do that, that's too nasty for me to do."

Seventeen hustlers stated they would act the role of the insertor during oral-genital sex; five said they would play the role of insertee. A similar limitation is noted for anal-genital sex. Fourteen indicated they would be the insertor during anal sex, whereas only one agreed to be the insertee.

I'm a straight man. There ain't no doubt about that. It means I wouldn't get fucked by nobody and suck nobody's dick. I'd fuck them and let 'em suck my dick. (Speed)

Well, there is a couple of things I don't do. I tell them and they understand. And if they still want to do something, they tell me what they want to do. And if it's alright with me then we go do it. I don't get screwed and sometimes I don't give head. (Bill).

One dude asked me to piss on him. I told him I couldn't do it. I couldn't piss on another human being. Shit, I wouldn't want nobody pissing on me. (Ricky)

He wanted me to go home with him, stay all night and handcuff me to a bed and beat the fuck out of me. I looked at him and said I don't get into that kind of sex. (James)

By establishing boundaries to limit the range of homosexual activity they willingly engage in, hustlers "restrict the display of those failings most centrally identified with the stigma" (Goffman 1963, p. 103). Thus, restricting oneself to certain sexual acts allows the nonhomosexual self to remain intact.

Covering with Significant Others

Erving Goffman (1963) suggests that individuals with a secret do not want to be caught directly in the act, lest their cover be lifted. Since these hustlers define themselves as nonhomosexual, it is essential to them that any stigmatizing behavior remain unknown to most people, as revealed in the following:

Well, there is a lot of secrecy. You don't want nobody to find out. (James)

If he's got a house we go over to his house. Somewhere off the streets. Somewhere nobody could see us. (Mike C.)

You would go away from society. You would go where you wouldn't have any attention. (Henry)

Discovery can have devastating effects for the individual. To prevent himself from becoming damaged socially, the hustler limits the locations where he will engage in homosexual acts. Reporting they have sex inside of cars, motels, and the houses of their tricks, hustlers maintain the important separation of their personal and social identities.

To reduce the chances that significant others may learn of his discrediting behavior, one approach taken is to limit the number of people who know his secret. The most obvious way to accomplish this is not to share information, especially with family members. For example, Glenn stated: "I just don't say nothing about it around her [mother]. I tell everybody else who knows about it don't let his git out."

A second method for preventing significant others from learning of one's involvement in prostitution is to disguise the source of money. James fabricated stories to keep his mother from discovering he hustled, thereby preserving his secret deviant identity. Speaking of his mother, James stated: "I tell her a lie and I hate to lie. She always asks me where did I git it at and I tell her I worked for someone. I'll make up any damn thing and tell her."

A third information control strategy is restricting the time spent in the prostitution area. Mitch, speaking of his wife, said: "I just didn't let her know. I didn't have to hang around downtown a lot because I had a lot of phone numbers." The benefits derived from use of the telephone to arrange sexual encounters include not being required to operate on the street, reducing the possibility of being observed by the wife, and decreasing the prospects of arrest.

Some hustlers recognize that their girlfriends would judge them negatively if their secret became known. Speaking of the importance of controlling his girlfriend's knowledge, Henry stated: "I have a couple of girlfriends that I don't want them to know because I feel if they know, they would judge me different because of what I've heard them say before. It's up to you to control it."

The fourth strategy for controlling information is for the hustler to reaffirm the evaluation others have of him. Boo stated: "I try my best to. Like if they say 'I hate faggots,' I'll say I hate them too, which I do." This strategy presents an image of the hustler as normal, professing to others an adherence to social norms by reaffirming to self and others that he is indeed what he appears to be.

Becoming Involved in Hustling

Most of these hustlers were introduced to street prostitution by a friend or sibling. Many were teenagers at the time, a stage of social-psychological development where young people search for an identity separate from that of their parents. Since significant others constitute an important reference group, people will mimic the behavior of their friends. These hustlers were asked if, prior to street hustling, they had knowledge of a friend's involvement in prostitution. Nine reported they knew that the individual who introduced them to street hustling was engaged in prostitution. Six stated they did not know their friend was a hustler.

But when associating with friends who hustle, juveniles do indicate their need for money, at which time the prostituting friend might reveal his involvement in homosexual prostitution. In one such example, Bill said: "I know this friend. I said damn, I need some money. He said, I know how to get it. He showed me the tricks so that I would know what to do. So I tried it and the guy gave me money." Assessing the strength of a friendship, the hustler has to decide whether he should share his secret with a nonhustling friend. He will share it if he believes that revelation of this secret will not place the friendship in jeopardy, otherwise he will not. Thus, yet another technique for passing is to divide one's world into two distinct arenas. Restricting the number of people who know of one's secret increases the individual's chance of maintaining that secret.

Most hustlers experience their initial homosexual encounter during their first act of prostitution: Twelve hustlers interviewed reported no previous homosexual experience prior to their entry into hustling; five others admitted to previous homosexual experiences. Speed, a 16 year old, said: "Once before. It was a long time ago. I let *one* suck me off." Tony admitted to several homosexual encounters prior to becoming a street hustler. While a resident of a juvenile home, according to Tony, another young resident would "suck off a couple of the guys," including Tony.

How did the young hustlers described here feel about their first homosexual encounter? Their expressions were somewhat diverse, ranging from feeling "great" to "wanting to kill the person." Ten hustlers felt "nervous," "bad," or "scared." Henry stated, "I was jumpy and nervous which I usually am when trying something new." Being nervous when confronting a new or different kind of situation is one thing, but engaging in behavior in violation of the law increases this nervous sensation. Glenn said: "I didn't want to do it. I was scared. I didn't know what was going to go down or nothing." Mink said he: "thought this guy might rape me or something. He might be the type of guy that will kill you." Boo, on the other hand, believed he was misleading women stating "[I] was doing women wrong in a way and I felt in a way I was gay but I know that I ain't." Boo initially thought that if he engaged in homosexual sex, this would indicate he was homosexual. Boo quickly rejected this idea, however, stressing that "he ain't." Mike "C" said: "It made me feel bad for what I had done. You know I been brought up thinking it was bad. I believe in not doing this shit." Ricky said "I felt guilty or something, it freaked me out." These expressions of guilt indicate Mike and Ricky have internalized the perception of prostitution others hold and, in turn, they are influenced by these attitudes.

Self Attitudes toward Homosexuality

People are assigned to acceptable and nonacceptable categories and the reactions and treatment accorded to them affect the perception others have of them. Because most hustlers have limited homosexual experience prior to becoming street hustlers, they do not define themselves, nor are they defined by others, as being homosexual. When asked what they thought of homosexuals before they began prostituting, eleven of eighteen stated they held an unfavorable, negative view. However, this perception changed once they became involved in street hustling. Initially, those expressing negative views reflected on the attitudes of their significant others, especially parents, other adult family members, or friends. James presented his views of gays and identifies their origins, stating: "At first, I thought I don't want a gay around me, I'll kill him. I just don't like them. I always heard my uncle sitting around and saying they hated a faggot. They hate this and they hate that."

James adopted the perspective of his relatives and continued to believe this way until he became a regular participant in the "life." Similarly, Bill adopted the opinions of significant others when formulating his initial opinion of gays: "I didn't like them too well. Since I was a kid *all* the grown-ups called gay people 'faggots' and I didn't like gay people."

Although eleven hustlers changed their views of homosexuals from unfavorable to favorable, three others were less accepting of this lifestyle. Sam stated: "I just think it's pitiful for a man to try to come on to another man 'cause the world ain't made for all that kind of shit. I ask some of them why they gay and they can't tell me nothing but one reason that's I like men." Sam's view of the homosexuals' world was more absolute than that of the other hustlers. For Sam, specific behavior is either right or wrong, a view that Sam is unlikely to alter. Still, despite his dislike of homosexuals, the money and other benefits derived from hustling did not prevent Sam from hustling males.

The reason for changing one's opinion of homosexuals may be found in the learning process. Through learning the attitudes and values held by others, their social perspective becomes a permanent part of the self. As people advance in age and maturity, their experiences change; previously held views also are subject to change. Since these hustlers had limited prior contact with homosexuals, their knowledge was based on a negative symbolic imagery transmitted to them by family members, friends, and others significant to them. After becoming involved in prostitution, however, hustlers were able to evaluate the truth or falsity of these views. As a result, many young males modified this previous perception. Mitch stated: "I used to didn't believe in gay people. You know now I realize that there is nothing wrong with being gay."

The trick also may influence this newly based perception. In many situations, the trick presents himself as someone who cares about the hustler, thereby creating a question in the hustler's mind: Should the hustler maintain the views of homosexuals held by significant others, or should he modify his attitude to reflect an evaluation based on personal experience? The hustler, we believe, changes his view of homosexuals because personal experience influences his decision to do so.

DISCUSSION AND CONCLUSION

Although the hustler may become more accepting of homosexuals, he may not perceive himself as such nor does he want others to view him as homosexual. Street hustlers place limits on the type of sex acts they engage in, and they strive to prevent family members and others from learning the secret.

Although it appears to be obvious that previous experiences influence the street hustler's value of self as nonhomosexual, the benefits associated with the behavior exceed the perceived liabilities. However, Pinkerton and Abramson (1992) contend it seems wholly irrational for anyone to continue to engage in risky sexual behavior given the tremendous suffering caused by AIDS. Superficially, this statement seems plausible. No one desires to contract the AIDS virus. However, this overly simplistic view fails to reveal the complexity of the dynamics involved. These young males are not immune to what occurs in the larger society. For example, exposure to advertising, such as that provided by Nike and FuBu, provides a commonality of values among young American males that by wearing a particular kind of tennis shoe or tee shirt one's chances of meeting and dating the girl of their dreams will be enhanced. In addition to being bombarded with fashion statements, they are influenced by peer behavior. Thus, many hustlers use drugs and drink alcohol as a part of the learning process. Many date women and desire to provide their girlfriends with material things. Although such commodities are expensive, homosexual prostitution provides the economic means through which enough money is easily earned to purchase whatever is desired.

Is street hustling a social problem? If so, what can be done about it? We propose several initiatives that can be undertaken to reduce street hustling. First, this behavior can be redefined as nondeviant, thereby removing legal restrictions and sanctions against homosexuality. Although difficult to achieve in a realistic sense, this proposal at least merits serious discussion.

Second, legitimate job opportunities that are both attractive and financially sufficient to make homosexual prostitution less desirable need to be created. To accomplish this goal, factors such as the kind of work, work schedules, and the meaningfulness of the task should be considered. Even people with little education need to survive.

Third, if a reduction in the use of illicit drugs is really a socially desirable and reasonable goal, then de-emphasizing the use of licit drugs such as coffee, nicotine, and Rogaine also should occur. As members of a drug-consuming society, young people do not understand that good drug use can and should be limited to specific medically related problem. Until youth accept that drug consumption is not a necessary social function, deviant expressions such as homosexual prostitution will continue to flourish.

Fourth, opportunities for youths to engage in meaningful activities both within and outside the school could diminish the effect of what now appears to be an attractive street life. The recent introduction of midnight basketball represents a step in this direction. However, other similar activities need to be identified, and the appropriate programs for monitoring youth-oriented activities should be considered.

Finally, the school experience should be evaluated from the youth's perspective. This is not to imply that students should have an opportunity to determine the nature of educational curricula, but to suggest that alternative learning strategies and teaching methods must go beyond reaching only high achievers. Not all individuals share similar life goals, but it is important to recognize that each possesses pride, dignity, and a desire to achieve success.

NOTES

1. The principal of reflected appraisals "holds that people, as social animals, are deeply influenced by the attitudes of others toward the self and that, in the course of time, they come to view themselves as they are viewed by others" (Rosenberg 1979, p. 83). Through

interaction with significant others, individuals become aware of, and seek to fulfill, social expectations.

2. Social comparison refers to "the fact that people judge and evaluate themselves by comparing themselves to certain individuals, groups, or social categories" (Rosenberg 1979, p. 68). Two types of comparisons are employed. The first marks the individual as superior or inferior to another in terms of some criterion of excellence, merit, or virtue, whereas the second refers primarily to deviance or conformity. Thus, the self results from self-observation and the corresponding outcome associated with specific behavior (Rosenberg 1979).

3. The information upon which this case chapter is based was collected during a three-month period in a medium-size city located in the southern portion of the United States. Ranging in age from 13 to 22 years, fifteen of the interviewees were white and three were black.

REFERENCES

Boyer, Debra. 1989. "Male Prostitution and Homosexual Identity." *Journal of Homosexuality* 17: 151–184.

Brown, Jan, and Victor Minichiello. 1995. "The Social Meanings Behind Male Sex Work: Implications for Sexual Interactions." *British Journal of Sociology* 46: 598–622.

Calhoun, Thomas C. 1988. "Theoretical Considerations on the Entrance and Stabilization of Male Street Prostitutes." Ph.D. diss., University of Kentucky.

———. 1992. "Male Street Hustling: Introduction Processes and Stigma Containment." *Sociological Spectrum* 12: 35–52.

Calhoun, Thomas C., and Greg Weaver. 1996. "Rational Decision-Making Among Male Street Prostitutes." *Deviant Behavior* 17: 209–227.

Caukins, Sivan E., and Neil R. Coombs. 1976. "The Psychodynamics of Male Prostitution." *American Journal of Psychotherapy* 30: 441–451.

Coleman, Eli. 1989. "The Development of Male Prostitution Activity Among Gay and Bisexual Adolescents." *Journal of Homosexuality* 17: 1–2, 131–149.

Coombs, Neil K. 1974. "Male Prostitution: A Psycho-social View of Behavior." *American Journal of Orthopsychiatry* 44: 782–789.

Ginsburg, Kenneth N. 1967. "The Meat Rack: A Study of the Male Homosexual Prostitute." *American Journal of Psychotherapy* 21:170–184.

Goffman, Erving. 1963. *Stigma: Notes on the Management of Spoiled Identity*. New York: Simon and Schuster.

Heider, F. 1980. The Psychology of Interpersonal Relations. New York: Wiley.

Hoffman, Martin. 1972. "The Male: Prostitute." *Sexual Behavior* 2:19–21.

Kinsey, A. C., W. B. Pomeroy, and C. E. Martin. 1948. *Sexual Behavior in the Human Male*. Philadelphia: W. B. Saunders.

Mills, C. Wright. 1940. "Situated Actions and Vocabularies of Motive." *American Sociological Review* 5: 904–913.

Pinkerton, Steven D., and Paul R. Abramson. 1992. "Is Risky Sex Rational?" *Journal of Sex Research* 29: 561–568.

Reiss, A. J. 1961. "The Social Integration of Queers and Peers" *Social Problems* 9:102–120.

Rosenberg, Morris. 1979. *Conceiving the Self*. New York: Basic Books.

Ross, H. Laurence. 1959. "The Hustler in Chicago." *Journal of Student Research* 1: 13–19.

Salamon, Edna. 1989. "The Homosexual Escort Agency: Deviance Disavowal." *British Journal of Sociology* 40:1–21.

Stryker, Sheldon, and Avi Gottlieb. 1981. "Attribution Theory and Symbolic Interactionism: A Comparison." In J. H. Harvey, W. C. Ickes, and R. F. Kidd, eds., *New Directions in Attribution Research*, vol. 3, pp. 425–458. Hillsdale, N.J.: Erlbaum.

Thio, Alex. 1998. *Deviant Behavior* 5th ed. New York: Addison-Wesley Educational Publishers, Inc.

13

Career Criminals

Ronald E. Jones

INTRODUCTION

Despite the magnitude of the crime problem in the United States, it has been recognized generally that career criminals constitute a relatively small category of all criminals, commit a disproportionate amount of crime, and their criminality lasts well into adulthood (Barkan 1997, p. 275). It is also recognized that career criminality is more common among those with little education and sparse job prospects, which are most characteristic of the urban lower class. There are some scholars who take exception to the notion that offending lasts well into adulthood (Gottfredson and Hirschi 1988), but there is a general agreement that this concept is valid for a small number of offenders.

The issue of how far into adulthood the career criminal remains active also has major social policy implications in view of the recent trend in the United States of adopting "three strikes and you're out" legislation for three felony convictions. Since imprisonment would continue long after the active criminality of most offenders, based on knowledge of the age patterning of crime, it appears on the surface that such legislation would only increase prison populations without reducing crime (Tonry 1994).

The existence of habitual or career criminals has been noted as far back as the Wolfgang, Figlio, and Sellin study of arrest records in the mid-1940s, wherein they found that 6 percent of the cohorts studied were responsible for 52 percent of all arrests (Wright 1996, p. 258). The recent shift in penological practice toward incapacitation as a crime prevention strategy has been, in large part, propelled by increasing focus on habitual criminals. Incapacitation ranges from collective (long sentences given indiscriminately) to selective (long sentences targeted at those who commit the most crimes). The drawback to selective incapacitation is that its effectiveness depends on the validity of the risk assessment instrument.

OVERVIEW OF THE CAREER CRIMINAL PROBLEM

With only 5 percent of the world's population, the United States has under incarceration approximately 25 percent of the world's imprisoned population. At the end of the millennium, America's prisons house approximately two million people. This recent figure, released by the Justice Policy Institute compares to midyear 1997, when an estimated 1,725,842 persons were incarcerated in the United States (1,158,763 in state and federal prisons; 567,079 in local jails). Between midyear 1996 and midyear 1997, the incarcerated population grew by 4.7 percent. While significant in itself, this increase was below the annual average for the decade of the 1990s (7.7 percent). In 1997, the incarceration rate per 100,000 U.S. residents was 645—up from 458 in 1990 (Bureau of Justice Statistics Bulletin 1998, p. 1). It is generally accepted that the United States has the highest incarceration rate in the world, having long passed both the (former) Soviet Union and South Africa.

The issue of career criminals looms large in modern America. Economic conditions have fostered this development insofar as poverty and crime are related. As urban job markets have deteriorated and virtually collapsed in the inner-city areas, the economic and social conditions for future increases in criminality are significant. In 1959, approximately one-third of the poverty population lived in metropolitan areas. By 1991, the central cities included almost half of the poverty population (Wilson 1996, p. 11). The ability of urban neighborhoods to maintain effective social control has deteriorated substantially in recent years.

There has been a growing popular concern that crime, criminals, and large prison populations threaten the democratic fabric of American society. One consequence of this concern has been a shift in penological practice away from rehabilitation to incapacitation. Part of this shift has been due to the stark realization that, after thirty years of effort and billions of dollars expended, the recidivism rate has not changed. It has remained basically at 30 to 35 percent for the past thirty years (Irwin and Austin 1996, p. 279). As Thomas (1994) has noted, since Robert Martinson's 1973 study that concluded no rehabilitation effort had an appreciable effect on recidivism, there has been a dramatic shift toward incapacitation as the dominant penological practice. In no area has this trend been more noticeable than in the selective incapacitation of career criminals. While there is general agreement that selective incarceration of society's worst offenders should have a significant effect on the crime rate, there is little consensus on the process by which the selections are made.

Recent years have also been witness to the proliferation of books that take the social sciences to task for failure to have much impact on the issue of crime and deviance. Byron Roth (1994) has argued that social scientists have become too cozy with government funds and programs and "must maintain a certain independence of mind so that they can objectively critique popular views and government programs" (p. 27). Others have pointed out that the failure to understand the role of compassion has blinded social scientists (Wilson and Herrnstein 1985, p. 519) or the omission of moral poverty as a legitimate topic for research has exacerbated the problem of crime itself (Bennett, DiIulio, and Waters 1996).

However, whatever the causes and consequences, the fact remains that the United States has a large, career criminal population that is not only taxing our financial well-being but our social well-being as well. How we have arrived at this point with a large prison population in general and a large career criminal group in particular has been one of the thorniest issues in social science for many decades.

Theoretical Explanations

A myriad of theoretical perspectives have been put forth to explain the emergence and continuation of deviant behavior in general and career criminality in particular. One of the most influential has been Robert Merton's (1968) theory of anomie. According to Merton, deviant and criminal behavior is elaborated as a socially constructed phenomenon. The amount of illicit behavior and its distribution depends on variable access to legitimate goals and the amount of anomie in a society. In Merton's view, socially approved or institutionalized means of access to legitimate means for achieving approved cultural goals are not equally distributed throughout the social structure. In essence, the lower social classes (which often tend to be disproportionately ethnic minorities) represent significantly disadvantaged social locations in the social structure. Higher rates of criminal activity are to be found in those classes that experience the lowest levels of education and occupational opportunity.

Albert K. Cohen's (1955) theory of delinquent behavior centers on the notion that middle-class goals are largely unobtainable by working-class males and therefore become meaningless. Since the problems of working-class males are similar to those of all persons in the social structure—acquisition of status and self-respect—adaptive mechanisms are brought into play by which they can be accomplished. To Cohen, the adaptive mechanism is the gang as an alternative status system, which provides status criteria that can be met by working-class males. Compulsory public schools are ideal environments to create gangs because schools are largely middle class in orientation and the class background of the staff is middle class. It is not surprising that delinquent gangs totally repudiate the public school system and middle-class values standards in general.

Kai Erikson (1968) views personal development as a maturational cycle wherein each stage of development contains a central problem to be solved. In adolescence, this problem amounts to the establishment of a "sense of identity" (Rettig, Torres, and Garrett 1977, p. 247). During adolescence the individual seeks to clarify his role in society. If society does not help clarify the adolescent's role and does not reward him/her with status, then the adolescent is likely to define himself through rebellion. Erikson hints, but does not elaborate, that there are societal forces that may very well, by design, engender deviant behavior.

Whereas the primary emphasis of Merton is the instigation of using illegitimate means as a way of adapting to anomie, Richard Cloward and Lloyd Ohlin (1960) point out that access to illegitimate means is also differentially distributed within the social structure. Thus, the acquisition of specific alternatives to legitimate means is dependent upon this differential access. What is important is that "the societal reaction makes it somewhat certain that particular forms of deviant behavior will occur in areas where there is asocial support for those particular forms of criminal or rebellious behavior" (Rettig, Torres, and Garrett 1977, p. 251).

The labeling or interactionist view of human behavior rests on the notion that deviancy is not something inherent in the act itself, but is created by the definitions of those who are responsible for defining and enforcing social standards of behavior. For Becker (1963) there is a sequence of events in the experience of a deviant career and factors exist that either move along or retard this development. Thus, the status of the deviant is maintained and reinforced not only by social forces but also by the individual's commitment to that societal identity.

For Kai Erikson (1964) as well as Becker, deviance is not something inherent in certain forms of behavior. It is a property that is conferred upon these forms by the audiences that either directly or indirectly witness the behavior itself. Thus, the audience is critical in the study of deviance since it is the audience that determines what is to be labeled as deviant (Erikson 1964, p. 10).

Three concepts are pivotal to this view of deviance—screening devices, boundary maintaining mechanisms, and deployment patterns. In Erikson's view, the screening device is the process whereby behavior is either allocated or not allocated to the category of deviance. Community definitions of what is acceptable, or not, as behavior is exercised through the boundary maintaining mechanisms. The transactions between the deviant and agencies of social control whereby the deviant is relegated or deployed to a caste or class are called deployment patterns. Viewing deviance through this perspective has led one noted author to conclude "that a wide variety of our social organizations are programmed so as to inhibit significant segments of our adolescent population from learning socially acceptable, responsible, and personally gratifying roles" (Rettig, Torres, and Garrett 1977, p. 255). Indeed, it may be that agencies of social control even foster negative role development. Certainly, as several authors have pointed out, "the government has an interest in seeing that the existing criminal justice system's response to crime is not significantly altered in purpose or function" (Kappeler et al. 1996, p. 77).

CAREER CRIMINALS: A CASE STUDY

For the purposes of this study, career criminal is defined as someone currently incarcerated for at least the third time, and who has served at least fifteen years inside an adult prison. A random sample of inmates so classified was drawn from a southern prison. Two series of interviews were conducted with each inmate. The first was to obtain and verify basic information such as demographics and social background. The second, of much longer duration, was designed to ascertain and identify the screening devices, boundary maintaining mechanisms, and deployment patterns within the correctional setting that serve to promote and maintain the status of career criminal. Subjects were questioned about their experiences with the police, courts, and correctional institutions to elicit their perception of, and adaptation to, screening devices, boundary maintaining mechanisms, and deployment patterns.

Fifteen inmates were randomly selected to participate in the study; three declined without a promise that participation would shorten their sentences. For the twelve participating career criminals the average age was 49.9 years. The average number of years spent in adult incarceration was 20.5 years. The average number of distinct incarcerations was 4.8 (including both state and federal sentences). Of the twelve remaining in the study, 75 percent were black and 25 percent were white. These percentages reflect the general racial characteristics of the long-term inmates in this particular prison population, which is approximately 60 percent black for first offenders.

The family, economic, educational, and social background of the twelve participants turned out to fit the general stereotype of career criminals. Only two of the twelve participants were raised by both parents; two were raised in foster homes; a mother, grandmother, or both raised the remaining eight. In terms of education, only two of the twelve had completed high school prior to their first incarceration. Four had completed GEDs while in prison, and one had completed two years of college while in prison and before the program was abolished for prison inmates. Significantly, none of the twelve had ever served in the military in any capacity.

The second interview phase was structured in such a way as to elicit responses from the participants in regard to screening devices, boundary maintaining devices, and deployment devices, not only within the correctional setting, but prior to and between incarcerations within the police and court institutions. An effort was also made to elicit the various coping mechanisms and adaptations employed by the participants in their effort to offset the stereotyping functions of these devices and soften their relegation to the status of career criminal. Needless to say, the participants did not recognize their experiences within the context of these three categories. They did, however, possess a wealth of experience stretching over many years of using these strategies to cope with the police, court, and correctional institutions. It is the adaptive mechanisms employed by career criminals in response to these devices that is the subject of the research.

The Police

A typical screening device utilized by the police is the practice of "rounding up the usual suspects." Every participant in this study related one or more episodes wherein they were picked up by the police as a suspect for no other reason than that they had prior convictions. Alonzo H. related the enormous difficulty of holding a job under these conditions and the considerable strain it placed on his relationships with others around him. In an effort to adapt to this device, Alonzo moved to another state after his third felony conviction for burglary. After serving time in another state, he moved again only to wind up in a federal prison. Alonzo is currently serving a life sentence for robbery. This is his seventh felony incarceration as an adult.

The migratory nature of career criminals is well known. Over half of the participants in the study had served felony incarcerations in more than one state. On the one side, of course, the effort is spurred by a desire to avoid the roundup of usual suspects and/or avoid prosecution. On the other side, however, the migratory nature of career criminals is also an adaptive response to the screening device utilized by police organizations. As is common knowledge in sociology, one major reason for human migration is a desire to start one's life anew and attempt to construct a new, more presentable biography. The spread of police computers has made this adaptation increasingly difficult to accomplish successfully.

Another screening device utilized by the police was identified by a majority of the participants. Edward W. the oldest participant at 66, and who has spent over twenty-seven years in adult prisons, noted the dramatic change in police demeanor since his first conviction in 1954. Edward is currently serving thirty-five years for armed robbery. He expects to die in prison.

The last time I was on the street (1981) the cops didn't know me and I didn't know them. Used to be that a lot of small stuff would slide and the cops would give you a break. Now they lock you up for everything. I ran whiskey since I was 14 years old and got caught plenty of times but they [police] let me go. I was in my twenties first time I fell. Now they look for you and stalk you on the streets. It's hard for an ex-con to stay out these days.

The changes noted by Edward and many others in the study and the attendant consequences for criminals in general and career criminals in particular emanate from the professionalization movement of police organizations. As Uchida (1966, p. 86) has noted, the professionalization movement had two unintended consequences. First, it led to the development of a police subculture with pronounced boundary maintenance consequences. Second, especially with the importation of modern technology, was the removal of the officer from the streets and subsequent elimination from contact with citizens. Jerome Skolnick (1996, p. 90) notes that the police officer's role contains two principal variables—danger and authority. The element of danger seems to make the police officer attentive to signs indicating potential for violence or lawbreaking. As a result "the element of danger isolates the police socially from that segment of the citizenry that they regard as symbolically dangerous" (Skolnick 1996, p. 90). Thus, while the screening device employed by the police is a coping mechanism for their occupational role, it is also reinforces the status of the career criminal.

The boundary maintaining mechanisms utilized by the police in regard to career criminals were manifold and generally well known to the participants in this study. Virtually every subject made reference to the prohibition against gun ownership by any ex-felon. The research subjects who had no violent convictions in their record particularly pointed this out. John R., the only subject in the study with a demonstrable middle-class background, was particularly incensed. With six incarcerations for property offenses, he also served two gun possession cases, one at the state level and one at the federal level. In his view, a weapon was necessary for protection. As he related during the interview,

once you are classified as a career criminal you are forced to live around people just like you. A lot of them are dangerous. My best friend from the streets was shot in the street in Mobile five years ago, in front of a dozen witnesses, and nothing was ever done to the shooter. The cops don't care. They always do things to you to make sure you don't forget what you are. We are treated worse than dirt by the police on the streets. We need guns worse than the police. They are the ones that got gun laws passed against ex-felons owning guns.

Another inmate, Dewey P., who is black and serving a fifteen-year sentence for possession of controlled substance, became very agitated about this issue during the interview. He pointed out that black cops are worse than white ones in how they treat people on the street. As he stated during the interview, "I guess they [black cops] want to make sure that no one mistakes them for a crook. Some of the guys I grew up with became cops. They act like they don't know you anymore."

One of the ways that the subjects have coped with or adapted to this problem has been the development of an elaborate ideology by which the police are considered criminals in uniform. Every subject was eager to tell personal stories about police corruption, police involved in criminal acts, and police taking part in drug dealing. Virtually every subject had a similar point to prove that there is basically no difference between the police and career criminals.

When asked during the interviews about how the police would relegate a career criminal to an inferior status (deployment patterns), the response was almost unanimous—the role of "snitch." It is a common practice in police organizations to use known criminals or individuals that have been caught in some relatively minor crime as snitches. The practice is ubiquitous in drug cases. In the world of criminals, particularly career criminals, the status of snitch is the lowest form of human existence. Every participant related numerous attempts through their criminal career to be turned into a snitch by the police. Most indicated that this status was especially difficult to avoid while one was in some type of early release program (e.g., parole) when even minor technical violations (e.g., changing jobs without approval from the parole officer, receiving a traffic ticket) can lead to a trip back to prison.

One of the adaptations developed by career criminals to avoid this deployment pattern has been the use of federal lawsuits. The potential for public embarrassment of the police is one of the few defensive tools available to the career criminal to combat the effort to being turned into a snitch. Recent Supreme Court rulings and the 1996 Prison Litigation Reform Act passed by Congress, all of which have made the filing of lawsuits by inmates more difficult, were expectedly opposed by all the participants in the study as being a serious erosion of their adaptation and deemed to be unfair.

The Courts

When questioned about experiences with the court system, few areas of consideration drew more emotion and anger from the subjects in the study than that of defense counsel. Following a series of Supreme Court cases in the 1960s (*Gideon v. Wainwright*, 1963; *Escobedo v. Illinois*, 1964; *Miranda v. Arizona*, 1966) it became mandatory for defense counsel to be present during the interrogation of any suspect in custody and for the state to pay for such counsel should the suspect be unable to do so. Failure on the part of the state would constitute a violation of the Fifth Amendment protection against self-incrimination.

In response to specific questions about their particular experience with defense counsel (all subjects in the study had court appointed defense counsel), the most common response was derogatory in nature. Jefferson B. stated that his defense counsel "worked for the system and sold me down the river." All subjects perceived defense counsel as part of the screening devices. This is consistent with Blumberg's finding. "All court personnel, including the accused's own lawyer, tend to be coopted to become agent-mediators who help the accused redefine his situation and restructure his perceptions concomitant with a pleas of guilty" (Blumberg 1996, p. 195).

Another area where screening devices come into play is the process of plea-bargaining. It is common knowledge that the vast majority (90 percent) of criminal cases are resolved by the plea-bargain process. All but one of the subjects in the study is currently serving a plea-bargain case. Positive and negative inducements offered to the subjects during the court process in order to plead guilty and preclude a jury trial included threats of a harsher sentence, derogatory presentence investigations, recommendations for certain programs while in prison (e.g., substance abuse, education), and suppressing of previous incarcerations that might affect length of sentence in the current case.

A similar adaptation elicited from the subjects revealed another, extensive ideology replete with "first-hand" stories about lawyers as racketeers. Every subject in the study readily provided a case personally known to them whereby a lawyer had been convicted and/or disbarred from the legal profession.

The plea-bargaining process also serves to function as a boundary maintaining mechanism in that it defines what is acceptable on the part of the criminal. The plea-bargaining process is inevitably followed by the "cop-out" ceremony (Blumberg 1996, p. 202), which functions as a deployment pattern for the criminal. In the transaction between the court personnel (agents of social control) and the criminal, the end result is to relegate the criminal to a class of convicted felons. This process not only helps the accused redefine himself but also allows him to reiterate publicly his guilt for the benefit of others. The accused is further made to indicate that he is entering his plea of guilty of his own free will, voluntarily, and without any promises or commitments that may have been made to him by anyone. This deployment pattern is also important for the court bureaucracy as it shields them from any possible charges of coercion that may lead to future appeals on violation of due process. The guilty plea is only a temporary role adaptation (Blumberg 1996, p. 202) as the accused will in almost all cases assert his innocence and publicly proclaim that he pled guilty on advice of his lawyer, to get a shorter sentence, etc. That is why the vast majority of prison inmates, despite their recorded plea of guilty, vigorously profess their innocence.

The Prison

Upon entering the prison system, the first screening device encountered by inmates is the intake classification system. Based upon a myriad of factors such as length of sentence, number of incarcerations, type of crime, and age, the inmate's past behavior is used to allocate the individual into one of many classifications. Most career criminals are usually classified as requiring more than minimum custody housing, which greatly shrinks the availability of programs in which they can be placed. Every inmate interviewed in this study stated he did not agree with his initial classification. Ben W. is typical in this regard. Ben W. is serving a life sentence for first degree murder which is his fourth felony incarceration and third for violent offenses. Although he barely escaped a life-without-parole sentence (initiated a year after his current offense), he is indignant to be classified as a career criminal. According to Ben, he has filed at least one unsuccessful lawsuit in federal court attempting to overturn his classification. For that matter, every inmate in the study took exception with his initial classification as a career (habitual) criminal.

The next screening device encountered by prison inmates is the orientation/job assignment board at their permanent facility. In this ritual, past behavior is again assessed and used to define the inmate as high risk and in need of closer security than most inmates. Because of their relatively long sentences and minimal prognosis of eventual success outside prison, they are generally denied programs in the early years that are designed for the soon-to-be-released inmates. One adaptation generally employed by all inmates but most noticeable among the career criminals is incessant attempts to be medically and/or psychologically categorized to preclude any manual labor. One consequence of being classified as a career criminal is to be housed with others so classified. According to Sykes (1996, p. 248), "It is a situation which can prove to be anxiety-provoking even for the hardened recidivist." Virtually every inmate involved in the study expressed at least periodic anxiety in being housed around other, long-term inmates.

The major effort to cope or adapt to these screening devices, similar to coping with the police, is to file federal lawsuits to modify or otherwise ameliorate the consequences of their relegation. Ten of the twelve participants in the study had filed lawsuits challenging their classifications at some point in their careers. Every participant but one (John W.) was familiar with the *Sandin v. Conner* (1995) Supreme Court ruling that basically took away the vast majority of due process claims in the area of classification. Most noted that this case would make it much more difficult to challenge effectively their relegation to the status of career criminal.

Some boundary maintaining mechanisms within the correctional setting are very obvious. Inmates are required to wear uniforms, to use numbers for identification, and to comply with a plethora of grooming regulations. Inmates, particularly the career criminals, are exposed to an endless array of degradation ceremonies designed to "keep them in their place," to constantly remind them that they have foregone their rights to be trusted members of society. Two of the most common types of degradation ceremonies evolve around prison disciplinary proceedings and classification hearings.

Prison inmates are exposed to, and held accountable by, scores of administrative rules and regulations. Some are so nebulous (by design) that successful avoidance is virtually impossible. Usually, any staff member can initiate a disciplinary hearing against any inmate. While ostensibly available to maintain control and order of the inmate population, they very often gravitate into boundary maintaining mechanisms. In a great many cases, a disciplinary hearing comes down to the inmate's word against that of a member of the staff. The inmate almost always loses and has, since recent court rulings and the 1996 Prison Litigation Reform Act passed by Congress, little recourse to avoid the consequences of such hearings.

Another clear demarcation line between inmates and staff, of which inmates are constantly reminded, is the prohibition against ex-felons becoming correction officers. In virtually every confrontation between inmate and officer, the inmate is reminded of this salient fact of life. One of the adaptations to this boundary maintaining mechanism is that most administrative and criminal cases made against security staff that lead to dismissal and/or prosecution are initiated by inmate informants, usually career criminals. Not only are they more knowledgeable about what goes on inside the prison on a day-to-day basis, but because of their long tenure in correctional facilities they tend to be more conscious of, and resentful toward, the dichotomy between them and correctional officers. James R. pointed out during his interview that there had been changes in the type of officer inside the prison today from twenty years ago. James is in his twenty-first year of incarceration for his eighth felony. In his view the officers today spend a lot of time making sure that the line between officer and inmate is maintained at all times.

Among deployment devices employed inside the correctional setting, three are common and obvious to all inmates. They are the classification hearing, the psychological evaluation, and the Job Board. The classification hearing is the main vehicle by which the agents of social control relegate the inmate to a caste or class, although such hearings can also involve a psychological evaluation and Job Board action as well. Within the overall prison system and within any given institution at any given time there is an array of statuses available to the inmate that can be altered in short order, often with vary difficult results for the inmate. Custody is a function of the classification hearing. Custody not only determines what type institution one lives in but also under what conditions within a given institution. As a general rule, the higher the custody level, the fewer amenities and programs available and the more dangerous the other inmates around you. Inmates in minimum custody institutions, for example, are allowed to work outside without an armed guard, and in some cases with no guard at all. Medium custody can only be outside with an armed guard. Higher custody grades are usually confined to single cell status. Such allocations are a constant source of tension and anxiety to inmates, particularly those who fall into the habitual category. Alonzo H. has tried unsuccessfully for ten years to alter his classification as habitual/violent. Prior to his current life sentence for second degree robbery (no weapon involved), his previous six felony incarcerations were all property cases. Alonzo is only one of two inmates participating in the study who was raised by both parents. He reacts emotionally to being referred to as a career criminal. In Alonzo's view (he is now 44 years old), his childhood rebellion lasted longer than expected. He had filed a lawsuit previously in federal court to alter his classification without success. The reality of a classification hearing is that there has never been much recourse outside the prison system for the dissatisfied. Whatever due process rights were obtained by inmates in such hearings since the early 1970s, the *Sandin v. Conner* (1995) Supreme Court case erased. Since that time there has been no due process requirement for any type classification action.

The psychological evaluation is another deployment pattern visible to inmates. Most such evaluations are conducted at the request of either security staff or the parole board and are designed to serve a particular motive. This type of evaluation is probably the most nebulous encountered by inmates and is feared generally. Every inmate involved in the study has had one or more such evaluations during his incarceration. The most feared category to which any inmate can be relegated is that of sociopath. This psychological classification is tantamount to be condemned to prison for the rest of your life. While rarely used, it is always there as a threat. Its correct employment under the right conditions can bring the most recalcitrant miscreant to heel. Edward W. has been classified as a sociopath. After twenty-seven years in adult prison and working on his fifth incarceration, he is, at age 65, reconciled to dying in prison. The deployment patterns have been so effective in his case that he accepts the status as a matter of unalterable fact. His consolation is that the fear of growing old and worrying about medical care has been alleviated by the perceived permanence of his status.

The last deployment pattern explored with the career criminals was that of the Job Board. The inmate population of a prison has a fairly distinct hierarchy with distinct subgroups. As in all hierarchical structures there are a variety of statuses that are attached to one's job assignment. While there are other statuses available to prison inmates, this is the main status that involves constant transactions between the agents of social control and the individual. The Job Board usually consists of the warden, the inmate control system supervisor, and a staff member from the treatment division. All decisions are final and cannot be appealed. A particular inmate can be elevated or lowered in status instantaneously. Every inmate interviewed in this study fully understood the nature and consequences of this board. For career criminals who have and will spend a great deal of time in prison, the allocation of a prestigious status from the agents of social control is extremely important. A high prestige job such as warden's orderly, visiting room orderly, and inmate clerk carry with them access to powerful individuals and an ability to make requests for special considerations in regard to the numerous, mundane rules of everyday prison life.

DISCUSSION AND CONCLUSION

The police, court, and correction institutions are all bureaucratic in nature. In dealing with such structures the inmate, particularly the career inmate, will encounter various mechanisms—screening devices, boundary maintaining mechanisms, deployment patterns—that serve to relegate and reinforce the status of career criminal.

Based on in-depth interviews with twelve career criminals who are currently incarcerated, oral evidence was elicited that highlights and reveals these various mechanisms. Moreover, career criminals explained a variety of adaptations by which they attempt to offset the consequences of such relegation or avoid it altogether. What turned out to be significant from the career criminal's point of view was the increasing difficulty in ameliorating or avoiding such relegations. Every subject involved in the study noted the increasing difficulty and basically attributed it to recent court rulings. Less strict rules of evidence, greater difficulty in filing appeals and lawsuits, and the elimination of many due process rights in prison have all served to increase anxiety among the subjects about their future.

Given the elaborate and effective mechanisms available to the police, courts, and correction institutions, and given the recent decrease in the rate of prison population growth (due to several years of reduced crime rates and demographic changes), the concern among career criminals of never being released from prison is real. It may very well turn out that an ever-increasing population of career criminals will be with us despite whatever else happens in our society.

REFERENCES

Barkan, Steven E. 1997. *Criminology: A Sociological Understanding*. Upper Saddle River, N.J.: Prentice-Hall.

Becker, Howard S. 1963. *Outsiders*. New York: The Free Press.

Bennett, William J., John J. DiLulio Jr., and John P. Walters. 1996. *Body Count: Moral Poverty and How to Win America's War against Crime and Drugs*. New York: Simon and Schuster.

Binder, Arnold, Gilbert Geis, and Dickson Bruce. 1988. *Juvenile Delinquency: Historical, Cultural, and Legal Perspectives*. New York: Macmillan.

Blumberg, Abraham S. 1996. "The Practice of Law as A Con Game." In Barry Hancock and Paul M. Sharp, eds., *Criminal Justice in America*, p. 193–212. Upper Saddle River, N.J.: Prentice-Hall.

Bureau of Justice Statistics Bulletin. 1998. *Prison and Jail Inmates at Midyear 1997*. Washington, D.C.: U.S. Department of Justice.

Cloward, Richard, and Lloyd Ohlin. 1960. *Delinquency and Opportunity*. Glencoe, Ill.: The Free Press.

Cohen, Albert K. 1955. *Delinquent Boys: The Culture of the Gang*. Glencoe, Ill.: The Free Press.

Erikson, Kai T. 1964. "Notes on the Sociology of Deviance." In Howard S. Becker, ed., *The OtherSide*, pp. 7–21. Glencoe, Ill.: The Free Press.

Gottfredson, Michael R., and Travis Hirschi. 1988. "Science, Policy, and the Career Paradigm." *Criminology* 24: 213–234.

Irwin, John, and James Austin. "It's about Time: Solving America's Prison Crowding Crisis." In Barry Hancock and Paul M. Sharp, eds. *Criminal Justice in America*, pp. 275–288. Upper Saddle River, N.J.: Prentice-Hall.

Justice Policy Institute. "The Punishing Decade: Prison and Jail Estimates at the Millennium." <http://www.ctcj.orgpunishingdecade/punishing.html>.

Kappler, Victor, Mark Blumberg, and Gary Potter. 1996. "The Social Construction of Crime Myths." In Barry Hancock and Paul M. Sharp, eds., *Criminal Justice in America*, pp. 373–387. Upper Saddle River, N.J.: Prentice-Hall.

Merton, Robert K. 1968. *Social Theory and Social Structure*. Glencoe, Ill.: The Free Press.

Miller, Walter. 1958. "Lower Class Culture as a Generating Milieu of Gang Delinquency." *Journal of Social Issues* 14:15–19.

Rettig, Richard P., Manuel J. Torres, and Gerald R. Garrett. 1977. *Manny: A Criminal-Addict's Story*. Boston: Houghton Mifflin Company.

Roth, Byron M. 1994. *Prescription for Failure: Race Relations in the Age of Social Science*. New Brunswick, N.J.: Transaction Publications.

Skolnick, Jerome. 1996. "A Sketch of the Police Officer's 'Working Personality.' " In Barry Hancock and Paul M. Sharp, eds., *Criminal Justice in America*, pp. 89–113. Upper Saddle River, N.J.: Prentice-Hall.

Sykes, Gresham. 1996. "The Pains of Imprisonment." In Barry Hancock and Paul M. Sharp, eds., *Criminal Justice in America*, pp. 242–251. Upper Saddle River, N.J.: Prentice-Hall.

Thomas, Andrew Peyton. 1994. *Crime and the Sacking of America: The Roots of Chaos*. Washington, D.C.: Brassey's, Inc.

Tonry, Michael. 1994. *Malign Neglect: Race, Crime, and Punishment in America*. New York: Oxford University Press.

Uchida, Craig D. 1996. "The Development of the American Police." In Barry Hancock and Paul M. Sharp, eds., *Criminal Justice in America*, pp. 73–88. Upper Saddle River, N.J.: Prentice-Hall.

Wilson, James Q., and Richard J. Herrnstein. 1985. *Crime and Human Nature*. New York: Touchstone Books.

Wilson, William Julius. 1996. *When Work Disappears: The World of the Urban Poor*. New York: Alfred A. Knopf.

Wright, Richard A. 1996. "In Support of Prisons." In Barry Hancock and Paul M. Sharp, eds., *Criminal Justice in America*, pp. 252–266. Upper Saddle River, N.J.: Prentice-Hall.

14

Mass Murder

Thomas A. Petee, Kathy G. Padgett, and Thomas S. York

INTRODUCTION

He arrived at the printing plant at 8:30 A.M. on Thursday, September 14, 1989. Joseph Wesbecker, 47, had been a pressman for the Standard Gravure Printing Corporation in Louisville, Kentucky, for seventeen years before the company placed him on permanent disability leave the previous February because of psychiatric problems. He suffered from manic depression and was taking medication (including Prozac) to help him control his mental illness. Wesbecker was angry with what he perceived to be his mistreatment at the hands of Standard Gravure officials. He believed that the company had discriminated against him by assigning him to stressful jobs that exacerbated his psychiatric condition. Carrying an arsenal of weapons that included an AK-47 rifle, three semiautomatic pistols, a .38 caliber revolver, a bayonet, and hundreds of rounds of ammunition, Wesbecker entered the company's reception area and took an elevator to the third floor.

As the elevator doors opened, Wesbecker began firing the AK-47, hitting two receptionists, one of whom died from her wounds. Employees immediately began to scramble to get out of the gunman's way. Some hid in their offices, crouched under desks or tables. Others frantically attempted to exit the premises. Wesbecker moved methodically through the third floor area—a witness later told the police that he was walking very deliberately, taking his time as he stalked the reception area—shooting three more employees in the process. He then went down a stairwell to the building's basement, firing his rifle along the way.

In the basement Wesbecker encountered several former co-workers. One of those former colleagues, John Tingle had a long-standing friendship with Wesbecker. Tingle had heard the gunfire and stepped around the press he was working at in order to see what the commotion was. As Wesbecker came around the corner, he acknowledged Tingle by stating "Hi John . . . I told them I'd be back. Get away from me." When Tingle questioned what Wesbecker was doing, he swore at Tingle, and warned him "Get back, I don't want to hurt you." Tingle escaped the incident without injury, apparently spared because of his friendship with the gunman. Others were not so fortunate. In the basement area, Wesbecker killed two employees and wounded three others. One of the slain victims was shot five times before Wesbecker stepped over the body to continue his onslaught.

Wesbecker next moved up a stairwell to the first floor. The first floor contained a pressroom that was leased by the *Louisville Courier-Journal*. At this point in time there were more employees than usual in the first floor area because of a shift change. As he came to the top of the stairwell, Wesbecker saw several of these workers and fired upon them, killing two press operators. Proceeding to the company's break room, Wesbecker burst through the door and opened fire on a handful of employees who had been taking a coffee break, hitting two workers who were sitting at a nearby table. As the remaining workers scrambled for cover, Wesbecker walked back into the pressroom, pulled out one of the semiautomatic pistols he was carrying, and shot himself in the face. The entire incident had lasted less than thirty minutes. In all, Wesbecker killed seven former colleagues and wounded thirteen others (Adams 1989; McDonough and Weronka 1989; McDonough and Willis 1989; Scanlon and Wolfson 1989).

OVERVIEW OF THE MASS MURDER PROBLEM

Mass murder, defined as the killing of three or more people in one place at one time, has certainly captured public attention over the last several years, thanks largely to a number of high profile incidents (e.g., James Huberty's rampage in a San Ysidro, California, McDonald's in 1984; Patrick Purdy's massacre of school children on a Stockton, California, playground in 1989; the killing of "feminist" engineering students by Marc Lépine in Montreal in 1989; the murders perpetrated by George Hennard at Luby's Cafeteria in Killeen, Texas in 1991).[1] Catastrophic incidents of mass murder pervade the public consciousness because people become enthralled with the sheer magnitude of the event in terms of the number of victims. Moreover, the seemingly random nature of target selection gives many people an exaggerated sense of their own risk. Consequently, these kinds of cases become the basis for how the public perceives mass murder in general. As Fox and Levin point out, when most people are asked to imagine a mass murderer, they "think of killers who suddenly 'go berserk' or " 'run amok' " (1994, p. 127). Indeed, over the last few years a stereotype of sorts has emerged for the mass murderer that draws upon some of the more highly publicized cases—a deranged and/or disgruntled white male, in his thirties or forties, who often has a fascination with guns, and who usually commits suicide at the conclusion of the murder event.

In many ways, Joseph Wesbecker fits this conception of mass murderers. He apparently had become a serious collector of firearms—the police had discovered that he had begun stockpiling weapons about the time he was forced to go on disability leave—and may have had an interest in the survivalist movement (McDonough and Willis 1989). He was also clearly enraged at Standard Gravure management, and likely had targeted his bosses, although they just happened to be out of town the day of the massacre. These, and other situational factors surrounding the offense, as well as his demographic profile make Wesbecker almost the personification of the stereotype. The concept of mass murder has become so familiar to Americans that the notion of a "disgruntled employee" who seeks revenge on his employer has really become part of the cultural landscape, perpetuated by cases like Wesbecker or any of the post office murders that have occurred over the last decade.[2]

CONSTRUCTING MASS MURDER: A CASE STUDY ANALYSIS

It should probably not be surprising that the imagery surrounding this kind of homicide may not be very accurate in describing most incidents of mass murder. Issues related to crime and deviance seem to be especially prone to misrepresentation and stereotyping (see Pepinsky and Jesilow 1984). Bound by selected or limited exposure to these issues, people often have opinions and beliefs that are exaggerated or distorted. This appears to be precisely what occurs with public perceptions about mass murder.

There is a substantial body of literature within sociology that focuses on the social construction of crime, deviance, and other social problems (see Spector and Kitsuse 1987). Essentially, the constructionist approach sets out to determine how various groups or other mechanisms within society can influence the definition and perception of these social problems (Spector and Kitsuse 1987; Best 1989; Ben-Yehuda 1990; and Jenkins 1994). Of particular interest for our purposes is the emphasis placed by some constructionists on the framing of social problems for public consumption. Framing involves the selection, presentation, and accentuation of an event or issue so as to place it in a comprehensible package (Papke 1987) On one hand, these events have to be put in context so that the selected audience can be familiar with it (Jenkins 1994). On the other hand, this framing must occur in such a way as to maintain the interest of the audience.

While there are numerous agencies, entrepreneurs, and interest groups that might be involved in the framing process, the mass media may be especially relevant for crime-related phenomena. There are a number of studies within the constructionist perspective that demonstrate how depictions of crime in the mass media shape public attitudes and perceptions (see, for example, Soothill and

Walby 1991; Sparks 1992; Surette 1992). The popular press, particularly television, has the capacity to reach a massive audience and the representation of crime and related issues by these media sources can play a significant role in how the public views various kinds of lawbreaking. As Jenkins (1994) has noted, the dissemination and interpretation of social problems through the news media needs to be critically analyzed in order to understand the social construction of that problem. Mass murder should certainly be no exception to this caveat.

With mass murder, the kinds of cases that come to the public's attention are going to be those that are more sensationalistic, essentially because the media plays such a major role in determining which events it will expose to the public. More mundane cases (in relative terms) are less likely to be judged "newsworthy" and consequently will draw less attention from media outlets. By contrast, catastrophic events conform to conceptions of what is "newsworthy," thereby garnering more intense scrutiny.[3] The Wesbecker massacre is a case in point.

All of the major networks gave select coverage to the slayings on their evening news programs, broadcasting Wesbecker's image to millions of viewers across the country. The incident also made national headlines and generated numerous op-ed treatments on topics ranging from the need for gun control to the efficacy of Prozac. For several days following the murders, any information related to the case was potentially a "top" news story. However, the impact of the media goes beyond mere exposure. How these events are described and characterized can also be critical. News coverage tends to use language that draws attention to the story. Unfortunately, it is often this kind of language that can sway people's preconceptions about issues and events. With headlines that made use of terminology such as "disturbed," "tormented," and "crazed" to describe Wesbecker, the general tone of the coverage of that incident only served to further entrench the stereotype for mass murder. In the end, even the high-profile cases may become somewhat distorted. When this is coupled with the likelihood that less sensational cases receive comparatively little media coverage, we may have a less than complete picture of the mass murder phenomenon.

Even academic treatments of mass murder seem to buy into this stereotype. While research on mass murder is relatively limited, those studies that have explored this form of homicide have generally focused on the deranged/disgruntled type of killer. Dietz (1986), for example, bases his analysis of mass murder specifically on sensational homicide cases. He characterizes mass murderers as being paranoid or depressive and claims that most of the offenders either commit suicide or force the police to kill them. Other studies (e.g., Holmes and Holmes 1994; Rappaport 1988) reach similar conclusions, in effect creating an image of mass murderers that is congruent with media depictions. This is exacerbated when academics cross over into the media realm. When experts from academia are interviewed on television or in newspapers, they typically foster the conventional depiction of mass murder. After a rash of post office massacres in 1991, several well-known criminologists appeared on news programs and talk shows to discuss the "typical" offender (i.e., deranged/disgruntled white male, etc.), further promulgating the stereotype.

It should be recognized that the stereotype for mass murder may also serve a political end. Certainly the image of a deranged killer with a large arsenal of weapons plays into the rhetoric of gun control advocates. The gun control debate often centers on the accessibility of firearms for criminals and the mentally ill. Whenever a catastrophic event occurs involving a mentally unstable offender (e.g., Wesbecker, Purdy, Huberty, Lépine, and Hennard), there is invariably a flurry of news items on how the murderer managed to obtain the weapons used in the offense. This is usually followed by editorial commentary in support of gun control. In some cases even serious discussions in the legislature ensure. Again, the Wesbecker case serves as an illustration of this process.

The day after the murders, the local newspaper (the *Louisville Courier-Journal*) ran several stories on how Wesbecker had acquired the guns he had used in the massacre, with headlines such as "Sledgehammer of A Gun Can Be Bought Easily" and "Killer Began Stocking up on Weapons A Year Ago" (McDonough and Weronka 1989; McDonough and Willis 1989). Wesbecker had been able to purchase his weapons legally despite the fact that he was manic depressive because the law prohibited firearms to be sold to anyone who had been "adjudicated mentally defective" or committed to a mental institution, neither of which applied (McDonough and Willis 1989).

For several days after the news stories on the firearms purchases were run, a series of editorials began appearing in newspapers across the country in support of tighter regulations concerning access to firearms. Both locally and nationally, gun control arguments took center stage. The sense of concern over the Wesbecker murders effectively served to legitimize the claims of gun control advocates. At the same time, because of the attention being focused on the incident by the media and various interest groups, the characterization of Wesbecker commonly became accepted as representative of mass murder cases.

Examining the Stereotype

The imagery of the deranged/disgruntled mass killer is consistent with what has been labeled the "anger/revenge" type of offender (Petee, Padgett, and York 1997; see also, Douglas et al. 1992). This kind of mass murderer is motivated by vengeance and will typically plan the offense. Sometimes the target(s) for the offender is a specific person(s) or place (as with Wesbecker), but in other situations the targets are more diffuse and often simply convenient. It is from this latter context that the perception that mass murder involves random victimization seems to emanate. Offenders of this type are also more likely to suffer from mental illness and have a greater probability of committing suicide (Petee, Padgett, and York 1997).

Many of the higher profile mass murder cases seem to fall into this anger/

revenge category. Wesbecker would certainly be classified as this type of a killer, as would George Hennard, James Huberty, Marc Lépine, Patrick Purdy, and numerous other infamous mass murderers. But this is far from an accurate representation of the typical mass killer. Mass murder is an extremely diverse phenomenon, both motivationally and situationally. Characteristics such as age, race, offender background, and context of the offense vary greatly across offender categories (Petee, Padgett, and York 1997). Some mass murderers are young, many are nonwhite. Motivation for the murders involves everything from greed to politics. In fact, the anger/revenge type of offender represents a relatively small fraction of all mass murderers. Far more common are mass homicides that result from a family-related argument, or from the commission of a another (usually property-related) felony. The circumstances and patterns seen with these latter types of mass murder are dramatically different from the anger/ revenge form of multicide. Yet these more frequent modes of multiple homicide do not seem to be represented adequately in the socially constructed image of mass murder. Instead, more compelling but comparatively infrequent incidents are what tend to influence widely held beliefs about this type of offense. The predominance of the anger/revenge killer hardly seems warranted given the variability found in mass murder cases.

Domestic-related cases probably represent the most frequent form of mass murder. Levin and Fox (1985) estimate that this type of homicide constitutes almost half of all mass murders, although this proportion is likely even higher, since they include serial and spree murder in their definition of mass murder.[4] Often these family slayings are motivated by some type of marital problem or family dispute. The case of Rodolfo Meinguer is illustrative of this kind of mass murder. On August 19, 1990, Los Angeles police forced their way into the apartment that Meinguer shared with his common-law wife, Maria Ortiz, and their three children after Ortiz's sister notified authorities that she had been unable to contact anyone in the family for two days. When the police entered the premises, they found all five family members dead (Hirabayashi and Boyer 1990).

Police were able to determine that two days before the bodies were found, Meinguer had stabbed Ortiz to death, then shot and killed their children before taking his own life. Meinguer and Ortiz had reportedly been experiencing domestic problems, and Meinguer apparently believed that his common-law wife was romantically involved with another man. By all accounts, Meinguer was extremely jealous, constantly questioning the wife's fidelity. According to the police, Meinguer, who had been heavily drinking, attacked Ortiz in their bedroom with a butcher knife, stabbing her repeatedly. After finishing the assault, he went into the living room where the three children, Rodolpho, 8, Rosalyn, 6, and Joe, 3, were sleeping on the floor, and shot each of them with a large caliber handgun. Later (two days after the killings), Meinguer shot himself with the same handgun he had used on the children (Hirabayashi and Boyer 1990; McMillan and Wilkinson 1990).

In comparison to the stereotype, Meinguer could hardly have been character-ized as deranged or disgruntled. He appears to have been a relatively stable and reliable person with no documented history of mental health problems. Although Meinguer was apparently motivated by jealousy, the dynamics of this motivation are distinct from the blind rage that is frequently seen in cases such as Wes-becker's. Moreover, Meinguer did not seem to have any particular affinity for firearms. The only gun he owned was the one used to kill his children and himself. Finally, in regard to demographic characteristics, Meinguer did fit the age profile for the stereotype (he was 40 years old), but he did not fit the race characterization (he was Hispanic). Overall, the Meinguer case is fairly repre-sentative of domestic-related mass murders. Our research indicates that most of these offenders have a specific target with limited victimization (i.e., the family) and commit their murders in a private setting (i.e., their home), which is not at all consistent with the notion of a killer "run amok."[5]

The inaccuracies in the common representation of mass murder are even more apparent with felony-murder. The image of three or more people being killed during a robbery or burglary attempt is probably not what comes immediately to mind when most people think of mass murder. Nevertheless, together robbery and burglary represent one of the more frequent forms of mass homicide (Petee, Padgett, and York 1997). The robbery of a Popeye's Chicken restaurant in Gads-den, Alabama, in 1994 by Robert Melson and Cuhuatemoc Peraita is typical of this form of mass murder. The two offenders entered the restaurant through an unlocked rear door late one evening as employees were preparing to close for the night. Melson and Peraita caught the workers off-guard, waving their guns menacingly as they looted the restaurant's cash registers. After gathering all of the money, the robbers herded the four workers into a walk-in cooler located in the rear of the building and opened fire on them. Three of the employees were killed, and a fourth was critically wounded (Nabberfeld and Bryant 1994; Rabiroff 1994).

With robbery murder, the primary motivation for the offense is monetary gain. However, the murders usually result either from the offender(s) losing control of the situation and panicking or from a perceived need to eliminate witnesses. The latter was clearly the case in the Gadsden murders. Peraita had once been employed at the restaurant (and was familiar with store procedures—hence the knowledge that the rear door would be unlocked at closing time) and all of the victims knew him. In fact, once the robbers left the premises, the surviving employee managed to crawl to a telephone to contact the police and immediately identified Peraita as one of the assailants.

The differences between incidents like the Melson/Peraita robbery murder and the Wesbecker case are especially striking. First of all, like Meinguer, neither Melson nor Peraita could be described as insane or disgruntled. The two of-fenders lacked any prior history of mental illness, and although Peraita had been an employee at the restaurant, the police quickly ruled out revenge as a motive for the murders. For the most part, Melson and Peraita are similar to most other

Table 1

Comparison of Selected Cases to the Stereotypical Representation of Mass Murder

	Stereotypical Representation	Wesbecker Case	Meinguer Case	Melson & Peraita Case
MOTIVATION	Disgruntled	Disgruntled	Jealousy	Monetary Gain
MENTAL HEALTH PROBLEMS	Yes	Yes	No	No
OFFENDER'S AGE	30-49	47	40	22/17
OFFENDER'S RACE	White	White	Hispanic	White/Hispanic
WEAPONS BACKGROUND	Yes	Yes	No	No
COMMITTED SUICIDE	Yes	Yes	Yes	No

felony-related mass murderers in this regard. Only rarely are offenders of this type mentally ill. Additionally, unlike both the Wesbecker and Meinguer cases, neither of the two robbers even attempted to commit suicide. Nor was there any suggestion that Melson and Peraita had any weapons background. Again, this is representative of felony-murder offenders. Our research indicates that this kind of mass murderer almost never commits suicide and only rarely has any special firearms experience (Petee, Padgett, and York 1997).

Two particular aspects of felony-related mass murders, which are reflected in the Melson/Peraita case, clearly delineate this type of homicide from the stereotype. First, Melson and Peraita were both considerably younger (22 and 17 years of age respectively) than the typical representation of mass murderers. In fact, overall felony-related killers tend to be in the 16–25 year-old age range, which is consistent with the age profile for offenders who commit property crime in general (Federal Bureau of Investigation 1996). Second, like the Melson/Peraita case, felony mass murder incidents are much more likely to involve multiple offenders. In a previous study, we found that an accomplice was present in more than 50 percent of cases of this type (Petee, Padgett, and York 1997). However, this may be the very reason why this form of mass murder is often overlooked. Indeed, some definitions of mass murder preclude having multiple offenders in order for a multiple homicide to qualify as a recognized case (see Dietz 1986; and, Gresswell and Hollin 1994), although this stipulation seems quite arbitrary given the frequency of multiple offenders for other forms of multicide such as serial and spree murder.

Table 1 summarizes the comparison of case studies utilized in this analysis. While there are common aspects to all of the cases, the differences are especially compelling. Only Wesbecker could be characterized as disgruntled—Meinguer was motivated by jealousy and Melson and Peraita by profit. Likewise, Wesbecker was the only one of the four offenders examined who had a weapons background or any discernable mental health problems. Although much has been made about the suicidal tendencies of mass murderers (see Dietz 1986; Holmes and Holmes 1994), Melson and Peraita clearly never had any intention of committing suicide.[6] Finally, even race and general age range varied across offenders. Both the Meinguer and the Melson/Peraita cases clearly demonstrate the diversity in offender and offense characteristics for mass murder.

DISCUSSION AND CONCLUSION

The stereotypical representation of mass murder, while based upon factual information from actual cases, gives us a somewhat distorted view of this phenomenon. The image of an insane or enraged, white, middle-aged offender does not take into account adequately the differences found in mass murder incidents. Many mass homicides involve sane offenders with identifiable motivations. Moreover, most offenders do not fit the demographic profile suggested by the stereotype. Mass murderers come from a variety of age groups and racial/ethnic categories. Even representations about the suicidal tendencies of these offenders, or their suggested proclivity for firearms, does not apply to all, or even most cases.

It is not difficult to understand how the stereotype for mass murder has developed. Because incidents like the Wesbecker case result in such horrifying carnage and involve a great deal of intrigue, they naturally attract the attention of the media. Consequently, as such cases achieve a higher level of visibility, people tend to generalize these cases as being representative of all incidents of mass murder. This process can be compounded by the topic becoming politicized. When sensational incidents occur, interest groups, such as gun control advocates, focus on the case to promote their political agenda. Typically, any pronouncements by these interest groups will accentuate exactly those features that are central to the stereotype (i.e., a deranged firearms enthusiast). This not only further increases the visibility of the case, but also serves as a confirmation of the stereotype in the public consciousness.

In conclusion, it should be clear that mass murder is not a singular phenomenon. The fact that one particular type of offender tends to dominate the public perception of this form of homicide results in a lack of understanding about this kind of crime. While the study of mass murder is admittedly a relatively new area, we need to be careful not to contribute to any further misunderstanding of this phenomenon by focusing exclusively on sensational cases.

NOTES

1. Mass murder is distinct from serial murder and spree murder. Serial murder involves the killing of three or more people over an extended period of time with a

"cooling-off" period between murders (Hickey 1997; Holmes and DeBurger 1988; Holmes and Holmes 1994). Spree murder is defined as the killing of three or more people over a relatively short period of time (several hours or a few days), with the homicides considered to be part of a continuous series of actions (Petee, Padgett, and York 1997). The victim criterion (three or more murder victims) is based upon the more recent convention used in the literature on multiple homicide (see Holmes and Holmes 1994).

2. The phrase "going postal," which had been used to describe the act of mass murder committed by a disgruntled employee, has even made its way into the popular vernacular.

3. According to Jenkins (1994), newsworthy stories should offer excitement or shock value and evoke an emotional response such as fear, outrage, or pity. Most of the high profile cases meet these criteria simply by the amount of carnage that typically occurs.

4. It is difficult to enumerate the exact number of different types of mass murder. The best source for homicide data, the Supplementary Homicide Reports, can be problematic in evaluating mass murder incidents due to misleading coding for the victim/offender relationship that occurs with multiple homicides, and because of a lack of detail on the location of the offense (see Fox 1996).

5. Collateral victimization with domestic-related incidents of mass murder almost exclusively occur in public settings. These incidents, however, are relatively rare—constituting a small percentage of even those incidents which occur in a public setting (Petee, Padgett, and York 1997).

6. Our research indicates that the vast majority of mass murderers do not commit suicide.

REFERENCES

Adams, Jim. 1989, September 15. "Tormented Man Driven by His Secret Stresses." *The Louisville Courier-Journal*, pp. A1, A16.

Ben-Yehuda, Nachman. 1990. *The Politics and Morality of Deviance: Moral Panics, Drug Abuse, Deviant Science, and Reversed Stigmatization.* Albany, N.Y.: SUNY Press.

Best, Joel. 1989. *Images of issues.* Hawthorne, N.Y.: Aldine de Gruyter.

Dietz, Park E. 1986. "Mass, Serial and Sensational Homicides." *Bulletin of the New York Academy of Medicine* 62: 477–491.

Douglas, John E., Ann W. Burgess, Allen G. Burgess, and Robert K. Ressler. 1992. *Crime Classification Manual: A Standard System for Investigating and Classifying Violent Crimes.* New York: Lexington Books.

Federal Bureau of Investigation. 1996. *Crime in the United States—Uniform Crime Reports—1995.* Washington, D.C.: U.S. Government Printing Office.

Fox, James A. 1996. *Uniform Crime Reports (United States): Supplementary Homicide Reports, 1976–2994* (ICPSR 6754). Ann Arbor, Mich.: Inter-university Consortium for Political and Social Research.

Fox, James Alan, and Jack Levin. 1994. *Overkill: Mass Murder and Serial Killing Exposed.* New York: Plenum Press.

Greswell, David M., and Clive R. Hollin. 1994. "Multiple Murder: A Review." *The British Journal of Criminology* 34: 1–14.

Hickey, Eric W. 1997. *Serial Murderers and Their Victims.* Belmont, Calif.: Wadsworth.

Hirabayashi, Bernice, and Edward J. Boyer. 1990, August 20. "Hollywood Man Kills 4 in Family, Then Himself." *The Los Angeles Times*, pp. B1, B6.

Holmes, Ronald M., and James DeBurger. 1988. *Serial Murder.* Newbury Park, Calif.: Sage Publications.

Holmes, Ronald M., and Stephen T. Holmes. 1994. *Murder in America.* Thousand Oaks, Calif.: Sage Publications.

Jenkins, Philip. 1994. *Using Murder: The Social Construction of Serial Homicide.* Hawthorne, N.Y.: Aldine de Gruyter.

Kennedy, James H. 1994, April 20. "Pair Accused in Gadsden Killings Denied Bond." *Birmingham (Alabama) News,* p. 4A.

Levin, Jack, and James Alan Fox. 1985. *Mass Murder: America's Growing Menace.* New York: Plenum Press.

———. 1996. "A Psycho-Social Analysis of Mass Murder." In T. O'Reilly-Fleming, ed., *Serial and Mass Murder: Theory, Research, and Policy,* pp. 55–76. Toronto: Canadian Scholars' Press.

McDonough, Rick, and Bill Weronka. 1989, September 15. " 'Sledgehammer' of A Gun Can Be Bought Easily." *The Lousiville Courier-Journal,* p. A16.

McDonough, Rick, and Cary B. Willis. 1989, September 16. "Killer Began Stocking Up on Weapons A Year Ago." *The Louisville Courier-Journal,* pp. A1, A9.

McMillan, Penelope, and Tracy Wilkinson. 1990, August 21. "Relatives Think Man's Jealousy Led Him to Kill Wife, Children." *The Los Angeles Times,* pp. B1, B4.

Nabbefeld, Joe, and Walter Bryant. 1994, April 17. "Restaurant Heist Leaves 3 Dead, One in Hospital." *Birmingham (Alabama) News,* p. 1A.

Papke, David Ray. 1987. *Framing the Criminal.* Hamden, Conn.: Archon Press.

Pepinsky, Harold A., and Paul Jesilow. 1984. *Myths that Cause Crime.* Cabin John, Md.: Seven Locks Press.

Petee, Thomas A., Kathy G. Padgett, and Thomas S. York. 1997. "Debunking the Stereotype: An Examination of Mass Murder in Public Places." *Homicide Studies: An Interdisciplinary & International Journal* 1:317–337.

Rabiroff, Jon. 1994, April 18. "Faith Eases Pain for Mother of Gadsden Victim." *Birmingham (Alabama) News,* p. 1A.

Rappaport, Richard G. 1988. "The Serial and Mass Murderer: Patterns, Differentiation, Pathology." *American Journal of Forensic Psychiatry* 9: 39–48.

Scanlon, Leslie, and Andrew Wolfson. 1989, September 15. "Disturbed Worker Kills 7 and Wounds 13 in Rampage with AK-47 at Louisville Plant." *The Louisville Courier-Journal,* pp. A1, A13.

Soothill, Keith, and Sylvia Walby. 1991. *Sex Crime in the News.* London: Routledge.

Sparks, Richard. 1992. *Television and the Drama of Crime: Moral Tales and the Place of Crime in Public Life.* Bristol, Pa.: Open University Press.

Spector, Malcolm, and John Kitsuse. 1987. *Constructing Social Problems.* Hawthorne, N.Y.: Aldine de Gruyter.

Surette, Ray. 1992. *Media, Crime and Criminal Justice: Images and Realities.* Pacific Grove, Calif.: Brooks Cole/Wadsworth.

15

Serial Killers

James A. Sparks

INTRODUCTION

Serial murder represents one form of violent, deviant behavior that has gained widespread public attention. Although the magnitude of this problem is unknown, serial murder has been recognized as a part of the American experience since the early 1900s. Since that time more than fifty major serial killers have been identified; estimates of the number of victims involved range from five per killer to more than 100 (Holmes and DeBurger 1988). Yet another estimate suggests that as many as 5,000 people per year may fall victim to serial murderers (Holmes and DeBurger 1985).

Serial murderers often kill for several years without detection. Steven Egger (1990) explains this situation, noting that investigations of serial murder are slowed by the difficulty in coordinating various interested divisions of law enforcement. Defining the problem as "linkage blindness" or the inability of law enforcement agencies to share information, serial murderers can change location and even their modus operandi without undo concern with being caught. Despite this historical limitation, some information is known. Holmes and DeBurger (1988), for example, found that serial killers have some characteristics in common stating, "The serial murderer is between the ages of 25 and 35, usually white males who kill white females, the serial murder occurs in areas of high transience and population change, involve people of similar status, and usually involves the killing of a total stranger" (pp. 23–24).

Motivated to kill to satisfy a personal need, serial murderers strike without warning, usually seek a victim who is unknown to them and, in many instances, commit a heinous crime that remains unsolved. Another aspect of the serial murder problem is that the killer often seeks single, unattached individuals who are vulnerable and of low social worth.

Serial murder has been described by the characteristics identified as a part of the murderer's methods. These include repetitive homicides, a brief one-on-one encounter or relationship with the victim, and the motivation to kill. According to Ressler, Burgess, and Douglas (1988, p. 122), more specific characteristics for at least two types of serial killers can be identified, namely the organized killer and the disorganized killer. The organized serial killer is of good intelligence, is socially competent, prefers skilled work, is sexually competent, has a high birth-order status, had a father whose employment was stable, experienced inconsistent childhood discipline, has a controlled mood during commission of the crime, experiences precipitating stress, uses alcohol during commission of the crime, lives with a partner, is mobile with a car in good condition, follows reports of the crime in the news media, and may change jobs or leave town. Characteristics of the disorganized killer, on the other hand, include average intelligence, social immaturity, a poor work history, sexual incompetence, minimal birth order status, unstable employment history of father, childhood experience of harsh parental discipline, anxious mood during commission of the crime, minimal use of alcohol, minimal stress, lives alone, lives or works near the crime scene, minimal interest in news media reporting of the crime, and minimal change in lifestyle (p. 122).

However, the organized and disorganized murderer categories are not believed to be mutually exclusive in that aspects of both types have been identified in certain serial killers. Characterized by Ressler and Schachtman (1992) as a combination type, an organized killer may become disorganized prior to being detected, a fact that may also account for the killer eventually being apprehended. On the other hand, a disorganized offender may become highly organized upon becoming effective at committing the crime while evading detection. In the case of John Wayne Gacy, considered the most prolific serial killer of the twentieth century (Hickey 1991), characteristics of both types can be identified.

Defining Serial Murder

Although several definitions of serial murder have been advanced, most analysts of this problem agree that a series of three victims must first be linked to a single killer or killers before the phenomenon serial murder is thought to exist (e.g., Egger 1990; Hickey 1991). Cormier et al. (1972) were the first to describe serial murder, using the term multicide. Defined as a number of murders committed by one individual over a period of time, the multicide offender is characterized by these analysts as having a psycho-pathological personality.

By 1982, a new term, "serial killer," was used by Federal Bureau of Investigation agent Robert Ressler who wrote that serial murder occurs when one or more persons commit an act of homicide with time lapses between each murder

(Ressler and Schactman 1992). Ressler, Burgess, and Douglas (1988) later re-defined the meaning, stating that serial murder involves the killing of separate victims with time breaks between victims. These time breaks, or "cooling off" periods, can be several days or may be separated by weeks or months.

Yet another student of this problem (Norris 1988) wrote

The serial murderer murders in an episodic frenzy that can strike without warning. He often preys on the most vulnerable victims in his area and then moves on, leaving the police to find the missing persons and search for traces of the scant clues left behind. Because his killing is not a passion of the moment but a compelling urge that has been growing within him sometimes for years, he has completely amalgamated this practice into his lifestyle. It is as though he lives to kill, surviving from one murder event to the next, stringing out his existence by connecting the deaths of the victims. Without this string of murders, he feels he will fall apart, that he will disintegrate psychologically. The remainder of his life is devoted to maintaining the mask of normalcy and sanity. (p. 19)

Perhaps the most comprehensive definition of serial murder was developed by Steven Egger (1985, p. 4):

A serial murder occurs when one or more individuals (males, in most cases) commit a second and/or subsequent murder; is relationshipless (no prior relationship between vic-tim and attacker); is at a different time and has no apparent connection to the initial murder; and is usually committed in a different geographical location. Further, the motive is not for material gain and is believed to be for the murderer's desire to have power over victims. Victims may have symbolic value and are perceived to be prestigeless and in most instances unable to defend themselves or alert to their plight, or are perceived as powerless given their situation in time, place or status within their immediate sur-roundings (such as vagrants, prostitutes, migrant workers, homosexuals, missing children, and single and often elderly women).

According to Egger (1990), most serial killers become sexually involved with their victims, while Hickey (1991, pp. 11–13) observed that serial killers also engage in one or more of the following activities: animal torture; anthropophagy (eating the victim's flesh or slicing off parts of the body); coprophilia (the offender may receive sexual gratification from touching or eating urine or ex-crement); fetishism (sexual gratification by substituting objects for a partner); gerontophilia (seeking out elderly people of the opposite sex for sexual gratifi-cation); mixoscopia (experiencing sexual pleasure from watching others engage in sex); necrofetishism (a fetish for dead bodies); necrophilia (having sexual intercourse with a corpse); pedophilia (having sexual intercourse with children); pederasty (having anal intercourse with children); using photographs or record-ings; using pornography, rape, torture, sadomasochism (inflicting mental or physical pain on others or oneself); voyeurism (sexual gratification achieved by peeping through windows to watch people); and lust murder (murdering sadistically and brutally, including the mutilation of body parts, especially the gen- italia).

Types of Serial Killers

Four distinctive types of serial killers have been identified: (1) visionary; (2) mission-oriented; (3) power/control-oriented; and (4) hedonistic. The visionary type responds to "voices" or "visions" and a demand that certain people or group of people be destroyed. Visionary killers interviewed by Holmes and DeBurger (1988) believed that an evil force called them to act, while others believe God told them to kill. One example of a visionary killer is David Berkowitz, also known as "Son of Sam," who killed both men and women because he believed his neighbor's dog instructed him to do so.

The mission-oriented killer has a goal of eliminating a particular group of people. Engaging in a "mission" to rid the world of undesirables (Holmes and DeBurger 1988). One example of a mission-oriented serial killer is Robert Hansen, a man who killed prostitutes because of his belief that prostitutes debase society.

The power/control-oriented serial killer derives satisfaction from having the ability to determine the victim's fate. Sexual abuse also may be associated with power/control (Holmes and DeBurger 1988). Ted Bundy, who traveled the United States seeking out women to control, exemplifies the power/control type killer.

The final hedonistic serial killer category includes two subtypes. Oriented toward pleasure and/or thrill-seeking, type one, the hedonist, is directly or in-directly rewarded and reinforced by the sense of pleasure or well-being achieved through commission of a crime (Holmes and DeBurger 1988). One example of this type of serial killer is Richard Ramirez, also known as "The Night Stalker" who, during the early 1980s, killed both men and women for pleasure. While in prison Ramirez stated that he loved the sight of blood (Newton 1990).

Subtype two, the lust killer, becomes sexually aroused, achieving emotional gratification as an integral part of the homicidal act (Hazlewood and Douglas 1980). Edmund Kemper, who killed college coeds and his mother during the 1970s, derived such sexual gratification. Concerned only with personal needs and desires, human life is irrelevant to the lust killer whose ultimate goals or desires include power and sexual gratification. This category may best describe John Wayne Gacy who serves as the case study example for this chapter.

E. Hickey (1991) describes the lust killer as a sexual psychopath who desires to sexually ravage the victim. J. P. deRiver (1958) suggested that lust murder and necrophilia, an act which involves masturbation while touching or fondling the corpse, is symbolic in that the lust murderer derives pleasure through post-mortem mating.

Hazlewood and Douglas (1980) further categorize lust murder into two distinctive types. Type one, the organized serial killer, is an asocial person who exhibits complete indifference to the interests and welfare of society, displaying an irresponsible and self-centered attitude. While disliking people in general, the organized killer does not avoid them. Instead, he is capable of displaying an amiable facade for as long as it takes to manipulate people into position to achieve his goal. Methodical and cunning, the lust killer is fully cognizant of the effect such acts have on society (p. 18).

The second type of lust murderer is a disorganized asocial person who, according to Hazlewood and Douglas (p. 19), exhibits characteristics of societal aversion. Typically a loner, this individual experiences difficulty in negotiating interpersonal relationships and consequently feels rejected. Lust murderers are less likely to grow up in an environment of love or understanding; they are more likely to have been abused or neglected during childhood. In the following case study, I focus on one type serial murderer, namely the lust killer. The symbolic world of John Wayne Gacy is described and a social-psychological profile is created to demonstrate the complexity involved in attempting to control this kind of social deviant.

JOHN WAYNE GACY: A CASE STUDY

The data upon which this case study is based were gleaned from personal interviews conducted with John Wayne Gacy, relatives of Gacy, personal letters, and previously published sources. Other information was obtained from former Gacy correspondents which include data relating to Gacy's family life and personal ideology. Police reports, Gacy's confession, the court case (*People v. Gacy* 1984), other court reports and excerpts, autopsy reports, witness reports, and medical reports developed prior to Gacy's trial also represent sources of information useful to develop a case profile of John Wayne Gacy.

I first met Gacy through a letter I sent to the Menard Correctional Facility. Gacy responded defensively, stating there were many sides to his story and one should not assume that everything printed about him was true. Gacy wrote of his innocence, stating also that 80 percent of the news media material represented fantasy. I again wrote to Gacy who invited me to visit. Eleven interviews were conducted with Gacy between August 1992 and the time of his execution in May 1994. Covering a broad range of topics relating to murder, alibis, and homosexuality, Gacy sent a list of acceptable questions to me prior to our initial visit, during which time he presented set answers providing his interpretation of the facts surrounding the case. Each interview was similar; Gacy would respond to questions, but never in a straightforward manner.

At the time the interviews were conducted I was unaware that a personal relationship with the research subject is central to good fieldwork. Ressler and Schachtman (1992) make this point, noting: "To extract information, the interviewer needs to be taken seriously by the inmate, and to achieve a level of trust so that the inmate will talk freely. And to do that, you have to earn the inmate's respect" (p. 50). Although naïve about such things at the time, in retrospect I believe each of these important points were achieved.

John Wayne Gacy was cooperative, but he had a tendency to change facts. Changing the description of the events leading to his arrest and even the accounts of his involvement during each interview, the only consistency noted throughout the interview process was Gacy's insistence that no statement or confession was made that he had, in fact, killed anyone. For this reason, interviews with other individuals were conducted to verify facts surrounding the Gacy case. Then, once Gacy was executed, a petition was filed through the Freedom of Information Act that provided me with a detailed confession in which Gacy admitted to killing thirty-three young men and adolescent boys.

Gacy's Early Background

Born on March 17, 1942, to John and Marion Gacy, John Wayne was the second of three children and the couple's only son. John Gacy's mother was born in Wisconsin to parents of Scandinavian descent. She was a pharmacist by vocation but, after the marriage, Marion gave up her career to raise the couple's three young children (Cahill 1987).

Gacy's father, a skilled machinist, was a Chicago native and the son of Polish/German immigrants. According to Gacy's sister, Karen, John Stanley Gacy was a quiet, self-contained individual. An alcoholic who committed violent acts, the elder Gacy was described by Karen as a man who, although strict, loved his family. John Wayne, on the other hand, described his father as a Jekyll-Hyde personality.

Gacy's relationship with his father was lacking in warmth. Never satisfied with his son's accomplishments, the elder Gacy frequently called John Wayne a "pansy" because of his affinity for cooking and working in the flower bed. According to Gacy, father and son never bonded primarily because the elder Gacy expected far more from John Wayne than he was able to produce. John Wayne supposedly led a normal youth although there were episodes during which delinquent acts occurred.

Levin and Fox (1985) cite childhood behaviors found to be common in the background of adult criminals that include bed-wetting, pyromania, and the torture of animals. Kenneth Bianchi, one of two men responsible for the California hillside strangling, had a childhood bed-wetting problem, and he also engaged in animal torture. David Berkowitz's childhood fascination with setting fires perhaps could have been a predictor of his adult criminal behavior. John Wayne's childhood also may lend some modest support for this contention. As a child, Gacy lived near a neighbor who raised turkeys. Torturing the turkeys by throwing balloons filled with gasoline and then igniting them, Gacy stated the resultant scene was one of the funniest he ever witnessed (interview, December 12, 1992).

John Wayne was popular as a teenager. However, his father did not approve of at least one of John's friends based on the feminine behavior exhibited, informing John Wayne that if he continued to befriend this individual John, too, would "become a fairy."

Gacy's sister described John's relationship with his mother and sisters as good. According to Gacy's mother, Marion, John was just like her. He could not sleep more than four hours a night, was overweight, was concerned for others, and disliked being alone.

Gacy attended Chicago public schools for grades one through six during 1947–1952. By the third grade, however, Gacy's teachers complained of his lack of attention. Gacy then transferred to a parochial school. Experiencing blackouts and easily distracted, John Wayne appeared to be unsuitable for either public or private school. He later attended four different vocational schools, earning a diploma in 1959.

Employment History

Gacy began to earn money at an early age. He had a paper route, mowed lawns during the summer, and shoveled snow in the winter. By age 14, Gacy worked part time in a grocery store and had saved enough money to purchase a used car. However, his father intervened informing John Wayne that he would assist in purchasing a new car because he did not want John to buy someone's junk. After his father fulfilled the commitment to purchase the new car, the vehicle sat in the driveway for three months until John Wayne could afford insurance. Then, after John applied for and received coverage for the automobile, his father either took away the car keys or removed the distributor cap so the car could not be driven.

Ultimately, John's desire for independence could not be restrained. Learning that people admired those who did charity work, at age 17, Gacy organized a school civil defense squad and made himself captain. Now John had a symbolic reason to place a flashing blue light similar to that used in law enforcement on the dash of his car (Time Life, 1992).

At age 19, John fell behind by one car payment to his father who threatened to take away the vehicle. Tired of his father's threats, one day John picked up his mother from work, informed her of the need to put air in the tires, and left the city of Chicago heading for Las Vegas. Upon arriving in Las Vegas, however, John was financially destitute. Pulling over to the side of the road to rest, Gacy passed out from the intense heat. When he awoke in a hospital, John learned he had suffered a mild heat stroke. Without money or a job, Gacy asked officials of the ambulance service if he could work to pay off the hospital bill. Because John Wayne was only 19 years of age, his new employer assigned Gacy to the mortuary service where he swept floors and assisted in preparing corpses for funerals.

While employed in Las Vegas, Gacy engaged in necrophilia, an activity he also engaged in with some of his later murder victims. Gacy's former employer stated that when Gacy worked on the premises, bodies were found undressed and, on at least one occasion, employees found clothes in which a corpse had been dressed folded and lying next to the casket (Time Life 1992). Curious about dead bodies, Gacy even laid in a coffin with a body to perform sexual acts. When arrested for his later crimes, Gacy readily admitted to having sexual relations with corpses.

Gacy worked in Las Vegas for several months, but soon tired of the work. He telephoned his mother to determine whether his father would allow him to return home. The senior Gacy agreed, whereupon the relationship between father and son improved. Gacy attended business college while working in a shoe store to support himself during this same period (Cahill 1987), an initiative that released John from his father's control. He graduated in 1963.

Sexual Background

John Wayne developed an early attraction for silk, and at the age of three or four he hid his mother's underwear. As a teenager, John Wayne continued to hide his mother's silk clothing in his bed and, at age 14, Gacy stole some underwear from neighborhood clothes lines. Gacy's mother discovered this underwear in his bed and punished him.

John experienced his first sexual contact at the age of 5 when a 15-year-old mentally retarded female took Gacy to her house, pulled down his pants, and played with his penis (Wilkinson 1994). His second sexual encounter occurred at the age of 7 when John Wayne and a neighborhood brother and sister were discovered "playing doctor." Gacy's father punished him (Cahill 1987).

It is well documented that many male sexual deviants were themselves sexually abused as children (see, for example, Groth 1979) and some evidence exists that this was true also for John Wayne. At age 8, Gacy was sexually abused by a housing contractor who bought young Gacy ice cream and gave him rides in a truck. The contractor demonstrated wrestling moves; Gacy's head always ended up between the man's legs.

Gacy began dating at age 16 at which time he approached his mother for advice. She informed the teenager that sex was a gentle, special experience between two people in love that should be shared and must never be forced. Gacy remembered that during his initial attempt to have sex he was overcome with excitement and fainted. Overcoming this problem, he experienced sexual intercourse for the first time at age 18.

John Wayne married in 1964. This also was the year a homosexual encounter was experienced for the first time. While his wife was in the hospital giving birth to their first child, Gacy went to a bar with a friend. The conversation soon turned to sex and a friend mentioned that it must have been quite sometime since Gacy had seen any "action." His friend confided that he was not choosy and each time he went out on the town the chance of "being laid" was 100 percent, whereas Gacy only had a 50 percent chance. Indicating he did not understand the comment, the friend explained to Gacy that if he did not have sex with a female he would have sex with a male. The two men continued drinking and eventually ended up at Gacy's home where they engaged in sex.

Shortly after being married John and his bride moved to Waterloo, Iowa, to manage his father-in-law's Kentucky Fried Chicken stores. John Wayne was active in the local Jaycees and eventually became the group's chaplain (Kneeland 1978). John Wayne and his wife also became involved with a spouse-swapping couple.

As a restaurant manager, Gacy was well liked. He set up a recreation area in the house where young male employees met often to play pool and to drink. Soon Gacy challenged the boys to a game of pool in exchange for oral sex. When that ploy did not work, he informed the boys that he was secretly commissioned by the governor of the state of Illinois to conduct a homosexual experiment. To the boys who claimed their heterosexual orientation, Gacy offered his wife in exchange for oral sex being performed on him (Sullivan and Maiken 1983).

Having relationships with young boys eventually led to criminal sodomy charges and a subsequent conviction. Gacy received a ten-year sentence and was incarcerated in the Iowa State Reformatory. That same day, Gacy's wife filed for divorce.

Because of previous convictions for assault and burglary, Gacy was ordered to submit to a psychiatric evaluation. Diagnosed with an antisocial personality disorder, Gacy was described as "bisexual and as a person whose behavior was thrill-seeking or exploitative and not as an exploitative fixation on abnormal sexual objects" (Lindecker 1980, p. 37). Nevertheless, Gacy's greatest fear was being victimized by homosexual rape. Informing other inmates that he despised homosexuals, Gacy requested protection to avoid being sexually assaulted (Lindecker 1980).

While in prison, John worked in the kitchen and was befriended by the prison guards. Soon Gacy began to receive special passes and was extended the privilege of obtaining canteen items unavailable to other inmates. He organized a Jaycee chapter and was given responsibility for building a miniature golf course (Cahill 1980).

Further taking advantage of a bad situation, Gacy attempted to learn everything he could about business practices. He read the the *Wall Street Journal*, informing inmate friends that someday he would establish a luxurious restaurant (Lindecker 1980). Paroled in June 1970, John Wayne's psychological profile listed him as a low-risk recidivist, further indicating the likelihood of Gacy committing another offense was negligible (Sullivan and Maiken 1983).

The Serial Murders

Upon returning to Chicago after being released from prison, Gacy moved into his mother's house and began working in a restaurant. During this period, Gacy met Jack Handley, a Chicago Police Department officer whose name Gacy later used to identify one of four "alter personalities" (Sullivan and Maiken 1983). Later, he entered into a partnership establishing a painting and decorating business, but this partnership soon dissolved. Gacy exhibited violent outbursts, once attacking his business partner with a claw hammer. By way of explanation for this assault, Gacy indicated he experienced a sudden urge to kill.

Soon thereafter Gacy committed the first murder. Picking up a young male at the Chicago Greyhound bus station, Gacy inquired whether the young man would like to party. The young man agreed, and the two drove to Gacy's home where they engaged in sex. Gacy then stabbed and buried the victim.

Gacy again began dating and eventually married a former high school friend. Within months of this marriage, however, Gacy killed a second time. The victim was strangled and placed in a closet.

In 1974, Gacy began cruising the Chicago gay area, initiating a six-year process during which time a series of murders would eventually include thirty-three victims. Soon Gacy's marriage began to deteriorate. On Mother's Day, 1975, Gacy informed his wife that their sex life was over (Time Life 1992). Meanwhile, Gacy's homosexual encounters continued. Gacy believed the sexual act committed with a man was just an act; it involved no love and orgasm represented the ultimate desire. Having sex with a male, according to Gacy, was similar to experiencing sex with a woman and the act never moved above the belt. Perhaps most symbolic, Gacy further stated the sexual act always was between two consenting adults; his vocabulary of motive was based on his view that he never forced anyone to have sex.

Gacy generally performed oral sex, stating that he had sex with fifty males prior to allowing anal sex to be performed with him. This event occurred only after the partner assured Gacy he would not be injured during the sexual act with Gacy carefully checking out the size of the man's penis. However, Gacy did admit to being a passive or feminine partner with other men whom he trusted (personal interview April 1, 1994).

Gacy's next victim was an employee, a 16-year-old youth who one day stopped at Gacy's house to seek payment for work completed. Gacy refused to pay, an argument ensued and the youth left. Later that night a cruising Gacy observed this same individual. Persuading the young employee to return to his house to settle the disagreement, the two talked and drank. Gacy then persuaded the youth to put on a pair of handcuffs but, once handcuffed, Gacy began to argue with the victim who stated he would kill Gacy once he was released from the handcuffs. Gacy then placed a rope around his neck, inserted a stick and strangled the teenager.

During May 1976, Gacy committed a double murder. Two youths, ages 14 and 15, became victims number six and seven. After killing six more victims, Gacy committed a second double murder during October 1976. Gacy picked up a 14 year old and a 16 year old, taking the two juveniles to his house where the youths stated they wanted to have a good time. Gacy had sex with each, performed magic tricks, and eventually placed them in handcuffs. Later, he strangled both youths.

By 1977, Gacy had murdered twenty-six young men and boys. Although questioned about the disappearance of two boys who worked for him, the police failed to run a background check into Gacy's past. During this same year, Gacy experienced his first encounter with a transvestite. John Wayne stated the man "danced like a broad and was very weird," and that "God did not put people on the earth to do things like that." After engaging in sex, Gacy strangled the young man.

One 19-year-old victim thought Gacy was a police officer. Observed at a bus stop, Gacy asked the young man for identification and when the youth bent over the passenger door of the automobile, Gacy pulled out his gun and ordered the victim into the car. Once inside the car, Gacy placed handcuffs on the young man and drove home (Sullivan and Maiken 1983). Gacy began to drink heavily and informed the victim he (Gacy) did not receive enough respect. Gacy offered the youth a drink which was refused; Gacy threw the drink in his face and informed the young man that when offered something, one should take it (Sullivan and Maiken 1983). After this event Gacy told the youth that if he fought he would be killed. Gacy led the young man to the bathroom, placed a rope around his neck, and held his head under the bathtub water.

The youth was subjected to a night of torture as Gacy alternately held the boy's head under water until he lost consciousness, displayed photos of naked women and men, placed a gun Russian roulette–style to his head, urinated in the youth's face, and brutally sodomized him until he passed out. When the youth awoke, he asked Gacy why he had not killed him. Gacy responded he would do so in due time and inquired how it felt to know he was going to die (Sullivan and Maiken 1983).

Gacy continued to threaten the young man as he led him out of the house and into the car. Gacy drove to a downtown store and, prior to releasing the victim, Gacy told the youth that if he went to the cops he would be hunted down and killed. The victim promptly reported the incident to the police who arrested Gacy on suspicion of deviate sexual conduct. Although Gacy did not dispute the victim's story, the police were informed the sex was consensual (Sullivan and Maiken 1983). Questioned by an assistant state attorney, the charges were later dropped (Sullivan and Maiken 1983). Approximately one month after this incident, Gacy killed victim number twenty seven, and buried him in the house crawl space (interview, September 16, 1994).

In March 1978, Gacy picked up a 26-year-old male homosexual. Once inside Gacy's car, the victim was given some marijuana and matches. Later, Gacy placed a chloroformed cloth over the victim's mouth. When the victim awoke, Gacy placed a torture device on him. Leather whips, fireplace tools, metal clamps, and dildos were placed around the victim's body and then Gacy chloroformed him. When the victim awoke, Gacy forced him to perform fellatio while shouting obscenities. Gacy then chloroformed the victim once again. When the victim woke, Gacy repeatedly sodomized him with a fireplace poker until he passed out. After hours of sadistic torture and rape, Gacy chloroformed him a third time and when the man awoke he was lying at the base of a park statue (Rignall and Wilder 1979).

The final serial victim was a 15-year-old male who died in December 1978. Gacy soon came under suspicion because he was known to have discussed hiring the youth. When interviewed, Gacy was uncooperative and, based on this lack of cooperation and his previous record for sodomy charges, a warrant to search Gacy's house was issued. While searching, the police found a receipt for a roll of film, articles of clothing that did not fit Gacy, jewelry, a high school class ring with the initials J. A. S., pornographic magazines depicting homosexual acts, and recreational drugs. A twenty-four-hour surveillance was initiated and the assistant district attorney obtained a second search warrant. Before this search warrant could be executed, Gacy was arrested for possession of marijuana with intent to distribute. When Gacy's house was searched a second time, a technician found the crawl space and within fifteen minutes discovered a body. Gacy was arrested.

John Wayne Gacy admitted killing thirty-three individuals, some of whom were buried in his crawl space while others were thrown into the Des Plaines river. It is perhaps again symbolic that Gacy's confession contained statements in which he indicated each of the victims was either homosexual or bisexual, none were female, and that most victims were picked up in the Chicago area. Gacy's car had a radio and spotlight which caused many victims to believe he was a police officer. For this reason they agreed to do what was asked of them. Many victims, according to Gacy, would sell their bodies for $20.00 and he told them that this could get them killed. Gacy said that when he picked up potential sex partners, they agreed on a price not to exceed $30.00. If they requested more money after the act, they would "have something done to them."

Gacy had affairs with 150 people, stating each were paid. He also informed the police that he was bisexual and that he never used force during "consensual sexual" acts. Gacy further informed authorities of his four personalities. Jack, who was very cruel, was one of these personalities. Jack did not like homosexuals.

The defense attorney entered a plea of not guilty on the grounds that Gacy was insane, but the prosecution successfully argued that Gacy was sane during the commission of the crimes, characterizing Gacy as a methodical, manipulative killer. On March 13, 1980, Gacy was found guilty of twelve counts of murder and sentenced to death. He was executed on May 10, 1994.

DISCUSSION AND CONCLUSION

John Wayne Gacy, a wealthy contractor operating in the Chicago area during the 1972–1978 period, was convicted in 1980 of the murder of thirty-three young men and boys and sentenced to death. Incarcerated in 1980, he was executed by lethal injection on May 10, 1994.

Gacy represents an extreme example of a social deviant whose killing style is suggestive of the hedonistic serial killer type, especially the lust killer. He also experienced a sexual identity crisis. Based on the profile developed by Ressler, Burgess, and Douglas (1988), Gacy may be characterized as a "mixed" type in that the killings did not appear to interfere with his organized lifestyle. Intelligent, socially competent, and mobile, Gacy followed news media reports of his crimes and lived with a partner during the period when he committed a majority of the murders. He also was a man with a mission.

Holmes and DeBurger (1988) observe that hedonistic killers experience pleasure without remorse. Within this context, Gacy did not demonstrate regret to officials nor did he apologize to the families of the victims. Gacy appeared to have enjoyed the sense of power experienced when he controlled other males, a control which he exercised in other ways as well. Posing as a police officer to entrap victims, using handcuffs, and the lure of money, Gacy was able to entice young victims into sexual encounters. Controlling his victims through kidnap and torture, Gacy did not murder quickly. Consistent with the hedonistic lust killer category, Gacy symbolically transferred aspects of the emotional conflict experienced through interactions with his father to the victims. According to Bryant (1982): "in sexual homicide the murder or violence can be more stimulating than sexual gratification attributed to the crime. The act of violence may allow the acting-out of some internalized and generalized hostility, and the sexual activity involved may even be something of an afterthought" (p. 357).

Another important factor was the type of victim chosen. Gacy selected victims in a manner similar to the way Ted Bundy chose victims. Although Bundy picked up attractive women, Gacy selected physically attractive, well-conditioned young men, victims he could never be like while he grew up.

Plagued with thoughts that he was what he hated most, a homosexual, Gacy enjoyed the power he exercised over male victims. Although stating he was bisexual, when discussing sexual relationships Gacy preferred to talk of males. Gacy's homosexual denial syndrome appears to be consistent with Tripp's (1975) assessment: "in both heterosexual and homosexual relations, many men feel their manliness would be jeopardized if they inverted their dominant role, even for a moment" (p. 21).

Another factor that may have taken on symbolic meaning while affecting Gacy's ideas is that he grew up during a period when homosexuality was considered an extreme social taboo. Gacy was, in the tradition of labeling theory described by Coleman (1972), a secret social deviant, a secret homosexual of middle-class background, married, employed, and skilled at playing a heterosexual role. Gacy concealed his homosexuality, rationalizing this behavior by stating he was bisexual. Admission to this sexual orientation also could prove disorganizing to his business and public life, a point Gacy emphasized to the Des Plaines, Iowa, police. Gacy supposedly enjoyed having sex with women, but he preferred men because no strings were attached.

Gacy's homosexuality also may be linked to his close maternal relationship. During childhood, children may develop a mother-fixation or mother-domination caused by an overprotective and overindulgent mother (Rushing 1975). During Gacy's childhood, his mother served as a protector from his father's abuse (interview with Karen Kuzma, March 27, 1995).

Gacy's father perceived his son as less than a real man because John Wayne did not engage in "manly things." Rather than participating in sports, Gacy preferred planting flowers and cooking, activities Gacy's father thought would make him "fruity" (interview with K. Kuzma, March 27, 1995). Although the father and son grew closer after the younger Gacy married and fathered a son ("It was as if John finally proved that he was a man"), John believed that no matter how hard he tried, he was unable to gain his father's approval. By internalizing his father's hatred for homosexuals, Gacy was capable of separating the concept from the act.

The symbolism nature of homosexuality is clear throughout Gacy's adulthood. During the period when Gacy was incarcerated, known homosexuals were not allowed to participate on his work team, again indicating a strong aversion toward gays (Sullivan and Maiken 1983). However, after being released from prison, returning to Chicago, and his eventual second marriage, the sexual desire for young boys was prevalent. After one year of marriage, Gacy began to bring young men home and the urge to kill began to emerge.

Some homosexuals experience a stage of denial. In Gacy's case he may have suffered from the gender-role umbrella described by Tripp (1975, p. 126) who states:

Many men feel free to respond to other males if and when they are able to maintain a masculine role in their own eyes by avoiding emotional expressions that imply an investment in the partner, and by otherwise perceiving their actions as free of effeminate characteristics. They preserve their male image by being the dominant partner in anal intercourse, or by lying back to be fellated. That both acts are highly phallic, that neither is receptive, and that both could occur with a heterosexual partner all support the rationalization that what they are doing is not really homosexual.

This case study illustrates that serial murder presents a special kind of problem for both the public and for law enforcement. Most serial murder victims are strangers, prostitutes, runaways, elderly people, and homosexuals, people who hold little community status or attachment. Gacy engaged in what he perceived to be a desirable social ritual, eliminating "punks" and "fags," especially young street hustlers who sold their bodies for money (Ressler and Schachtman 1992). John Wayne Gacy engaged in a symbolic ritual during which he sought to appease the disdain for homosexuals held by his father. Indeed, Gacy sought to rid the world of what he perceived his father thought to be "trash." Gacy's attempt to satisfy his father's anger toward homosexuals, as described by Katz (1988), represents an attempt by the perpetrator to overcome humiliation and powerlessness. Gacy believed that, as the aggressor, he was in control. Thus the murders also appear to symbolize Gacy's desire to restore what he thought to be good and socially proper. Gacy also killed homosexuals because of that part of him which he hated most (J. Gacy, confession statement, December 26, 1978).

Combating serial murder is difficult because no specific programs exist to address this social problem. When a serial murderer will strike is an unknown factor and there is no evidence that serial murderers look, or in many respects, act any differently from anyone else. That is, analysts of this problem have yet to catalog distinctive physical features or special social characteristics that set serial murderers apart from other members of society. Finally, the Gacy case illustrates the need for cooperative efforts between law enforcement agencies. If linkage blindness is not eliminated, then serial murder will continue as a major social problem.

REFERENCES

Bryant, Clifton D. 1982. *Sexual Deviancy and Social Proscription: The Social Context of Carnal Behavior.* New York: Human Sciences Press, Inc.

Cahill, T. 1987. *Buried Dreams.* New York: Bantam Books.

Coleman, J. 1972. *Abnormal Psychology and Modern Life.* 4th ed. Glenview, Ill.: Scott, Foresman and Company.

Confession statement of John Wayne Gacy: December 22–26, 1978.

Cormier, B., C. Anglicker, R. Boyer, and G. Mersereau. 1972. "The Psychodynamics of Homicide in a Semispecific Relationship." *Canadian Journal of Criminology and Corrections* 14: 335–344.

de River, J. P. 1958. *Crime and the Sexual Psychopath.* Springfield, Ill.: Charles C. Thomas.

Egger, Steven. 1985. "An Analysis of the Serial Murder Phenomenon and the Law Enforcement Response." Ph.D. diss. Sam Houston State University, Huntsville, Texas.

———. 1990. *Serial Murder: An Elusive Phenomenon.* New York: Praeger.

Groth, Nicholas. 1979. *Men Who Rape: The Psychology of the Offender.* New York: Plenum.

Hazlewood, R., P. Dietz, and J. Warren. 1993. "The Criminal Sexual Sadist." *FBI Law Enforcement Bulletin* 61:12–20.

Hazlewood, R., and J. Douglas. 1980. "The Lust Murderer." *FBI Law Enforcement Bulletin* 49:1–5.

Hickey, E. 1991. *Serial Murderers and Their Victims.* Pacific Grove, Calif.: Brooks/Cole Publishing Company.

Hirsley, M. 1978, December 31. " 'It Is Better to Know'—Father of Murdered Teen." *Chicago Tribune*, p. A3.

Holmes, R., and J. DeBurger. 1985. "Profiles in Terror: The Serial Murderer." *Federal Probation* 49: 29–34.

———. 1988. *Serial Murder.* Newbury Park, Calif.: Sage.

Katz, Jack. 1988. *Seductions of Crime.* New York: Basic Books.

Kenney, B., and K. Heide. 1994. "Serial Murder: A More Accurate and Inclusive Murder." Paper presented at the 46th annual meeting American of the Society of Criminology, Miami, Florida.

Keppel, R. 1989. *Serial Murder.* Cincinnati: Anderson.

Kneeland, Douglas E. 1978, December 27. "Four More Bodies Found under House of Contractor, Bringing Total to Nine." *New York Times*, p. 12.

Levin, Jack, and J. Fox. 1985. *Mass Murder*. New York: Plenum.

Lindecker, C. 1980. *The Man Who Killed Boys*. New York: St. Martin's Press.

Newton, M. 1990. *Hunting Humans*. Port Washington, Wash.: Loompanics.

Norris, J. 1988. *Serial Killers: The Growing Menace*. New York: Doubleday.

People v. Gacy, 468 N.E. 2d 1171 (IL. 1984).

Ressler, R., A. Burgess, and J. Douglas. 1988. *Sexual Homicide*. Lexington, Mass.: Lexington Books.

Ressler, R., and T. Schachtman. 1992. *Whoever Fights Monsters*. New York: St. Martin's Press.

Rignall, J., and R. Wilder. 1979. *29 Below*. Chicago: Wellington Press, Inc.

Rushing, William. 1975. *Deviant Behavior and Social Process*. New York: Rand-McNally Publishing Company.

Sullivan, T., and P. Maiken. 1983. *Killer Clown: The John Wayne Gacy Murders*. New York: Windsor Publishing.

Thio, Alex. 1983. *Deviant Behavior*. 2nd ed. Boston: Houghton Mifflin Company.

Time Life Books. 1992. *Serial Killers*. Alexandria, Va.: Time Life Books.

Tripp, C. A. 1975. *The Homosexual Matrix*. New York: McGraw-Hill Book Company.

Wilkinson, Alec. 1994, April. "Conversations with a Killer." *The New Yorker* 70, no. 9, pp. 58–75.

Index

About the Editors and Contributors

Audwin L. Anderson is a graduate of Texas A&M University and currently associate professor of sociology at Southwest Texas State University. His wide range of teaching and research interests include medical sociology, race and ethnic relations, deviance, sport, education, and sickle cell anemia. Dr. Anderson has presented numerous professional papers on these topics and has a number of publications in the applied area.

John M. Bolland is an assistant professor of political science and a research social scientist in the Institute for Social Science Research at the University of Alabama. An accomplished research scholar, Dr. Bolland is the recipient of numerous grants for which he served as principal investigator and project director and he has authored or co-authored numerous journal articles and a well-received book now in its second edition.

Thomas C. Calhoun is an associate professor of sociology and interim associate vice chancellor for academic affairs at the University of Nebraska-Lincoln where he has taught methodology deviance, criminology, and minority relations. An active academic researcher, Dr. Calhoun is the author of numerous journal articles and he served as co-editor of *Sociological Spectrum*, the official journal of the Mid-South Sociological Association. He is co-editor of *Readings in Deviant Behavior* and contributes to several professional associations through presentations of papers and in numerous official roles.

Norman A. Dolch is a professor of sociology at Louisiana State University in Shreveport, a position he has held since 1974. He is co-editor of *Readings in Sociology* (1975) and co-author of several research reports and practice-oriented journal articles as well as numerous book reviews. Dr. Dolch has extensive experience in the applied sociology area, and he has volunteered his services to many local community organizations.

Julie Ezernack is an undergraduate student at Louisiana State University in Shreveport. Ms. Ezernack was previously instrumental in establishing a needs center for pregnant women.

Kimberly A. Folse is a graduate of Oregon State University and the University of Alabama. She has presented numerous papers at professional conferences, many of which have been published in sociology journals. Dr. Folse was among the first to recognize the importance of the child support compliance issue, which she continues to evaluate in her role as associate professor at Texas A&M International University.

Gerald Globetti is emeritus professor of sociology at the University of Alabama where he served with distinction for more than two decades. The author of numerous publications in the area of alcohol and drug studies, Dr. Globetti served as editor of one of the primary publication outlets in this area.

Larry D. Hall is a professor of sociology at Spring Hill College. Dr. Hall's interest in institutional discrimination serves him well as an expert witness in jury selection cases, an area in which he also has published. He has co-authored a book on practical approaches to computing in the social sciences and he is a frequent presenter of papers at professional meetings.

Ronald E. Jones holds a Ph.D. in sociology from the University of Missouri. Interested in issues relating to social control, Dr. Jones has more than twenty-five years of administrative experience in the field of corrections, and he served as commissioner of the Alabama State Department of Corrections. The co-author of several publications in the area of deviant behavior, Jones continues to analyze male inmates in his present position as adjunct professor of sociology at Auburn University at Montgomery.

Celia Chun-Nui Lo serves as an assistant professor of sociology at the University of Akron where she specializes in the teaching of deviant behavior and research techniques. Dr. Lo's research interest is primarily in the area of alcohol use and she has published in a variety of interdisciplinary research journals.

Debra M. McCallum is an adjunct professor of psychology and Director of the Institute for Social Science Research at the University of Alabama. Dr. McCallum conducted needs assessment of healthy families, the homeless, and health care issues. She is an accomplished writer who has authored numerous scholarly publications and research monographs.

Penelope A. McLorg is a doctoral candidate in the Department of Anthropology at Southern Illinois University at Carbondale. She is specializing in biological anthropology, with interests in human biology, aging, women's health, and epidemiology. Her current research concerns assessment of bone variability, as well as aging patterns in blood glucose among rural female Maya Indians. Topics of published works include infant feeding practices, gender socialization in eating disorders, and bone anatomy and measurement. Her research appears in such journals as *Medical Anthropology, International Journal of Anthropology,* and *Deviant Behavior.*

Melanie L. Miller is the director of the Women's Center at the University of Alabama where she earned degrees in social work and community counseling. Her extensive professional background includes serving as executive director of a domestic violence/sexual assault program and program manager and program coordinator of a mental retardation facility and mental health center respectively. Mrs. Miller has extensive volunteer experience, and she frequently serves as a facilitator for domestic violence and violence self-advocacy group issues.

Mary-Rose Mueller earned a Ph.D. in sociology from the University of California, San Diego. Currently, she is an assistant professor in the School of Nursing at the University of California, San Francisco. Dr. Mueller also holds two degrees in nursing. An expert in the analysis of the AIDS problem, her publications in this area are found in a number of health-related and social science journals.

Kelly E. Orr is a M.S.W. graduate of Tulane University and is currently a social worker in Richlands, Virginia. Ms. Orr has evaluated a program for teen-age mothers and is certified in the use of a feeding and teaching scale.

Kathy G. Padgett holds B.S. and M.S. degrees in sociology with a specialization in criminology. She is currently a graduate teaching assistant at Florida State University and a freelance writer. Active in professional work, Ms. Padgett has authored and co-authored several publications.

Dennis L. Peck, a graduate of Washington State University, is currently a professor of sociology at the University of Alabama. Dr. Peck's areas of teaching and research include deviant behavior, evaluation, and social policy research, and law and society—areas in which he has extensively published. Dr. Peck currently serves on a number of editorial boards, is associate editor of the forthcoming *Encyclopedia of Criminology and Deviant Behavior*, and has served as book review editor of *Deviant Behavior*, and as editor of *Sociological Inquiry*.

Thomas A. Petee is director of the criminology program and associate professor of sociology at Auburn University. His teaching excellence recently was recognized by an Outstanding Faculty award for the College of Liberal Arts. His criminology experience was recognized by an appointment to the editorial board of *Homicide Studies*, as a reference for many academic journals, as an expert witness, and as a lecturer.

James A. Sparks holds an M.A. degree in criminal justice from the University of Alabama. His research on serial killers continues when he is able to take time away from his current position as a juvenile officer of the court.

Diane E. Taub is an associate dean of the College of Liberal Arts and associate professor of sociology at Southern Illinois University at Carbondale. Dr. Taub also holds cross-appointments in the Department of Psychology and in the Department of Behavioral and Social Sciences, School of Medicine. Her current research focuses on eating disorders in women and the lived experience of women with physical disabilities. She has published articles in such journals as the *Sociological Quarterly, Sociology of Sport Journal, American Journal of Drug and Alcohol Abuse*, and *Deviant Behavior*.

Beverly E. Thorn serves the University of Alabama with distinction as professor of psychology, director of Clinical Training for the Department of Psychology, and is Sexual Harassment Officer in the College of Arts and Sciences. Dr. Thorn is a licensed practitioner in two states. In addition to her considerable department, college, university service, and clinical consultation activities, Dr. Thorn has authored numerous journal articles and book chapters, as well as contributed papers to professional symposiums.

Greg S. Weaver is an assistant professor of sociology at Auburn University. Dr. Weaver earned a Ph.D. from the University of Nebraska-Lincoln where he specialized in the areas of crime and deviance, areas in which he also has published.

N. Ree Wells is an assistant professor of sociology at Missouri Southern State College in Joplin, Missouri. Her teaching specialties include gender issues, stratification, domestic violence and health and illness, which are areas of her current research and publication.

Thomas S. York is a recent M.A. graduate of Auburn University with a specialty in criminology. With the promise of future scholarship, Mr. York is active through his participation in professional meetings and publication in a scholarly journal.